Programming
Microprocessor Interfaces
for Control
and Instrumentation

Programming Microprocessor Interfaces for Control and Instrumentation

MICHAEL ANDREWS
Colorado State University
Fort Collins, CO

Prentice-Hall, Inc., Englewood Cliffs, New Jersey 07632

Library of Congress Cataloging in Publication Data

Andrews, Michael
    Programming microprocessor interfaces for
control and instrumentation.

    Bibliography: p.
    Includes index.
    1. Microprocessors—Programming.
2. Computer interfaces. I. Title.
QA76.6.A54   001.64'04   81-5932
ISBN 0-13-729996-6   AACR2
ISBN 0-13-730242-8 (Limited paperback edition)

Editorial/production supervision and interior design by Mary Carnis
Cover Design by Mario Piazza
Manufacturing Buyer: Joyce Levatino

Printed in the United States of America

10 9 8 7 6 5 4 3

Prentice-Hall International, Inc., *London*
Prentice-Hall of Australia Pty. Limited, *Sydney*
Prentice-Hall of Canada, Ltd., *Toronto*
Prentice-Hall of India Private Limited, *New Delhi*
Prentice-Hall of Japan, Inc., *Tokyo*
Prentice-Hall of Southeast Asia Pte. Ltd., *Singapore*
Whitehall Books Limited, *Wellington, New Zealand*

To Sandy, Jenny, Chris,
Ginger, and Becky

Contents

Contents   **xiii**

Preface

Microprocessors are a truly versatile design tool. This new dimension literally expands the horizon of applications beyond imagination. Yet to capture the power of microprocessors, you must understand both the hardware and the software aspects of these machines. Unlike any other computer technology, the microprocessor is available to everyone because of its low cost. Unfortunately, few recognize the hidden costs of software development. As in large computers, we can be plagued by code that is illogically structured, very application dependent, and totally undocumented. The new generation of microprocessor architectures and software architectures leaves us no room for writing bad code. It is my hope that you will come away from this book with a clearer grasp of modern programming methods, which, when consistently applied, minimize frustration, errors, and programs which are expensive to maintain.

This book is written for the technician, engineer, or programmer who must design or employ a microprocessor in the many applications of signal processing and control. Nine chapters carry you through the basics of a popular 8-bit microprocessor, illustrating each point with examples and programs. The book also serves as a technical reference for the designer of microprocessor-based equipments. Only a modest electronics background is necessary to understand the easy interfacing principles. Hence, practicing engineers, scientists, and programmers will find this book useful in their applications. The many examples and exercises at the end of each chapter should help the instructor using this book as a class text.

The book is divided into two parts. The first half develops the hardware and software architecture of a microprocessor system centered about the 6809 microprocessor unit. The second half first develops software through modern programming techniques. Later chapters describe many practical applications for microprocessors. Chapter 1 establishes themes for each remaining chapter, with each section serving as the entry point to topics more fully developed later in the text. This chapter is your road map to further study throughout the text. Chapter 2 introduces the software and hardware architecture of the popular 6809 microprocessor. Here I present the essential features of each architecture, which will help you to understand the power of this device. Only the important factors and properties crucial to the design and implementation of microprocessor units are included, thus enabling you to incorporate the microprocessor unit in your design as quickly as possible. Later in the chapter, the important notions of position independence and structured programming are developed.

Interfacing a microprocessor to the real world is no small effort. Most devices have numerous control and timing signals, which must be clearly understood before any interface can be developed. In Chapter 2 I also analyze the 6809 signal set and electrical characteristics. My intent is to introduce important control signals which lead to better designs. Here you will find discussion on the address, data, and control buses. In all microprocessor systems, there are master synchronization signals, from which all peripherals are clocked in step. In this chapter I explain such use of the E and Q signal functions in the 6809.

In Chapter 3 I discuss procedures for configuring a microprocessor system, related to bus loading and expansion. Finally, I analyze the all-important memory interface techniques between ROMs, RAMs, and the MPU.

The true personality of a microprocessor is its instruction set. In Chapter 4 we study several of the important instructions in a microprocessor taken from four classes: *data movement, data manipulation, program movement,* and *program status.* Here we see how registers, memory locations, and stacks are employed in microprocessor programs. My goal is to develop your understanding of data and instruction flow to the microprocessor unit through the various buses. At the same time, you will learn how cycle times in a microprocessor are used. In the last half of this chapter I describe assembler and editor features that support the 6809 code development.

Chapter 5 is the most important chapter. By example, I show you how code should be written. This chapter on modern programming methods consistently employs modular programming techniques, develops your understanding of position independency, and describes recursive and reentrant programs. These programs stress structure and position independence because I have seen the unbearable cost of generating code without these attributes. There is literally no excuse for developing code that is not modular and structured. By employing such techniques, you can reap many benefits from code that is easily maintainable and debuggable, resilient to misapplication, readily understandable, and clearly documentable. In this chapter I have included many useful programs necessary for such vital tasks as floating-point arithmetic, multibyte multiplication and division routines, and text string searches. Because most applications require fast execution in minimal storage, a good solution is to program at the assembly language level. For these reasons, in this text I have focused on programming topics at the machine language level. Even so, the techniques so described apply equally well to high-level language development. Should you enjoy the luxury of a high-level language such as BASIC, FORTRAN, PASCAL, or PL1, the material should be beneficial.

Chapter 6 is our turning point from the software architecture dimension to the interface design dimension in a microprocessor system. Here I develop simple single-wire interfaces which lay the foundation for parallel, serial, and analog interfaces. All of these interfaces are described in this chapter with numerous examples using a combination of software and hardware approaches. In this chapter you will find interfaces with the 6821 PIA and the 6850 ACIA.

In Chapter 7 we complement the hardware focus on interfaces with the software requirements necessary for input/output programming. All important topics as real-time programming, interrupts, and interrupt-driven systems are described. From this chapter you will gain considerable insight into the need for counting cycle time and the number of program bytes in memory.

The microprocessor plays a pivotal role in the design and implementation of data acquisition and control systems. Chapters 8 and 9 present essential topics in signal sampling and conversion. In Chapter 8 I discuss transducers, standard industry functions for instrumentation, determination of aperture time for sampling analog signals, and popular codes for A/D and D/A conversion. My goal is to make you aware of design requirements for the front end of microprocessors, including low-pass filtering, noise reduction, and signal averaging. In Chapter 9 several important digital control algorithms for the 6809 with actual programs are presented. A useful development technique for translating mathematical descriptions of a control system from its Laplace model to the difference-equation form, and finally to its digital control implementation suitable for programming, are also described. The useful control topics include proportional–integral–derivative control and deadtime compensation. As with all chapters, a number of examples with actual microprocessor programs is offered.

I have chosen the 6809 architecture for a variety of reasons. First, the 6800 family of microprocessors is very popular. Second, its instruction sets closely resemble those found in many larger computers, thus enabling the minicomputer and maxicomputer user to rapidly grasp concepts in the microprocessor world. Third, the instruction set of the 6809 is powerful, permitting the invocation of modern programming methodology. Its instruction consistency, versatility, and flexibility will help you to generate quality code. Even though I have focused upon the 6809, much of the material in this text can be applied to other architectures and microprocessor systems. However, I have found in practice that demonstrating the power of one real machine is worth far more than generalizing over abstractions that may have no practical relevance.

I gratefully acknowledge contributions from Lothar Stern, Tim Ahrens, and Bob Burlingame of Motorola Semiconductor Products, Inc., for technical assistance and for permission to reprint from several fine data specification bulletins. In addition, Lynn Schimanuki, Bruce McGreggor, Jonathan Dust, and Vish Dixit contributed much to the generation of several programs. I appreciate the support of Terry Ritter and Lloyd Maul of Motorola for many stimulating discussions and contributions to this text. Without their guidance, this effort might well have fallen short of its desired objectives. Finally, I acknowledge the typing support of Todd Gale, a most enthusiastic person and my wife, Sandra, for her loving devotion to me.

Michael Andrews

Programming
Microprocessor Interfaces
for Control
and Instrumentation

1

Introduction to the Microprocessor World

1.1 WHERE DO WE FIND MICROPROCESSORS?

Everywhere! Look at your wrist. In the kitchen. What awoke you up this morning? Do you know how the tuner works on your television? How did you compute your monthly budget? In countless situations today, we enjoy the power, flexibility, and convenience of microprocessors. Following are just a few of the recent applications of microprocessors:

Microwave ovens	TV games
Digital watches	Calculators
Digital clocks	Telephones
Smart oscilloscopes	Educational toys
Intelligent terminals	Radios
Small computers	CB scanners
Data-acquisition modules	Home computers
Patient-monitor systems	Gas chromatographs
Energy-management systems	Telecommunications
Process controllers	TV tuners
Modems	

Process Control

The list of applications illustrates two significant points. First, micro-computers (microprocessors with other devices to make a "system") are not only replacing minicomputers in some applications, but more important, microprocessors are creating many new market areas. Second, microprocessors are a truly versatile design tool. The low cost, small size, and lower power consumption of microprocessors increasingly convinced designers to utilize them in a wide range of applications. Furthermore, the growing tendency among users is to desire local control by microcomputer application rather than to employ large centrally located computers remotely controlled. Many separate locations create an ever-widening demand for microprocessors, especially in distributed microprocessing. Local operators can control, monitor, and visually oversee the actual effect of the microprocessor's operation instantly, with little inherent delay. Microprocessors increasingly replace large centrally located mini- or maxi-computers previously used in process control applications.

The use of microprocessors as local microcontrollers at various stages of a process has several advantages. They provide convenient access by local line personnel to correct problems and fine-tune a system. Miles of expensive cabling are eliminated, costs go down, and communication between local operators and remote operations is reduced, thereby also reducing the possibility of communication errors. The trend to return control to the actual process site through the use of local microcontrollers is thus very strongly based.

In process control applications, we typically find hundreds of measurement points, such as temperature, pressure, line speed, and other process data. In operation, numerous analog circuits can be automatically selected and digitized under the control of a microprocessor. The microprocessor performs the computation and processing operations at lightning speeds, switching inputs and digitizing the analog data. It is not uncommon to find a microprocessor also generating tens of analog signals via digital-to-analog converters driving actuators in manufacturing processes to complete the real-time computer-aided process loop. Microprocessors can also send the return data to local monitoring stations. They can process status and display it on bar graphs via a color cathode ray tube (CRT) while simultaneously displaying several process variables on digital meters.

Instrument Panels

Microprocessors are a natural choice for smart instruments. They conveniently scan the many pushbuttons on the user's panel, monitor input signals, and generate digitized output signals—all while annunciating data on light-emitting diodes (LEDs). The digital voltmeter in Figure 1.1 and the synthesizer/function generator in Figure 1.2 are typical of the micro-processor implementation in modern instrumentation. Microprocessors help

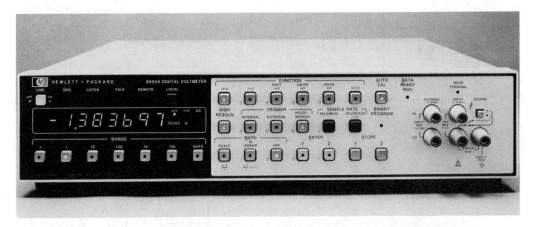

Figure 1.1. Digital Voltmeter. (*Courtesy of Hewlett-Packard Corp.*)

Figure 1.2. Synthesizer. (*Courtesy of Hewlett-Packard Corp.*)

develop user understanding of complex instruments by consolidating and simplifying user controls on the front panel. Simultaneously, inadvertant sequences of pushbutton actuations are detected and noted in readable format on LEDs. Even the oscilloscope screen itself becomes alive with alphanumeric data generated by the microprocessor.

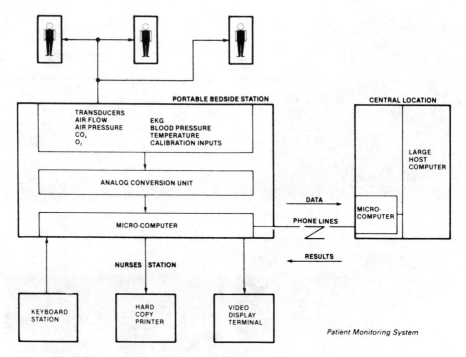

Figure 1.3. Patient-Monitor System. (*Courtesy of Datel-Intersil*)

Data Acquisition

The birth of microprocessors has significantly reduced the cost of hospital patient-monitoring systems. At each bedside station, measurements cater to the exact needs of a patient. Nearby monitoring terminals at the nurse's station provide immediate access to the physiological status of the patient. Bedside stations monitor many parameters, including gas flow, pressure, gas analyzers, and gas mixtures. Long-term drifts typically found in such analog interfaces are automatically compensated by the microprocessor on line. Elaborate patient-monitoring systems use the microprocessor to transmit data via phone lines to a centrally located computer. This computer performs the front-end task for a large host computer specifically programmed for patient-monitor tasks. Blood pressure, heart rate, respiratory rate, lung resistance, and compliance are but a few of the signals such systems can monitor and control. Figure 1.3 depicts a typical patient-monitoring system.

Signal Processors

Coupled with ultrafast video analog-to-digital converters, microprocessors perform well in such signal-processing applications as distortion analyzers and radar signature analysis. A fast digital memory records elusive transients

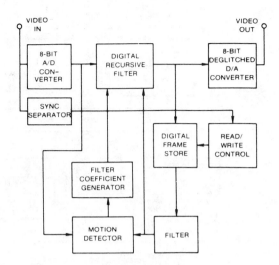

Figure 1.4. Digital Noise Reducers.
(*Courtesy of Datel-Intersil*)

such as those encountered in shock and explosion testing, nuclear magnetic resonance, high-speed chemical reactions, and power-line disturbances. Digital noise-reduction systems similar to the one shown in Figure 1.4 can reduce picture noise by 9 to 15 decibels (dB) and at reasonable cost. A noise-reduction algorithm averages over several frames to eliminate noise. For moving images the process is inhibited by comparing the illuminance of each element (pixel) of one picture with its earlier counterpart in the previous frame. When little change or no change occurs in illuminance, the filter-noise algorithm in the microprocessor is employed. When illuminance from frame to frame at each element changes rapidly, the algorithm is inhibited. The same system can perform time-based correction, frame synchronization, and still-picture projection, all at costs much lower than disc-based all-electronic systems.

Scientific Research

Microprocessors can be found in such exotic applications as weather research. In Figure 1.5, cloud climatology experiments combine active and passive remote observation techniques to infer cloud parameters. A Cloud Physics Radiometer (CPR) is an eight-channel scanning radiometer with seven channels in the near infrared and one channel in the thermal infrared. A Cloud Lidar System (CLS) employs a two-wavelength polarized scanning laser radar. This expensive instrumentation can be carried aboard aircraft. Since physical size and weight are constraints, the small microprocessor is an advantage. Performing data acquisition, the microprocessor can monitor system power supplies, temperature, pressure, laser water flow and temperature.

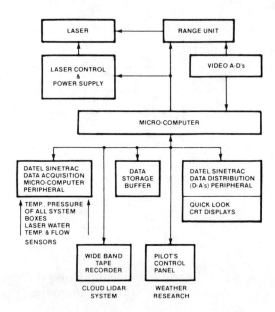

Figure 1.5. Microprocessor-Based
Weather Monitor System.
(*Courtesy of Datel-Intersil*)

Figure 1.6. Energy-Management System.
(*Courtesy of Horizon Technology Corp.*)

Energy Management

In the comfortable setting of our own homes we find the microprocessor controlling our lights, heat, and kitchen appliances. The energy management unit depicted in Figure 1.6 is typical of the many residential uses. Here the microprocessor is called upon to monitor kilowatt loads at different points in the home, enabling or disabling circuits when the instantaneous, average or peak load has been exceeded. Both visual output through liquid crystal displays (LCDs) and audio alarm output warn the occupant of load changes.

In summary, microprocessors can be found in the full spectrum of applications from dedicated usage to fully general purpose. Why? First, because microprocessor hardware is relatively inexpensive. Second, software engineering costs can be amortized over several hundred or thousands of units, so volume production generates potentially large profit incentives. Third, microprocessors are flexible because they are programmable. A product definition change generally requires a simple alteration because reprogramming is much easier than rewiring. Fourth, one product leads to another with only an incremental cost in software engineering. In fact, the replacing of hardware by software is one of the key advantages, since software itself is a nonrecurring cost.

1.2 WHAT IS A MICROPROCESSOR?

This ubiquitous device can be readily understood by examining the microprocessor (MPU) *block diagram* and the *programming model*, which represent the hardware and software architectures, respectively. From a hardware viewpoint, the quickest way to visualize the structure is to study the block diagram available from the manufacturers. Figure 1.7 provides us with essential information to determine the input/output structure of the device, the internal configuration, possible data and address paths internal to the device, the type of technology, power requirements, and size of the registers. In fact, all of the available resources employable by the hardware designer within the device itself are generally shown. Occasionally, additional registers may be depicted to illustrate the timing relationships or the data flow internal to the MPU itself. Using these aids, the hardware designer can almost determine whether certain instructions exist and how they behave.

In our MPU diagram, we show an arithmetic logic unit (ALU), an accumulator, a register called TEMP (accumulator and TEMP are input/output to the ALU), the instruction register (IR), and the program counter (PC). In this simple figure, we see that the address lines are connected to the PC and the data lines are connected to the accumulator (ACC). In actual devices, the block diagram may show more detail than this simple hardware architecture.

The software engineer looks at the programming model, again provided

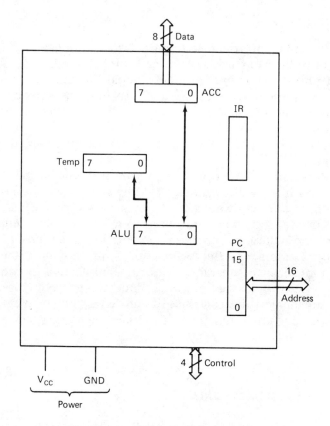

Figure 1.7. MPU Block Diagram.

by microprocessor manufacturers. The programming model also depicts essential resources, but this time *only* those that the programmer can access, use, or alter. Any registers not available to the programmer would not normally be shown. If register TEMP in the block diagram of Figure 1.7 could not be accessed by the programmer, it would not be shown in the programming model for that machine. We see in Figure 1.8 a typical programming model which contains four general-purpose registers (GPRs), an index register stack pointer (SP), and the program counter. This uncluttered picture readily provides the programmer with the essential software architecture of the machine. Coupled with the instruction set definitions, the software engineer has a complete snapshot of the microprocessor itself.

In our programming model, we also see that the GPRs are 8 bits wide, indicating that the data bus is an 8-bit-wide bus and the program counter is 16 bits wide, indicating that the address bus is also 16 bits wide. This means that our memory can span 65K locations. The full 16-bit index register and stack pointer can work in the entire memory space. Such essential information quickly gives the software and hardware designer a capsule view of the power (or deficiencies) of the particular microprocessor.

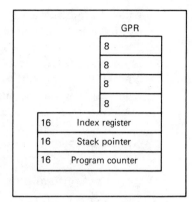

Figure 1.8. Programming Model.

1.3 MICROCOMPUTER SYSTEMS

The microprocessor unit (MPU) is the basic processing unit of the micro-computer system. By itself, not much is possible. So the MPU is connected to memory and input/output as shown in Figure 1.9. The memory unit may consist of several devices, called read/write or random-access memory (RAM) and read-only memory (ROM). Memories store necessary programs for the particular application of the microprocessor. The primary connection to external devices such as keypads, Teletypes, or CRTs is accomplished through the input/output (I/O) unit. This basic interfacing unit of the microcomputer system is implemented with one or more special chips provided by the microprocessor manufacturers. The microcomputer system moves necessary information through three buses: the address bus, data bus, and control bus.

In early microprocessor devices, these buses were sometimes shared in time (time-multiplexed). In all second- and third-generation microprocessors these buses are available independently. The address bus commonly is 16 bits

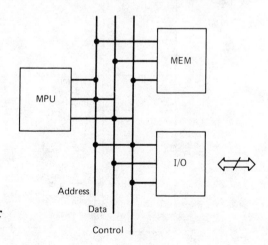

Figure 1.9. Microcomputer System.

wide. In microcomputer systems this same address bus serves to select devices by decoding particular address values for specific devices called device select addresses. The data bus is the main highway for information transfer to and from the MPU. Eight- and 16-bit bidirectional lines are now common. The control bus of a microcomputer system generates the timing, synchronization, isolation, and direction of data transfer for the memory and I/O devices.

Main design considerations in developing a microcomputer system consist of specifying the following:

Bus configuration
Expandability
Power requirements
Physical size

1.4 HOW IS A MICROCOMPUTER SYSTEM CONFIGURED?

Configuring a microcomputer system is a two-step process. After selecting the necessary components, you, as a system designer, must first allocate specific addresses to select I/O devices and memory units. Next, you must determine the electrical loading requirements on all your buses. The first task involves memory management. You want to produce a memory map such as the one shown in Figure 1.10. Part of the map will already be specified by

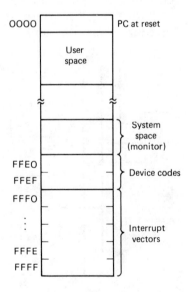

Figure 1.10. Memory Map.

the manufacturer for locations the MPU necessarily accesses in certain situations. In our map we show locations FFFF and FFFE through FFFO as interrupt vectors. These reserved locations are used by the MPU at the start of interrupts. Program memory location OOOO is also a special location. Here the microprocessor would start executing upon entering a RESET state. User locations are available to allocate device selection codes in unallocated memory. In our memory map we chose locations FFEO through FFEF as special addresses for selecting certain devices.

Most microprocessors view memory and I/O devices similarly. Hence, the system designer can organize the configuration by allocating specific addresses to individual units, regardless of functional usage. But it is wise to place device select codes at addresses around natural memory boundaries. Memory devices normally come in units of contiguous 1K, 2K, 4K, and 16K words. A 1K-word device has a natural 1K-word boundary. Usually the number of words in the device dictates the size of the memory page.

Decoding the Address Bus

Once you have mapped out your memory space, you proceed to decode the specific addresses for the various I/O devices and memory units. In small systems it is possible to use a "partial" decoding technique. On large microcomputer configurations, a "full" decode is necessary.

The partial decoding technique simply uses less than the full set of address lines to decode specific device selection lines. In Figure 1.11 we depict devices A, B, and X selected with address bits A15, A9, A1, and A0. The 4-to-1 decoder will enable 1 of 16 output lines when a particular value appears on the four input lines. This combinational logic device activates one unique output line and hence selects one unique device. Both memory and I/O devices can be selected in this manner. Selection is made via chip enable (CE) or chip select (CS) input pins of devices. When asserted, the device is enabled, permitting data to be transferred to or from the device.

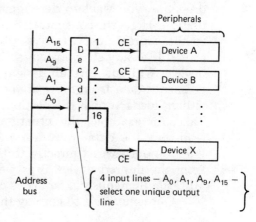

Figure 1.11. Partial Decode Selection.

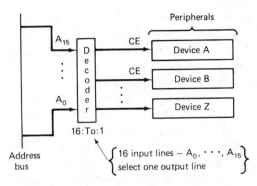

Figure 1.12. Full Decode Selection.

Partial decoding is simple, uses less random logic, and subsequently needs less wiring, but device selection is not uniquely specified by a single address! For example, in Figure 1.11 more than one address can select a particular device since address bits A14 through A10 and A8 through A2 are not specified. This ambiguity presents a hidden trap to the programmer, who may unknowingly use addresses which inherently access memory locations and input/output devices simultaneously.

We can resolve this ambiguity with the *full decode* technique. Here the full 16 bits of address are input to decoders. Every output line is needed to select a unique device, as in Figure 1.12. A full decode is certainly more expensive because larger decoders are necessary and more wiring is required, but the full decode is by far the safest technique to use because no ambiguity occurs in device selection. Decoders come in various sizes. Figure 1.13 depicts some popular devices.

Bus Isolation

Once you have generated your memory map and have decoded the address bus, you want to determine the signal path behavior within the configuration. Here we concentrate on the data bus. The same procedure applies to the address bus. Our task is to ensure that data transferred to and from the MPU at any given instant are received from or transmitted to one unique device. Without careful design, it is possible to simultaneously "read" erroneous data from more than one source. This multiplicity of signal inputs either "loads" down the destination or generates an ambiguous signal value. Take, for example, the situation in Figure 1.14. Suppose that we wish to read only the data from device B into the MPU. If device A and B output lines are both wired directly to the data bus of the MPU, the output signal from the desired device B as well as that of device A may be read by the MPU simultaneously. Erroneous data are transmitted.

Our solution is to employ three-state or tri-state devices on the data bus

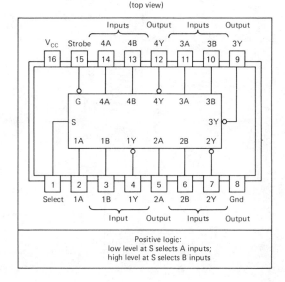

SN54157, SN54LS157, SN54S157 . . . J or W package
SN54L157 . . . J package
SN74157, SN74L157, SN74LS157, SN74S157 . . . J or N package
(top view)

SN54LS158, SN54S158 . . . J or W package
SN74LS158, SN74S158 . . . J or N package
(top view)

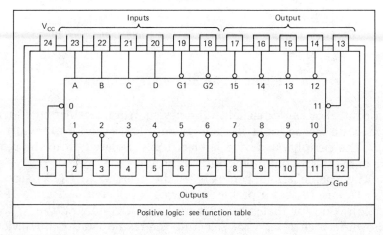

Figure 1.13. Popular Decoders. (*Courtesy of Texas Instruments, Inc.*)

as shown in Figure 1.15. These devices isolate signal paths among devices on the bus, thus preventing erroneous data transfer. Tri-state devices employ an enabling signal to make the connection through the device (placing the device in an active state). In Figure 1.15 our tri-state devices are bidirectional, thus permitting signal flow in both directions. The direction is determined

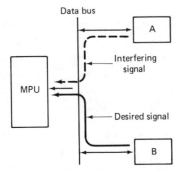

Figure 1.14. Nonbuffered Configuration.

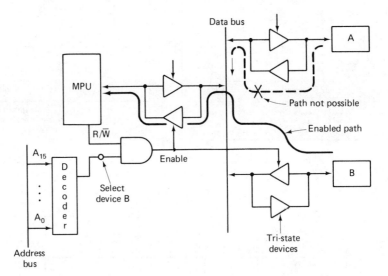

Figure 1.15. Buffered Configuration.

by a control or *enable* signal to the device. When disabled in either direction, the tri-state device looks like a large impedance (and is in the off state). As a result, the peripheral device is electrically isolated from the remaining circuits in the microcomputer configuration.

The enable signal generally is the read/write $(R/\overline{W})$ signal from the MPU. To ensure that a particular device is selected, a decode of the address selection code for that particular device is ANDed with the $R/\overline{W}$ signal. This is shown in Figure 1.15 for selecting the read operation on device B. $R/\overline{W}$ is one way to generate the enable signal for tri-state devices. As we shall see in a later chapter, there are many alternatives. One word of caution. *Never "tri-state"* control signals since they must always be in an active state, never in the off state. Tri-state devices can have desirable characteristics such as the following:

    High speed
    Low power

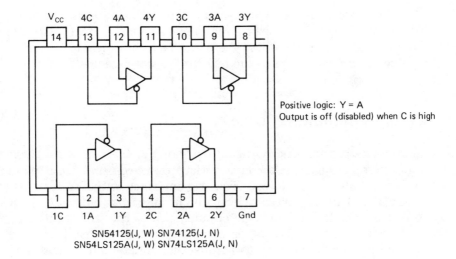

Positive logic: Y = A
Output is off (disabled) when C is high

SN54125(J, W) SN74125(J, N)
SN54LS125A(J, W) SN74LS125A(J, N)

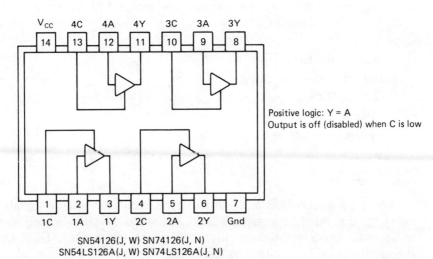

Positive logic: Y = A
Output is off (disabled) when C is low

SN54126(J, W) SN74126(J, N)
SN54LS126A(J, W) SN74LS126A(J, N)

Figure 1.16. Quadruple Bus Buffer Gates with Three-State Outputs. (*Courtesy of Texas Instruments, Inc.*)

Single power supply voltage
Bus-compatibility with MPU and devices
High impedance in the off state
Low leakage current in the off state
Low undershoot voltages

Common tri-state devices are depicted in Figure 1.16. The 74LS367 hex buffer is unidirectional (for address buses). When a single wire or device pin must function in both directions (read and write), a bidirectional tri-state device, or bus transceiver is used (for data bus), as shown in Figure 1.16.

You have now seen two general steps in configuring a microcomputer system. When specific interface requirements must be met, help comes from a number of available devices. These interface chips help us to perform many complex interfacing tasks to the real world, as we see next.

1.5 INTERFACING TO THE REAL WORLD

Microprocessors are strictly digital devices. Yet the real world is seldom digital. External signals take on a variety of waveforms, from pulsed codes to continuous analog levels. You can interface with the real world using powerful I/O devices already available in numerous chips. I/O devices may consist of simple random logic circuits such as the tri-state devices we saw previously, or they may be as complex as devices that take serial digital information and convert it to parallel digital data and devices that convert analog signals to digitized signals (and vice versa). I/O devices commonly perform the following tasks:

> Data conversion
> Data storage or latching
> Data buffering
> Timing
> Control

Analog Interfaces

In data acquisition and control it is vital that analog signals be processed by the microprocessor. To do so, we convert the analog signal input to the microprocessor with an analog-to-digital converter (ADC). This device, shown in Figure 1.17, converts the analog signal to an 8-bit digital equivalent. An ADC requires one control signal and one status signal. The control signal, start of conversion (SOC), initiates the conversion process inside the ADC. The status signal, end of conversion (EOC), informs the microprocessor that the conversion process is complete and data are available. In all the applications discussed earlier in the chapter, the ADC was an integral part of the system.

In many control applications, the microprocessor must also generate an analog signal. This is accomplished with a digital-to-analog converter (DAC), as depicted in Figure 1.18. Here, an 8-bit digital input from the data bus is converted to a single-wire analog signal output from the DAC. Most DACs do not require control or status signals. Selecting an ADC or DAC for a particular application is straightforward, and numerous procedures are available from vendors. Such important specifications as linearity, drift, conversion

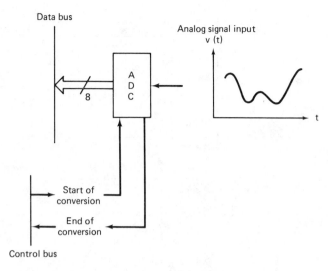

Figure 1.17. Analog-to-Digital Conversion.

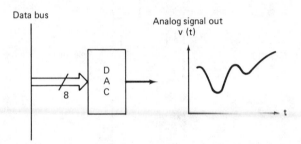

Figure 1.18. Digital-to-Analog Conversion.

time, and code structure are readily available. Figure 1.19 depicts a typical ADC and a DAC.

Serial Interfaces

A very common microprocessor interface is the serial-to-parallel input and parallel-to-serial output depicted in Figure 1.20. The serial input device takes a single digitized signal train and sequentially loads the information into the device shift register synchronized by a clock (CLK) signal. The parallel output of the shift register is then transferred in parallel to the data bus of the microprocessor system. Transfer to the data bus is accomplished only after the shift register is fully loaded. During loading, a shift start signal must be sent to the shift register. The serial data output device first receives a digital data word loaded parallel into the shift register. The serial data output is then sequentially shifted out of the shift register, again with a shift

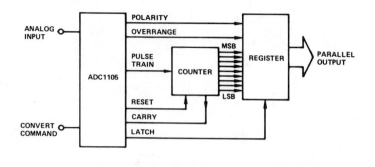

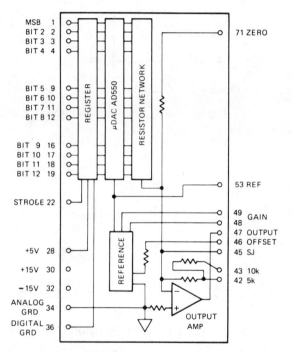

Figure 1.19. Typical ADC and DAC. (*Courtesy of Datel-Intersil*)

control signal. Serial-to-parallel and parallel-to-serial converters are called universal asynchronous receiver-transmitters (UART) and universal synchronous, asynchronous receiver-transmitters (USART), and are depicted in Figure 1.21.

Programmable Devices

In general, peripheral device interfaces perform two functions, the function of latching data and the function of control. The control procedures are called handshaking.

As we have already seen with regard to ADCs, DACs, and serial data

Introduction to the Microprocessor World

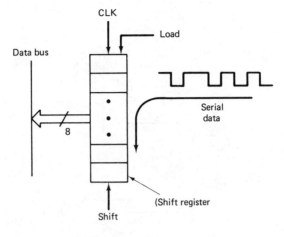

(a) Serial to parallel

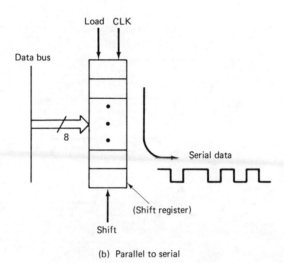

(b) Parallel to serial

Figure 1.20. Serial Interfaces.

converters, status and control signals are part of the handshake or protocol functions available in peripheral devices. For peripheral devices to perform these essential tasks, certain resources are required. These are shown in Figure 1.22. Typically, a *data register* (DR) interfaced to the data bus is available to latch input or output data. Also, many peripheral devices are bidirectional and can be programmed to operate as input or output ports by using a *data direction register* (DDR). This register specifies the direction of each bit or all bits as input or output in the data register. The third resource is a *status* and/or *control register* (CSR). This register is connected to the control bus of the microprocessor system. The control status register may also be connected to control or status lines of the peripheral hardware. Peripheral devices come in a variety of packages, but the essential features of

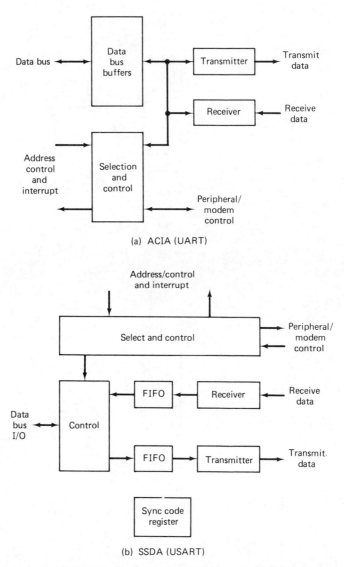

(a) ACIA (UART)

(b) SSDA (USART)

Figure 1.21. Universal Asynchronous and Universal Synchronous, Asynchronous Receiver-Transmitters. (*Courtesy of Motorola Semiconductor Products, Inc.*)

most can be examined by studying the data, data direction, and control status registers.

Interface Units

To increase the power of the interface capability in a microprocessor, manufacturers also provide programmable peripheral devices. The device in Figure 1.22 is programmable. We can program the direction of a data line as

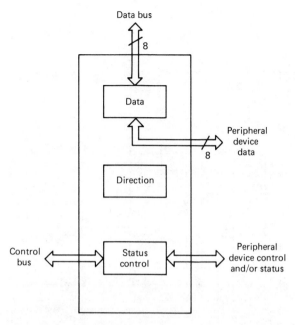

Figure 1.22. Block Diagram of Microprocessor Interface Units.

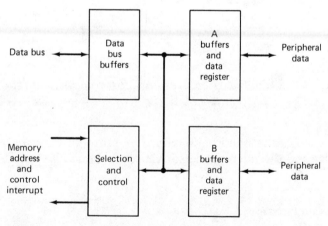

Figure 1.23. PIA Device. (*Courtesy of Motorola Semiconductor Products, Inc.*)

input or output. We can also program certain control signal patterns. In Figure 1.23 you see a programmable interface adapter (PIA) device. This 6821 device actually has two ports and four control lines available to the peripheral device. These independent ports, ports A and B, are nearly identical except for some minor differences. Also, by programming the CSR, you

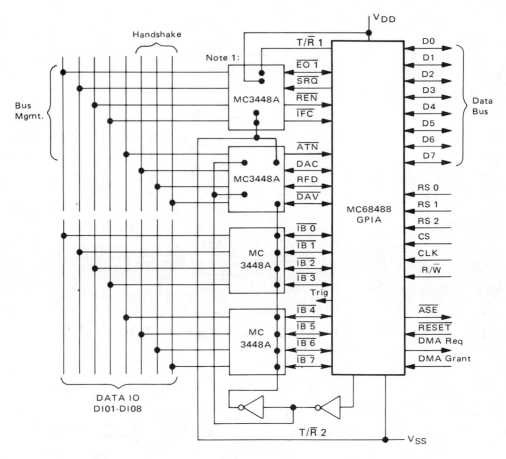

Figure 1.24. GPIA. (*Courtesy of Motorola Semiconductor Products, Inc.*)

can specify the handshake nature or protocol between the actual peripheral device and the microprocessor via control lines CA1, CA2, CB1, and CB2.

Standard Interfaces

In the microprocessor world, popular buses have now appeared, among them the S-100 and IEEE 488 bus configurations. These de facto standards are found predominantly in the personal computing environment and in scientific instrumentation, respectively. These standards go further than simply specifying timing and control. They also formulate recommended electrical operating ranges for signal behavior. The MC68488 general-purpose interface adapter (GPIA) depicted in Figure 1.24 is typical of the powerful family of interface chips available for standard interfaces. The GPIA can automatically handle all handshake protocol needed on typical instrument buses. Characteristics include:

> Single or dual primary address recognition
> Secondary address capability
> Complete source and acceptor handshakes
> Programmable interrupts
> Serial and parallel polling
> Talk-only and listen-only capability
> Selectable automatic features to minimize software
> Synchronization trigger output

IEEE 488 Bus: The IEEE 488 instrument bus standard which the 68488 can handle is a bit-parallel, bit-serial bus structure designed for communications to and from intelligent instruments. The flexibility of this standard interface is seen in the multiplicity of interconnection and control configurations which can be established, both remotely and automatically. Data may be taken from, sent to, or transferred between instruments. A bus controller such as the 68488 dictates the role of each device by making an attention line true and sending "talk" or "listen" addresses on the instrument bus data lines. Only those devices having appropriately decoded addresses are activated. In typical communications, the controller first activates the attention line. Then the instrument bus demands are sent to single or multiple GPIAs. Next, information is transmitted on the instrument bus data lines under sequential control of three handshake lines. Many instrument bus protocol functions are easily handled automatically by the GPIA, thus reducing additional MPU action. Since GPIAs contain many internal registers, minimum MPU response is possible.

Software versus Hardware: Which Way to Go?

Interface designs are application-sensitive. Your choice of peripheral devices will depend strictly on the intended task. Realize that microprocessors can also "do" with software what it is possible to do with hardware in most cases. But you choose a software technique over hardware when the cost of the hardware per unit (product) is greater than the cost of software amortized over the total number of units. Such costs are not always obvious. Then, in most cases, the convenience of implementing the peripheral device outweighs the programming task of simulating the device itself. Sometimes, the software technique is too slow. Our only alternative then is to implement the interface task with the specific peripheral device.

1.6 PROGRAMMING MICROPROCESSORS

Programming is your first step toward learning the personality of a microprocessor. For it is here that you encounter the true character of your

Table 1.1   Typical Instruction Groups

Data manipulation	Data movement
Add	Load
Subtract	Store
Logical	Page addressing
Rotate	File movement
Transfer	Indexing
Arithmetic	Stack operations
Program manipulation	Program status manipulation
Call subroutines	Carry, overflow
Interruption	Zero and negative status
Subroutine nesting	Test and skips
Conditional branches	Test and branches
Unconditional branches	Interrupt enable
Program jumps	Stack overflow
	Set mask
	Program status register command

machine, the instruction set. If we analyze instruction sets, we can find four general classes in each set. These are data manipulation, data movement, program manipulation, and program status manipulation. By examining the actual instructions of your microprocessor, you can gauge the programming power by identifying the group to which each instruction belongs. From this approach, you determine the inherent capacity of the microprocessor to manipulate or move data and programs. Table 1.1 illustrates the typical instructions found within each group.

Data Manipulation

All instructions have a specific format that helps us to describe its structure and addressing mode. For example, the format of an ADD instruction is shown in Figure 1.25. This data manipulation instruction, ADD

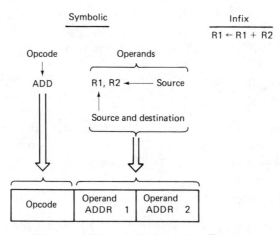

Figure 1.25. An Instruction Format.

R1,R2, consists of the operation code (OPCODE) and its operands. This symbolic notation of the ADD operation is a mnemonic which tells us that the two operands R1 and R2 are added together, placing the SUM in R1. Other instruction formats are similarly structured. We discuss instruction formats in greater detail in Chapter 4.

Data Movement

It is important to understand how instructions manipulate the contents of the MPU registers, memory, and devices. In Figure 1.26 we see the essential load (LDA) and store (STA) data movement instructions, which load the MPU from memory and store data from the MPU into memory. Another data movement instruction, the transfer instruction, TFR, is also shown. In load and store instructions, data are typically transferred between the accumulator registers external to the MPU. With the transfer instruction, data between general-purpose registers internal to the MPU are being exchanged. In Figure 1.27 we see some typical data manipulation instructions. Here the complement accumulator (CMPA) instruction causes the accumulator to be complemented. Another instruction, increment accumulator (INCA), increments the contents of the accumulator.

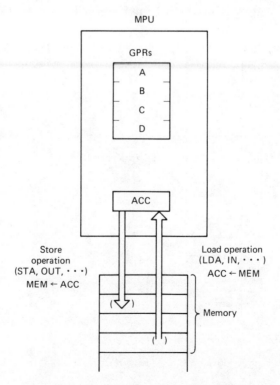

Figure 1.26. Typical Data Movement.

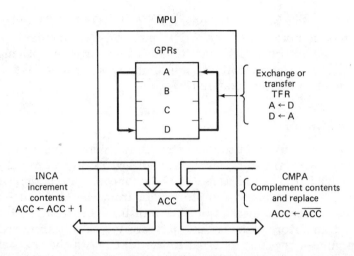

Figure 1.27. Data Manipulation.

In many microprocessors, data movement instructions also operate with a stack. Figure 1.28 illustrates typical stack operations. Here we see the PUSH onto the stack, STA -(SP). This instruction first decrements the stack pointer (SP), then transfers data from the accumulator into the new stack pointer location. This PUSH instruction loads the stack with data from the

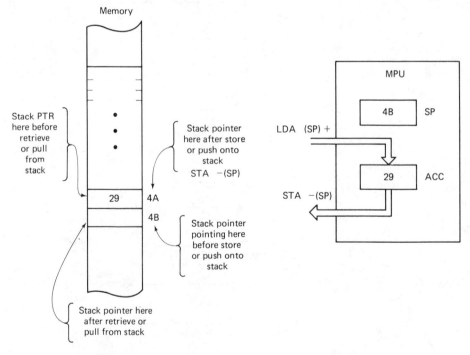

Figure 1.28. Data Movement (Stack Operations).

source. When we retrieve data from the stack we use a PULL or POP instruction. In Figure 1.28, LDA (SP)+ also takes data from the stack and places them in the accumulator. Next, the stack pointer is incremented. A stack instruction involves two tasks. In the PUSH operation we store data, then decrement the stack pointer. In the PULL operation we increment the stack pointer, then retrieve the data. Our last-in, first-out (LIFO) stack operates in a pre-decrement store, post-increment load addressing mode. Using stack instructions makes data transfer through contiguous memory locations trivial. With a single instruction, you transfer data and adjust the pointer itself.

Program Manipulation

Program manipulation instructions operate on microprocessor resources as shown in Figure 1.29 for the program counter manipulation. Here we see two instructions, branch (BRA) and jump (JMP). Branch instructions cause a program to move to another location in memory *relative* to the current contents of the program counter (PC). Jump instructions cause a program to move to any location (not necessarily a location relatively addressed from the current PC). Branch instructions cause "relative" movement, whereas jump instructions cause "absolute" movement.

Program Status Manipulation

The program status manipulation instructions test and/or change conditions in the microprocessor to alter the instruction sequence. In Figure 1.30 we see the instruction ORCC 10. (In this text and in most literature, numbers as operands in instructions are considered hexadecimal. As we shall see in Chapter 4, special symbols will denote the base of the representation.) This instruction sets the interrupt (I) mask in the condition code register of the MPU. The condition code register contains the current status of the microprocessor during program execution. Our condition code register has eight flags or masks, including zero (Z), overflow (V), carry (C), and negative (N) flags. These four flags indicate the result of arithmetic activity in the accumulator. Hence, a zero, overflow, or carry from the most significant bit, and a negative word in the accumulator is "remembered" by these four flags, respectively. The interrupt (I) mask permits us to ignore or disable interrupt requests. In Figure 1.30 we have set this mask, thus disabling further interrupts.

We have seen only a few instructions in a microprocessor. In a subsequent chapter we examine these instructions further. As we do, you should understand which resources are being used and how they change. This basic knowledge will help you to utilize more efficiently MPU registers, memory locations, stacks, and I/O devices. A typical design takes into account the number of cycles that each instruction takes in the program. Do not forget

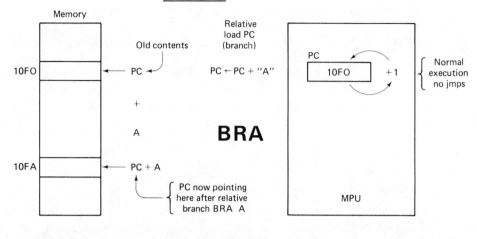

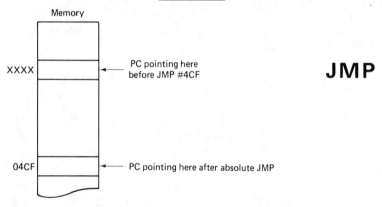

Figure 1.29. Program Manipulation.

that most designs also require minimal memory. Microprocessor systems consider memory and time to be precious commodities.

Addressing Modes

Most instructions can affect various resources in the microprocessor, from MPU registers to memory locations. You select these resources in a particular instruction with addressing modes available to the instruction set. For instance, the data movement instructions LDA and STA in Figure 1.26 access memory locations. These instructions use the several address modes, including direct, inherent or register, indirect, immediate, and absolute. The increment accumulator instruction in Figure 1.27 references the accumula-

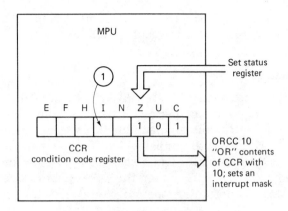

Figure 1.30. Program Status
Manipulation.

tor. The latter instruction employs an *inherent* mode of addressing. The address of the source is implied by the opcode itself. The transfer instruction employs the *register* mode. Here, two MPU registers are utilized by the instruction. The stack operations use the autodecrement and autoincrement mode of addressing. The branch and jump instructions use the relative and absolute mode of addressing. There are many other addressing modes, some of which are:

Inherent	Extended
Accumulator	Register
Immediate	Indexed
Absolute	Relative
Direct	

The important modes—inherent, register, direct, immediate, relative, and absolute—can be found in most microprocessors. Only a few have all the modes typically found in large computers. We discuss addressing modes in greater detail in Chapter 4.

1.7 MODERN PROGRAMMING PRACTICES FOR MICROPROCESSORS

There is no excuse today for generating code that cannot withstand rigorous implementation in a variety of applications. Code portability or the inherent property of a program to be readily implemented in different microprocessor systems or different applications is highly desirable and easily attainable with many microprocessor instruction sets. Designing microprocessor code that is structured, well documented, and portable should be the objective of the software engineer. Structure and documentation lead to easily understandable, maintainable, and debuggable programs.

Position Independence

Position-independent code (PIC), that can be moved around in memory without reprogramming, permits us to use the same ROM, as illustrated in Figure 1.31. In this application, three electronic boards are interfaced to several printers with similar yet different characteristics. These characteristics could be motor running speed, startup time, word width, and buffer requirements. PIC code in the same ROM can be employed in all three boards. More importantly, the PIC code in one ROM may permit you to

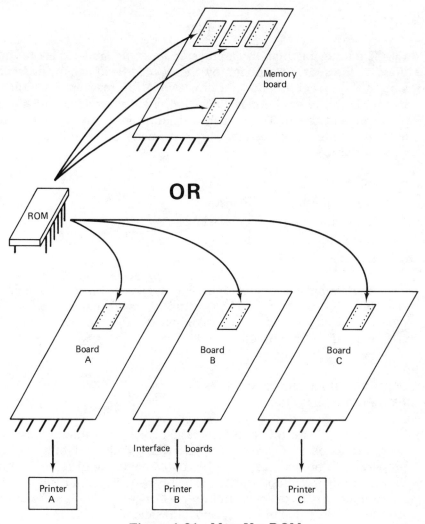

Figure 1.31. Mass-Use ROM.

Introduction to the Microprocessor World

insert the same ROM into different integrated-circuit (IC) sockets on the same memory board, even if each socket represents a different page or memory bank.

Structured Methodology

We develop structure by employing a *top-down* design, starting with a task definition, leading into the algorithmic development, and terminating with the actual program code. This front-end "decomposition" process naturally helps us to generate structured code. Your principal challenge is to *bound the complexity* of the problem at each step. Each additional step in Figure 1.32 is then an elaboration of the previous step, with greater detail and complexity. A structured process generates many benefits.

1. Each step is independent of other steps, thus allowing you to isolate your checks at each step.
2. Each step may be checked stage by stage through the structured process, from task definition to program code.
3. Errors are detectable in a systematic manner.
4. At any point, only a small amount of information has to be remembered and manipulated by a software engineer.
5. Structure helps to prove rigorously the correctness of the entire algorithm.

A top-down design is easy to apply within a software team approach to program development. The project leader can define the task and definition phase, directing the team members toward separate algorithm development, and, in turn, the team members can direct the program code tasks. This attractive engineering approach achieves all the desirable benefits just noted.

The top-down approach is aided considerably by applying software sup-

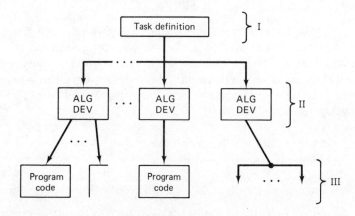

Figure 1.32. Top-Down Design.

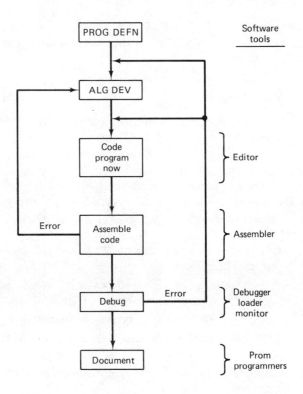

Figure 1.33. Typical Program-Generation Process.

port tools. Software tools are necessary for rapid generation of large, complex programs, whose steps are as those shown in Figure 1.33. Such tools also provide clear, consistent output understandable to each team member.

What Are the Software Tools of the Trade?

If you have written more than 10 lines of code for a microprocessor, you already know that there is more to programming than simply loading hexadecimal numbers into memory. There are also many error-prone clerical tasks that must be performed. Software support tools help us to minimize errors, increase proficiency, and encourage good coding practices. Popular software tools include:

Editors	Assemblers
Debuggers	Compilers
Interpreters	Loaders

Editors help us to make textual changes in our microprocessor program without reloading or rewriting it. They perform such useful functions as adding or deleting a line or character, all automatically. Editors are friendly software support tools, especially when corrected errors can be inserted without retyping the entire program. *Assemblers* are program translators that map or translate assembly language code into machine language code. Most microprocessor programs will be written at the assembly level. Assembly language programs permit us to tailor our programs to unique applications. At the assembly level we can trade off execution time for minimal usage of memory locations in a particular application.

The *debugger* is an extremely useful diagnostic tool that permits us to analyze programs while they are running. Before "fixing" the code, we would insert *breakpoints* (temporary program halts) at critical points to obtain information about registers and memory locations. Then, as the program stops at these points, we automatically examine register and memory contents, making appropriate modifications at that time.

Like assemblers, *compilers* convert source code (your entered code) to binary object code (machine code), subsequently run on the microprocessor. In fact, the compiler process follows essentially the same procedures as those used by an assembler. However, compilers generally convert source code written in a high-level language such as FORTRAN or ALGOL. Some compilers actually optimize the code during compilation, sometimes eliminating redundant instructions, and at other times eliminating code that generates no results.

Like the assembler and compiler, the *interpreter* is a translator which connects a source program (written by the user) into object code (executable by a computer). But an interpreter translates one instruction at a time, executing that instruction in place. When repeated execution of a statement is required, the interpreter automatically repeats the translation process, together with the execution, as many times as required. Even though the process is inherently slower, programs written in an interactive environment such as where BASIC might be found are quite acceptable in this execution procedure.

Even with only one software support tool, the assembler, the programmer's productivity increases measurably. Assemblers remove the tedious errors that human beings tend to make. An alternative solution is to code at the high level. But going beyond assembly language programs and choosing higher-level languages is sometimes not an easy decision, although one that should be made even with a microprocessor. Higher-level languages are readily understood by a wider class of users. More important, most programmers already know at least one high-level language among the several available (FORTRAN, BASIC, ALGOL, PL1, PASCAL).

Why Should You Use an Assembler?

Imagine yourself translating words from Chinese to English. You take each character, look in the Chinese/English dictionary, find the English equivalent, return for the next character, and translate it, proceeding from

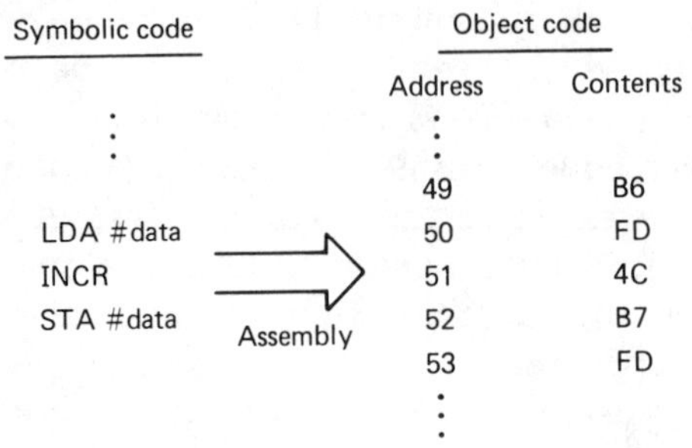

```
Symbolic code                         Object code

                              Address       Contents
        .                        .
        .                        .
        .                        .
                                49             B6
  LDA #data                      50             FD
  INCR              ⟹            51             4C
  STA #data    Assembly          52             B7
                                53             FD
                                 .
                                 .
                                 .
```

Figure 1.34. Translation Process.

one word to the next. Recall that some words have several different meanings, depending on the connotation as well as the denotation. Translating assembly machine language into object code is much the same process. Assemblers do this automatically, by taking symbolic code and translating it into object code. In Figure 1.34 the assembler loads data from memory into the accumulator, increments the accumulator, and stores the accumulator back in memory.

The symbolic code consists of three lines. The object code is a hexadecimal listing after the translation process. Can you recognize the hexadecimal code? No, not unless you have memorized the many hexadecimal codes for your particular instruction set.

Assemblers do more than just translate. An assembly process keeps track of where instructions reside in memory, where symbols are used and their values, and the translation process itself, transforming opcodes and symbols into machine language equivalents. Assemblers can:

1. Keep track of registers, locations, data, instructions, and flags.
2. Accept binary, octal, and hexadecimal numbers.
3. Determine where to put code.
4. Generate addresses.
5. Assign symbols to information.
6. Build tables that equate symbols with values.
7. Generate diagnostics.
8. Produce a standard documentation file which includes the symbolic code, comments, program sequence numbers, and machine object code.

Translating from source to object code involves the use of symbolic references or mnemonics. You have already seen symbolic code—LDA, STA, BRA, and JMP. You assemble or write a program with mnemonics one source statement at a time in the microprocessor source language, which usually consists of:

Label (optional)   Operand or variable field
Opcode   Command field (optional)

The label is only needed when we reference a line of code by other statements. Labels define a location in the program, the name of a common storage element or common parameter, data storage space, or a constant. Labels are unique within any program and must not be duplicated. The opcode is a legal instruction executable by the microprocessor, such as LDA, STA, BRA, and JMP. The operand field may contain expressions consisting

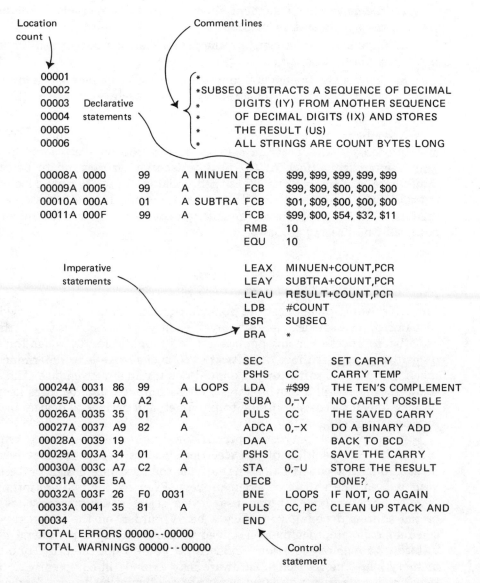

```
Location                          Comment lines
count

    00001                    ┌ *
    00002                    │ *SUBSEQ SUBTRACTS A SEQUENCE OF DECIMAL
    00003   Declarative      │ *    DIGITS (IY) FROM ANOTHER SEQUENCE
    00004   statements       ┤ *    OF DECIMAL DIGITS (IX) AND STORES
    00005                    │ *    THE RESULT (US)
    00006                    └ *    ALL STRINGS ARE COUNT BYTES LONG

    00008A 0000      99    A MINUEN FCB   $99, $99, $99, $99, $99
    00009A 0005      99    A        FCB   $99, $09, $00, $00, $00
    00010A 000A      01    A SUBTRA FCB   $01, $09, $00, $00, $00
    00011A 000F      99    A        FCB   $99, $00, $54, $32, $11
                                    RMB   10
                                    EQU   10

    Imperative                      LEAX  MINUEN+COUNT,PCR
    statements                      LEAY  SUBTRA+COUNT,PCR
                                    LEAU  RESULT+COUNT,PCR
                                    LDB   #COUNT
                                    BSR   SUBSEQ
                                    BRA   *

                                    SEC            SET CARRY
                                    PSHS  CC       CARRY TEMP
    00024A 0031 86   99    A LOOPS  LDA   #$99     THE TEN'S COMPLEMENT
    00025A 0033 A0   A2    A        SUBA  0,-Y     NO CARRY POSSIBLE
    00026A 0035 35   01    A        PULS  CC       THE SAVED CARRY
    00027A 0037 A9   82    A        ADCA  0,-X     DO A BINARY ADD
    00028A 0039 19                  DAA            BACK TO BCD
    00029A 003A 34   01    A        PSHS  CC       SAVE THE CARRY
    00030A 003C A7   C2    A        STA   0,-U     STORE THE RESULT
    00031A 003E 5A                  DECB           DONE?
    00032A 003F 26   F0  0031       BNE   LOOPS    IF NOT, GO AGAIN
    00033A 0041 35   81    A        PULS  CC, PC   CLEAN UP STACK AND
    00034                           END
    TOTAL ERRORS 00000--00000
    TOTAL WARNINGS 00000--00000              Control
                                             statement
```

Figure 1.35. Typical 6809 Assembler Output Listing. (*Courtesy of Motorola Semiconductor Products, Inc.*)

of characters, integers, numbers, and special symbols, or combinations of these arithmetic operators such as plus and minus. The meaning and format of the operand is dictated by the particular opcode and the current addressing mode.

Assemblers employ three types of source statements: declarative, imperative, or control.

1. The *declarative* statement allocates space for symbols or values and assigns contents to locations.
2. *Imperative* statements are the actual machine instructions coded in symbolic form.
3. *Control* statements are commands to the assembler by the programmer to manipulate the assembly process itself.

Assemblers use a *location counter* (LC) during assembly much as a microprocessor uses a program counter during program execution. The location counter keeps track of the next instruction or operand to be placed somewhere in memory. The LC is then updated as each symbolic statement is translated. At printout time the assembler would list the translated code together with the contents of the location counter. A typical assembler output is shown in Figure 1.35.

SUMMARY

The wide world of applications for microprocessors is convincing evidence that microprocessors are here to stay. Yet in your decision as to whether to use a microprocessor in any application you should carefully weigh the costs of hardware against those of software. Your challenge is to determine how much hardware or software you should employ in any given task. The eventual "design" is still a moving target. Microcomputer architectures keep improving, memory costs continue to plummet, and peripheral devices become increasingly intelligent.

Developing a microcomputer (a microprocessor system) requires thoughtful consideration of the electrical load as well as memory management. Your first concern (loading) affects the hardware design process and your second, the software design process. Even so, the two are intimately coupled. For example, if you use device select codes sparingly (as with partial address decode), you place a heavy burden on the programmer to generate software that must not inadvertently call up a peripheral device instead of a memory location. Similarly, if you do not carefully lay out the memory map, the respective hardware may explode in complexity. Modern structured code in a noise-free hardware configuration is very forgiving to hastily designed microcomputer systems.

The software dimension in the design process should always be kept within the bounds of modern programming. You should try to develop structured microprocessor programs. For many applications it is highly desirable to maintain position-independent coding throughout. Software development tools help increase productivity—but they do more. They indirectly maintain your code because such tools generate standard records that have some organization (location count, field designations, line comments, etc.). Only in "very" private microcomputer systems (personal computing, hobbyist, homes) may such tools be ignored.

EXERCISES

1. In your own work, identify areas where microprocessors are currently used. Explain carefully the task(s) the microprocessor is performing in each application.

2. In your own work, identify areas where microprocessors are *not* currently used. Why?

3. What two essential pieces of information must you have to understand the generalities of a specific microprocessor? If you are currently familiar with a microprocessor, examine this information. Could you use them to explain to a co-worker what features your microprocessor has?

4. What is the difference between a microprocessor and a microcomputer?

5. What are the two main design considerations in organizing the bus structure of a microcomputer?

6. Identify the advantages and disadvantages of:
   a. Partial decode for device selection.
   b. Full decode for device selection.

7. What resources will most peripheral devices (chips) contain?

8. In designing a microcomputer, we can minimize the amount of hardware or the amount of software, but not both simultaneously. Why?

9. List and briefly describe microprocessor software development tools.

10. From a human-factor (or engineering) viewpoint, why are the software development tools adequate?

11. What useful functions do tri-state devices perform?

12. Suppose that all microcomputer components (MPU, RAM, ROM, peripheral devices, etc.) can "tri-state" their input/output. Explain why you would or would not need tri-state buffers and/or transceivers in a typical system design.

13. Control directives inform the assembler how to "operate." Without looking up a specific assembler, list and describe useful control directives that might be found.

14. What is the major task involved in a top-down design of any problem?

BIBLIOGRAPHY

BRODERICK, WILLIAM J. "How to Minimize Hardware/Software Partitioning Risks," *Electronic Design News*, Dec. 15, 1978, pp. 21-22. Uses five categories of LSI-based designs to introduce design hints that minimize risk.

CRESPI-REGHIZZI, STEFFANO, PIERLUIGI CORTI, AND ALBERTO DAPRA. "A Survey of Microprocessor Languages," *Computer*, vol. 13, Jan. 1980, pp. 48-67. Describes a classification that helps the user choose among various microprocessor languages and dialects.

CUSHMAN, ROBERT H. "How Development Systems Can Speed Up the Microprocessor Design Process," *Electronic Design News*, Apr. 20, 1976, pp. 63-72. A teletype interface and typical program exercise demonstrates the use of development systems in debugging microprocessor systems.

ELMQUIST, KELLS A. "Standard Specification for S-100 Bus Interface Devices," *Computer*, vol. 12, July 1979, pp. 28-52. An IEEE committee member describes the S-100 preliminary bus standard.

ERDMANN, ROBERT E., JR. "A Serial Data Analyzer for Locating Faults in Decentralized Digital Systems," *Hewlett-Packard Journal*, Oct. 1979, pp. 23-28. The microprocessor in this instrument makes the front panel easy to use while performing complicated tasks.

GLADSTONE, BRUCE. "Ease Painlessly into Microcomputer Operation with In-Circuit Emulation," *Electronic Design News*, Sept. 20, 1977, pp. 89-97. Uses the hardware development tool (ICE) to check prototype hardware, gradually shifting from applications software into the hardware/software configuration.

GRAY, LAWRENCE. "What Type of Programming Language Best Suits OEM Designs?" *Electronic Design News*, June 20, 1978, pp. 78-84. Describes BSAL, a new high-level programming language for microcomputer applications, with justification for the use of BSAL as a block-structured language.

Joint Special Issue on Microprocessors and Microcomputers, *IEEE Transactions on Computers*, vol. C-29, no. 2, Feb. 1980. This highly technical journal is devoted to modern applications of microprocessors. Over 10 papers by leading researchers describe the current state of the art.

LINGANE, PAUL J. "Interactive Modulation Analyzer Control," *Hewlett-Packard Journal*, Nov. 1979, pp. 26-30. A microprocessor is employed to help perform many analog tasks in this sophisticated instrument, such as frequency tuning and tracking.

LUNCH, FRANK, AND CLAY SHOWEN. "Choosing Microprocessors for Reduced Parts Counts," *Digital Design*, Nov. 1977, pp. 18-24. Describes an alternative solution to random logic implementations for floppy disc control.

MACKEEN, JACK. "Minis or Micros? It's the Application That Really Counts," *Digital Design*, Aug. 1978, pp. 18-20. Identifies software/hardware issues involved in choosing a minicomputer over a microprocessor.

MANO, M. MORRIS. *Computer System Architecture*, Englewood Cliffs, N.J.: Prentice-Hall, 1976. This introductory and well-presented text describes the fundamental architectural considerations of computers in general.

MENNIE, DON. "Self-contained Electronic Games," *IEEE Spectrum*, vol. 14, Dec. 1977, pp. 20-25. Describes novel applications for microprocessors.

MILLER, GREG. "Using Microprocessor Development Systems," *Digital Design*, Sept.

1977, pp. 101–104. A comparative analysis of microprocessor development systems and logic analyzers is made.

OGDIN, CAROL A. "Making the Transition to Micros," *Mini-Micro Systems*, Oct. 1977, pp. 32–37. Describes the essential differences between large systems and microprocessors with regard to hardware and software.

PATTERSON, D. A., AND C. H. SEQUIN. "Design Considerations for Single-Chip Computers of the Future," *IEEE Transactions on Computers*, vol. C-29, Feb. 1980, pp. 108–116. The future of new microprocessor architectures may be predicted by these considerations. This volume contains many interesting microprocessor-related topics in relation to new directions for applications.

PINES, KEN. "What Do Logic Analyzers Do?" *Digital Design*, Sept. 1977, pp. 55–70. A survey of applications for the logic analyzer in debugging microprocessor systems.

"Use Your Microcomputer as a Hands-on Learning Tool," *Electronic Design News*, Nov. 20, 1976, pp. 155–161. Describes a resident monitor for generating a learning experience tool in your microprocessor.

WARREN, CARL. "Minis versus Micros: Are They Really Different?" *ICP Interface, Small Business Management*, Fall 1979, pp. 6–11. Suggests several striking similarities between minis and microcomputers.

WEISBERG, MARTIN J. "Microprocessor Development Systems," *Digital Design*, Dec. 1979, pp. 80–85. Describes the number of choices in the universality of functionality of several hardware development systems available for microprocessors, including the Tektronic 8001 and the HP 6400, and in circuit emulators (ICE).

2

Architecture and
Signal Characteristics
of the 6809

2.1 INTRODUCTION

Every microprocessor system has two organizations, the hardware architecture and the software architecture. The block diagram of a microprocessor generally depicts the hardware architecture of the microprocessor device itself. In this block diagram we can find the registers and the arithmetic logic unit visible to a user. Most block diagrams indicate the types of buses being used. In the 6809 we have three buses: an address bus, a data bus, and a control bus.

Block diagrams help us understand what hardware architectural features are available. Sometimes a microprocessor block diagram includes registers that are not directly available to the user but help us to understand the function of the MPU and some instructions. In the 6809 we do not see any extra registers.

The software architecture of a microprocessor is portrayed by the programming model. The programming model, similar to the block diagram, tells us what registers and processor elements are directly available to the programmer. Extra resources are seldom indicated in the programming model. This stripped-down version of software architecture, like the hardware architecture, helps us to grasp quickly the programming features of a microprocessor. In this chapter we look at the block diagram and programming model of the 6809.

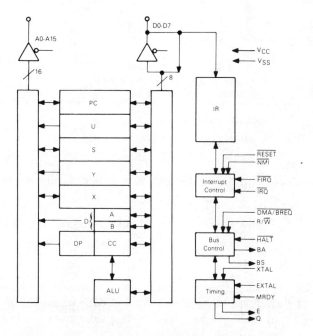

Figure 2.1. 6809 Expanded Block Diagram. (*Courtesy of Motorola Semiconductor Products, Inc.*)

6809 Block Diagram

The 6809 device is a second-generation microprocessor with greatly improved hardware characteristics over earlier versions. Simpler clocking, resetting, and control signals are used. The internal configuration is shown in Figure 2.1.

We use the block diagram as a quick aid to determine possible instructions and grasp the internal architecture. For example:

1. A connection exists from S to D0–D7. This implies that some instruction using these may exist in the instruction set.
2. The direct page register, DP, is connected to address pins. This implies that DP may serve as a source of address.
3. There are no general-purpose registers except for A and B, which are really accumulators. Also, D is a concatenation of A and B.
4. Control signal functions are easily identified.

What Are Some of the Powerful 6809 Features?

These features include hardware and software improvements to facilitate the design of a 6809 microcomputer system:

1. More powerful control signals.
2. Powerful architecture features.

   a. Direct page register to support postion-independent code generation and modular programming.
   b. Doubles the index register and stack pointer capabilities.
   c. Genuine user stack.
   d. 16-bit accumulator instructions.
   e. Expanded addressing capability.

3. The minimal 6809 system needs virtually no random logic because:

   a. The RESET circuits are simpler.
   b. Elaborate clock circuits are unnecessary.

6809 Minimal System

An essential feature of any microprocessor system is the number of chips or devices that we could get by with to make the system run. But this is not a "minimal" system. We define a minimal system as:

Definition: A 6809 minimal system is defined as any system within the basic load limitation of the MPU.

The 6809 minimal system shown in Figure 2.2 can handle eight 68xx loads plus one Schottky or four low-power Schottky TTL devices. A typical system (not minimal) is limited by the electrical driving or loading characteristics on the input/output pins. Of course, if our application demands less power, we must eliminate chips. At the very least, any microprocessor system should have a microprocessor, clock circuitry, memory, and input/output.

Programming Model

Two important characteristics of any microprocessor are its electrical or hardware capabilities and its software capabilities. Microprocessor vendors use programming models to help us understand what software capabilities exist for particular microprocessors. The 6809 programming model appears in Figure 2.3.

The 6809 programming model has subtle hardware improvements which play significant roles in new product designs. Principal among these are:

1. Two 16-bit index registers (X, Y).
2. Two stack pointers (U, S), with U cleanly available to the user.
3. A double accumulator, D, which is actually A and B handled together.

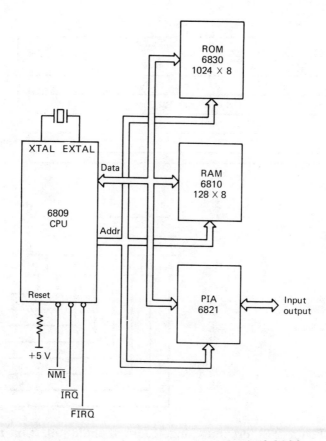

Figure 2.2. Block Diagram of a Typical 6809
System.

4. A direct page register, DP (cleared to zero by every RESET).
5. Two CCR bits: F, used to mask FIRQ interrupts, and E, which specifies the interrupt registers stacking condition.
6. Addressing modes (indirect, pre/post-indexing, program counter relative, PCR).

Applications that find use for these new resources include:

Applications	Resource
Position-independent code	PCR, Long Branch
Reentrant code	DP, U
Modular programming	DP, U, X, Y
Stack machines	DP, E, $\overline{\text{FIRQ}}$, U, S
Multimicroprocessing	DP, U, S, $\overline{\text{FIRQ}}$

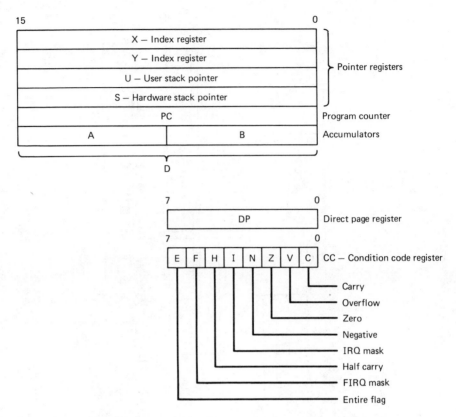

Figure 2.3. Programming Model of the 6809. (*Courtesy of Motorola Semiconductor Products, Inc.*)

The Stack

Nearly all applications require us to store information rapidly and automatically with few instructions. Single-instruction operations working with a stack do just that. Interrupts especially need this capability. Since the S pointer is occasionally used for interrupts, its current pointing location can change both by events in programs as through hardware. The 6809 has a "free" pointer, U, aptly called the user pointer. Stack operations are depicted in Figure 2.4. In a later chapter, we demonstrate the efficient use of each stack pointer.

The PUSH operation stores registers from the microprocessor, or MPU, in sequentially decreasing memory locations (toward location zero). The opposite occurs with the PULL operation.

The stack operations, push and pull, have a nice feature which saves time. You do not have to stack all MPU registers every time because the second byte of the stack instruction, called the postbyte, specifies which registers to save.

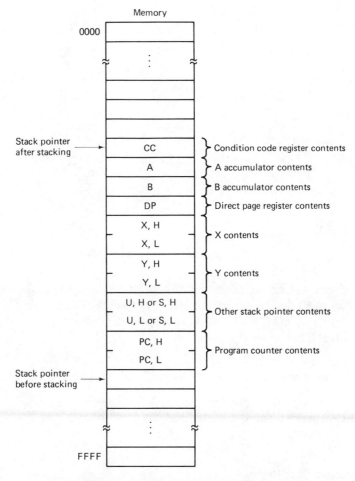

Figure 2.4. 6809 Stacking Order.

EXAMPLE 2.1

This code does the following:

> PSHS—MNEMONIC for pushing information with the S pointer.

> B, X, DP—these registers in the microprocessor are stored on the stack.

This code stored in memory as shown in Figure 2.5 will save X, DP, and B in that *order*, even though you did not list it that way in your manual coding. This is a property of a good assembler. Hardware automatically stores these registers in proper order. Note that you only used eight cycles to execute it. Why? The MPU used five machine cycles for the PSHS and three

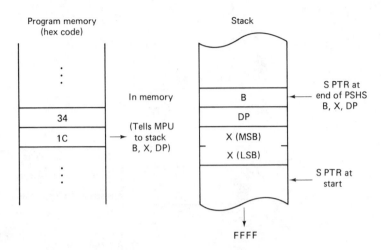

Figure 2.5. PUSH S Pointer or PSHS.

machine cycles to stack all the bytes. The push/pull postbyte (shown in Figure 2.6) designates which registers to save. Note that if we execute PSHU, or the U pointer, the stack will save the S pointer if requested, but not the U pointer! This raises the question.

How can I save the U pointer when I use the PSHU?

Answer: You can put U into X or Y before the PSHU is executed. Then that respective saved register has the U pointer in the U stack. This need will rarely occur.

Condition Code Register

The 6809 has two new condition bits (not available in the 6800), the E flag and the F mask. Note that the other flags have maintained their relative position and functional usage in both the 6809 and 6800. The E flag when set to one indicates that the complete machine state was stacked. *Remember:* The E flag of the stacked CC is used on a return from an interrupt (RTI) to determine the extent of the stacking or pushing. The F bit masks out the

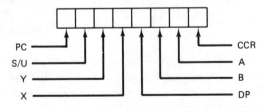

Figure 2.6. PUSH/PULL Postbyte.

interrupts caused by the $\overline{\text{FIRQ}}$. The F bit is also affected by the other interrupts listed below.

Interrupts	F Value after Interrupt
$\overline{\text{NMI}}$	1
$\overline{\text{FIRQ}}$	1
SWI	1
$\overline{\text{RESET}}$	1
$\overline{\text{IRQ}}$	No affect
SWI2	No affect
SWI3	No affect

The remaining CCR bits are affected as follows:

N: Set if and only if the most significant bit of the result is set (this would be the 2's complement of the "sign" bit).

Z: Set if and only if all the bits of the result are clear (the result is exactly 0).

V: Set if and only if the operation causes a 2's-complement overflow. Notice that the expression (N exclusive ORed V) will give the correct sign, even if the sign is not properly represented in the result. This expression is very useful if you want to generate another method to check arithmetic results.

C: 1. Set if the operation causes a carry from the most significant bit (for ADD, ADC).

2. Set if the operation does not cause a carry from the most significant bit of the arithmetic and logic unit for subtraction-like operations (SUB, SBC, CMP—carry flag represents a borrow), *or*

3. Set according to rules for rotate or shifts, *or*

4. Set if bit 7 of the result is set (for MUL).

Besides the E and F bit differences, the 6809 CCR does more than the 6800 CCR because:

1. The 6800 does not have a multiply instruction, whereas the 6809 does.

2. Also, the 6809 CCR sets flags properly for multibyte operations (CCR bits are affected by MSB).

3. The C flag is not the simple result of the carry in the 8-bit arithmetic and logic unit, but depends on the type of operation performed. The 6809 has double accumulator instructions which affect the CCR.

2.2 HIGH-PERFORMANCE PROGRAMMING CAPABILITIES OF THE 6809

Instruction Consistency

The 6809 microprocessor is designed to facilitate powerful programming methods. Instruction consistency or the expected similar behavior of instructions should help the user programmer both to understand the 6809 quickly and to implement programs rapidly. Among these powerfully consistent features are address manipulation, stack operations, and interruption.

Modern programming methods require easy use of pointer operations. The 6809 enhances pointer operations by enforcing a consistent rule for pushing and pulling (through pointers) in all stacks. All instructions that automatically point and move the pointer behave similarly. There also exist autoincrementing and autodecrementing modes of addressing that can mimic stack pointers. The push stack operation decrements the pointer, then stores the word. The pull stack operation loads the word, then increments the pointer. The autodecrement feature first decrements the pointer, then stores the word. The autoincrement feature first loads the word, then increments the pointer.

In fact, Figure 2.4 indicates the stacking order not only for the push and pull operation but also for all other stacking operations with the 6809 instructions. Even if we desire not to push all the active registers (which we can do with the postbyte), the order of pushing or pulling remains the same for stack operations with the user and hardware stack pointers, with active register preservation and restoration by interrupts, and with autodecrement/increment operations.

One register in the 6809 that cannot (purposely) be changed easily is the direct page register, DP. In fact, there is no load immediate instruction for DP. To change DP we must load another 8-bit register and perform an exchange or transfer operation into DP. This cumbersome method is intentional. DP should not be changed frequently. Hence, this operation is discouraged by intentionally making the operation difficult.

Stack Operations

Modular programs are best, because programs so designed are easy to debug and maintain. Structure is also important. In most instances, we make programs modular by using subroutines. Structure is easy to build into 6809 subroutines. Consistent stacking procedures are thus important. Since parameter passage as well as local storage are vital to subroutines, the useful stack configuration shown in Figure 2.7 is recommended in the 6809. Note that the calling routine establishes parameter locations on the stack prior to the subroutine call. Upon subroutine call, the subroutine should establish space on the stack for local variables (only if necessary).

A consistent handling of the stacks is very important. Two distinct and safe procedures are recommended. First, in the calling routine, save the old

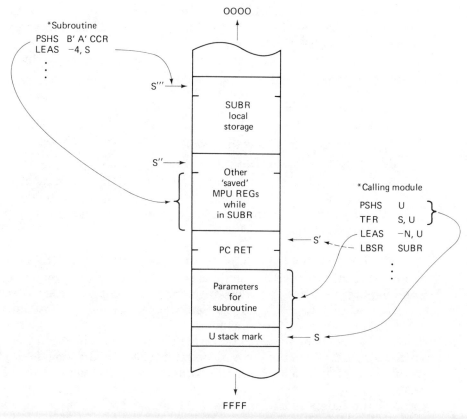

Figure 2.7. Consistent 6809 Stack Picture.

stack mark, U, and generate the parameter space for the subroutine (LEAS
−N, U). Be sure that the S stack pointer is above the parameter space. Second, upon entering the subroutine, immediately save old MPU registers likely
to be altered by the subroutine itself (PSHS B, A, CCR). Also, generate stack
space for local storage required by the subroutine. In Figure 2.7, we have
saved B, A, and CCR, because the subroutine will alter these registers. Also,
four local storage locations have been set up (LEAS −4, 5).

Position Independency

A very attractive property of the 6809 is the ability to support the
generation of position-independent code. There are five attributes designed
into the 6809 to enhance the generation of code which make ROM programs
highly portable without requiring complete regeneration of software. This
"ROMability" of the 6809 now permits us to generate "mass-use" ROMs
that can be used over several applications without requiring program regeneration. That means that manufacturers who incorporate the 6809 in dedicated applications and users who intend to support software can expect

high-quality routines which are universally applicable. Furthermore, the original software can be made modular, permitting the software to grow without affecting later code generation.

Generation of position-independent code is supported by position-independent operations via:

1. Control transfer
2. Temporary storage
3. Access to constants within code
4. Access to tables within position-independent code
5. Dual access to constants located in ROMs, outside of position-independent code, and global variables located in memory whose addresses are unknown at the assembled time of the position-independent code

Control transfers are made position-independent through the use of long and short relative branch instructions across the full address map in memory. The temporary storage is made position-independent by using workspace on the stack, as in Figure 2.7. Position-independent access to constants is possible with the indexed addressing mode made relative to the program counter. Position-independent access to tables is possible using a load effective address instruction, LEAX, in the program counter relative addressing mode. In fact, the starting or base address of the table or constants can be loaded into X relative to the program counter, and then accesses can be made possible through the index addressing mode. These valuable features are employed frequently in later examples.

2.3 6809 SIGNAL CHARACTERISTICS

We have now seen the software and the hardware architecture of the 6809. These architectures tell us about the internal configuration of the 6809 MPU. Every microprocessor needs some interconnection to other devices or peripheral chips. Now we analyze the important interface connections to the control bus, address bus, and data bus. A designer needs to know how the signals will behave on these buses from and to a 6809. Furthermore, any design will require an interface to memory as the first step. Memories employ both the address bus and data bus, as well as the control bus.

Microprocessor system designs become complicated only when an excessive number of devices are attached to the buses. When we stay within the minimal configuration, the design is generally straightforward. When we employ either slow devices or a large number of chips, we need to alter the design.

The objective of this chapter is to determine what important electrical characteristics are necessary for designing beyond the minimal configuration.

Complete understanding of any microprocessor requires us to know the electrical properties. No interfacing can be done until we know how the MPU signals behave electrically. Address and data bus behavior is vital to our understanding. Let us examine the address bus first.

Address Bus Behavior

Addresses become valid on the rising edge of Q, as shown in Figure 2.8. We use this edge to latch addresses into peripheral devices such as ROMs or RAMs.

The address bus has certain load specifications that must not be violated. Each address pin can drive one Schottky TTL load and typically 90 picofarads (pF). Since most 68xx devices have approximately 10 pF of input capacitance, a minimal 6809 system can safely drive eight 68xx devices *plus* one Schottky TTL device (with no buffering required) at the specified clock frequency. It is possible to drive more devices at a lower clock speed, but any design should be tested and analyzed carefully. However, when a buffered address bus is necessary, the circuit of Figure 2.9 can be used with 8T97's.

We can use output control signals BA and BS from the MPU to tell devices what the address bus is doing. HALT, as well as DMA/$\overline{\text{BREQ}}$ and the SYNC instruction, place the address pins of the 6809 in the off state or in high impedance.

Data Bus Behavior

The load specifications for the data bus are similar to those of the address bus, but not identical. The maximum load for data lines of the MPU

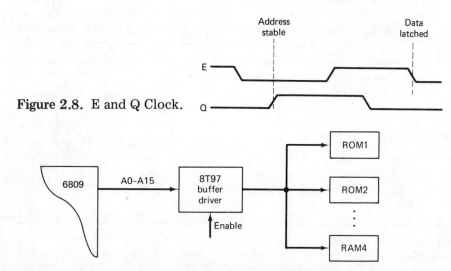

Figure 2.8. E and Q Clock.

Figure 2.9. Typical Buffered Address Bus Load.

is one Schottky TTL load plus 130 pF. (*Note:* Since a typical 68xx device has approximately 10 pF, 12 68xx are possible.) A frequent question is:

How can I verify if a particular loading configuration is satisfactory?

Answer:

1. From 6809 specifications (which we will examine next), obtain worst-case current specifications. Perform the analysis for both logical "1" and "0" levels (I_{OH}, I_{OL}). This is dc (static) loading.
2. Obtain the maximum allowable capacitive loading of the address and data bus at your desired frequency of operation. This is ac (dynamic) loading.
3. Add all load current requirements and capacitive loads of the peripheral devices and verify that these are within the 6809 specifications.

EXAMPLE 2.2:   Load Verification on a Nonminimum Data Bus Configuration

Suppose that we must have six ROMs, two RAMs, and four PIA devices in the system, all of which are in the 68xx family.

Can we operate a 6809 at 1 MHz without bus drivers (8T97's)?

Answer: *No!* Without any analysis, we already know that the 6809 in minimum configuration drives approximately eight 68xx devices plus one TTL load.

We know that device signal voltages have specific valid operating ranges. There is an undefined region for all technologies. TTL is shown in Figure 2.10.

The 6809 electrical characteristics (see Appendix B) specify a supply voltage, V_{CC}, at 5 volts (V) ± 5%. This specification is interpreted by the equivalent circuits shown in Figure 2.11.

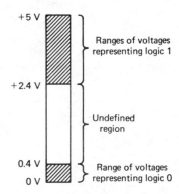

Figure 2.10. Output-Voltage Ranges (TTL Devices).

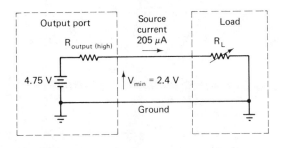

(a) Output high

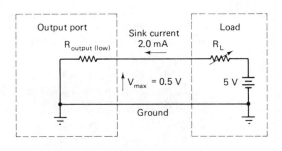

(b) Output low

Figure 2.11. Worst-Case Loading of 6809 Output Port.

EXAMPLE 2.3:   Load Verification on a Data Bus

How many 74LSxx TTL inputs will a 6809 output line drive?

Answer: From the 6809 electrical characteristics we see that for D0–D7, the logical "1" voltage, VOH, can deliver a maximum of

$$I(\text{load}) = 205 \text{ microamperes } (\mu A)$$

before we can no longer distinguish the logical 1. The 6809 output may drop below 2.4 V dc if we try to pull more than 205 μA from each output line.

According to Table A.2 in Appendix A, each 74LSxx can receive 20 μA:

$$20 \ \mu A \times 10 = 200 \ \mu A < 205 \ \mu A$$

or ten 74LSxx inputs can be operated at a logical 1 from a 6809 output line.

What about logical 0? A 74LSxx will feed 0.36 mA back into a 6809. Hence

$$0.36 \text{ mA} \times 5 = 1.90 \text{ mA} < 2.0 \text{ mA} \qquad \text{(maximum 6809 current at logic 0 output)}$$

so only five 74LSxx devices can be operated, not ten!

Control Signal Behavior

All microprocessors have a set of control signals to facilitate peripheral device activity. The 6809 has certain control signals that help the 6809 perform. They include:

Input Timing Signals	Important Features
$\overline{\text{RESET}}$	1. Lets peripherals come out of reset prior to MPU (not like 6800).
	2. Uses simple *RC* circuit for entire system.
$\overline{\text{HALT}}$	1. Useful for cycle steal, burst DMA, or single-instruction execute.
	2. Current instruction always completed.
DMA/$\overline{\text{BREQ}}$	1. Quick memory access or multiprocessing applications.
	2. Opens 15 consecutive bus cycles to user.
	3. Gets bus within one clock cycle.

The previous signals essentially place the address and data bus in particular states. But, more important, devices like to know when the address and data are truly valid. E and Q serve this purpose, as shown in Figure 2.12. We should expect a valid address on the address bus before the end of an interval equal to t_{AVS} from the start of any memory reference cycle.

Two useful signals permit us to interpret 6809 states. They are BA and BS. We can use $\overline{\text{BA}} \wedge \text{BS}$ and the least 4 bits of the address bus to detect which interrupt is being handled. Table 2.1 lists the intended uses of BA and BS.

The 6809 has three interrupt signals, which operate as follows:

Interrupt Control Signals	Important Features
$\overline{\text{NMI}}$	1. Saves entire machine.
	2. Must be low at least one E cycle.
	3. After RESET, $\overline{\text{NMI}}$ is recognizable only after first program load of hardware stack pointer.
$\overline{\text{FIRQ}}$	1. Recognizable if F mask in CCR is zero.
	2. Stacks only CCR and PC.
$\overline{\text{IRQ}}$	1. Recognizable if I mask in CCR is zero.
	2. Stacks all active registers.

Architecture and Signal Characteristics of the 6809

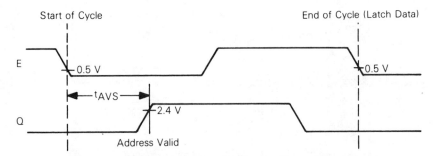

Figure 2.12. E, Q Latch Data/Address Times.

Table 2.1   MPU Output
Status Signals: BA, BS

BA	BS	MPU State
0	0	Normal (running)
0	1	Interrupt acknowledge
1	0	SYNC acknowledge
1	1	HALT or bus grant

Two signals useful for memory reference are read/write ($R/\overline{W}$) and MRDY or Memory Ready:

Memory Control Signals	Important Features
$R/\overline{W}$	1. Use it to switch bidirectional bus drivers in proper direction (low for writing onto data bus). 2. Valid on rising edge of Q.
MRDY	1. Stretches E to allow MPU to wait for a slow device (integrals of $\frac{1}{4}$ bus cycle). 2. Maximum stretch of 10 microseconds (μs). 3. Note that Q is stretched relative to E.

If we perform a memory reference operation, we are assured that the $R/\overline{W}$ line is set properly (high for READ, low for WRITE) at least t_{AQ} nanoseconds (ns) before Q goes high (see Figure 2.13). If we desire to stretch E, the minimum MRDY setup time is t_{PCSR} before E begins to "stretch" (see Figure 2.14).

6809 Clock Circuits

A simple circuit suffices for the 6809 clock and Figure 2.15 depicts one candidate. An AT-cut crystal in the parallel resonant mode works well for the 6809. Make the crystal operate at four times the bus frequency, since

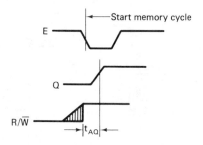

Figure 2.13. R/$\overline{\text{W}}$ Signal Timing.

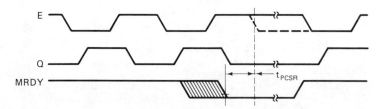

Figure 2.14. MRDY Signal Timing.

Y1	C_{in}	C_{out}
8 MHz	18 pF	18 pF
6 MHz	20 pF	20 pF
4 MHz	24 pF	24 pF

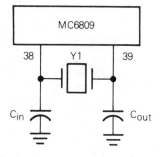

Figure 2.15. 6809 Clock Signal Circuit. (*Courtesy of Motorola Semiconductor Products, Inc.*)

a "÷4 circuit" is built into the 6809 MPU. In a 6809 microprocessor system, the crystal clock circuits can take up to 100 ms after power-on before oscillating at the necessary voltages.

2.4 GENERAL TIMING RULES

Nearly all timing with the 6809 MPU can be related to E and Q. E is the master 68xx bus system timing signal. In general, the interval assignments of Figure 2.16 and the data and address bus rules below will apply. They are recommended by the 6809 designers. Notice that phase 2 ($\phi 2$) in the 6800 MPU corresponds approximately to E, while Q in the 6809 has no counterpart in the 6800 MPU.

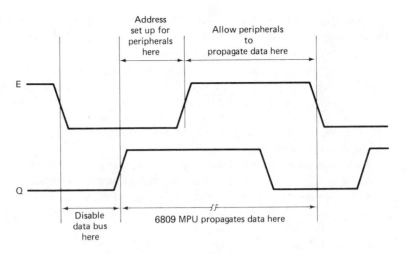

Figure 2.16. E, Q Interval Assignments.

Data Bus Rules

1. Use the interval $\overline{E} \wedge \overline{Q}$ to tri-state the data bus for data bus turnaround without contention.
2. Allow peripherals to propagate data during E.
3. Expect the MPU to start propagating data to data bus with the leading edge of Q.
4. Use the falling edge of E to latch data in receiving devices.

Address Bus Rules

1. Addresses are stable with the rising edge of Q.
2. Use $\overline{E} \wedge Q$ as address setup time for peripherals.

SUMMARY

Microprocessors are not unlike computers in general. In fact, most of the powerful features found in large-scale computers have now telescoped down into a single chip. However, even though we have shrunk the physical real estate, by no means have we, in general, eliminated the complexity and intricacies of computers. To understand this paradigm, we should look at essential block diagrams only. The block diagram of any microprocessor provides us with the macroscopic view of the hardware architecture. The programming model does the same for its software architecture. These "snapshots" help us to assess the power of the microprocessor.

All manufacturers provide minimal configurations for their microprocessors. These tell us how many RAMs, ROMs, and peripheral devices we can interconnect to the microprocessor without requiring any buffering or tri-state logic. We can, of course, make a smaller system, but to develop a larger system we must now include additional hardware to accommodate the electrical signals and increased loading.

As we scan the horizon of microprocessor architectures, our main thrust should be to identify the salient software attributes (powerful features of its instruction set) that enable us to employ modern programming practices. In this chapter we have emphasized the high-performance characteristics of the 6809: flexible stack addressing, consistent instruction behavior in the various addressing modes, the ability to support modularity, and the enhancement of position-independent coding. This chapter briefly introduces such notions and lays the groundwork for further application later in the text.

Every microprocessor has a master synchronization signal, SYNC. This timing signal propagates throughout the entire microcomputer. Its source is either clock circuitry external to the MPU or a signal emanating from within the MPU. In the case of the 6809 we have the E signal. (The 6800 uses phase 2 of the two-phase clock. In fact, all data transfer occurs with phase 2 in the 6800, leaving phase 1 for some interesting applications, such as staggered direct memory access.) The 8080 also uses a two-phase clock relationship which propagates through the entire system.

For any microprocessor you must know how to use the master synchronization signals. Only then will all devices march in lock-step to this specific timing signal. Microprocessors include an additional quadrature signal which either leads or lags the SYNC signal by an integral amount. In the 6809 we have the Q signal, which is staggered one half-cycle from the E signal. These two signals can overlap. This is not allowed in other MPUs. For example, phase 1 and phase 2 are not allowed to overlap in the 6800 and 8080 systems.

MPUs utilize a number of control signals that reduce design effort when interfacing incompatible peripheral devices (too-slow, too-fast). The DMA/$\overline{\text{BREQ}}$ signal, memory read (MRDY), signal, and $\overline{\text{HALT}}$ are typical of the timing signals that are available. DMA/$\overline{\text{BREQ}}$ allows for quick memory access. In fact, you can grab the bus within one clock cycle. Unfortunately, you must "let go" of the bus within 15 cycles. In contrast, the $\overline{\text{HALT}}$ signal does not release the bus to you instantly, but only after the current instruction is executed. Now, however, you have the bus for an indefinite period of time.

You must be aware of the manufacturer's voltage specifications in any interface design. For the 6809 the manufacturer guarantees successful MPU execution at the rated supply voltage, $V_{CC} \pm .5$ V. This 10% tolerance should always be used pessimistically (that is, $V_{CC} - 5\%$) in load analyses. In this chapter we consider a worst-case loading program of the 6809 output port with TTL logic. Notice that we assume the source voltage from the MPU to be 4.75 V, which is the rated low side of V_{CC} according to the manufacturer. As you perform other load verifications on the system, you should assume likewise.

EXERCISES

1. What is the minimal configuration for a 6809?

2. Which registers have a 16-bit length in the programming model?

3. What is the purpose of the direct page register?

4. How do we specify the number of "saved" registers when we execute a stack instruction?

5. What are the significant differences between the 6809 CCR and the 6800 CCR?

6. How do the associated stack pointer instructions in the 6809 differ from those of the 6800?

7. How does the S pointer differ from the U pointer? Why is the U pointer called the user pointer?

8. How much current can E and Q deliver to a load?

9. What are the specific functions of MRDY and BREQ? How do they differ? Can they be used interchangeably?

10. What circuit can be used to distinguish between $\overline{\text{HALT}}$ and BUS GRANT by using BA, BS, and/or $\overline{\text{HALT}}$?

11. What is the minimum resistance to ground, R(L), that can be hung on a 6809 data line yet still ensure that the logic 1 output voltage will be greater than 2.4 V?

12. How many 74LSxx inputs will a 6809 output line drive?

13. $\overline{\text{BA}} \wedge$ BS indicates an interrupt acknowledge. It is also asserted after a $\overline{\text{RESET}}$. How do you use $\overline{\text{BA}} \wedge$ BS to distinguish a true interrupt ($\overline{\text{NMI}}$, $\overline{\text{FIRQ}}$, $\overline{\text{IRQ}}$, SWI, SWI2, SWI3) from a $\overline{\text{RESET}}$?

BIBLIOGRAPHY

BELL, GORDON, AND ALLAN NEWEL. *Computer Structures: Readings and Examples.* New York: McGraw-Hill, 1971. This comprehensive anthology of computer architectures describes the many abstract notions surrounding computers, starting at the instruction set processor (ISP) level.

CUSHMAN, ROBERT H. "Special-Architecture One-Chip Microcomputers Aim for Versatility and Power," *Electronic Design News*, June 20, 1979, pp. 119-127. Surveys one-chip microcomputers in the middle range of the one-chip world limited to 8-bit machines.

FARRELL, JAMES J., III. "MC6801 Offers Versatility," *Digital Design*, vol. 10, Mar. 1980, pp. 58–65. Describes a companion member of the 6800 family of microprocessor architectures.

KRAFT, GEORGE D., AND WING N. TOY. *Mini/Microcomputer Hardware Design*. Englewood Cliffs, N.J.: Prentice-Hall, 1979. This comprehensive text covers the design considerations and architecture employed in the design of the internal hardware mechanisms in a microprocessor. Chapter 7 describes the frequency of instruction execution timing cycles in considerable detail.

ROTHMULLER, KENNETH. "Comparing Microprocessor Architectures," *Mini-Microsystems*, Jan. 1979, pp. 74–79. Applies an evaluation process using high-level programming primitives instead of benchmark programs to the problem of comparing microprocessor architectures. The programming primitives include expression evaluation, control structures, and program modules. Makes a case for comparing the 6800 to other architectures.

SNIGIER, PAUL. "Microprocessor Selection, Some Do's and Don'ts," *Digital Design*, May 1979, pp. 28–34. Sixteen-bit micros are surveyed and guidelines are provided for selecting a particular micro.

SNIGIER, PAUL. "Single-Board Computers and Single-Chip Microcomputers—Some Do's and Don'ts," *Digital Design*, vol. 10, Mar. 1980, pp. 48–56. The powerful features of one-board computers are analyzed.

3

Microprocessor
Timing Specifications

3.1 INTRODUCTION

The most important interface in any microprocessor system is the memory interface. Without properly timing the address and data information, neither the microprocessor nor the memory will capture the respective information. In this chapter we focus on the analysis of matching the 6830 ROM and the 6810 RAM to the 6809.

3.2 THE 6809 AC CHARACTERISTICS

The major contributing factor which "slows down" a microprocessor system is the capacitive effects on timing requirements. As more devices are connected to the address and data bus, the capacitance on the bus increases. The MUP must now drive a heavier load, which slows down the dynamic response. The delay time (interval during which the signal reaches 50% of its final value) becomes significant. This effect is shown in Figure 3.1 for light and heavy loads (many devices) on output signals from the 6809. At the 50% point, the voltage threshold has been reached whereby the receiving device can discriminate a logical 1 from a logical 0 with considerable noise immunity.

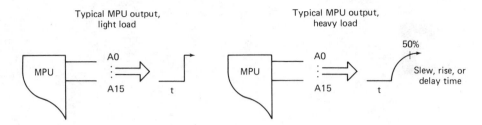

Typical MPU output,
light load

Typical MPU output,
heavy load

MPU   A0 ⋮ A15   t

MPU   A0 ⋮ A15   t

50%

Slew, rise, or
delay time

Figure 3.1. Capacitive Loading.

Matching MPU Timing to Devices

Following are steps for matching MPU timing to devices:

1. To estimate the capacitive effect and determine the correct clock cycle, simply add up the total capacitive load of devices.
2. Calculate the remaining delay times in other relevant circuit paths.
3. Refer to the MPU ac characteristics (see Figure 3.2) to find the permissible worst-case delay time for address, data, and $R/\overline{W}$.
4. Use the MRDY or DMA / $\overline{BREQ}$ appropriately with software if you need to "slow down" the MPU *or*
5. Reduce the MPU clock rate to the tested level, *or*
   Choose a faster 6809, such as the 68A09 or the 68B09.

Manufacturers supply "load" specifications similar to those shown in Figure 3.2. This is typical for many microprocessors. Note that the precise

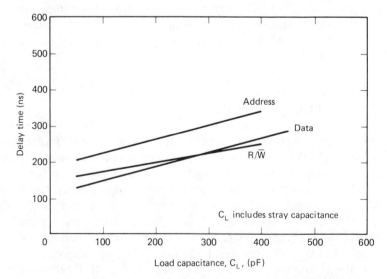

Figure 3.2. Approximate AC Loading Specifications for an MPU. (*Courtesy of Motorola Semiconductor Products, Inc.*)

operating conditions (I_{OL}, I_{OH}; or current at output low voltage, current at output high voltage) are always stated. All regions below each respective curve are the only valid regions of operation. Therefore, you can employ the data in Figure 3.2 to determine the effect of load capacitance on the data and address pins. As you increase the load, you increase the load capacitance. Hence, the data and address signals will be delayed proportionally.

Three-state Bus Considerations

Many system applications require a large number of devices to be connected to the bus structures. In most microprocessor systems there are three buses that must be considered: the address, data, and control buses. In Figure 3.3 we show several ROMs, RAMs, and PIAs that attach to the data bus together with an MPU. If we can accept the time delay associated with data buffers, the loading problems are reduced considerably. But suppose that we do not want to use data or address buffers.

One important question arises: How do several devices share the same bus? In response to this question, manufacturers provide a type of logic called three-state logic, in which the output of a device is either in an active state (1-state or 0-state), or in the high-impedance (off) state. Hence, if several devices are connected to a bus and only one device is operating, the remaining devices should be held in the high-impedance state. The purpose of three-state logic is to isolate components from the buses of a microprocessor system, thus creating a shared bus.

We must provide a control signal to place a device into the high-impedance state. In 6809 designs, the three-state devices that we can use for the data bus are bidirectional bus drivers such as the 8T26's or 8T28's shown in Figure 3.4. The address bus does not normally require bidirectional bus drivers (only if DMA is used).

The 6809 product specifications use three-state notation. For most purposes, I_{tsi}, the three-state (off state) input current found in the 6809 product specifications, is satisfactory for designing systems. Note that the maximum input current leakage into the 6809 data pins is 10 μA, whereas that for the address pins is 100 μA (only when such pins are in the high-impedance state).

How, then, do we ensure that the loading requirements for three-state logic have not been exceeded? The analysis for both active and off states is rather simple. Each of the logic devices will have a specification for "accepting" source current in the high-impedance mode. The procedure described below is equivalent to our solution in Example 2.3 (for active states).

Active-State Analysis

1. Sum up all of the input currents to the devices when they are in the off state.
2. Verify that this does not exceed the maximum allowable specifica-

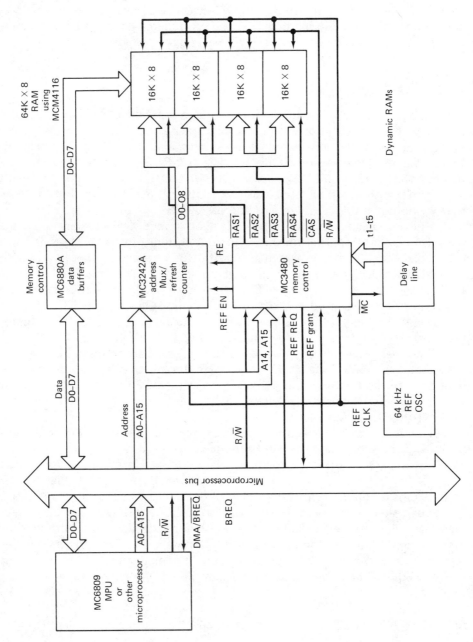

Figure 3.3. Microcomputer System. *(Courtesy of Motorola Semiconductor Products, Inc.)*

64

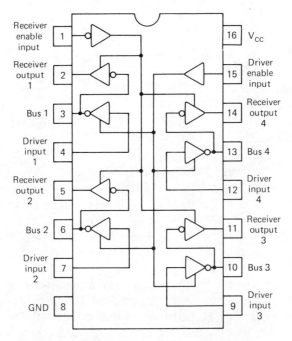

Figure 3.4. 8T28 Bus Driver. (*Courtesy of Motorola Semiconductor Products, Inc.*)

tions for the data bus drivers if they are used or the 6809 data pins if tied directly.

The 6809 data pins can deliver up to 205 μA to either active- or off-state devices. The 6809 address pins can deliver up to 145 μA.

High-Impedance-State Analysis

Repeat steps 1 and 2 above but use 10 μA for data pins and 100 μA for address pins. Most three-state design considerations will depend on the loading of the address and data bus. However, if your design is smaller than the minimal system configuration of your microprocessor architecture, you probably will not perform a three-state analysis. Hence, your design analysis is much simpler.

Matching the ROM to the MPU

Device Selection: When choosing a ROM to be interfaced to the MPU, the first consideration should be to decode the address bits and the MPU control signals that select such devices. Note our need for more than address bits. From the 6809 architecture, it is possible, although not necessary, to use E ORed with the Q signal, as shown in Figure 3.5. The OR gate output

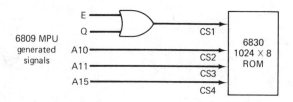

Figure 3.5. Typical Chip Select Connections.

could then be tied to CS1 or chip select pin 1. For a 6830, it is only necessary to use E directly into CS1. One reason we choose to use the leading edge of Q to select a device (i.e., CS1) is that this provides the maximum time for data access in the 6830. For our configuration, address bits A15, A11, and A10 are used to implement the chip select for our particular ROM. Here we have selected a 6830 ROM and assumed that it will function as page 8C in our memory map.

Decoding Delays: Suppose, however, that we must design a large system with many peripheral devices attached to the address bus. In this case it might be necessary to introduce some additional decode logic between the address, data buses, and the 6830. This additional logic increases the path delay, as shown in Figure 3.6, another interfacing scheme. This path delay is equivalent to some time interval, t_{DL}, which we must take into consideration

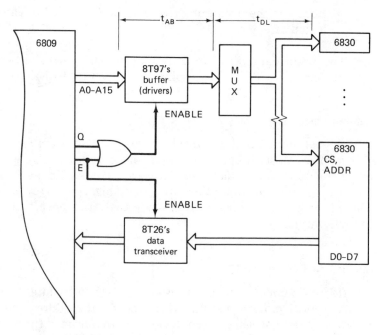

Figure 3.6. Additional Path Delay, t_{DL}.

Microprocessor Timing Specifications

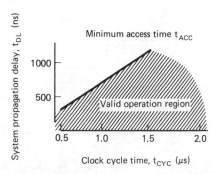

Figure 3.7. Propagation Delay versus 6809 Clock Period.

in the design of the total system. The usual path delay, t_{AB}, in buffered systems represents the requirements for devices that constitute the address bus. These could be 8T97 devices.

Of course, if the decode logic introduces significant additional path delay, we must refer to another specification from the 6809 manufacturer, shown in Figure 3.7, because we must expect to operate the 6809 at slower-than-maximum rated speeds. In this figure we see that as the 6809 clock period increases, the minimum access time, which starts at 695 ns for the 6809 data specifications currently provided, increases as the clock period increases. When we use Figure 3.7 in our timing analysis, we are assuming that the address signals to the devices are available at the start of the t_{ACC} interval of the 6809. When the address signals are enabled to a device by E ORed with Q, a different specification is necessary. Here, we would use, not t_{ACC}, but $t_{ACC} - t_{AD}$. This will become clearer in the timing analysis of the 6830 we are about to perform.

The slope of the curve shown in Figure 3.7 is only approximate, and you should refer to the manufacturer's actual specifications. This is important because only points under the curve are valid operating points for your system clock period. You must either slow down the clock, reduce the decode logic delay (t_{DL}) or use a faster device to ensure that your operating point lies below the curve. The principal specification affected by t_{DL} is access time, t_{ACC}.

Many manufacturers assume that satisfactory reading from a device by the MPU requires that the time interval from address-line activation or valid address time to output access time lies below the curve shown in Figure 3.7. You must realize, however, that all the timing specifications provided by the manufacturer assume that you are operating with a specific load and that the waveforms are rather clean on both the rising and falling transitions. If you violate the load test conditions as well as the waveform purity, the analysis must change to include settling and rise times of the signals. The 6809 specifications assume that all devices have 10 ns rise and fall times. All analyses in this chapter assume that devices are operating in this manner.

The major timing concern will be to verify that all ROM operations can be performed in the intervals provided by the MPU. A READ operation in

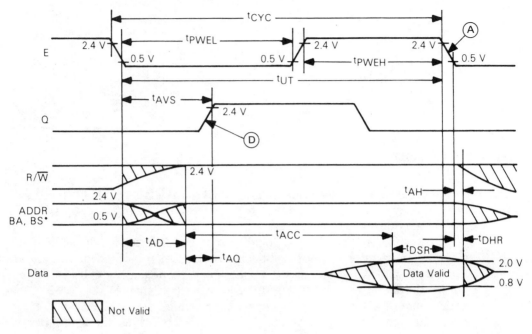

Figure 3.8. Read-Cycle Timing for the 6809. (*Courtesy of Motorola Semiconductor Products, Inc.*)

our 6830 configuration requires only a "clean" address. A R/$\overline{W}$ signal and timing are used when we must share the data bus. In any case, we need two sets of timing specifications, those for the MPU and those for the ROM. Our final "system" specification for timing must fit within both of these sets. For read operations, we must use Figure 3.8 (MPU) and Figure 3.9 (typical ROM). Again, we are assuming the interface shown in Figure 3.5.

Our objective is to ensure that data from the ROM appear at the proper instant to the MPU data pins. This instant occurs at the end of the memory reference cycle, point A in Figure 3.8. Region B in Figure 3.9 must overlap point A in Figure 3.8.

A and B line up at the right side of the timing interval. But we need to determine what parameters to line up on the left side. Well, the ROM does nothing until the CS pins are activated. This is the initiation instant, point C in Figure 3.9. The MPU initiates the chip select at point D in Figure 3.8.

Our timing analysis must verify that if points C and D line up, so do points A and B within some specified tolerance. If so, the ROM will run at the MPU rated clock speed. If not, we must slow down the MPU or choose another ROM. Let us go through an analysis with the 6830.

Timing Considerations, $t_{DL} = 0$: Let us assume for Example 3.1 below that the OR gate of Figure 3.5 introduces insignificant delay over the total response time of the system design. *What, then, are the important timing questions concerning matching ROMs to the MPU?* First we must determine

AC Operating Conditions and Characteristics
(Full operating voltage and temperature unless otherwise noted)
(All timing with $t_r = t_f = 20$ ns. load)

Characteristic	Symbol	Min	Max
Cycle time (ns)	t_{cyc}	500	—
Access time (ns)	t_{acc}	—	500
Data delay time (read)(ns)	t_{DDR}	—	300
Data hold from address (ns)	t_{DHA}	10	—
Data hold from deselection (ns)	t_H	10	150

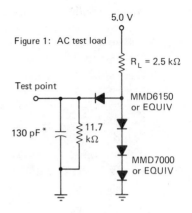

Figure 1: AC test load

*Includes fig. capacitance

Timing Diagram

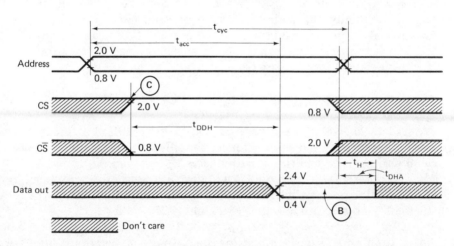

Figure 3.9. Read-Cycle Timing for the 6830 ROM. (*Courtesy of Motorola Semiconductor Products, Inc.*)

how fast the ROM can respond to the MPU access. Any memory device, when called to do a READ operation, will respond to the address selection as well as to the control signal. When we examine most memory timing diagrams of ROM devices, we see three important parameters: cycle time, t_{CYC}; access time, t_{ACC}; and delay time, t_{DDR}.

In some specifications, you may find t_{DDR} redefined as t_{CO} and called chip select to output delay. To ensure proper operation between the ROM and the MPU, then, we need to verify that these timing specifications fit within the 6809 requirements.

EXAMPLE 3.1: Analysis of a 6809-to-6830 Interface

Peripheral Read Access Interval, t_{acc}: When an MPU attempts to read data from a ROM, it must activate both the ROM address lines and control lines according to the timing of Figure 3.8. From Figure 3.5 we found that address bits A15, A11, and A10, as well as control signals E or Q, will select our particular 6830. Now if we refer to the timing diagram (Figure 3.8) for the 6809, we can determine when the valid address appears. This occurs at the rising edge of Q. From the 6830 timing diagram, the device access time, t_{acc}, of the device must comply with the equivalent 6809 specifications. To be precise, t_{acc} of the device must never exceed the maximum duration that could be required of the device to permit the data to appear at the device output pins. We must ensure that the maximum t_{acc} of the 6830 is always less than the minimum access time of the MPU, t_{ACC}:

$$t_{acc} \text{ (device)} < t_{ACC} \text{ (MPU)} \qquad (3.1)$$

From the specifications we find that at rated clock speeds of 1 MHz the MPU time of 695 ns is always greater than the device time of 500 ns.

Device Cycle Interval, t_{cyc}: We also see that the cycle time of the device, t_{cyc}, is essentially the address up-time or valid time. For the 6830, t_{cyc} is 500 ns and is the minimum time at which that ROM can operate. From the MPU diagram, we find that the equivalent specification is $t_{CYC} - t_{AD}$ (address delay). We must satisfy

$$t_{cyc} \text{ (device)} < t_{CYC} \text{ (MPU)} - t_{AD} \text{ (MPU)} \qquad (3.2)$$

From data specifications, we find that 1000 - 200 ns is greater than the 500 ns required of the 6830. Hence, the 6830 will perform adequately with the 6809, given no additional path delays.

To determine if path delays will have a serious effect, we need to calculate the total propagation delay. Then this delay must be subtracted from the right-hand side of equations (3.1) and (3.2).

Data Delay Interval, t_{CO} or t_{DDR}: Another important timing specification is the duration of time required for the output data to appear after we select a ROM itself, t_{DDR} or t_{CO}. For the 6830 this is 300 ns maximum. The equivalent specifications in the 6809 require that this time, t_{DDR}, be less than $t_{ACC} - t_{AQ}$:

$$\begin{matrix} t_{CO} \text{ (device)} \\ \text{or} \\ t_{DDR} \text{ (device)} \end{matrix} < t_{ACC} \text{ (MPU)} - t_{AQ} \text{ (MPU)} \qquad (3.3)$$

When we substitute actual values we find that 695 - 25 ns is greater than 300 ns; and again we find that the ROM will perform satisfactorily at the rated clock speed for the 6809. This same procedure must be carried out for any ROM device you choose.

Data Hold Interval, t_{DHA} or t_H: Since our circuit (E ORed with Q) is used as a chip select, when E goes low, for all practical purposes the ROM is deselected. The question arises: Does the ROM hold its data long enough for the MPU to capture it? In other words, is equation (3.4) satisfied?

$$t_{DHA} \ (MIN) < t_{DHR} \tag{3.4}$$

At rated MPU clock speeds, t_{DHR} is 10 ns. The ROM device holds its data for no less than 10 ns.

The MPU latches whatever data are on the bus when E goes low. Because both clock and data signals are buffered throughout the system, some skew may exist between the clock and data on the processor pins and the external latch and enable signals in both the processor and the peripheral devices.

To compensate for internal processor skew, *read* data must remain valid *on the processor data bus pins* for 10 ns after the falling edge of E. Since the sending device will go from a valid low-impedance state to a very high impedance state, correct data should remain on the bus long after the sending device is disconnected. These are *valid data* and will generally remain valid until another device sends data on the bus. For most situations, t_{DHR} is not a limiting factor on a 6809 bus.

Matching the RAM to the MPU

When we interface a RAM to the MPU, the chip select considerations are identical to those of the ROM as shown previously. However, the timing specifications for the RAM are more complex than that of the ROM because we need to also verify that the write operation of the RAM is satisfactory for our purpose. What important considerations are there for the write operation in a RAM? The WRITE timing specifications for the MPU are depicted in Figure 3.10.

EXAMPLE 3.2:   Analysis of a 6809-to-6810 Interface

Let us use a specific RAM device, the 6810. This 128 × 8 static device has seven specific timing parameters, which we must analyze as shown in Figure 3.11 for the write cycle. Again, we assume that E ORed with Q is tied to a CS pin of the 6810. The analysis for t_{cyc} is identical to that of the 6830 ROM device we saw previously. The other parameters, however, must be considered separately.

Address Setup Interval, t_{AS}: There is a relationship between the chip select and address valid time, t_{AS}, or the setup time. The MPU must be able to energize the chip select lines no sooner than 20 ns after the address valid time, as we see from the 6809 write-cycle timing diagram (Figure 3.10). In our assumption that the chip select lines are activated by both address lines and E or Q, as shown in Figure 3.5, we can assume that the time that Q goes high is the time at which the chip select lines are activated, and the address

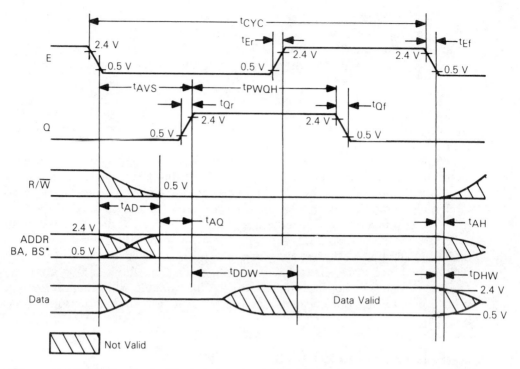

Figure 3.10. Write-Cycle Timing for the 6809 MPU. (*Courtesy of Motorola Semiconductor Products, Inc.*)

lines become valid no later than t_{AQ} prior to Q going high. This constraint is satisfied at the rated clock speed for the 6809:

$$t_{AS} \text{ (device)} < t_{AQ} \text{ (MPU)} \qquad (3.5)$$

Write Chip Select Interval, t_{WCS}: There is also a minimum time duration between activating the write line and asserting the chip select lines for many RAM devices. For the 6810, however, t_{WCS} or write-to-chip select delay time can be 0. In spite of this, the 6809 equivalent time, t_{AQ}, is nonzero. Hence, equation (3.6) will always be satisfied for a 6809 operating at a rated clock speed with a 6810 in the write mode for this time parameter.

$$t_{WCS} \text{ (device)} < t_{AQ} \text{ (MPU)} \qquad (3.6)$$

Chip Select Pulse Width: The chip select lines must be held activated for a minimum duration, t_{CS}. For the 6810 this is 300 ns. Since we are using address bits and the E, Q combination, the shortest duration expected is the length of Q overlapped with E. This is approximately equivalent to $t_{CYC} - t_{AVS}$ in Figure 3.10.

$$t_{CS} \text{ (device)} < t_{CYC} - t_{AVS} \qquad (3.7)$$

Write cycle

Characteristic	Symbol	MCM6810AL		MCM6810AL1	
		Min	Max	Min	Max
Write cycle time (ns)	t_{cyc} (W)	450	–	350	–
Address setup time (ns)	t_{AS}	20	–	20	–
Address hold time (ns)	t_{AH}	0	–	0	–
Chip select pulse width (ns)		300	–	250	–
Write to chip select delay time (ns)	t_{WCS}	0	–	0	–
Data setup time (write) (ns)	t_{DSW}	190	–	150	–
Input hold time (ns)	t_H	10	–	10	–

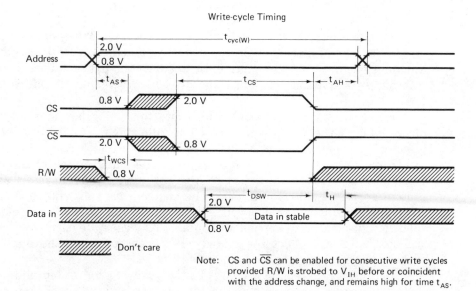

Note: CS and $\overline{CS}$ can be enabled for consecutive write cycles provided R/W is strobed to V_{IH} before or coincident with the address change, and remains high for time t_{AS}.

Figure 3.11. Write-Cycle Timing for the 6810 RAM. (*Courtesy of Motorola Semiconductor Products, Inc.*)

For the 6809 at rated clock speed, $t_{CYC} - t_{AVS} = 1000 - 250 = 750$ ns, which, is of course, greater than the minimum acceptable time for the 6810 of 300 ns for t_{CS}.

Data Setup Interval, t_{DSW}: To write into the device, we must ensure that the data on the data bus are stable for a sufficiently long interval to be latched accurately by the RAM device. The data setup time, t_{DSW}, for the 6810 is 190 ns minimum, and is the minimum interval prior to deactivation of the chip select lines upon which the data must remain stable. Since our chip select lines are disabled approximately the same time the address lines are disabled (which is very close to the end of the write-cycle time) and the data have been stable ever since Q went high minus t_{DDW}, the data stable time for the 6809 is much longer than that required by the 6810. To be precise, then, we need to satisfy

$$t_{DSW} \text{ (device)} < t_{CYC} \text{ (MPU)} - t_{AVS} \text{ (MPU)} - t_{DDW} \text{ (MPU)} \qquad (3.8)$$

For the 6809 at rated clock speed, the right-hand side of (3.8) is 1000 – 250 – 225 or 525 ns. The 6810 requirement (left-hand side) is 190 ns.

Input Hold Interval, t_H: Another important parameter is the input hold time, t_H, of the device. For the 6810 this minimum time is 10 ns. The equivalent specification for the 6809 is t_{DHW}, output data hold time, and is minimally 30 ns. Hence, for the 6809 and the 6810 operating at rated clock speeds, equation (3.9) is satisfied.

$$t_H \text{ (device)} < t_{DHW} \text{ (MPU)} \qquad (3.9)$$

The data receiver (e.g., memory or peripheral) latches whatever data are on the bus when E goes low. Since both clock and data are buffered throughout the system, some skew may exist between the data sender and the data receiver. In a minimal system, skew does not exist and therefore is not a factor.

However, since the specifications cite that valid data must be present *on the pins* of the data receiver for 10 ns following the falling edge of E, the effect of this specification is greatly reduced in a real system. On an actual bus, capacitance to ground tends to store the value presently on the bus; when the data sender switches to the off mode, only device leakage is present to affect this stored level. The charged bus will tend to decay, but with a time constant that is typically much longer than a bus cycle. Noise that may occur due to capacitive coupling may generate narrow glitches but will not adversely affect the stored charge, except when the bus is being actively driven.

Because the levels on a charged data bus will tend to be valid until the next data sender comes out of the off mode, data hold time is not a significant factor in real 6809 systems.

3.3 PROPAGATION DELAY

If any of the previous timing specifications are not satisfied, we have several alternatives: slow down the clock of the MPU, get a faster device, or use an MRDY control signal to the MPU. This signal can be generated by the peripheral devices themselves in some manner. Recall, however, that if we have many devices on the address and data bus, we must consider the *total* propagation delay between MPU and the memory device.

If the additional decoding devices introduce significant delays or if the capacitive loading effects introduce sufficient propagation delays, we must utilize some additional manufacturers' data in order to proceed. These

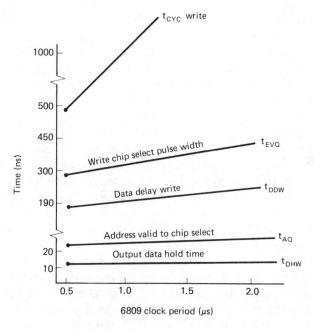

Figure 3.12 6809 Write Timing Specifications versus Clock Period (Approximate).

data must represent the functions of the timing parameters for the write cycle as a function of the clock-rate in the system architecture. Figure 3.12 is representative of such data available from manufacturers. Here the change of the important write timing parameters as a function of clock period is specified and *all RAM devices must then operate below each curve* for the respective time parameter.

SUMMARY

At the start of a design process, you must determine whether data and addresses will arrive at their respective destinations in time. In this chapter we have examined the importance of timing relationships in a microprocessor system. We have in mind two situations. In the first case we assume that we are exceeding the minimal configuration of the manufacturer's specification for the microprocessor, and therefore that additional logic between the MPU and peripheral devices is necessarily required. A potential increase in the propagation delay of data and address information is expected. In the second case we assume that our peripheral devices are too slow for the microprocessor. Here we need to slow down the microprocessor, skip cycles, or choose another peripheral device.

You analyze the timing for your configuration by searching through the manufacturer's specifications for the ac characteristics of the MPU and the peripheral devices. In the 6809 technology, a 50% threshold point is assumed above and below which a voltage threshold indicates that a receiving device can discriminate a logical 1 from a logical 0. The 50% threshold increases the noise immunity and is a conservative measure. To illustrate this point, we have performed a stepwise analysis of a ROM and RAM interface to the 6809. Hopefully, in most cases you will not have to go to such great lengths to verify a design. But it is wise to be thorough!

Matching timing relationships between an MPU and devices is a process that estimates the total capacitive load of the devices on an MPU pin, searching for the longest delay. The procedure shown in this chapter is identical to a critical path analysis. Here we identify the path that has the greatest capacitive loading and, in principle, the longest propagation delay. Once that is determined, we verify the need to extend the clock cycle. As alternatives we could use MRDY and DMA/$\overline{\text{BREQ}}$ control signals to slow down the MPU. Another alternative is to increase the MPU clock rate, because even though manufacturers supply chips at a rated clock speed, in many instances you can increase that rate considerably. However, your design must be checked out at an acceptably tested level. Run the MPU at the fast rate, but exhaustively check (wring out) the system. In any event, you can always choose an even faster MPU, such as the 6809A and 6809B.

In an interface design, the timing must be examined from a precise starting point. In our RAM and ROM interface we have assumed the positive transition of Q as our starting point for analysis. Remaining data hold and address stable intervals are then analyzed from this leading edge. Should you use a different starting point, such as the rising or falling E signal transition, all equations shown will change, but the analysis procedure is similar. You must determine that the device specifications are compatible with the MPU specifications.

EXERCISES

1. How do you determine bus delay times for a particular system design?

2. Suppose that 8T97 buffers are used between 6809 address pins and a 6830 ROM. Let E ORed with Q enable 8T97's. What are the important timing equations?

3. Suppose that only address lines select a 6830 as well as generate A0–A9. No buffers or decoders are used. Neither are the E and Q signals. What are the important timing equations?

4. Repeat Exercise 2 for the 6810 operating in the read cycle.

5. Repeat Exercise 2 for the 6810 operating in the write cycle.

6. Suppose that 16 RAM and ROM devices are needed in a particular system. Design appropriate MUX and address decoder circuitry to select the devices. How are you handling path delay?

7. Why do we employ E ORed with Q as a chip select signal to RAMs? Is it necessary for all RAM devices?

8. Why do we employ E alone as a chip select timing signal to ROMs since the READ is asynchronous?

9. Why do we employ E ORed with Q as a chip select timing signal to ROMs (again, since the READ is asynchronous)?

BIBLIOGRAPHY

"CPU Boards—A Matter of Bits, Buses and Basic Basic," *Electronic Design News*, Nov. 20, 1977, pp. 144-150. Describes briefly popular bus standards for the microcomputer world, including S100, PROLOG, INTEL and LSI11.

KRAFT, GEORGE D., AND WING N. TOY, *Mini/Microcomputer Hardware Design*. Englewood Cliffs, N.J.: Prentice-Hall, 1979. Chapter 3 describes the internal organization and data transfer gating logic for microprocessors. Identifies basic computer organization.

"The Microsystem Game Plan—Design in and Win," *Electronic Design News*, Nov. 20, 1977, pp. 135-138. Part 1 of a series of articles describing the development of a micro-based product for a small business application.

SCHREIER, PAUL G. "Offering Little Standardization and a Wide Choice of Configurations, Microcomputer Systems Don't Make Life *That* Easy," *Electronic Design News*, Nov. 20, 1977, pp. 104-117. Describes several one-board computers and gives a rationale for choosing each.

SCHWARTZ, MEL. "Bank-Switchable Memory for LSI-11s," *Digital Design*, vol. 10, Mar. 1980, pp. 38-40. Many microprocessor applications require large memory, which bank-switchable solutions described here can provide.

4

6809 Instruction Set

4.1 INTRODUCTION

The 6809 microprocessor is the result of considerable effort by hardware and software engineers. Their first goal was to upgrade the 6800 to form a new processor that would be better than others, especially for business and word-processing applications. The power of the device is evident in the instruction set, but the address enhancements make the 6809 an exceptional microprocessor. This chapter focuses on these topics.

The 6809 inherited much of its character from its parent chip, the 6800. (A chip off the old block, you might say.) Most of all, the 6809 was designed to be highly compatible with the 6800 (but only at the assembly language-compatible). This helped the designers to remap the opcodes of the 6809 to provide more efficient machine execution.

There were additional improvements over the 6800:

Powerful addressing modes

Simpler timing and control signals

A second stack available to the user

A second index register

Program relative addressing over full memory

Support for true position-independent code generation

The basic instructions of any computer are strengthened by powerful addressing modes. The 6809 has a very large set of modes. There are 59 basic instructions, and 1464 different variations of instructions and addressing modes. All features support modern programming methods. The addressing modes include:

Inherent	Indexed
Immediate	Zero Offset
Direct	Constant Offset
Extended	Accumulator Offset
Extended Indirect	Indexed Direct
Register	Relative
	Short/Long
	Program Counter Relative

For your convenience, the instructions and their various address modes are tabulated in Tables 4.1 to 4.8. The notation for the 6809 assembler and

Table 4.1   8-Bit Accumulator and Memory Instructions

Mnemonic(s)	Operation	Implied	Immediate	Direct	Extended	Extended Indirect	Indexed	Indexed Indirect	Relative	Relative Indirect
ADCA, ADCB	Add memory to accumulator with carry	−	X	X	X	X	X	X	X	X
ADDA, ADDB	Add memory to accumulator	−	X	X	X	X	X	X	X	X
ANDA, ANDB	And memory with accumulator	−	X	X	X	X	X	X	X	X
ASL	Arithmetic shift left memory location	−	−	X	X	X	X	X	X	X
ASLA, ASLB	Arithmetic shift left accumulator	X	−	−	−	−	−	−	−	−
ASR	Arithmetic shift right memory location	−	−	X	X	X	X	X	X	X
ASRA, ASRB	Arithmetic shift right accumulator	X	−	−	−	−	−	−	−	−
BITA, BITB	Bit test memory with accumulator	−	X	X	X	X	X	X	X	X
CLR	Clear memory location	−	−	X	X	X	X	X	X	X
CLRA, CLRB	Clear accumulator	X	−	−	−	−	−	−	−	−
CMPA, CMPB	Compare memory with accumulator	−	X	X	X	X	X	X	X	X
COM	Complement memory location	−	−	X	X	X	X	X	X	X
COMA, COMB	Complement accumulator	X	−	−	−	−	−	−	−	−
DAA	Decimal adjust A-accumulator	X	−	−	−	−	−	−	−	−

Table 4.1   (Continued)

Mnemonic(s)	Operation	Implied	Immediate	Direct	Extended	Extended Indirect	Indexed	Indexed Indirect	Relative	Relative Indirect
DEC	Decrement memory location	—	—	X	X	X	X	X	X	X
DECA, DECB	Decrement accumulator	X	—	—	—	—	—	—	—	—
EORA, EORB	Exclusive or memory with accumulator	—	X	X	X	X	X	X	X	X
EXG R1, R2	Exchange R1 with R2 (R1, R2 = A, B, CC, DP)	X	—	—	—	—	—	—	—	—
INC	Increment memory location	—	—	X	X	X	X	X	X	X
INCA, INCB	Increment accumulator	X	—	—	—	—	—	—	—	—
LDA, LDB	Load accumulator from memory	—	X	X	X	X	X	X	X	X
LSL	Logical shift left memory location	—	—	X	X	X	X	X	X	X
LSLA, LSLB	Logical shift left accumulator	X	—	—	—	—	—	—	—	—
LSR	Logical shift right memory location	—	—	X	X	X	X	X	X	X
LSRA, LSRB	Logical shift right accumulator	X	—	—	—	—	—	—	—	—
MUL	Unsigned multiply (AXB → D)	X	—	—	—	—	—	—	—	—
NEG	Negate memory location	—	—	X	X	X	X	X	X	X
NEGA, NEGB	Negate accumulator	X	—	—	—	—	—	—	—	—
ORA, ORB	Or memory with accumulator	—	X	X	X	X	X	X	X	X
ROL	Rotate memory location left	—	—	X	X	X	X	X	X	X
ROLA, ROLB	Rotate accumulator left	X	—	—	—	—	—	—	—	—
ROR	Rotate memory location right	—	—	X	X	X	X	X	X	X
RORA, RORB	Rotate accumulator right	X	—	—	—	—	—	—	—	—
SBCA, SBCB	Subtract memory from accumulator with borrow	—	X	X	X	X	X	X	X	X
STA, STB	Store accumulator to memory	—	—	X	X	X	X	X	X	X
SUBA, SUBB	Subtract memory from accumulator	—	X	X	X	X	X	X	X	X
TST	Test memory location	—	—	X	X	X	X	X	X	X
TSTA, TSTB	Test accumulator	X	—	—	—	—	—	—	—	—
TFR, R1, R2	Transfer R1 to R2 (R1, R2 = A, B, CC, DP)	X	—	—	—	—	—	—	—	—

Note: A and B may be pushed to (pulled from) either stack with PSHS, PSHU (PULS, PULU) instructions. See Table 4.3.

Table 4.2   16-Bit Accumulator and Memory Instructions

Mnemonic(s)	Operation	Implied	Immediate	Direct	Extended	Extended Indirect	Indexed	Indexed Indirect	Relative	Relative Indirect
ADDD	Add memory to D accumulator	—	X	X	X	X	X	X	X	X
CMPD	Compare memory with D accumulator	—	X	X	X	X	X	X	X	X
EXG D, R	Exchange D with X, Y, S, U, or PC	X	—	—	—	—	—	—	—	—
LDD	Load D accumulator from memory	—	X	X	X	X	X	X	X	X
SEX	Sign Extend	X	—	—	—	—	—	—	—	—
STD	Store D accumulator to memory	—	—	X	X	X	X	X	X	X
SUBD	Subtract memory from D accumulator	—	X	X	X	X	X	X	X	X
TFR D, R	Transfer D to X, Y, S, U, or PC	X	—	—	—	—	—	—	—	—
TFR R, D	Transfer X, Y, S, U, or PC to D	X	—	—	—	—	—	—	—	—

Table 4.3   Index Register/Stack Pointer Instructions

Mnemonic(s)	Operation	Implied	Immediate	Direct	Extended	Extended Indirect	Indexed	Indexed Indirect	Relative	Relative Indirect
CMPS, CMPU	Compare memory with stack pointer	—	X	X	X	X	X	X	X	X
CMPX, CMPY	Compare memory with index register	—	X	X	X	X	X	X	X	X
EXG R1, R2	Exchange D, X, Y, S, U, or PC with D, X, Y, S, U, or PC	X	—	—	—	—	—	—	—	—
LEAS, LEAU	Load effective address into stack pointer	—	—	—	—	X	X	X	X	X
LEAX, LEAY	Load effective address into index register	—	—	—	—	X	X	X	X	X
LDS, LDU	Load stack pointer from memory	—	X	X	X	X	X	X	X	X
LDX, LDY	Load index register from memory	—	X	X	X	X	X	X	X	X
PSHS	Push any register(s) onto hardware stack (except S)	X	—	—	—	—	—	—	—	—
PSHU	Push any register(s) onto user stack (except U)	X	—	—	—	—	—	—	—	—

Table 4.3 (Continued)

Mnemonic(s)	Operation	Implied	Immediate	Direct	Extended	Extended Indirect	Indexed	Indexed Indirect	Relative	Relative Indirect
						Addressing Modes				
PULS	Pull any register(s) from hardware stack (except S)	X	—	—	—	—	—	—	—	—
PULU	Pull any register(s) from hardware stack (except U)	X	—	—	—	—	—	—	—	—
STS, STU	Store stack pointer to memory	—	—	X	X	X	X	X	X	X
STX, STY	Store index register to memory	—	—	X	X	X	X	X	X	X
TFR R1, R2	Transfer D, X, U, or PC to D, X, S, U, or PC	X	—	—	—	—	—	—	—	—
ABX	Add B-accumulator to X (unsigned)	X	—	—	—	—	—	—	—	—

Table 4.4 Branch Instructions

Mnemonic(s)	Operation	Implied	Immediate	Direct	Extended	Extended Indirect	Indexed	Indexed Indirect	Relative	Relative Indirect
						Addressing Modes				
BCC, LBCC	Branch if carry clear	—	—	—	—	—	—	—	X	—
BCS, LBCS	Branch if carry set	—	—	—	—	—	—	—	X	—
BEQ, LBEQ	Branch if equal	—	—	—	—	—	—	—	X	—
BGE, LBGE	Branch if greater than or equal (signed)	—	—	—	—	—	—	—	X	—
BGT, LBGT	Branch if greater (signed)	—	—	—	—	—	—	—	X	—
BHI, LBHI	Branch if higher (unsigned)	—	—	—	—	—	—	—	X	—
BHS, LBHS	Branch if higher or same (unsigned)	—	—	—	—	—	—	—	X	—
BLE, LBLE	Branch if less than or equal (signed)	—	—	—	—	—	—	—	X	—
BLO, LBLO	Branch if lower (unsigned)	—	—	—	—	—	—	—	X	—
BLS, LBLS	Branch if lower or same (unsigned)	—	—	—	—	—	—	—	X	—
BLT, LBLT	Branch if less than (signed)	—	—	—	—	—	—	—	X	—
BMI, LBMI	Branch if minus	—	—	—	—	—	—	—	X	—

Table 4.4 (Continued)

Mnemonic(s)	Operation	Implied	Immediate	Direct	Extended	Extended Indirect	Indexed	Indexed Indirect	Relative	Relative Indirect
						Addressing Modes				
BNE, LBNE	Branch if not equal	—	—	—	—	—	—	—	X	—
BPL, LBPL	Branch if plus	—	—	—	—	—	—	—	X	—
BRA, LBRA	Branch always	—	—	—	—	—	—	—	X	—
BRN, LBRN	Branch never (3, 5 Cycle NOP)	—	—	—	—	—	—	—	X	—
BSR, LBSR	Branch to subroutine	—	—	—	—	—	—	—	X	—
BVC, LBVC	Branch if overflow clear	—	—	—	—	—	—	—	X	—
BVS, LBVS	Branch if overflow set	—	—	—	—	—	—	—	X	—

Table 4.5 Miscellaneous Instructions

Mnemonic(s)	Operation	Implied	Immediate	Direct	Extended	Extended Indirect	Indexed	Indexed Indirect	Relative	Relative Indirect
ANDCC	AND condition code register	—	X	—	—	—	—	—	—	—
CWAI	AND condition code register, then wait for interrupt	—	X	—	—	—	—	—	—	—
NOP	No operation	X	—	—	—	—	—	—	—	—
ORCC	OR condition code register	—	X	—	—	—	—	—	—	—
JMP	Jump	—	—	X	X	X	X	X	X	X
JSR	Jump to subroutine	—	—	X	X	X	X	X	X	X
RTI	Return from interrupt	X	—	—	—	—	—	—	—	—
RTS	Return from subroutine	X	—	—	—	—	—	—	—	—
SWI, SWI2, SWI3	Software interrupt (absolute indirect)	X	—	—	—	—	—	—	—	—
SYNC	Synchronize with interrupt line	X	—	—	—	—	—	—	—	—

Table 4.6   Hexadecimal Values of Machine Codes

OP Mnem[a]	Mode	Cycles[b]	Bytes[c]	OP Mnem[a]	Mode	Cycles[b]	Bytes[c]
00 NEG	Direct	6	2	30 LEAX	Indexed	4+	2+
01 *	↑			31 LEAY	↑	4+	2+
02 *				32 LEAS	↓	4+	2+
03 COM		6	2	33 LEAU	Indexed	4+	2+
04 LSR		6	2	34 PSHS	Inherent	5+	2
05 *				35 PULS	↑	5+	2
06 ROR		6	2	36 PSHU		5+	2
07 ASR		6	2	37 PULU		5+	2
08 ASL/LSL		6	2	38 *			
09 ROL		6	2	39 RTS		5	1
0A DEC		6	2	3A ABX		3	1
0B *				3B RTI		6/15	1
0C INC		6	2	3C CWAI		20	2
0D TST		6	2	3D MUL		11	1
0E JMP	↓	3	2	3E *			
0F CLR	Direct	6	2	3F SWI	Inherent	19	1
10 Page 2	—	—	—	40 NEGA	Inherent	2	1
11 Page 3	—	—	—	41 *	↑		
12 NOP	Inherent	2	1	42 *			
13 SYNC	Inherent	2	1	43 COMA		2	1
14 *				44 LSRA		2	1
15 *				45 *			
16 LBRA	Relative	5	3	46 RORA		2	1
17 LBSR	Relative	9	3	47 ASRA		2	1
18 *				48 ASLA/LSLA		2	1
19 DAA	Inherent	2	1	49 ROLA		2	1
1A ORCC	Immed	3	2	4A DECA		2	1
1B *	↕			4B *			
1C ANDCC	Immed	3	2	4C INCA		2	1
1D SEX	Inherent	2	1	4D TSTA		2	1
1E EXG	↕	8	2	4E *			
1F TFR	Inherent	6	2	4F CLRA	Inherent	2	1
20 BRA	Relative	3	2	50 NEGB	Inherent	2	1
21 BRN	↑	3	2	51 *	↑		
22 BHI		3	2	52 *			
23 BLS		3	2	53 COMB		2	1
24 BHS/BCC		3	2	54 LSRB		2	1
25 BLO/BCS		3	2	55 *			
26 BNE		3	2	56 *			
27 BEQ		3	2	56 RORB		2	1
28 BVC		3	2	57 ASRA		2	1
29 BVS		3	2	58 ASLB/LSLB		2	1
2A BPL		3	2	59 ROLB		2	1
2B BMI		3	2	5A DECB		2	1
2C BGE		3	2	5B *			
2D BLT		3	2	5C INCB		2	1
2E BGT	↓	3	2	5D TSTB		2	1
2F BLE	Relative	3	2	5E *			
				5F CLRB	Inherent	2	1

Table 4.6 (Continued)

OP Mnem[a]	Mode	Cycles[b]	Bytes[c]	OP Mnem[a]	Mode	Cycles[b]	Bytes[c]
60 NEG	Indexed	6+	2+	90 SUBA	Direct	4	2
61 *				91 CMPA		4	2
62 *				92 SBCA		4	2
63 COM		6+	2+	93 SUBD		6	2
64 LSR		6+	2+	94 ANDA		4	2
65 *				95 BITA		4	2
66 ROR		6+	2+	96 LDA		4	2
67 ASR		6+	2+	97 STA		4	2
68 ASL/LSL		6+	2+	98 EORA		4	2
69 ROL		6+	2+	99 ADCA		4	2
6A DEC		6+	2+	9A ORA		4	2
6B *				9B ADDA		4	2
6C INC		6+	2+	9C CMPX		6	2
6D TST		6+	2+	9D JSR		7	2
6E JMP		3+	2+	9E LDX		5	2
6F CLR	Indexed	6+	2+	9F STX	Direct	5	2
70 NEG	Extended	7	3	A0 SUBA	Indexed	4+	2+
71 *				A1 CMPA		4+	2+
72 *				A2 SBCA		4+	2+
73 COM		7	3	A3 SUBD		6+	2+
74 LSR		7	3	A4 ANDA		4+	2+
75 *				A5 BITA		4+	2+
76 ROR		7	3	A6 LDA		4+	2+
77 ASR		7	3	A7 STA		4+	2+
78 ASL/LSL		7	3	A8 EORA		4+	2+
79 ROL		7	3	A9 ADCA		4+	2+
7A DEC		7	3	AA ORA		4+	2+
7B *				AB ADDA		4+	2+
7C INC		7	3	AC CMPX		6+	2+
7D TST		7	3	AD JSR		7+	2+
7E JMP		4	3	AE LDX		5+	2+
7F CLR	Extended	7	3	AF STX	Indexed	5+	2+
80 SUBA	Immed	2	2	B0 SUBA	Extended	5	3
81 CMPA		2	2	B1 CMPA		5	3
82 SBCA		2	2	B2 SBCA		5	3
83 SUBD		4	3	B3 SUBD		7	3
84 ANDA		2	2	B4 ANDA		5	3
85 BITA		2	2	B5 BITA		5	3
86 LDA		2	2	B6 LDA		5	3
87 *				B7 STA		5	3
88 EORA		2	2	B8 EORA		5	3
89 ADCA		2	2	B9 ADCA		5	3
8A ORA		2	2	BA ORA		5	3
8B ADDA		2	2	BB ADDA		5	3
8C CMPX	Immed	4	3	BC CMPX		7	3
8D BSR	Relative	7	2	BD JSR		8	3
8E LDX	Immed	3	3	BE LDX		6	3
8F *				BF STX	Extended	6	3

Table 4.6 (Continued)

OP Mnem[a]	Mode	Cycles[b]	Bytes[c]	OP Mnem[a]	Mode	Cycles[b]	Bytes[c]
C0 SUBB	Immed	2	2	F0 SUBB	Extended	5	3
C1 CMPB		2	2	F1 CMPB		5	3
C2 SBCB		2	2	F2 SBCB		5	3
C3 ADDD		4	3	F3 ADDD		7	3
C4 ANDB		2	2	F4 ANDB		5	3
C5 BITB	Immed	2	2	F5 BITB		5	3
C6 LDB	Immed	2	2	F6 LDB		5	3
C7 *				F7 STB		5	3
C8 EORB		2	2	F8 EORB		5	3
C9 ADCB		2	2	F9 ADCB		5	3
CA ORB		2	2	FA ORB		5	3
CB ADDB		2	2	FB ADDB	Extended	5	3
CC LDD		3	3	FC LDD	Extended	6	3
CD *				FD STD		6	3
CE LDU	Immed	3	3	FE LDU		6	3
CF *				FF STU	Extended	6	3
D0 SUBB	Direct	4	2	1021 LBRN	Relative	5	4
D1 CMPB		4	2	1022 LBHI		5(6)	4
D2 SBCB		4	2	1023 LBLS		5(6)	4
D3 ADDD		6	2	1024 LBHS/LBCC		5(6)	4
D4 ANDB		4	2	1025 LBCS/LBLO		5(6)	4
D5 BITB		4	2	1026 LBNE		5(6)	4
D6 LDB		4	2	1027 LBEQ		5(6)	4
D7 STB		4	2	1028 LBVC		5(6)	4
D8 EORB		4	2	1029 LBVS		5(6)	4
D9 ADCB		4	2	102A LBPL		5(6)	4
DA ORB		4	2	102B LBMI		5(6)	4
DB ADDB		4	2	102C LBGE		5(6)	4
DC LDD		5	2	102D LBLT	Relative	5(6)	4
DD STD		5	2	102E LBGT	Relative	5(6)	4
DE LDU		5	2	102F LBLE	Relative	5(6)	4
DF STU	Direct	5	2	103F SWI/2	Inherent	20	2
				1083 CMPD	Immed	5	4
E0 SUBB	Indexed	4+	2+	108C CMPY		5	4
E1 CMPB		4+	2+	108E LDY	Immed	4	4
E2 SBCB		4+	2+	1093 CMPD	Direct	7	3
E3 ADDD		6+	2+	109C CMPY		7	3
E4 ANDB		4+	2+	109E LDY		6	3
E5 BITB		4+	2+	109F STY	Direct	6	3
E6 LDB		4+	2+	10A3 CMPD	Indexed	7+	3+
E7 STB		4+	2+	10AC CMPY		7+	3+
E8 EORB		4+	2+	10AE LDY		6+	3+
E9 ADCB		4+	2+	10AF STY	Indexed	6+	3+
EA ORB		4+	2+	10B3 CMPD	Extended	8	4
EB ADDB		4+	2+	10BC CMPY		8	4
EC LDD		5+	2+	10BE LDY		7	4
ED STD		5+	2+	10BF STY	Extended	7	4
EE LDU		5+	2+	10CE LDS	Immed	4	4
EF STU	Indexed	5+	2+	10DE LDS	Direct	6	3

Table 4.6   (Continued)

OP Mnem[a]	Mode	Cycles[b]	Bytes[c]	OP Mnem[a]	Mode	Cycles[b]	Bytes[c]
10DF STS	Direct	6	3	118C CMPS	Immed	5	4
10EE LDS	Indexed	6+	3+	1193 CMPU	Direct	7	3
10EF STS	Indexed	6+	3+	119C CMPS	Direct	7	3
10FE LDS	Extended	7	4	11A3 CMPU	Indexed	7+	3+
10FF STS	Extended	7	4	11AC CMPS	Indexed	7+	3+
113F SWI/3	Inherent	20	2	11B3 CMPU	Extended	8	4
1183 CMPU	Immed	5	4	11BC CMPS	Extended	8	4

[a]Asterisk denotes unused opcode. All unused opcodes are both undefined and illegal.
[b]Number of MPU cycles (less possible push/pull or indexed-mode cycles).
[c]Number of program bytes.

memory addressing notation used in our examples is listed in Tables 4.9 and 4.10. (*Note:* In the 6809, during the current instruction execution, the PC always points one byte past the last byte of the instruction opcode and thus at the beginning of the next instruction.)

4.2 ADDRESSING MODES

The 6809 retained all of the 6800 modes and added many more. These new modes mean that we have many types of addressing modes to reach across the memory with ease, whether we are in a subroutine or in the main program.

Register Addressing

In this address mode, the effective address is an MPU register. In some literature, the inherent and accumulator modes are also considered as register modes.

TFR X,Y   Transfer MPU register X to MPU register Y.

Inherent Addressing

In this addressing mode, the opcode of the instruction itself contains all the addressing information necessary. These are the one-byte instructions, such as:

ABX   Adds register B to index register
DAA   Decimal adjust
SWI   Software interrupt
ASRA   Arithmetic shift right on ACCA

Table 4.7   Indexed Addressing Modes

Type	Forms	Nonindirect				Indirect			
		Assembler Form	Postbyte Opcode	Cycles[a]	Bytes[a]	Assembler Form	Postbyte Opcode	Cycles[a]	Bytes[a]
Constant offset from R (signed offsets)	No offset	,R	1RR00100	0	0	[,R]	1RR10100	3	0
	5-bit offset	n,R	0RRnnnnn	1	0	Defaults to 8-bit			
	8-bit offset	n,R	1RR01000	1	1	[n,R]	1RR11000	4	1
	16-bit offset	n,R	1RR01001	4	2	[n,R]	1RR11001	7	2
Accumulator offset from R (signed offsets)	A–register offset	A,R	1RR00110	1	0	[A,R]	1RR10110	4	0
	B–register offset	B,R	1RR00101	1	0	[B,R]	1RR10101	4	0
	D–register offset	D,R	1RR01011	4	0	[D,R]	1RR11011	7	0
Auto increment/decrement R	Increment by 1	,R+	1RR00000	2	0	Not allowed			
	Increment by 2	,R++	1RR00001	3	0	[,R++]	1RR10001	6	0
	Decrement by 1	,–R	1RR00010	2	0	Not allowed			
	Decrement by 2	,--R	1RR00011	3	0	[,--R]	1RR10011	6	0
Constant offset from PC	8-bit offset	n,PCR	1XX01100	1	1	[n,PCR]	1XX11100	4	1
	16-bit offset	n,PCR	1XX01101	5	2	[n,PCR]	1XX11101	8	2
Extended indirect	16-bit address	—	—	—	—	[n]	10011111	5	2

R = X, Y, U, or S   X = 00   Y = 01
X = don't care   U = 10   S = 11

[a] Number of additional cycles and bytes for the particular variation.

Table 4.8   Indexed Addressing Postbyte Register Bit Assignments

Postbyte Register Bit								Indexed Addressing Mode
7	6	5	4	3	2	1	0	
0	R	R	X	X	X	X	X	EA = ,R ± 4 bit offset
1	R	R	0	0	0	0	0	,R +
1	R	R	1	0	0	0	1	,R + +
1	R	R	0	0	0	1	0	,-R
1	R	R	1	0	0	1	1	,--R
1	R	R	1	0	1	0	0	EA = ,R ± 0 offset
1	R	R	1	0	1	0	1	EA = ,R ± ACCB offset
1	R	R	1	0	1	1	0	EA = ,R ± ACCA offset
1	R	R	1	1	0	0	0	EA = ,R ± 7-bit offset
1	R	R	1	1	0	0	1	EA = ,R ± 15-bit offset
1	R	R	1	1	0	1	1	EA = ,R ± D offset
1	X	X	1	1	1	0	0	EA = ,PC ± 7-bit offset
1	X	X	1	1	1	0	1	EA = ,PC ± 15-bit offset
1	R	R	1	1	1	1	1	EA = ,Address

```
                    Addressing mode field
                    Indirect field
                    Sign bit when bit 7 = 0

                    Register field
                      00:R = X
                      01:R = Y
                      10:R = U
                      11:R = S
                    X = don't care
```

Immediate Addressing

In this mode the effective address of the data is in the program location immediately following the opcode. Instructions in this mode are two-byte instructions, at the very least. Since data are coming from memory, we also call this mode memory immediate. We can use both 8- and 16-bit immediate values. Typical code looks as follows:

```
LDA  #$20      Load ACCA with the value of $20.
LDX  #$F000    Load index X with the value of $F000.
```

Table 4.9   6809 Assembler Notation

Symbol	Meaning
#	Immediate addressing byte(s) follow(s)
$	Hex value follows
%	Binary value follows
<	Before indexing: force one-byte offset form (for known forward reference)
	Before absolute address; force direct addressing (obtain warning if SETDP ≠ MS byte value)
	Before indexing; force two-byte offset form
>	Before absolute address; force extended addressing
,	Indexing symbol
[ ]	Indirection

Table 4.10   6809 Operand Formats

Operand Format	M6809 Addressing Mode
<<expression>	Direct
><expression>	Extended
[<expression>]	Extended indirect
<expression>,R	Indexed
<<expression>,R	8-bit offset indexed
><expression>,R	16-bit offset indexed
[<expression>,R]	Indexed indirect
<[<expression>,R]	8-bit offset indexed indirect
>[<expression>,R]	16-bit offset indexed indirect
Q+	Auto increment by 1
Q++	Auto increment by 2
[Q++]	Auto increment indirect
-Q	Auto decrement by 1
--Q	Auto decrement by 2
[--Q]	Auto decrement indirect
W1, [W2, . . . ,Wn]	Immediate

Source: Motorola Semiconductor Products, Inc.

Extended Addressing

An extended mode instruction uses the next two bytes in the program to specify a 16-bit effective address used by the instruction. This is one of the few addressing modes where you cannot generate position independency.

LDD $2000   Load register D with data in the absolute address of $2000 and $2001.

4.3 MORE POWERFUL ADDRESSING MODES

From the programming model we saw in Chapter 2, additional registers are found in the 6809. We will use these registers to demonstrate features of the 6809. One impressive feature includes the direct page register, DP. The 8 bits that are contained in the DP register become the effective address for the upper 8 bits of the 16-bit addresses. With the DP set to zero (it automatically is at RESET), the 6809 direct page addressing is equivalent to that of the 6800.

Indexed Addressing

A major addition to the addressing modes is the ability to do many variations of indexed addressing. The many types are illustrated in Table 4.7. Indexed addressing requires at least a second byte, the postbyte, to determine the effective address. Let us look next at five modes.

Constant Offset: The "constant offset from R" mode is not totally unlike the 6800. In the 6809 we can select one of three different lengths to be added to the "R" register and the value may be negative. The R register can be X, Y, U, or S. To form the effective address in this mode, add the offset to the contents of the specified register. This is the effective address. Remember that the pointer's initial content is unchanged by the addition. The three sizes of offset are:

5-bit 2's complement (−16 to +15)
8-bit 2's complement (−128 to +127)
16-bit 2's complement (−32768 to +32767)

Why would we have a two's complement 5-bit offset? Because it reduces the use of bytes and cycles. Examples are:

LDA 14,X   Temporarily add 14 to the contents of the index register X. Use this value as an address to fetch the data to load into register A.

LDX −2,S   Subtract 2 from the contents of the S stack pointer. Use this as an address to fetch the data from two consecutive locations to load into the X register.

Accumulator Offset: The "accumulator offset from R" mode of indexed addressing is almost identical to the previous mode, except that we use an accumulator to be added to the R register to form the effective address. Realize that A, B, or D must contain a 2's complement value. A neat feature is that the accumulator offset can be calculated at run time. An example is

LDX D,Y   Add the contents of the concatenated A, B registers to the Y register. Use this address to fetch two consecutive bytes to be placed into the X register.

Autoincrement/Decrement: The "autoincrement/decrement R" mode of addressing enables the programmer to automatically use all the index registers as stack pointers; additionally, it allows easy movement through tables and lists of data. The "by 1" or "by 2" features allow the user to stack either bytes or double bytes. The auto mode is a pre-decrement/post-increment type. In autodecrement, the R register is decremented first, then the new R contents are used as the effective address. Autoincrement uses the R register first as the effective address; then the R register is incremented. An example is:

LDA ,X+   Load a data word into ACCA pointed to by the X register, then increment X by one.

Indexed Indirect: The indexed addressing modes are greatly enhanced by the ability to perform a level of indirection after the index had been obtained. In indirect addressing, the effective address is contained at the location specified by the contents of the index register plus any offset. All modes of indexed indirect are included except the useless ones (autoincrement/decrement by 1 direct). The next example uses X and ACCA in this mode. The autoincrement and autodecrement modes can perform indirection as in the following examples.

LDA [,X++]   X points to a location. Fetch an address from this location and the following location. Go to that address, fetch the data to load into ACCA. Finally, increment X by 2.

LDD [,--X]   Decrement X by 2. Fetch an address using this newly decremented value as the pointer. Load the contents of this "pointed-to" location into the D register.

Extended Indirect: In this mode of addressing, the MPU fetches trap vectors for the various interrupts. However, we can also use this mode. In extended indirect, the two bytes following the postbyte of an indexed instruction contain the address of the data. An example is:

		Before execution
		A=XX (don't cares)
		X=$B000
$4C	LDA [$10,X]	/effective address is now $B010
	⋮	
$B010	$F1	/new effective address is $F150
$B011	$50	
	⋮	After execution
$F150	$AF	A=$AF

4.4 RELATIVE ADDRESSING

In most microprocessors we can find some form of relative addressing in the branch instructions. Here the jumps are made from a position in the program with respect to the current value in the program counter. This facility also exists in the 6809. The byte or bytes following the branch opcode are interpreted as a signed offset to be added to the program counter. If the current branch test passes, the calculated address is used as the new program location. Both short (one byte) and long (two bytes) relative branches are allowed in the 6809. In fact, all memory space can be reached in the long relative addressing mode since the effective address is interpreted modulo 2 (16). The significance of the long and short relative branches comes into play if the instruction other than branches can utilize the relative addressing mode. BRA and LBRA are extremely useful branch instructions relative to the PC. They facilitate position independency.

Position independency is possible in the 6809. The PC can be used as the pointer with 8- or 16-bit offsets. Program counter relative addressing, available in the 6809, means that the offset is added to the current PC to create the effective address. This effective address is then used as the address of the operand or data. Program Counter Relative (PCR) addressing is a necessity if we are to generate position-independent code. When subroutines need certain data, we sometimes must store the data in tables within the program. But if we need to move the subroutines elsewhere in the memory space, the tables will "follow" in the program, and the code will execute properly. Only if PCR addressing were used would this be possible. In a later chapter, we will see additional advantages to PCR addressing. An example of PCR is:

$24 LDA FIN,PCR   The effective address of FIN is calculated by adding the current value of the PC to constant value (computed by the assembler) which is FIN minus the location of the next instruction. This new value is used to point to the location to fetch data to load into ACCA.

Before execution
Address of FIN was $F000, ACCA=XX, $F000 contains $AF.

After execution
Absolute location $F000 is used to retrieve the data word $AF, which is finally loaded in ACCA.

Program Counter Relative Indirect Addressing

In the 6809 we can also employ one level of indirection in the PCR addressing mode. As an example we have:

$24 LDA [FIN,PCR]   This is the same as above except that the calculated value points to a location which contains an address, not a data word. This address is then used to fetch the data.

Before execution
Address of FIN was $F000, which contains 00; location $F001 contains $12, and location 12 contains $4F.

After execution
Absolute location $F000 is used to retrieve another address, 12, from which the data word 4F is fetched and loaded into ACCA.

Assembler Generation of Relative Addresses

It is vital to understand how the 6809 assembler handles offsets with the program counter. PCR addressing is somewhat like indexed addressing, where the PC is used as a base register for a constant-offset indexing operation. However, the 6809 assembler treats the PCR address field differently from that used in other indexed instructions. In PCR addressing, the assembly-time PC value is *subtracted* from the value of the desired symbol, yielding the (constant) value of the PCR offset. The resulting distance is the value placed into the machine language object code. Now the machine instruction contains the distance to the desired symbol. During execution, the processor adds the value of the run-time PC to that distance to get a position-independent absolute address. In the first example, we want to use an offset of 10 in the LEAY instruction. The assembled code generated by the 6809 assembler will compute the relative distance between 10 and the current value of PC, or 10 - 3 = 7. Seven will be the immediate value inserted in the assembled program after the LEAY instruction.

Source Code

PC	Opcode	
0000	LEAY	10,PCR

Assembled Code

PC	Opcode
0000	31
0001	8C
0002	07

In the following example, we will use a label, "THERE," in the LEAY instruction. Suppose that the label is in program location 6, as shown. The assembler generates an immediate value of 2, placing it after the opcode, since 6 - 4 = 2!

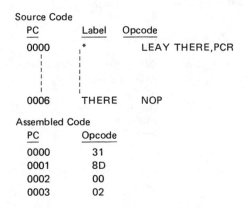

Source Code

PC	Label	Opcode
0000	*	LEAY THERE,PCR
0006	THERE	NOP

Assembled Code

PC	Opcode
0000	31
0001	8D
0002	00
0003	02

Note that 0002 has been inserted in locations 2 and 3 by the assembler. (The assembler allocates two bytes for the offset since, upon the first assembly pass, the location of THERE, a forward reference, is unknown and may be quite distant.) Suppose, however, that we had *manually* coded a program such as:

PC	Opcode	
0	32	LEAS
1	FC	PC ±7 bit offset, indirect
2	0A	Offset of 10
3	⋮	
D	12	Desired value for
E	34	S above

When this program is executed, the 6809 will compute an effective address that is used to retrieve the data to be placed in the S register. This effective address is 000D, since 0A + 03 = 0D. The value, 1234, will eventually be found in S. If you were to generate source code to do the equivalent task, you would use LEAS [$D,PCR]. The assembler would then place the immediate value, 0A, in location 2. Upon execution, the 6809 would add 0A to 03, obtaining 0D, the address from which we will fetch 1234. However, in practice, a label instead of 0D would be more appropriate.

4.5 HOW INSTRUCTIONS WORK

Now let us look at some specific examples of instructions and the types of addressing modes. As we examine each case, try to do the example with a different addressing mode. Our set of examples is grouped into four convenient categories: data movement types, data manipulation types, program manipulation types, and the miscellaneous category. Some from each type are analyzed. We begin with the data movement types. (*Note:* All characters in Examples 4.1 to 4.18 are hexadecimal.)

The accompanying figure in each example depicts data memory, program memory, and the MPU registers. Although data memory is separated from program memory, in actual practice this is not necessary, but may be in the same memory device or even on the same page. Each example demonstrates how the PC is changed, how active MPU registers are altered, and what affects the CCR. Recall that for all instructions the PC has been incremented to the next available instruction. Hence, operations involving the PC reflect this altered value. All symbols used are taken from Tables 4.9 and 4.10. Instruction opcodes can be found in Table 4.6. Addressing modes are found in Tables 4.7 and 4.8. All of the modes have been demonstrated at least once. We have assumed that memory is 8 bits wide. In all cases, a hexadecimal coded instruction is found in program memory.

DATA MOVEMENT INSTRUCTIONS

EXAMPLE 4.1:   8-Bit Transfer   TFR B,DP

This instruction is used to move data in the MPU. The two registers must be of equal length. Bits 7–4 of the immediate postbyte after the opcode define the source register. Bits 3–0 define the destination using the following postbyte assignment.

Postbyte Assignment for Data Movement Instructions

0000 = A:B or D	0100 = SP	1000 = A	1100 = undefined
0001 = X	0101 = PC	1001 = B	1101 = undefined
0010 = Y	0110 = undefined	1010 = CCR	1110 = undefined
0011 = US	0111 = undefined	1011 = DPR	1111 = undefined

In the case of TFR B,DP, the 1F opcode is fetched into the instruction register. Then the postbyte 9B is fetched, which tells us which registers are involved in the transfer. From the table we see that ACCB is to be transferred into the DP. Additional cycles are required to actually transfer the register. Note that the CCR is not affected by TRF unless a transfer is made to it.

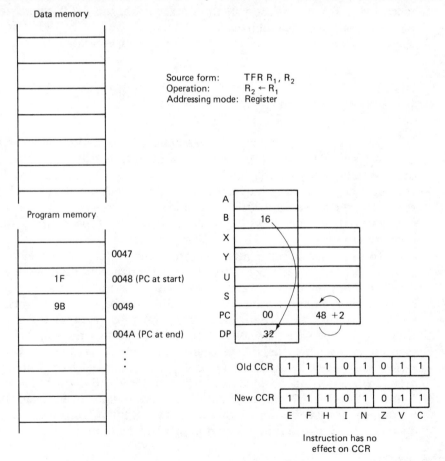

Source form: TFR R_1, R_2
Operation: $R_2 \leftarrow R_1$
Addressing mode: Register

Instruction has no
effect on CCR

EXAMPLE 4.2: 16-Bit Exchange   EXG Y,PC

This data movement instruction does more than the TFR instruction. It exchanges the contents of two equal-length registers in the MPU. For our specific case, Y and PC are exchanged. First the opcode (1E) is fetched into the instruction register. There it is decoded. Then the postbyte (25) is fetched and decoded per the preceding table used by all data movement types. The exchange is made. For this specific instruction the CCR is not affected. Note that the postbyte (52) would do the same thing.

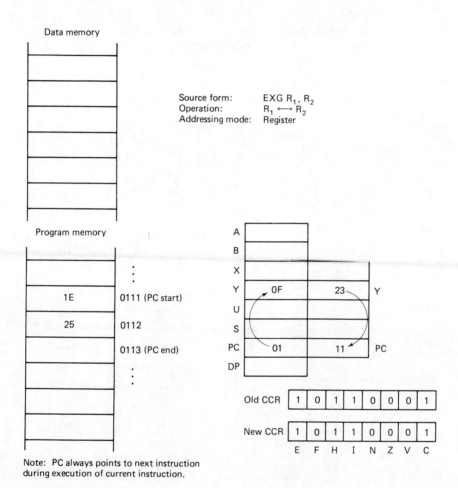

Source form: EXG R_1, R_2
Operation: $R_1 \longleftrightarrow R_2$
Addressing mode: Register

Note: PC always points to next instruction during execution of current instruction.

EXAMPLE 4.3: Load Effective Address LEAS -6,S

The load effective address instruction gives the 6809 programmer access to the address calculation hardware in the MPU. The 6800 did not have this feature. Let us see what our present example does. First the opcode (32) is fetched into the instruction register. After decoding the postbyte, we see from Table 4.8 that the postbyte, 7A, indicates our effective address EA = R+5 bit (2's complement) offset. R is the S register and the offset is -6. We set bits 4-0 in the postbyte to 11010, with bit 5 indicating the sign of the offset (when bit 7, B7,=0). Note that LEAS and LEAU do *not* affect the CCR, but LEAX and LEAY do affect the CCR. This instruction is quite useful for reserving local storage for subroutine variables. The instruction LEAS 6,S accomplishes the release or cleanup of the stack.

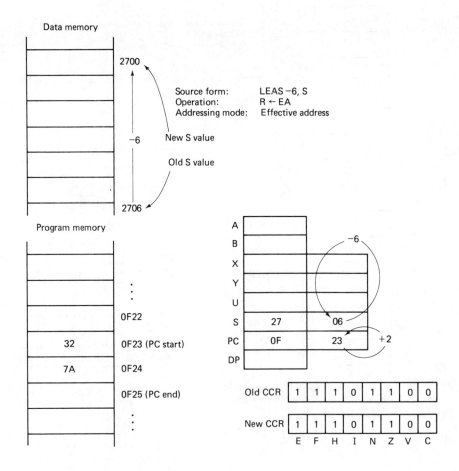

EXAMPLE 4.4: Register Push   PSHU A,X,CC

The 6809's push instructions give the programmer the ability to push any or all of the 6809 active registers onto the stack. The order of stacking is the same no matter how many registers you push, this being controlled by the hardware. For our example, after the opcode (36) is fetched and decoded, the postbyte is retrieved. This postbyte tells which registers are to be stacked. They are the X, ACCA, and CCR registers. These are now stacked. The CCR is *not* affected by the push. When the instruction is completely executed, the final contents of U are 0013.

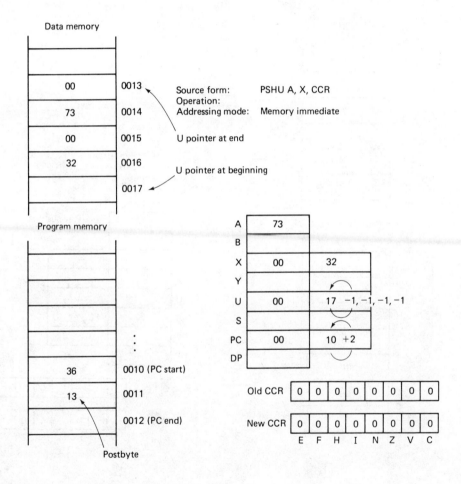

Data memory

00	0013
73	0014
00	0015
32	0016
	0017

Source form: PSHU A, X, CCR
Operation:
Addressing mode: Memory immediate

U pointer at end

U pointer at beginning

Program memory

36	0010 (PC start)
13	0011
	0012 (PC end)

Postbyte

A	73	
B		
X	00	32
Y		
U	00	17 −1, −1, −1, −1
S		
PC	00	10 +2
DP		

Old CCR	0	0	0	0	0	0	0	0
New CCR	0	0	0	0	0	0	0	0
	E	F	H	I	N	Z	V	C

DATA MANIPULATION INSTRUCTIONS

EXAMPLE 4.5:   16-Bit Load   LDS A,S

This example is a 16-bit load instruction. The postbyte (E6) tells the MPU that the A accumulator is an offset added to the S register. Data at this address are loaded into the stack pointer. Its previous contents are destroyed. N, Z, and V CCR flags are affected by this instruction. V is always cleared. Z in our present case is cleared and N is set.

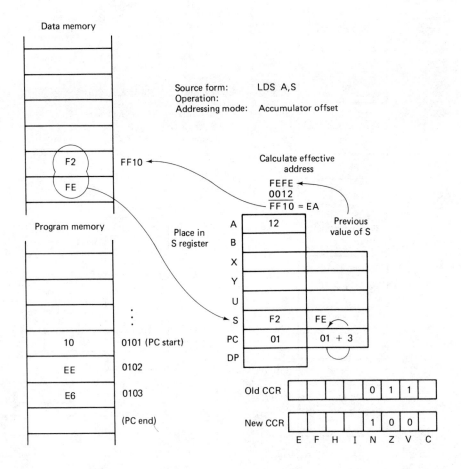

EXAMPLE 4.6: Sign Extended SEX

This special instruction is a definite asset to the programmer. SEX extends the arithmetic sign from ACCB (assumed to be the least significant bits of a 16-bit arithmetic word) through ACCA. Equivalently, this instruction converts an 8-bit signed number to a 16-bit signed number. For this example, ACCB·contains $F4, and ACCA contains $00. When this instruction gets executed, the negative sign from ACCB is propagated through ACCA, wiping out the previous contents (00), and installing the new contents ($FF). The N and Z flags of the CCR are affected. In this case, the N flag gets set to 1, since the result is negative. The Z flag gets cleared, since the result is nonzero. Finally the program counter is incremented to point to the next instruction. SEX is very useful when the programmer executes extended byte arithmetic.

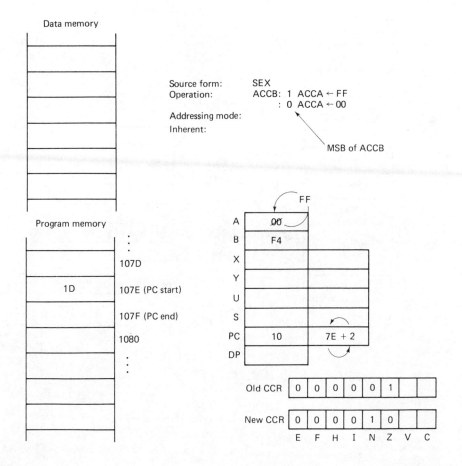

EXAMPLE 4.7: Subtract With Borrow SBCA MIN

This instruction is unchanged from the 6800 instruction. First the opcode is fetched. Then the subtraction is performed. Four of the CCR flags are affected, the C, V, Z, and N flags. In this case the carry flag is set to zero. The overflow and zero flags are cleared. See how the carry flag gets set if the operation did *not* cause a carry from bit 7 of the ALU.

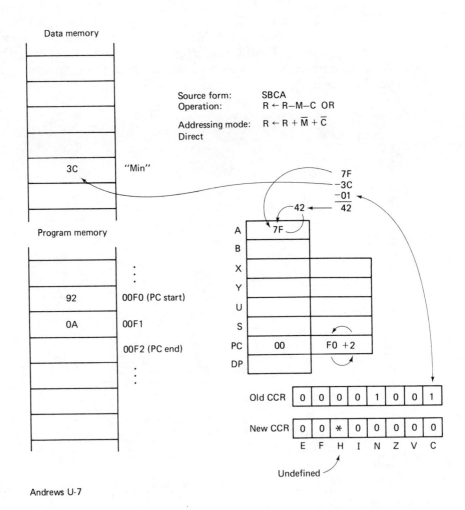

Andrews U-7

EXAMPLE 4.8: 8-Bit Unsigned Multiply   MUL

This instruction performs an 8-bit × 8-bit unsigned multiply. First the opcode is fetched. Then the multiplication is performed. In this case the multiplication is trivial, 6 × 13. The ACCA × ACCB result is placed in ACCD (=ACCA:ACCB). Only two of the CCR flags are affected, the Z and C flags. In this case, the zero flag is set to zero, because the result is *not* zero. The carry flag is set to zero. *Why?*

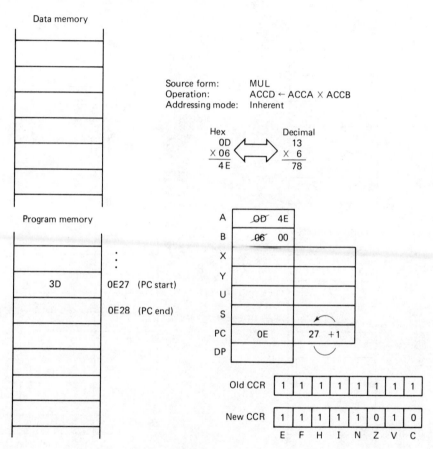

Data memory

Source form: MUL
Operation: ACCD ← ACCA × ACCB
Addressing mode: Inherent

```
Hex                Decimal
  0D                  13
X 06                X  6
────               ─────
 4E                   78
```

Program memory

```
    3D        0E27   (PC start)
              0E28   (PC end)
```

A   0D   4E
B   06   00
X
Y
U
S
PC 0E   27 +1
DP

Old CCR | 1 | 1 | 1 | 1 | 1 | 1 | 1 | 1 |

New CCR | 1 | 1 | 1 | 1 | 1 | 0 | 1 | 0 |
           E   F   H   I   N   Z   V   C

How do you round off to 8 bits?
Ans.   MUL
       ADCA #0

EXAMPLE 4.9: Arithmetic Right Shift   ASRA

This is just a normal shift instruction. It is the same in the 6809 as it was in the 6800. This instruction performs an arithmetic right shift of one bit. In this case it shifts $7C one bit for the result of $3E. The result is placed back in ACCA. The C, Z, and N flags of the CCR are affected by this instruction. In this case, the carry flag gets set to zero, because that is the value that was shifted out of ACCA. The zero and negative flags both get set to zero, because the result is not zero, nor is it negative.

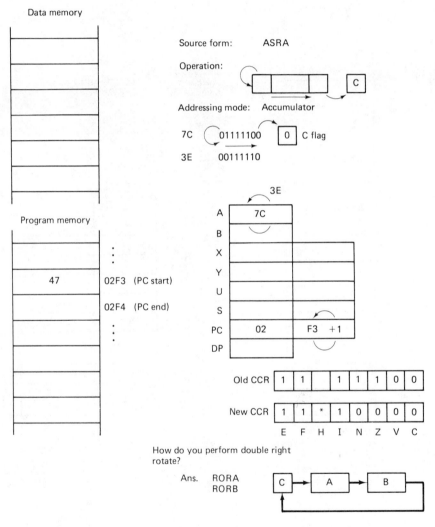

Note: Define your carry prior to this code.

PROGRAM MANIPULATION INSTRUCTIONS

EXAMPLE 4.10:   Load Effective Address   LEAX 10,X

This instruction does not perform any level of indirection. Hence, the calculated address 10+(X) is loaded directly into the X register. Only the zero flag is affected (it is cleared here).

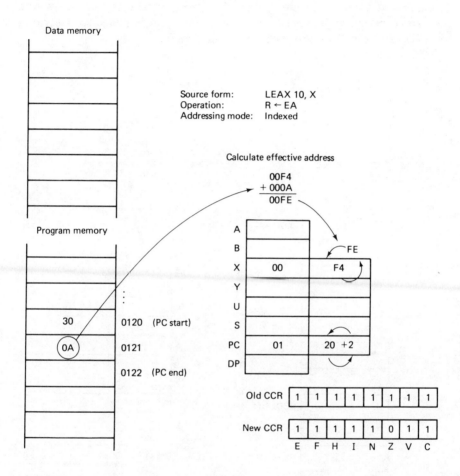

Source form: LEAX 10, X
Operation: R ← EA
Addressing mode: Indexed

EXAMPLE 4.11:   16-Bit Compare   CMPY 12,X

This instruction performs a comparison between the 16-bit Y index register and the two consecutive 8-bit memory bytes at 12 offset from the X index register. This instruction does not destroy any memory or register contents; it is just useful for setting up program flow. The lower 4 bits of the CCR are affected by this instruction. In this case, the negative flag gets set to one, and the overflow, and zero flags get set to zero. The CCR flag, C, is set if there is no carry from bit 15. First the two-byte opcode is fetched from memory. Then the address calculation is made to determine the effective address. The comparison is made next.

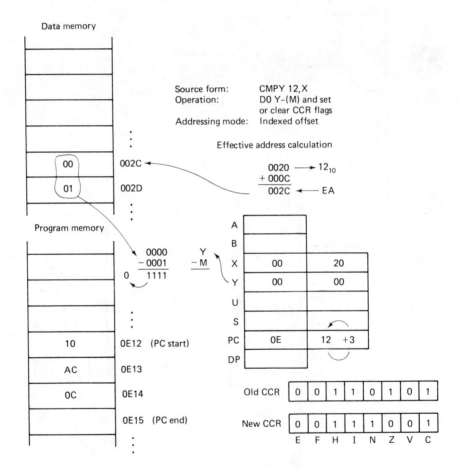

EXAMPLE 4.12: Short Branch If Equal   BEQ *-10

This instruction is a simple branch instruction. It checks for a particular combination of CCR flag settings, and if it finds these conditions, it branches to the new program counter-relative address. In this case, it checks to see if the zero flag is set to one before this instruction is executed. First the opcode is set fetched from memory. The zero flag is then checked. The offset [in this case it is $F6 (the 2's-complement form of –10)] is then added to the current program counter (which points to the byte after the offset). This sum is then placed back in the program counter to point to the next instruction.

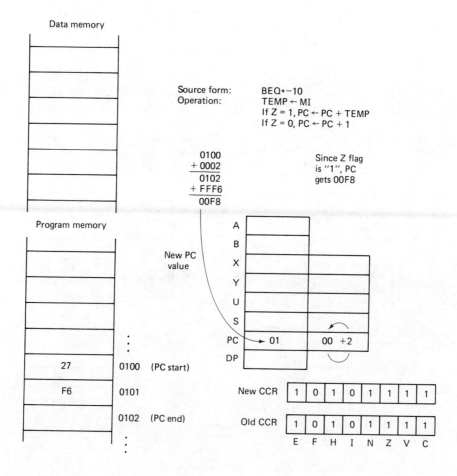

Data memory

Source form: BEQ*–10
Operation: TEMP ← MI
                If Z = 1, PC ← PC + TEMP
                If Z = 0, PC ← PC + 1

```
  0100
+ 0002
  0102
+ FFF6
  00F8
```

Since Z flag
is "1", PC
gets 00F8

Program memory

New PC
value

	A	
	B	
	X	
	Y	
	U	
	S	
PC	01	00 +2
	DP	

27	0100	(PC start)
F6	0101	
	0102	(PC end)

New CCR | 1 | 0 | 1 | 0 | 1 | 1 | 1 | 1 |

Old CCR | 1 | 0 | 1 | 0 | 1 | 1 | 1 | 1 |
         E   F   H   I   N   Z   V   C

EXAMPLE 4.13:   Long Branch to Subroutine   LBSR #$03E8

This instruction is used to transfer control to a subroutine. In the course of its execution, the PC is stacked on the hardware stack. First the opcode is fetched. Then the program counter is stacked. Then the address calculation is made, and then loaded into the program counter to point to the next instruction. Notice that LBSR and BSR use the S pointer. First S is decremented, then PCL is pushed onto the S stack. Next S is again decremented, and then PCH is pushed onto the S stack. Upon completion, S points to the location containing PCH.

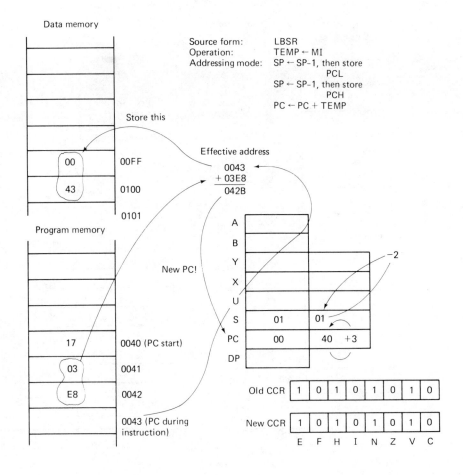

PROGRAM STATUS MANIPULATION

EXAMPLE 4.14: The No Operation NOP

This instruction is useful for taking up slack in your timing. First the opcode is fetched. When the opcode is decoded, no action is taken. The program counter is then incremented to point to the next instruction. The CCR remains unaffected by this instruction. This instruction is used in a program when a gap in time or program space is needed.

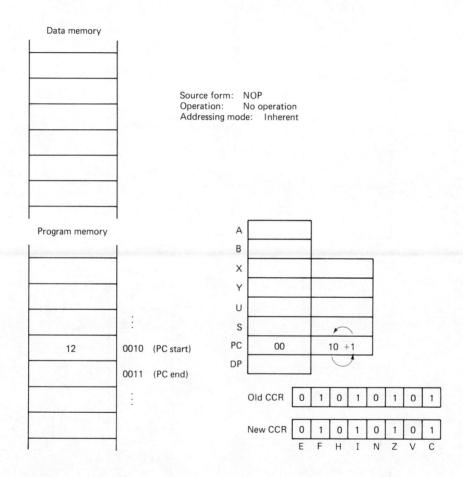

Source form: NOP
Operation: No operation
Addressing mode: Inherent

EXAMPLE 4.15:   Synchronize with I/O   SYNC

This instruction is used when a program needs to wait for a slower interrupting device. First the opcode is fetched. The program counter is next incremented to point to the next instruction. The processor then enters the wait state. If the interrupts are masked, then upon the next interrupt, processing will continue where the program counter is now pointing. If, however, the interrupts are not masked, then after the interrupt, the processor will execute the interrupt servicing routine first, and then continue with the first instruction after the SYNC instruction. The CCR is unaffected by this instruction.

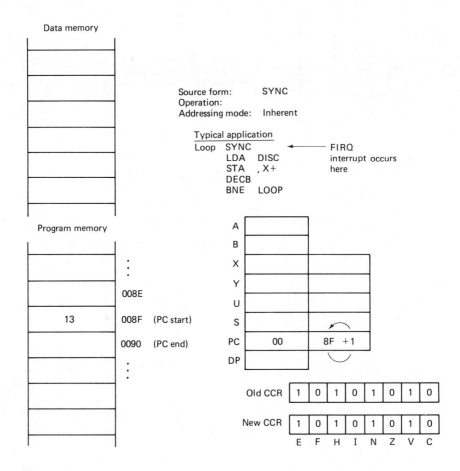

EXAMPLE 4.16: Clear Condition Codes ANDCC #$0D

This instruction will clear bits 7, 6, 5, 4, and 1 of the CCR and leave the other bits unchanged. First the opcode is fetched. The old CCR is then "AND"ed with the immediate byte $0D. In this case, the new CCR will be $00 after "AND"ing.

Note that one of the significant differences between the 6800 and the 6809 is that in the 6800 several one-byte instructions were provided to set and clear individual bits in the CCR, whereas in the 6809 only two-byte instructions have been provided. In the 6809, the programmer can either AND an immediate byte with the CCR, or OR an immediate byte to the CCR. It is evident that all of the old 6800 functions can be realized with the new 6809 instructions. Try to duplicate them for yourself.

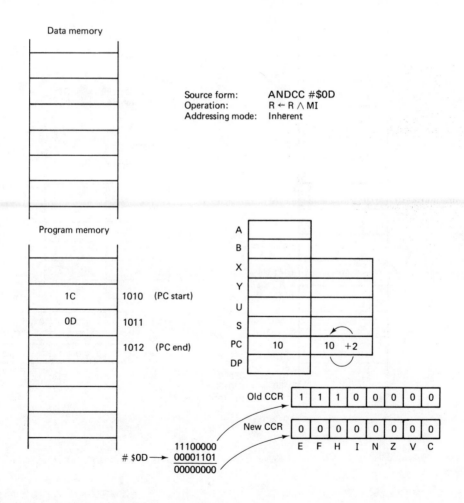

EXAMPLE 4.17: Set Condition Code ORCC #$50

This instruction is the companion to the ANDCC instruction discussed earlier. This instruction is used to selectively set bits in the CCR. First the opcode is fetched, and then the old CCR is "OR"ed with the immediate byte of data. This result is then stored as the new CCR. In this case, the "OR"ing produces a result of $55. Finally, the program counter is incremented to point to the next instruction.

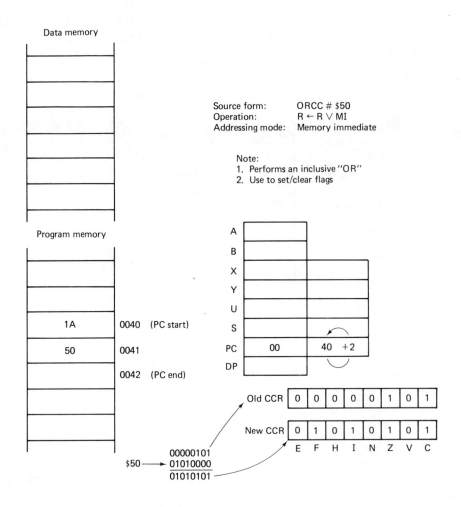

Source form: ORCC # $50
Operation: R ← R ∨ MI
Addressing mode: Memory immediate

Note:
1. Performs an inclusive "OR"
2. Use to set/clear flags

EXAMPLE 4.18: Clear and Wait   CWAI #$AF

This instruction puts the 6809 into an interrupt wait state. The opcode is fetched. Next the immediate byte of data is "AND"ed with the old CCR to form the new CCR. Next the program counter is incremented to point to the next instruction. Now the machine state is saved on the hardware stack. Finally the processor is put in a wait state. *Note:* In this example, the E bit is cleared, which suggests that the user expects only an $\overline{\text{FIRQ}}$. If the user were actually expecting any interrupt, especially an $\overline{\text{IRQ}}$, he or she should not clear the E flag with CWAI #$AF.

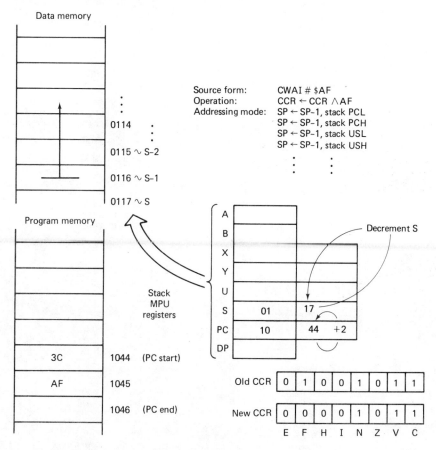

4.6 6800 CODE COMPATIBILITY

We define source code compatibility as follows:

> *Definition 4.1:* A machine is *source code-compatible* with another machine if the assembly language of the second machine will assemble and execute correctly on the first machine.

JMP	O,X	=	TFR	X,PC
		=	PSHS PULS	X PC
		=	PSHS RTS	X
LBRA	CAT	=	JMP	CAT,PCR
LBRA	*+5	=	JMP	2,PC
LBSR	DOG	=	JSR	DOG,PCR
LDX	#PIG	=	LEAX	PIG,PCR

↑   ↑
the loaded value will not   the loaded value will
change when executed in   change when executed in
different locations   different locations

PSHS (shorter)	A		STA (affects flags)	,−S
PULS (shorter)	A		LDA (affects flags)	,S+
RTI		=	PULS	ALL
		=	TST	O,S
			BMI	RAT
			PULS	CC,PC
		RAT	PULS	ALL

6800 Instruction	6809 Equivalent		
ABA	PSHS	B; ADDA	,S+
CBA	PSHS	B; CMPA	,S+
CLC	ANDCC	#$FE	
CLI	ANDCC	#$EF	
CLV	ANDCC	#$FD	
CPX	CMPX	P	
DES	LEAS	−1,S	
DEX	LEAX	−1,X	
INS	LEAS	1,S	
INX	LEAX	1,X	
LDAA	LDA		
LDAB	LDB		
ORAA	ORA		
ORAB	ORB		
PSHA	PSHS	A	
PSHB	PSHS	B	
PULA	PULS	A	
PULB	PULS	B	
SBA	PSHS	B; SUBA	,S+
SEC	ORCC	#$01	
SEI	ORCC	#$10	
SEV	ORCC	#$02	
STAA	STA		
STAB	STB		
TAB	TFR	A,B; TST A	
TAP	TFR	A,CC	
TBA	TFR	B,A; TST A	
TPA	TFR	CC,A	
TSX	TFR	S,X	
TXS	TFR	X,S	
WAI	*CWAI	#$FF	

Figure 4.1. 6809 Instruction Equivalence to 6800. (*Courtesy of Motorola Semiconductor Products, Inc.*)

The 6809 was intended to be source code-compatible with the 6800 assembly language code, but this is not always the case. Although all of the actions of the 6800 exist in the 6809, not all of the 6800 instructions exist in the 6809. Some instructions have been eliminated in favor of more efficient instructions. Some instructions have been changed slightly. And some instructions' mnemonics have changed their meanings.

Figure 4.1 lists all of the 6800 mnemonics that are not in the 6809 assembly language, and their 6809 equivalent replacements. Also, some 6809 equivalent code is listed for greater understanding.

Hardware Effects on Software

The stacking of the machine state in the 6809 is not the same as in the 6800. There are two reasons for this: (1) there are now more registers in the machine state, so any 6800 code that expects to find certain registers in positions relative to the top of the stack will not work correctly; and (2) the stack pointer now works differently. The stack pointer in the 6800 points to the *next* empty stackable location, whereas in the 6809, the stack pointer points to the last (top) stacked item.

Condition Code Register

There are a number of condition code register–related semantic differences between the 6800 and the 6809. The 6809 right shifts (ASR, LSR, and ROR) do not affect the overflow flag, whereas the 6800 right shifts set the overflow flag=b3 exclusive ORed with b0. The 6809 subtraction-like instructions (CMP, NEG, SBC, and SUB) do not define the status of the Half-carry flag, whereas the corresponding 6800 instructions clear the Half-carry flag. The 6809 CMPX instruction sets all the flags in the CCR correctly, whereas the 6800 CPX only sets the zero flag correctly.

4.7 SOFTWARE INCOMPATIBILITIES WITH 6800/6801/6802[1]

1. The new stacking order on the 6809 exchanges the order of ACCA and ACCB; this allows ACCA to stack as the MS byte of the pair.
2. The new stacking order on the 6809 invalidates previous 6800 code which displayed X or PC from the stack.
3. Additional stacking length on the 6809 stacks five more bytes for each NMI, IRQ, or SWI when compared to 6800/6801/6802.
4. The 6809 stack pointer points directly at the last item placed on the stack instead of the location before the last item, as in 6800/6801/6802. In general, this is not a problem because the most usual method of pointing at the stack in the 6800/6801/6802 is to

---

[1] Adapted from *MC6809 Programming Manual*, Motorola Semiconductor Products, Inc., Austin, Tex., © 1979.

execute a TSX. The TSX increments the value during the transfer, making X point directly at the last item on the stack. The stack pointer may thus be initialized one location higher on the 6809 than in the 6800/6801/6802; similarly, comparison values may need to be one location higher. Any 6800/6801 program that does all stack manipulation through X (i.e., LDX #CAT, TXS instead of LDS #CAT) will have an exactly correct stack translation when assembled for 6809.

5. Instruction timings in 6809 will, in general, be different from other 6800-family processors.

6. The 6809 uses the two high-order condition code register bits. Consequently, these will not, in general, appear as 1's on the 6800/6801/6802.

7. The 6809 MUL instruction sets the Z flag (if appropriate); the 6801 MUL does not.

8. The 6809 TST instruction does not affect the Z flag, whereas 6800/6801/6802 TST does clear the C flag.

9. The 6809 right shifts (ASR, ,LSR, ROR) do not affect V; the 6800/6801/6802 shifts set $V = b_7 \oplus b_6$.

10. The 6801 double-length shift instructions (ASLD, LSRD) are not exactly emulated by the 6800/6802/6809 sequences ASLB, ROLA; and LSRA, ROLB. In particular, the Z flag represents only the last 8-bit result, not the 16-bit quantity.

11. The 6809 H flag is not defined as having any particular state after subtraction-like operations (CMP, NEG, SBC, SUB); the 6800/6801/6802 clear the H flag under these conditions.

12. The 6800/6802 CPX instruction compared the MS byte, then the LS byte; consequently, only the Z flag was set correctly for branching. The 6801/6809 instructions (CPX/CMPX) set all flags correctly.

13. The 6809 instruction LEA may or may not affect the Z flag, depending upon which register is being loaded; LEAX and LEAY do affect the Z flag, whereas LEAS and LEAU do not. Thus, the User Stack does not exactly emulate the index registers in this respect.

4.8 EQUIVALENT INSTRUCTION SEQUENCES

The following equivalent instruction sequences are quite useful.[2]

```
LEAX   ,--X  =  LEAX  -2,X
LEAX   ,--Y  =  LEAY  -2,Y
                TFR   Y,X
```

[2] Reprinted from *MC6809 Programming Manual*, Motorola Semiconductor Products, Inc., © 1979.

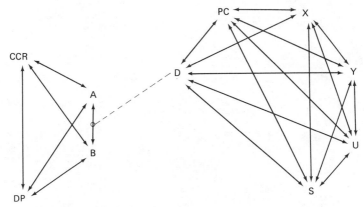

Figure 4.2. Legal 6809 Data Movement Internal to the MPU. (*Courtesy of Motorola Semiconductor Products, Inc.*)

```
LEAX   ,X++  =  LEAX   2,X
LEAX   ,Y++  =  TFR    Y,X
                LEAY   2,Y
NOP          =  TFR    X,X
                LEAX   0,X
```

Figure 4.2 shows the legal transfer and exchange paths.

4.9 THE 6809 ASSEMBLER

A variety of software support tools are available for the 6800 architecture family. These include an assembler, linking loader, and co-resident editor. All of these tools operate within a 6800 development system. Disc and tape versions are available which support the 6800, 6801, 6805, and 6809 microprocessors. In this section we examine the M6800 macroassembler which supports the 6809 available from Motorola, Inc.

Recall that the symbolic language which we used to code those programs is processed by an assembler. This symbolic language is actually the assembly language. The assembly language is a collection of mnemonic symbols, such as operations, symbolic names, operators, and special symbols. The assembly language also contains directives (commands to the assembler) necessary to operate the assembler itself. These assembly directives are not translated into machine language, but enable the programmer to manipulate the macroassembler itself.

Assembler Processing

Assembling symbolic language is a two-pass process. In the first pass the source program, that program which you actually write, is read by the

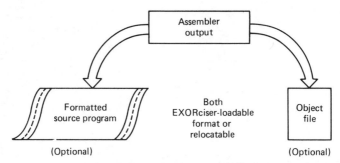

Figure 4.3. Assembler Output.

assembler. In this pass the assembler generates the symbol and macro tables. In the second pass, the object file is created using the tables developed in the first pass. Also at this time the source program listing is produced. During assembly processes, each source statement is processed completely before the next source statement is read. During this process, the assembler examines labels, operation code, and operand field. Any anomalous source language statement automatically generates an error. Error messages are produced by the M6800 assembler.

The assembly process can generate two outputs, the source program listing, which is optional, and the object file, as shown in Figure 4.3. The source program listing is formatted (annotated). which helps you and others to understand the actual program. The object file consists of the hexadecimal opcodes necessary for machine microprocesor operation. We can control the output listing through several directives, including PAGE, SPC n, and OPT. These operations direct the assembler to the top of the page, skip *n* lines, or produce specific outputs, depending on the option chosen. In the cassette/paper tape operation, we can retain or clear symbols, generate or suppress the assembly listing, and generate only the object tape with pass control options.

Source Statement Format

It is convenient to think of each of the source languages you generate as being composed of individual lines or source statements. Each source statement is a sequence of ASCII characters with the statement terminated in a carriage return. Source statements may contain five fields: a sequence number, label, operation, operand, and a comment. It is possible for an entire statement to be a line comment. In that case, a "*" indicates a comment line. The sequence number performs the same task as the location counter mentioned in Chapter 1. The sequence number is an optional field and can be deleted. Sequence numbers may consist of five decimal digits.

Each field is separated by a space. The label field is the first field of a source statement. It can be:

1. An asterisk as the first character to indicate that the source statement is actually the comment.
2. A space to indicate that the label field is empty.
3. A symbol character to indicate that the line has a label. Symbol characters are uppercase letters, A through Z, digits 0 through 9, and special characters (., $, _). Symbols may consist of up to six characters, the first of which must be alphabetic or the special character (.). Some symbols are reserved for the assembler (A, B, X, C, D, DP, PC, PCR, S, U, Y). These special symbols refer to the registers in the MPU and should not be used except for that purpose.

A label is generally assigned the value of the program counter of the first byte of the instruction or data being assembled. These values may be relocatable or absolute. Relocatable labels will then obtain absolute values during the link load process performed by the linking loader. Labels so generated are found in a symbol table which is automatically formed by the assembler.

The operation field must consist of one of the following three types:

1. Opcode of the valid 6809 instruction set.
2. Directives, which are special operation codes known by the assembler to control the assembler process.
3. Macrocall, indicating the selection of a previously defined macro to be inserted at the position of the macrocall.

The operation field consists of symbols, expressions, or combinations thereof separated by commas. The actual contents of the operand field depend on the contents of the operation. The operand field of machine instructions specifies the addressing mode of the instruction. In the 6809 the operand format is as shown in Table 4.10, where R is one of the registers PCR, S, U, X, or Y, and Q is one of the registers S, U, X, or Y. W_i ($i = 1$ to n) is one of the symbols A, B, CC, D, PC, S, U, X, or Y. All the addressing modes we saw earlier in the chapter apply to this operand field in the assembler.

The assembler will accept expressions which are combinations of symbols, constants, algebraic operators, and parentheses. An expression is used to specify a value to be used as an operand. In the 6809 assembler, expressions follow conventional rules of algebra. They may also be relocatable or externally defined. However, relocatable symbols or expressions cannot be multiplied, divided, or operated on with special two-character operators. Operators found in expressions obey certain rules of precedence. Parenthetical expressions are always evaluated first, with the innermost parentheses

Table 4.11   Two-Character Operators

!^	Exponentiation	The left operand is raised to the power specified by the right operand. If the right operand is zero, the resulting value will be "1," regardless of the value of the left operand.
!.	Logical AND	Each bit in the left operand is logically "ANDed" with the corresponding bit in the right operand.
!+	Inclusive OR	Each bit in the left operand is inclusively "ORed" with the corresponding bit in the right operand.
!X	Exclusive OR	Each bit in the left operand is exclusively "ORed" with the corresponding bit in the right operand.
!<	Shift left	The left operand is shifted to the left by the number of bits specified by the right operand. The left operand is zero-filled from the right.
!>	Shift right	The left operand is shifted to the right by the number of bits specified by the right operand. The left operand is zero-filled from the left.
!L	Rotate left	The left operand is rotated left by the number of bits specified by the right operand. The most significant bit is rotated into the least significant bit position of the left operand.
!R	Rotate right	The left operand is rotated right by the number of bits specified by the right operand. The least significant bit is rotated into the most significant bit position of the left operand.

Source: Motorola Semiconductor Products, Inc.

being processed before the outer one. Multiplication, division, and all two-character operators have precedence. Addition and subtraction operators have the lowest preference. The assembler allows a unary minus to occur only at the beginning of an expression or immediately before a left parenthesis. Operators of the same precedence are evaluated from left to right, with intermediate results in the computation of an expression truncated to a 16-bit integer value. Any expression result is also a 16-bit integer. The assembler recognizes many two-character operators that have the same precedence as multiplication or division. Each two-character operator begins with the exclamation point and takes two operands. Two-character operators are available as shown in Table 4.11.

The 6809 assembler allows symbols to take on the following properties:

1. Absolute attribute
2. Relocatable attribute
3. External reference (defined in another program)
4. Named common name
5. Undefined
6. SET symbol

There are certain symbols special to the assembler which can only be used in expressions. These include:

$$*, \quad \&, \quad \$, \quad H, \quad \%, \quad @, \quad '$$

Table 4.12   6809 Assembler Constants

Type	Valid	Invalid	Reason Invalid
Decimal	14	148762	More than five digits
Hexadecimal	$12	A602	No preceding "$"
Binary	%00101	01010	Missing percent
Binary	10100B	%2101	Invalid digit
Octal	1776	249Q	Invalid character
ASCII	' *	'INVALID	Too long

The asterisk (*) when used in an expression as a symbol represents the current value of the location counter. The ampersand (&) character precedes decimal constants. Hexadecimal constants are preceded by the dollar ($) sign or succeeded by the letter H. All binary constants that consist of a maximum of 16 ones or zeros must be preceded by the percent (%) sign or succeeded by the letter B. Octal constants are preceded by the commercial at-sign (@). Character constants are preceded by a single quote ('). We list some typical valid and invalid constant expressions in Table 4.12.

Relocation

A powerful feature of modern programming methods is the position independency of the eventual code. Programs written for microprocessors should be "portable" across the memory map. This is possible through code that is relocatable. Relocation is actually the process of specifying or "binding" a program to a set of memory locations *at a time other than during the assembly process*. We can make code relocatable in various ways. One procedure is always to reassemble the program to start at the new location. Another procedure is to use a relocating loader which accepts specific coded binary output from a relocatable assembly. Another procedure assumes that it is possible to have the program relocate itself after it is loaded. Finally, we can write a program that is position-independent from the start. The alternative, which produces an object module containing enough information so that another program (for instance, a linking loader) can easily assign a new set of memory locations to the module, is most attractive because:

1. Reassembly is not required.
2. The object module is generally smaller than the source program.
3. Relocation is faster than reassembly.
4. Relocation can be handled automatically by a linking loader.

The linking loader does more than permit program relocation. At times it is necessary for a calling routine to acquire some lower-level modules through the JSR instruction. Unfortunately, at assembly time the absolute value may not be known. However, the linking loader automatically deter-

Table 4.13   Desirable Assembly Capabilities

1. Program relocation
2. Multiple program linking
3. Easy development of programs for RAM/ROM environment
4. Easy specification of any addressing mode
5. Specification of uninitialized, blank common
6. Specification of initialized, named common

mines this address and resolves the reference to the call to the subroutine. This resolution process among interprogram references is actually called "linking." Good relocation and linking schemes should allow us to invoke the capabilities as shown in Table 4.13.

Assemblers and linking loaders operate on specific program sections. We define program sections to enable the assembler and linking loader to generate the correct starting addresses for calling routines and lower-level modules. You can define five different sections in the assembler language: absolute (ASCT), base (BSCT), blank common (CSCT), data section (DSCT), and program section (PSCT). Except for the absolute section, all other program sections are relocatable. The assembler directives, ASCT, BSCT, ..., are control statements to the assembler to assign particular sections to our source language program.

Assembler Directives

There are four types of assembler directives: assembler control, listing and output control, data definition/storage allocation, and symbol definition. Assembler directives are actually control statements to the assembler which are not translated into object code. Valid directives are recognizable by the 6809 assembler. The popular assembler control directives include NAM, ORG, and END. The first control directive assigns a program name to your source program. The ORG directive specifies the origin of the code in the actual memory map. The END control directive indicates to the assembler the end of source program. An optional expression in the operand field specifies the starting execution address of the program. To enable the relocation and linking schemes described earlier, we employ the five directives ASCT (absolute section), BSCT (base section), CSCT (blank common), DSCT (data section), and PSCT (program section).

A variety of assembler directives permit us to control the listing and output of the assembled code. We have already seen the PAGE, SPC, and OPT directives. The OPT control directive permits us to generate object code, load object code into memory, suppress loading of object code into memory, print the symbol table, suppress the symbol table listing, list the assemble data, or suppress the assemble data.

The group of assembly control directives that define the data and storage allocation include the ability to form a constant character (FCC), form a constant byte (FCB), form a double byte (FDB), and reserve memory byte (RMB). With these definition and allocation directives, we can store ASCII strings into consecutive bytes of memory; identify numerical constants, character constants, and/or symbols in either 8-bit or 16-bit values; and reserve blocks of memory for expressions.

Our last group, symbol definition control directives, include the frequently used equate (EQU) directive, which assigns permanent values to expressions in the operand field to the label. The EQU directive is one of the directives that assigns the value other than the program character label. Such labels cannot be redefined anywhere else in the program. The expression itself cannot contain any external references or undefined symbols. However, the expression may be relocatable. A typical assembler output listing is shown in Example 4.19.

EXAMPLE 4.19: Typical 6809 Assembly Output Listing

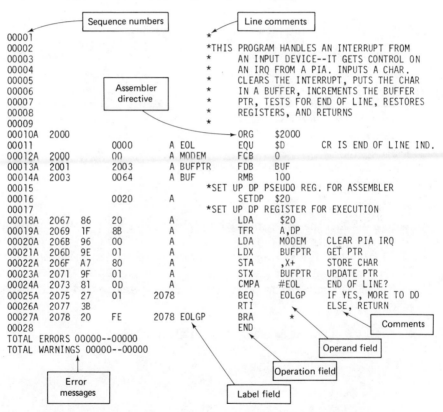

```
00001                          *
00002                          *THIS PROGRAM HANDLES AN INTERRUPT FROM
00003                          *     AN INPUT DEVICE--IT GETS CONTROL ON
00004                          *     AN IRQ FROM A PIA. INPUTS A CHAR.
00005                          *     CLEARS THE INTERRUPT, PUTS THE CHAR
00006                          *     IN A BUFFER, INCREMENTS THE BUFFER
00007                          *     PTR, TESTS FOR END OF LINE, RESTORES
00008                          *     REGISTERS, AND RETURNS
00009                          *
00010A  2000                   ORG    $2000
00011           0000    A EOL   EQU    $D       CR IS END OF LINE IND.
00012A  2000    00      A MODEM FCB    0
00013A  2001    2003    A BUFPTR FDB   BUF
00014A  2003    0064    A BUF   RMB    100
00015                   *SET UP DP PSEUDO REG. FOR ASSEMBLER
00016           0020    A       SETDP  $20
00017                   *SET UP DP REGISTER FOR EXECUTION
00018A  2067    86  20  A       LDA    $20
00019A  2069    1F  8B  A       TFR    A,DP
00020A  206B    96  00  A       LDA    MODEM    CLEAR PIA IRQ
00021A  206D    9E  01  A       LDX    BUFPTR   GET PTR
00022A  206F    A7  80  A       STA    ,X+      STORE CHAR
00023A  2071    9F  01  A       STX    BUFPTR   UPDATE PTR
00024A  2073    81  0D  A       CMPA   #EOL     END OF LINE?
00025A  2075    27  01  2078    BEQ    EOLGP    IF YES, MORE TO DO
00026A  2077    3B              RTI             ELSE, RETURN
00027A  2078    20  FE  2078 EOLGP BRA  *
00028                          END
TOTAL ERRORS 00000--00000
TOTAL WARNINGS 00000--00000
```

Assembler Error Messages

An important feature of many assembler programs is the capability to detect and print out certain assembly errors. In the 6809 assembler, the errors are displayed before the actual line containing the error is printed.

Table 4.14   Assembler Error Messages

Number	Meaning
201	NAM directive used in other than first source statement.
	NAM used twice in same program (ASM 1.2 only).
202	EQU directive syntax requires label (ASM 1.2 only).
204	Source statement syntax incorrect.
205	Label not allowed. Label syntax incorrect.
206	Symbol previously defined.
207	Invalid directive or op code mnemonic.
208	Destination beyond relative branch range.
209	Address mode not allowed with opcode.
210	Byte overflow. One-byte expression converts to value $>255_{10}$ or $<-128_{10}$.
211	Undefined symbol.
213	EQU directive requires label (ASM 1.2 error 213 = redefined symbol error).
216	Directive operand error.
218	Overwrite attempted into nonexistent memory.
220	Redefined label field symbol—pass 2 value differs from pass 1 value.
221	Symbol table overflow.

Source: Motorola Semiconductor Products, Inc.

Errors are also accumulated, with the total number of errors printed at the end of each source listing. Even when no source listing is requested, error messages are still displayed to indicate that the assembly process may have failed. The 6809 assembler generates warning messages as well as errors. Warning messages generally indicate that the resultant source program will execute on a 6809 microprocessor. Error messages are more disastrous, suggesting that the code will not run. A number of useful error messages exist in the 6809 assembler. These are tabulated in Table 4.14.

The format of the error is

$$****ERROR \quad XXX--YYYY$$

where XXX is the error message number and YYYY is the line number of the previously encountered error. A typical error message is depicted in Example 4.20. Here we see two errors, one at line 91, the other at line 96. Error 255 indicates that an error has occurred in the arguments. The format of warning messages is similar. The 6809 warning messages consist of six types, listed in Table 4.15.

EXAMPLE 4.20:   Typical Assembler Error Output

```
00096A 0000                    PIA      49
****ERROR 255--00091
                          FAIL *PIA > 48*
00097                 *
00098                 * THE LAST USE OF THE MACRO ILLUSTRATES
00099                 * THE ERROR  CHECK FOR TOO MANY ARGUMENTS
00100                 *
00101A 0000                    PIA      01, 04
****ERROR 255--00096
                          FAIL *TOO FEW OR TOO MANY ARGS*
00102                          END
```

Table 4.15   M6809 Warning Messages

Number	Meaning
1	Long branch not required
	A long branch instruction was used to branch to an address within the range −126 to +129. Although the long branch instruction could be changed to a short branch, it could result in other out-of-range short branches.
2	Extended addressing should be used
	Direct addressing was forced by using the "<" indicator. However, the direct page pseudo-register assigned by the SETDP directive indicated that the extended mode should have been used.
3	Duplicate register specification
	The same register name was specified more than once in a register list. Register D specified with either register A or B gives this warning.
4	Possible SETDP expression error
	The most significant byte of the expression in a SETDP directive was not zero. The direct page pseudo-register is assigned the value of the least significant byte anyway.
5	Extended addressing should be used
	Direct addressing was forced by using the "<" indicator with a CSCT, DSCT, or PSCT nonexternal expression. The expression will not be relocated by the M6800 Linking Loader.
6	Possible transfer error
	The TFR instruction was used with a transfer from a 16-bit register to an 8-bit register. The result of such a transfer is to move the least significant byte of the 16-bit register to the 8-bit register.

Source: Motorola Semiconductor Products, Inc.

4.10 6809 CO-RESIDENT EDITOR

Generating microprocessor programs that run the first time is a rare phenomenon. In fact, most microprocessor software is an ongoing process with much interaction among several programmers. To assist in this task, an editor software development tool is provided. The editor is an interactive program that can be used to create and modify source program statements written in assembler language. The 6809 editor can manipulate characters, character strings, and lines. An interactive editor such as the 6809 co-resident editor greatly reduces the time and effort required to write correct programs.

The 6809 editor uses a buffer in system memory in which to load source statements for expansion, deletion, or modification, all by means of the editor command. The input/output system configuration is shown in Figure 4.4. The resident editor accepts input text from either the system console device or system reader device. Commands are usually generated via the system control console device. Typical edit operations generate successive portions of input text which are transferred to the edit buffer. When complete, the buffer is transferred out the system punch or printer.

Editing is always performed with ASCII characters. A line in the assembler program is a collection of characters bounded by carriage returns. Nonprinting characters such as line feed (LF), null (NUL), and rubout (RUBOUT) are deleted on input to the edit buffer and will not appear in the edit buffer

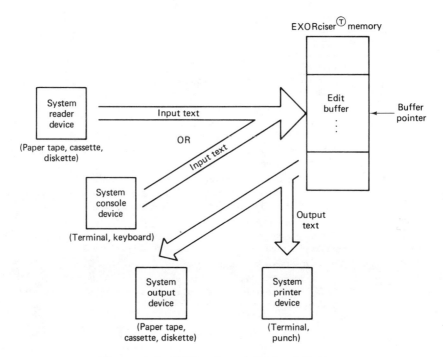

Figure 4.4. Editor Input/Output System.

text. We keep track of the current text locations we are editing with a *buffer pointer*. This pointer specifies the character location within the edit buffer we are editing. It is convenient to think of this pointer as being located between two characters.

Editor Commands

While running the resident editor, a @ appears in the left margin when the editor is prompting us or waiting for a command. Commands to the editor are single characters entered from the counsel device. Some characters may also have arguments; however, all commands must be terminated by two ESC characters. The second character causes the editor to begin execution.

There are three groups of editor commands: input/output operations, buffer pointer operations, and edit operations. Input/output operations cause the transfer of information between the edit buffer and the output devices. For example, the append (A) causes input text to be transferred from the system reader device to the edit buffer. The end (E) command terminates the edit operation and causes the edit buffer to be output to the punch or printer device. Buffer pointer operations manipulate the position of the edit buffer pointer. The beginning command (B) moves the edit buffer pointer to the beginning of the edit buffer, while the end of buffer command (Z) moves the edit buffer pointer to the end of the buffer. We can manipu-

Table 4.16   Editor Command Summary

Command	Description
A	Append. Appends input text from the System Reader Device to the edit buffer.
B	Beginning. Moves the edit buffer pointer to the beginning of the edit buffer.
Cstring1$ string2	Change. Replaces the first occurrence of "string 1" with "string 2."
nD	Delete. Deletes *n* characters from the edit buffer.
E (tape)	End. Terminates an edit operation by writing the contents of the edit buffer to the output tape and copying the remainder of the input tape to the output tape. Returns control to the editor.
E (disc)	End. Terminates an edit operation by writing the contents of the edit buffer to the output file and copying the remainder of the input file to the output file. Returns control to the disc operating system.
F (tape)	Tape Leader/Trailer. Writes 50 NULL characters into the system punch device.
F (disc)	The F command is ignored.
Istring	Insert. Inserts characters or lines of text into the edit buffer.
nK	Kill lines. Deletes *n* lines from the edit buffer.
nL	Line. Moves the edit buffer point *n* lines.
nM	Move character pointer. Moves the edit buffer pointer *n* characters.
Nstring (tape)	Search File. Searches file for first occurrence of "string."
Nstring (disc)	Search File. Searches file for first occurrence of "string." If "string" is not found, returns control to the disc operating system.
nP	Punch. Punches *n* lines from the edit buffer to the System Punch Device.
Sstring	Search. Searches the edit buffer for the first occurrence of "string."
nT	Type. Types *n* lines from the edit buffer to the System Console Device.
X (tape)	EXbug. Returns control to EXbug.
X (disc)	The X command is an illegal command in the disc version of the editor.
Z	End of edit buffer. Moves the edit buffer pointer to the end of the edit buffer.
Control H	Backspace. Causes the last character entered in the command mode to be typed on the System Console Device and deleted from the command.
Control X	Cancel. Causes all commands following the last prompt to be deleted and another prompt to be typed.

Source: Motorola Semiconductor Products, Inc.

late the pointer internal to the text with the move (M) command, which causes the buffer pointer to move a specified number of characters. The line (L) command moves the buffer pointer a specified number of lines.

The edit operations permit us to insert text into the buffer, delete text, or replace it. The insert command (I) inserts lines or characters at the position of the current buffer pointer. The delete character command (D) does the opposite, deleting characters at the current buffer pointer location. We change ASCII characters with the change command (C), which automatically searches the edit buffer from the current buffer pointer position and for the string we wish to change. Upon finding such a string, the editor replaces the old string with the new string. Example 4.21 depicts the use of these commands. The edit commands and messages are summarized in Tables 4.16 and 4.17.

Table 4.17   Editor Messages

Message	Description
M6800 RESIDENT EDITOR n.n	Printed upon initiation of editor. Revision is specified by n.n.
@	Prompt. Editor is waiting for a command.
????	Illegal command.
CAN'T FIND "string"	Editor cannot find the string specified by Search or Change command.
BELL	The editor rings the bell in the System Console Device when the user attempts to enter further commands into a full command buffer. The user must delete (backspace) two characters in order to terminate the command with two ESC characters.

Source: Motorola Semiconductor Products, Inc.

EXAMPLE 4.21:   Edit Commands in Use

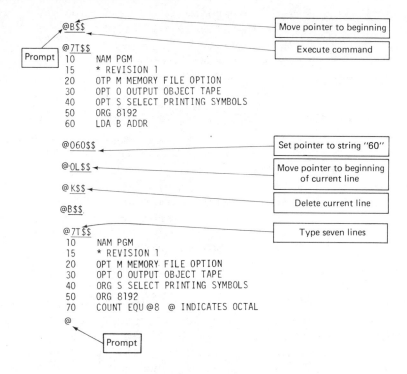

SUMMARY

In this chapter we have studied several instructions and addressing modes of the 6809. Only after much use will you grasp the powerful features of this second generation 8-bit microprocessor. We have seen how important facilities are necessary for position independent coding. Program relative branches are essential.

Employing available software support tools (for example, the assembler and editor) enhances program production. If not improving the rate of production, such tools contribute to a "standardization" of output. This documentation is readily understood by other programmers. Also, assemblers will identify and flag some errors likely to go unnoticed by hand-coded procedures.

EXERCISES

Now here's your chance to prove to yourself how well you understand the 6809!

1. What is the range of size (in bytes) for 6809 instructions?

2. Which 6809 addressing mode executes the fastest? Why is it the fastest?

3. Which addressing mode typically executes the slowest? Why does it take so much time?

4. How many cycles does it take for the 6809 instructions that execute in the least number of cycles?

5. Which instructions take the most number of cycles to execute? And what are they spending all of their machine cycles doing?

6. Write two blocks of equivalent code for the instruction JMP 0,X.

7. Write a block of equivalent code for the instruction RTI.

8. Write a block of equivalent code for SEX.

9. Write a block of equivalent code for the instruction SWI.

10. Write some equivalent code to have the effect of the instructions ASLD and LSRD.

11. Write a block of code to have the effect of the instruction NEGD.

12. Write a block of code to have the effect of the instruction LDDP 10,X, while not changing the current machine state.

13. Write some blocks of code that will implement these nonexistent instructions as macros:

```
IH  A,X
IL  A,Y
IH  B,S
IL  B,U
```

The I stands for insert. This instruction inserts the named 8-bit register into the high (H) or low (L) byte of the named 16-bit register.

14. Write some blocks of code that will implement these nonexistent instructions as macros:

```
EBL  A,X
EBH  A,Y
EBL  B,S
EBH  B,U
```

The EB stands for exchange byte. This instruction exchanges the named 8-bit register with either the high (H) or low (L) byte of the named 16-bit register.

15. This is a bit packing question. Write a routine that takes this input setup:

    (ACCA)=$ZX
    (ACCB)=$WY.   (where WXYZ are hexadecimal digits)

    and produces this output:

    (ACCA)=$XY.

16. Write a converse routine for Exercise 15. Write a routine that takes this input:

    (ACCA)=$XY.

    and returns this output:

    (ACCA)=$FX
    (ACCB)=$FY.   (where F=1111)

17. Signed 8-bit multiplication.
    The 6809 MULtiply instruction performs an 8-bit × 8-bit unsigned multiply. Write a subroutine that uses MUL to perform 8-bit × 8-bit signed multiplication (i.e., when the operation is completed, ACCD is in the correct 2's-complement form for its sign). Assume that ACCA and ACCB have been loaded with the two operands, and then this instruction calls your subroutine:

    JSR +20,PCR,

    and this instruction is at loc=$0040. In addition to writing the routine, calculate the total number of bytes in your routine, and the total number of cycles it will take to execute. Include these figures in your program header comments.

18. As powerful as the program counter relative addressing is in allowing position-independent code, there is a different way to accomplish the same goal. This other method of coding is better for program correction than the PC relative form of addressing. Could you write a routine that would be position-independent, but that did not use the program counter relative form of addressing? Describe how to implement this type of program coding that does not use PC relative addressing except for branches (which can only use forward relative branches), and which is still position-independent. (*Hint:* This addressing mode is sometimes known as base + displacement.)

19. How does the 6809 stack work?

20. What is the order of the 6809 stacking?

21. What will be the eventual effect of only stacking ACCA and PCR and then using a JMP to go to a subroutine? (That is, what will happen on the return?)

22. Why is timing (i.e., counting cycles) important?

23. Why isn't the NOP a wasteful instruction? Or is it?

24. There is more than one form of NOP. Write a line of code using a four-byte NOP.

25. How would you get a two-byte NOP?

26. List two ways to get an 8-bit value in ACCA into the direct page register.

27. How do I pull a single register and set the CCR flags accordingly?

28. How do I round after a multiply?

29. How do I execute a double right rotate on A, B?

30. Make a worksheet similar to Examples 4.1 through 4.18. Fill in the blanks in the worksheets for the following lines of code.

```
a.   100   JMP   [+10, S]    /assume S contains $42
b.   100   JMP   $FE, PCR
c.   A4    LDA   [10, PCR]
d.         DAA
e.         LEAX  -10, U
f.         LEAX  5, S
g.         LDA   , X++
h.         STD   , Y++
i.         LDB   , -Y
j.         LDX   , - -S
k.         LDA   [  , X]
l.         LDD   [10, S]
m.         LDA   [ B, Y]
n.         LDD   [ , X++]
```

BIBLIOGRAPHY

ANDREWS, MICHAEL, "Influence of Architecture on Numerical Logarithms," *Microprocessors and Microsystems*, vol. 2, June 1978, pp. 130-138. Describes the architecture and instruction set influence on the generation of numerical code-producing efficient and reliable programs.

FISCHER, WAYNE P. "Microprocessor Assembly Language Draft Standard," *Computer*, vol. 12, Dec. 1970, pp. 96-109. The IEEE Task P694/D11 proposes another standard language for microprocessors. Lists standard instruction memories for several microprocessors.

GUNDLING, WILLIAM E., AND PETER A. SCHADE, "Programmable Devices: Their Advantages and Disadvantages and Program Equipment, Part I," *Digital Design*, Sept. 1979, pp. 32-34. Describes a selection of EPROMs and FPLAs for ease of program use, reliability, and access time.

"Memory Systems—Forget-Me-Nots of the Digital World," *Electronic Design News*, Nov. 1977, pp. 155-166. Survey article describing memory, magnetic disc and floppy disc applications for microprocessors.

Micro Assemblers Reference Manual 6800, 6801, 6805, 6809, Motorola Inc., Integrated Circuits Division, *Microsystems*, P.O. Box 20912, Phoenix, Arizona, 85036, Document #M68MASR(D), © 1978.

M6800 Co-Resident Editor Reference Manual, Motorola Inc., Integrated Circuits Division, *Microsystems*, P.O. Box 20912, Phoenix, Arizona, 85036, Document #M68CRE(D), © 1977. The editor and assembler manuals describe the usage of the 6809 support software which operates on the EXORCISER.

5

Modern Programming Methods

5.1 INTRODUCTION

In this chapter we demonstrate, by example, the capabilities of the 6809 that help you to generate high-quality code. Structure, position independence, reentrancy, and recursion are hallmarks of modern programming methods. Of these, structure and position independence are paramount. Structure makes your code easily understandable and readily maintainable. Position independence permits code generated for one microprocessor system to be portable to another microprocessor system with little effort.

Most microcomputer systems do not support full development of structured programming found in larger computer systems. Notably lacking is the ability to indent actual code segments which have different functions. One reason for this is that microprocessor code is generally assembly language and no assembler has a control directive to change the column designations freely. Of course, high-level languages such as PASCAL very nicely provide indentation (to help us understand program behavior). So you should not expect to use the indentation mechanism to provide structured code. Rather, you must use line comments and blank lines to "partition" code segments to increase code "readability." Also, structured microprocessor code should be modular. That is, code segments should be assigned to "high-level" or "lower-level" modules. By doing so, your code will be clear to any user. But more important, you will make well-defined assignments to "global" and "local" variables. Parameter passage to/from higher-level modules will be easier. We will return to these important issues later in this chapter.

5.2 HIGH-QUALITY CODE

Let us assume that you are the programmer of a 6809. Your employer asks you to write programs to do such and such. If you know what a good program is and how to write one, you are doing your job. Anything less is inadequate. This chapter helps you to build high-quality code. Good programs are illustrated to show you their characteristics.

Many lists of qualities of a good program exist. Ours include:

1. Correctness
2. Minimum cost
3. Minimum speed and execution
4. Efficient use of memory and features
5. Good documentation and debugging capability
6. Modular
7. Maintainable
8. Adaptable

Correctness

Almost everyone, including your boss, will agree that correctness is the most important quality in a program. No one would care much about how short or how fast your program is if it does not work. And the program does not merely need to run; it must run according to the specifications given you.

Block structure, high-level language, and at the machine level, a regular architecture, consistent instruction set, and logical assembly language enhance correctness. The 6809 people have minimized the number of assembly language mnemonics and applied them consistently, both functionally and syntactically, to similar registers.

Cost versus Speed

The order of the remaining qualities will depend on the situation. Did your boss hand you a rush job or can you concentrate on efficiency? Will the program be used over and over or just once in a great while? Which is more expendable, computer time or your time?

Many factors need to be considered when minimizing cost. If the 6809 is just taking up space most of the time, execution speed may not be important. Your time would be more important, so it would be unwise to spend hours to save a minute of computer time. But if use of the machine is in constant demand, a fast program is more desirable. Both of the routines in Example 5.1 multiply NUMBER by 2 and place the answer in RESULT.

EXAMPLE 5.1: Slow and Fast Programs

Wrong Way	Number of cycles	Number of bytes	Right Way	Number of cycles	Number of bytes
LDA #2	2	2	CLRA	2	1
LDB NUMBER	4	2	LDB NUMBER	4	2
MUL	11	1	ASLB	2	1
STD RESULT	5	2	ROLA	2	1
	22	7	STD RESULT	5	2
				15	7

Notice that although the second set in Example 5.1 is one instruction longer, both take the same amount of memory, yet the first one is seven cycles longer! Discrete use of memory space is also related to minimizing cost and speed. Keep an eye on the number of bytes the instructions require. A detailed knowledge of the instruction set is most helpful, as shown in the following example.

EXAMPLE 5.2: Equivalent Programs

Wrong Way	Number of cycles	Number of bytes	Right Way	Number of cycles	Number of bytes
STA HOLDA	4	2	EXG A,B	8	2
STB HOLDB	4	2		8	2
LDA HOLDB	4	2			
LDB HOLDA	4	2			
	16	8			

Both sets accomplish the same thing, but the second is much shorter and faster. Features such as autoincrementing and autodecrementing of the index registers and powerful Push/Pull instructions are some of the other conveniences.

Documentation

A well-documented program is mandatory. Program boundaries and branch instructions need full clarification. Remember that your program will last long after you are gone.

It is not easy to judge the "goodness" of comments, but here are some guidelines. Comments should be:

1. Up to date
2. Accurate
3. Complete
4. Concise
5. Understandable

Misleading or absent comments waste time and money. Documentation helps to maintain and adapt programs. Be aware that others may someday utilize your routine and modify it to their needs or attach it to their own program. They must know exactly what it does and what it needs.

The following documentation standards[1] for the 6809 have been proposed by the designers. They represent a careful yet important collection of rules that you should follow.

1. Each subroutine should have an associated header block containing at least the following elements:

   a. A full specification for this subroutine—including associated data structures—such that from this description alone replacement code can be generated.

   b. All usage of memory resources must be defined, including:

      (1) All RAM needed from temporary (local) storage used during execution of this subroutine or called subroutines.
      (2) All RAM needed for permanent storage (used to transfer values from one execution of the subroutine to future executions).
      (3) All RAM accessed as global storage (used to transfer values from or to higher-level subroutines).
      (4) All possible exit-state conditions, if these are to be used by calling routines to test occurrences internal to the subroutine.

2. Code internal to each subroutine should have sufficient associated line comments to help in understanding the code.

3. All code must be non-self-modifying and position-independent.

4. Each subroutine that includes a loop must be separately documented by a flow chart.

5. The main program should be executable starting at the first location and should include an I/O jump table immediately thereafter.

[1] See *MC6809 Programming Manual*, Motorola Semiconductor Products, Inc., Austin, Tex., © 1979.

6. When any single routine begins to approach the length of one listing page, it becomes candidate for further subroutining.

Modularity and Maintenance

If a program were modular, maintaining and adapting it would be easier than if it were not. Modular programming partitions the program into pieces to write an independent module for each. As for the size of each module, common sense should prevail. For instance, suppose that a module consists of only two instructions and is called fewer than five times. It may be wiser to insert the two instructions directly into code instead of using JSR/RTS. It will not save space, but it will save execution time.

It is inevitable that someday one of your programs will be expanded or changed in some way, perhaps by using it as a subroutine attached to some other program. Whoever gets the job of modifying or adapting your program (it may even be yourself) will appreciate its modularity. Then it can be generated in sections, hopefully with only minor changes. Good programs are well structured.

How many times have you heard that the boss wants the program yesterday? Modular programs are easier to write and debug. They will save you time and effort as you concentrate on one portion at a time. Then the whole program can be verified after testing each module.

Modular programming means far more than slicing up code into reasonable modules. Writing code to do a well-defined task as in a subroutine means that (1) the subroutine must neither have nor generate hidden anomalies to other computation, and (2) the module operation must be fully understood by looking only at this module. We do this by establishing "local" as well as "global" variables. We say that a local variable is used for temporary data storage only while in a module. The local storage must be so organized that any WRITE to a local does not affect the later processing of other modules. A global variable is available to all modules. Notice that a module-in-error may change the value of a global, thus causing later program failure by modules not in error, and far removed from the error-causing troublemakers! Local storage implies the ability to use exactly the same variable names in different modules. There can be no modular-programming environment at all without local variables.

5.3 TOWARD MODERN STRUCTURED CODE

Many microprocessor applications require us to store data as contiguous pieces of information in memory. The data may be temporary (that is, subject to change) or they may be permanent. If they are permanent, you will probably store them in ROM. If not, you will store them in a RAM. We sometimes call these blocks of data tables. This activity is called data management, although there is more to it.

Modern Programming Methods

It is very important to be able to move these tables around the memory space. This is very easy in the 6809. It is also important to be able to allow the main program as well as subroutines to access tables, especially if arguments are to be passed from the main program to the subroutines, and vice versa.

6809 Modular Facilities

Programs can be viewed as a collection of modules and subroutines. A module can actually be a subroutine itself, but a subroutine cannot be a module. A module is the highest-level code in a software system. That is, modules generate storage for global variables, make passage to subroutines, and manage system movement through the code from the main program to subroutines and return.

Upon entry to subroutines, the absolute address, which is the return to the calling routine (somewhere in our module), should be on top of the stack. Inside the subroutine, we will probably use MPU registers. Therefore, at the beginning of the subroutine we should immediately execute a PSHS B,A,CCR (assuming that B, A, and CCR are to be used by the subroutine). In this manner, the previous contents of the MPU registers have been saved. Just before we exit the subroutine, execute a PULS CCR,A,B,PC. This restores the old MPU registers to their values before we entered the subroutine, and does the subroutine return as well.

Parameters can be passed to or from modules in two ways: by using MPU registers or by using a stack. When few parameters are required, use the MPU registers. When many parameters are passed, use a stack. Place them on the stack before calling a lower-level module. When the lower-level module needs to access these parameters, it simply uses an appropriate offset with respect to S. The offset consists of the number of bytes pushed (upon entry), two for the stacked return address and the remaining bytes for the data offset at the time of the call. Naturally, if the lower module returns more parameters than the calling routine provided space for, the calling routine should contemplate this need and initially generate sufficient stack space. The caller can use LEAS –N,S, where N is the number of additional parameter bytes.

The handling of local and global storage is described as follows. Local storage space is acquired from the stack for use within the present routine; the storage is then returned prior to exit. You should push registers to be used in later calculation by saving those registers in temporary local storage. Additional local storage can easily be acquired from the stack (for example, executing LEAS –256,S acquires a buffer area running from 0,S to +255,S inclusive). Any byte here can be accessed directly by any instruction that has an indexed addressing mode. At the end of the routine, you should release the local storage (e.g., LEAS 256,S) prior to the final pull.

Global storage is most effectively acquired by the stack, and the highest-level routine should establish it. Although local storage is the highest-level routine, it becomes "global" by positioning a register to point (stack mark pointer) at this storage. Now you let all modules pass that same pointer value when calling lower-level modules. Generally, it is convenient to leave the stack mark register unchanged in all modules because global accesses will become commonplace. Remember that if one module changes the stack mark register, other modules may have to be notified. For example, the highest-level routine executes the following sequence upon entry (to initialize the global area):

```
PSHS    U       Higher-level mark
TFR     S,U     New stack mark
LEAS    -9,U    Global storage
```

See how the U register acquires nine bytes of locally allocated (permanent) globals (which are -1,U through -9,U) as well as other external globals (2,U and below toward locations FFFF) which have been passed on the stack by the routine that called the standard package. Now, any global may be accessed by any module using exactly the same offset value at any level. Had any module changed this register, "global" access would be destroyed.

6809 Stack Operations

We use stacks to manage tables in the 6809. Stack pointers are markers that point to the stack and its internal contents. There are two obvious stack pointers in the 6809, the S or hardware stack pointer and the U or the user stack pointer. Both are 16-bit indexable registers in the 6809 MPU. Of the two, the MPU uses only the S register during interrupts.

Either stack pointer can be specified as a base address in indexed addressing. One nice feature is that the indirect mode using stack pointers allows addresses of data to be passed to a subroutine on a stack as arguments to a subroutine. The subroutine can now reference the data pointed to with *one* instruction. High-level language calls that pass arguments by reference are now more efficiently coded. Also, each PUSH or PULL operation in your program uses a postbyte (see Chapter 2) which specifies any register or set of registers to be pushed or pulled from either stack. With this option we greatly decrease the overhead associated with subroutine calls in both assembly and high-level language programs. In fact, with other instructions that use autoincrement and autodecrement (which we shall see shortly) the 6809 can very nicely emulate a stack computer architecture. But the principal advantage to the indirect addressing mode is the access to I/O devices in different systems.

Using the S or U stack pointer, the order in which the registers are pushed or pulled is given in Figure 5.1. Notice that we push "onto" the stack toward decreasing memory locations. The program counter is pushed first. Then the stack pointer is decremented and the "other" stack pointer is pushed onto the stack. We continue decrementing locations and storing

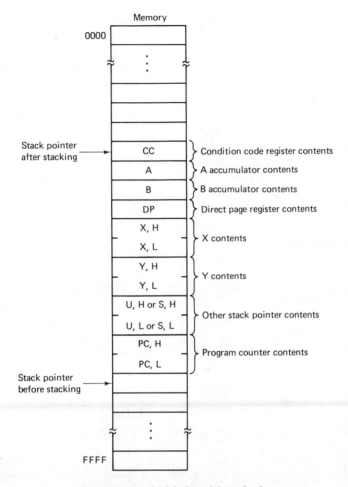

Figure 5.1. 6809 Stacking Order.

subsequent registers. Only those registers requested by the postbyte will be pushed onto the stack. The stack pointer points to the top of the stack now after the push operation. It does *not* point to the next available location in the stack (as in the 6800).

The stacking order is specified by the hardware and is identical to the order used by *all* hardware and software interrupts. Furthermore, the order is still the same even if a subset of all the registers is pushed.

Subroutine Linkage

In the highest-level routine, global variables may be considered local. Therefore, storage is allocated at this point, but access to these variables requires different offset values from the hardware stack pointer (S), depending on subroutine depth, since the return address for each subroutine is also stacked. Unfortunately, the subroutine depth dynamically changes from invocation to invocation. The distance to the desired globals may not be readily known beforehand. We solve this problem by assigning one pointer to "mark" a location on the hardware stack. For instance, we can use the instruction TFR S,U and do this immediately prior to allocating global storage. Then you can expect all variables to be available at a constant location positive offset from this stack mark. We actually call U the stack mark pointer.

Example 5.3 depicts a typical high-level subroutine linkage. Before calling this subroutine, you should push the addresses of two arguments and the answer onto the stack. Then jump to the subroutine (JSR puts the current program counter on the stack). See how the subroutine saves the old stack pointer, U, on the stack as well as preserving space on the stack for local variables used by the subroutine (Figure 5.2).

The subroutine body uses six locations during calculation. Here the

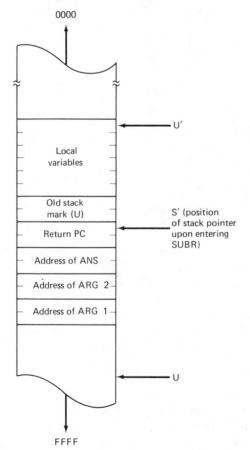

Figure 5.2. A Stack Mark Pointer.

stack mark pointer is set to new values for the subroutine. Primed variables denote that the value of the variable has been changed. For instance, U' is the new value of the user stack pointer. Notice that we are using the indexed addressing mode. The subroutine finishes with the answer in the D register. Before the subroutine exits, D is stored in the parameter space. It then loads the return address in PC and restores the previous stack mark pointer.

EXAMPLE 5.3: Use of Stacks on the 6809 Processor[2]

```
00006 0500 34 40      6 SUBR PSHS U       SAVE OLD STACK MARKER
00007 0502 32 66      5       LEAS -6,S    RESERVE LOCAL STORAGE
00008 0504 1F 43      6       TFR  S,U     GET NEW STACK MARKER
00009 0506 EC D8 0E  10       LDD  [14,U]  GET ARGUMENT 1
00010 0509 AE D8 0C  10       LDX  [12,U]  GET ARGUMENT 2
00011                       .
00012                       . SUBROUTINE BODY
00013                       .
00014 050C ED D8 0A  10       STD  [10,U]  SAVE ANSWER
00015 050F AE 48      6       LDX  8,U     GET RETURN ADDRESS
00016 0511 EE 46      6       LDU  6,U     RESTORE U
00017 0513 32 E8 10   6       LEAS 16,S    POP EVERYTHING OFF STACK
00018 0516 6E 84      3       JMP  ,X      RETURN
```

The following program also demonstrates the proper instruction sequences for the calling program (higher-level module) and the subroutine (lower-level module).

EXAMPLE 5.4: 8-Bit Restoring Division for Positive Integers

```
* THIS POSITION-INDEPENDENT CODE SUBROUTINE GENERATES THE
* QUOTIENT OF TWO 8-BIT POSITIVE OPERANDS.
* THE SUBROUTINE USES A, B, AND CCR.  ROUTINE REQUIRES 3N/2
* ADDITIONS, WHERE N=8.  (RESTORING METHOD IS USED)
* STACK PICTURE ON ENTRY
*        U + 0      OLD STACK MARK
*        U – 1      DIVISOR
*        U – 2      DIVIDEND
*        U – 3      COUNT ( = –8 INITIALLY )

* STACK PICTURE ON EXIT
*        U + 0      OLD STACK MARK
*        U – 1      QUOTIENT
*        U – 2      REMAINDER
*        U – 3      UNUSED
* CALLING ROUTINE SAVES STACK SPACE AND STACK MARK POINTER
* AND PASSES PARAMETERS
```

[2] Reprinted courtesy of Byte Publications, © 1979.

```
* CALLING ROUTINE SHOULD DO THE FOLLOWING
*         PSHS       U
*         TFR        S,U
*         LEAS       -3,S
*           .
*           .                                    STACK PARAMETERS
*           .
*         LBSR       RSDVSR
*         TFR        U,S
*         PULS       U,PC
* SUBROUTINE BODY FOR 8-BIT RESTORING DIVISION
RSDVSR PSHS       B,A,CCR                    PRESERVE MPU STATUS
       CLRA
       LDB        DIVD,U                     GET DIVIDEND
* ADJUST DIVIDEND AND QUOTIENT
* TRIAL SUBTRACTION: DIVISOR .LT.  DIVIDEND  ?
LOOP     ASLB                                ALIGN DIVIDEND AND QUOTIENT
         ROLA
         SUBA      DVSR,U
         BMI       NEGA                       DIVISOR .LT. DIVIDEND?
         INCB                                 YES, INC QUOTIENT
         BRA       ENDCHK                     SKIPOVER
* NO, RESTORE DIVIDEND : TRIAL FAILED
NEGA     ADDA      DVSR,U                     ADD DIVISOR BACK
* YES, NOW CHECK FOR EIGHT TRIALS
ENDCHK INC        CNT,U
       BLT        LOOP                       8 TRIALS?
       STA        RMDR,U                     STACK RESULTS
       STB        QUOT,U
DONE     PULS      CCR,A,B,PC                 RETURN
* END OF SUBROUTINE
* STACK OFFSET VALUES FOR PARAMETERS
CNT      EQU       -3                         COUNT
DVSR     EQU       -1                         DIVISOR
DIVD     EQU       -2                         DIVIDEND
RMDR     EQU       -2                         REMAINDER
QUOT     EQU       -1                         QUOTIENT
```

Software Stacks

Suppose that you need more than two stacks. Does the 6809 give us this capability? Yes, in fact, using the autoincrement and autodecrement mode of addressing we can generate many additional software stack pointers. This neat autoincrement and autodecrement feature is also available in indexed addressing in the 6809.

In autoincrement the value pointed to by the index register (X, Y, U, or S) is used as the effective address. Then, the index register is incremented. In autodecrement the index register is first decremented and then used to obtain the effective address. The 6809 always performs *pre*-decrement and *post*-increment, since this is equivalent in operation to the push and pull from a stack. This equivalence allows the X and Y registers to be used as software stack pointers. Indeed, the index addressing mode can also implement an extra level of post-indirection. This useful feature supports block moves and string commands.

In Example 5.5 we list a subroutine that searches a text buffer for the occurrence of an input string. See how we use autoincrement. The X register points to an input string in the text buffer with a byte containing a negative value. We pass the length of the input string to the subroutine in ACCB. When we leave the subroutine, Y contains the pointer to the start of the matched string +1 if the Z flag is set. If the Z flag has not been set, the input string was not found.

EXAMPLE 5.5: Text String Search Program[3]

```
00032                              *
00033                              * SEARCH LOOKS FOR A PARTICULAR TEXT STRING
00034                              *       IN A BLOCK OF DATA.
00035                              *       RETURNS Z=1 IFF FOUND.
00036                              *       X POINTS AT NEXT CHAR PAST STRING.
00037                              *
00038 1443 30   8D   0038   9 START   LEAX  BLOCK,PCR  DATA BLOCK START ADDR
00039 1447 33   8D   0061   9         LEAU  END,PCR   DATA BLOCK END ADDR
00040 144B 31   8D   005E   9         LEAY  STRING,PCR ADDR OF STRING TO BE FOUND
00041 144F C6   05          2         LDB   # LENGTH
00042 1451 8D   02          7         BSR   SEARCH
00043 1453 20   FE          3         BRA   *

00045 1455 34   74          11 SEARCH PSHS  U,Y X,B
00046                              *
00047                              * ( SP+0 ) = LENGTH
00048                              * ( SP+1 ) = RESTART BLOCK SEARCH ( H )
00049                              *            RESTART BLOCK SEARCH ( L )
00050                              * ( SP+3 ) = STRING ( H )
00051                              *            STRING ( L )
00052                              * ( SP+5 ) = END ( H )
00053                              *            END ( L )
00054 1457 AE   61          6 AGAIN  LDX   1,S
00055 1459 10AE 63          7         LDY   3,S        RESET STRING PTR
00056 145C E6   E4          4         LDB   0,S        RESET STRING LENGTH
00057                              * THIS LOOP SEARCHES AFTER MISMATCH
00058 145E AC   65          7 LOOP1  CMPX  5,S        END OF DATA?
00059 1460 2E   1A          3         BGT   EXIT       IF YES, EXIT NOT FOUND
00060 1462 A6   80          6         LDA   ,X+        GET BYTE AND INC
00061 1464 AF   61          6         STX   1,S        STORE RESTART LOCATION
00062 1466 A1   A4          4         CMPA  0,Y        SAME AS STRING?
00063 1468 26   F4          3         BNE   LOOP1      BRANCH IF NOT
00064 146A 31   21          5         LEAY  1,Y        POINT TO 2ND CHAR
00065 146C 5A              2         DECB
00066 146D 27   0D          3         BEQ   EXIT       FOR 1-BYTE SEARCH
00067                              * THIS LOOP SEARCHES AFTER MATCH
00068 146F AC   65          7 LOOP2  CMPX  5,S        END OF DATA?
00069 1471 2E   09          3         BGT   EXIT       IF YES, EXIT NOT FOUND
```

[3] Reprinted from *MC6809 Programming Manual*, Motorola Semiconductor Products, Inc., Austin, Tex., © 1979 (see Section 6.2).

```
00070 1473 A6  80      6          LDA    ,X+      GET BYTE AND INC
00071 1475 A1  A0      6          CMPA   ,Y+      SAME AS STRING?
00072 1477 26  DE      3          BNE    AGAIN    IF NO, START OVER
00073 1479 5A          2          DECB            DONE?
00074 147A 26  F3      3          BNE    LOOP2    IF NO, KEEP GOING
00075 147C 32  67      5   EXIT   LEAS   7,S      CLEAN UP STACK
00076 147E 39          5          RTS

00078 147F     54          BLOCK  FCC    / THIS IS A BLOCK OF DATIVE /
00079 1499     44                 FCC    / DATA TO BE SEARCHED. /
00080          14AC        END    EQU    *-1
00081 14AD     44          STRING FCC    / DATA /
00082          0005        LENGTH EQU    *-STRING
```

Do I have a problem because the stack pointer points to a location containing the last operand and not an available location (as in the 6800)?

Answer: NO. The 6809 uses other stack instructions accordingly. For example, TFR S,X will transfer the value in the stack pointer to the indexable register X. Now the first time you use the index register to "push" a value, employ the "autoincrement by one" addressing mode.

Do I have only two stack pointers?

Answer: NO. With all the autoincrement and decrement instructions on the indexable registers, you can create X and Y stacks. For example,

```
              STA    ,-X
```

uses the X index register as a stack pointer and pushes the contents of accumulator A onto this stack. The following instructions also simulate the PUSH. They push B, D, Y, U, and S onto a stack, respectively.

```
          STB    ,-X     Autodecrement by 1
          STD    ,--X
          STY    ,--X
          STU    .--X    Autodecrement by 2
          STS    ,--X
```

Then how do I pull with X, Y?

Answer: These instructions pull A, B, D, Y, U, and S from a stack, respectively.

```
          LDA    ,X+     Autoincrement by 1
          LDB    ,X+
          LDD    ,X++
          LDY    ,X++    Autoincrement by 2
          LDU    ,X++
          LDS    ,X++
```

Why should I stack A, B, then D?

Answer: You shouldn't.

Modern Programming Methods

5.4 A BETTER WAY TO CODE

Designers of the 6809 have incorporated many features to enable good programs to be written for the microprocessor. Some of them are powerful addressing modes, powerful Push/Pull instructions, two 16-bit stack pointers, and vectored interrupts. All of these features, properly used, can help us achieve position-independent, reentrant, and recursive routines, and suitable interrupt systems.

Position-Independent Code

Position-independent code (PIC) means that the same machine language code can be placed anywhere in memory and still function correctly. The 6809 has a long relative (16-bit offset) branch mode plus program relative addressing. This uses the program counter like an indexable register, which allows all instructions that reference memory to reference data relative to the current program counter. The 6809 also has LEA instructions that allow the user to point to data in a position-independent manner in order to gain access to it in the text of the program. PIC, also called "self-relative," goes far in making software portable.

Since PIC is self-relative, it is wise to use the BSR and LBSR instead of JSR internal to PIC code. One reason is that BSR and LBSR use addresses relative to PIC code. JSR can do much more (perhaps harmfully). JSR has seven addressing modes. To encourage clean PIC code, JSR should be avoided.

PIC Generation Rule

NEVER USE ABSOLUTE ADDRESSING

Global, permanent, and temporary values need to be easily available in a position-independent manner. Use the stack for these data since the stacked data are directly accessible. Stack the absolute addresses of I/O devices before calling any standard software package since the package can use the stacked addresses for I/O in any system.

We commonly need to gain access to tables or data or immediate values in the text of the programs; the LEA instructions allow us to point at data in a position-independent manner. For instance, suppose that our problem is to print out a message whose location is not known at the time we are generating our program. We can use the PCR mode of addressing as in Example 5.6.

EXAMPLE 5.6:

.
.
.

```
LEAX    MSG1,PCR
```

```
                    LBSR    PDATA
                             .
                             .
                             .

              MSG1    FCC    / PRINT THIS! /
```

Here we wish to point at a message to be printed from the body of the program. By writing "MSG1,PCR" we signal the assembler to compute the distance between the present address (the address of the next instruction following LSBR) and MSG1. This result is inserted as a constant into the LEA instruction which will be indexed from the program counter value at the time of execution. Now, no matter where the code is located, when it is executed, the computed offset from the program counter will point at MSG1. This code is position-independent. Example 5.7 is also position-independent code.

EXAMPLE 5.7: A Text Buffer Search[4]

```
00001                        NAM   AUTOEX
00003                        OPT   LLEN=80
00004            .
00005            ................................................
00006            .   COMPARE STRINGS SUB
00007            .
00008            .   FIND AN INPUT ASCII STRING POINTED TO BY THE
00009            .   X-REGISTER IN A TEXT BUFFER POINTED TO BY THE
00010            .   Y-REGISTER. THE BUFFER IS TERMINATED BY A
00011            .   BYTE CONTAINING A NEGATIVE VALUE. ON ENTRY
00012            .   A CONTAINS THE LENGTH OF THE INPUT STRING. ON
00013            .   EXIT, Y CONTAINS THE POINTER TO THE START
00014            .   OF THE MATCHED STRING + 1 IFF Z IS SET. IFF Z
00015            .   IS NOT SET THE INPUT STRING WAS NOT FOUND.
00016            .
00017            .   ENTRY:
00018            .      X POINTS TO INPUT STRING
00019            .      Y POINTS TO TEXT BUFFER
00020            .      A LENGTH OF INPUT STRING
00021            .   EXIT:
00022            .      IFF Z=1 THEN Y POINTS ITO MATCHED STRING + 1
00023            .      IFF Z=0 THEN NO MATCH
00024            .      X IS DESTROYED
00025            .      B IS DESTROYED
00026            .
00027            ................................................
00028            .
```

[4] Reprinted courtesy of Byte Publications, © 1979. See Terry Ritter and Joel Boney, "A Microprocessor for the Revolution: The 6809, Part I," *Byte Magazine*, Jan. 1979, p. 31.

```
00029 0100                          ORG    $100
00030 0100 E6 A0      6  CMPSTR  LDB    ,Y+        GET BUFFER CHARACTER
00031 0102 2A 01      3          BPL    CMP1       BRANCH IF NOT AT BUFFER END
00032 0104 39         5          RTS               NO MATCH, Z=0
00033 0105 E1 84      4  CMP1    CMPB   ,X         COMPARE TO FIRST STRING CHAR.
00034 0107 26 F7      3          BNE    CMPSTR     BRANCH ON NO COMPARE
00035                      · SAVE STATE SO SEARCH CAN BE RESUMED IF IT FAILS
00036 0109 34 32      9          PSHS   A,X,Y
00037 010B 30 01      5          LEAX   1,X        POINT X TO NEXT CHAR
00038 010D 4A         2  CMP2    DECA              ALL CHARS COMPARE?
00039 010E 27 0C      3          BEQ    CMPOUT     IF SO, IT'S A MATCH, Z=1
00040 0110 E6 A0      6          LDB    ,Y+        GET NEXT BUFFER CHAR.
00041 0112 2B 08      3          BMI    CMPOUT     BRANCH IF BUFFER END, Z=0
00042 0114 E1 80      6          CMPB   ,X+        DOES IT MATCH STRING CHAR?
00043 0116 27 F5      3          BEQ    CMP2       BRANCH IF SO
00044 0118 35 32      9          PULS   A,X,Y      SEARCH FAILED, RESTART SEARCH
00045 011A 20 E4      3          BRA    CMPSTR
00046 011C 35 B2     11  CMPOUT  PULS   A,X,Y,PC   FIX STACK, RETURN WITH Z
00047
00048           0000              END
```

Reentrant Programs

A program that can be executed by several different users sharing the same copy of it in memory is called reentrant. This is important for interrupt-driven systems. Especially for large routines, this method saves considerable memory space. Stacks are most handy for reentrant programs, and the 6809 has two of them. Also, the X and Y registers can be programmed to act as stack pointers if needed.

Stacks are simple and convenient mechanisms for generating reentrant programs. In contrast, routines that refer to parameters or temporary values in absolute memory locations are probably not reentrant. Subroutines should use stacks for passing parameters and results as well as for temporary storage of values. Stack addressing is quick. (Remember that the address is updated as part of the execution of the instruction.) When you add new data, you do not necessarily destroy the old data.

Pure code, or code that is not self-modifying, exemplifies reentrant code. No internal information within the code is subject to modification. Reentrant code is interruptable and restartable. Example 5.8 is reentrant.

EXAMPLE 5.8:   Convert ASCII Numeral to Decimal

```
* CONVERTS ASCII NUMERAL TO DECIMAL.  REENTRANT CODE.
* STACK PICTURE ON ENTRY AND EXIT
*         U + 0       OLD STACK MARK
*         U – 2       ADDRESS OF ASCII CHARACTER
*         U – 4       ADDRESS OF DECIMAL NUMBER
* SUBROUTINE USES A AND CCR
```

```
* SUBROUTINE EXITS WITH ALL ONES IN (U-2)
* IF INPUT IS ALPHA CHARACTER, ELSE A DECIMAL DIGIT
*


* CALLING ROUTINE SAVES STACK SPACE, STACK MARK
* AND PASSES PARAMETERS:
*        PSHS        U                   SAVE STACK MARK POINTER
*        TFR         S,U
*        LEAS        -4,S
*         .
*         .                              STACK PARAMETERS
*         .
*        LBSR        ACDEC
*        TFR         U,S
*        PULS        U,PC


* SUBROUTINE BODY FOR CONVERSION
ACDEC   PSHS        A,CCR               STACK OLD A, CCR
        LDA         [CHAR,U]            GET ASCII INPUT
        SUBA        #'0                 MINUS ASCII ZERO
        CMPA        #10                 RESULT .LT. 10 ?
        BLO         END                 YES, NUMERIC!
        LDA         #$FF                NO ALPHA
END     STA         [DEC,U]             SAVE IT
        PULS        CCR,A,PC            RETURN
* END OF SUBROUTINE


* STACK OFFSET VALUES FOR PARAMETERS
CHAR    EQU         -2                  ASCII INPUT CHARACTER
DEC     EQU         -4                  DECIMAL NUMBER RESULT
```

Recursive Programs

A recursive program is one that can call upon itself. Many programmers avoid writing them because they are subject to much confusion and require precise data manipulation. On occasion, however, they become quite convenient to use, such as for factorial computation. As with reentrant programming, stacks are very useful for this technique.

An example of a recursive routine follows next. This mathematical routine calculates the factorial function $N! = N*(N-1)*(N-2)*...*1$. Since we known that $N! = N*(N-1)!$ and $1! = 1$, we will use these properties recursively in the coding. This program does not compute $0!$ nor can $n!$ exceed $2**15$. The recursive nature of this program utilizes the S stack to save the return jumps from RETURN at the end of the FACT subroutine to PROD within the same subroutine. These internal jumps occur N-1 times. The U stack contains the numbers N, N-2, ..., 2 in decreasing stack locations. The X and Y stacks reserve temporary storage for intermediate calculation of $(N-I)*[(N-J)]$, where $1 < I < J$. The final result, $N!$, can be found in the X stack. All the stacks, X, Y, U, and S, store into decreasing stack locations. You must ensure that this "working space" is available prior to entering FACT.

Another factorial program can be found in Example 5.15. It is worthwhile to compare the two programs. Ask yourself which is more understandable, easier to debug, and well documented.

EXAMPLE 5.9: Recursive Factorial

```
* Enter:   X has address of last result
*          Y has address of current result
           A has or will have current number
* Exit:    same but updated
* This is the routine for calling the factorial
* subroutine. It initializes the storage in
* memory and prepares for the recursive subroutine.
* Enter: A had the number to find factorial product
* Exit:   X has address of final result, either
              RESLT1 or RESLT2
* Calling Routine

         CALFAC  LDX    #RESLT1        /set up pointer
                 LDY    #RESLT2        /set up pointer
                 LDB    MAXBYT
                 DECB                  /MAXBYT-1
         INIT    CLR    B, X           /clear storage
                 CLR    B, Y           /clear storage
                 DECB                  /decrement pointer
                 BNE    INIT           /storage cleared?
                 LDB    MAXBYT         /yes, restore B
                 DECB                  /MAXBYT-1

                 INC    B, X           /put in 1 for first multiplication
                 LBSR   FACT           /jump to Factorial subroutine
*                       .
*                       .
*                       .
* Subroutine
         FACT    CMPA   #1             /N=1
                 BLE    RETURN         / return when A=1, Factorial=1
                 PSHU   A              / put current number on U-stack
                 DECA                  /N-1
                 LBSR   FACT           /save next PC on S stack

         PROD    PULU   A              / put current number in A
                 LDB    MAXBYT         / initialize loop counter
                 DECB                  /next factor in stack (MAXBYT-1)
                 STB    BYTCNT         / store offset count in memory

         MULBYT  LDB    BYTCNT,X       / put a byte of last result in B
                 CLR    BYTCNT,X       / for future purposes
                 DEC    BYTCNT
                 MUL                   /8x8 multiply
                 ADDD   BYTCNT,Y       / add new partial result to current result
                 TST    BYTCNT         /BYTCNT-0=0?
                 BGE    MULBYT         / loop back if BYTCNT≥0

                 EXG    X, Y           / adjust addresses for exit
         RETURN  RTS                   /go to PROD, use S stack
```

5.5 SOME USEFUL PROGRAMS

In this section we present some useful programs that follow modern programming practices. Study them carefully, noting how the code is structured and whether it is or can be made position-independent.

EXAMPLE 5.10: 8-Bit Nonrestoring Division

```
* THIS POSITION-INDEPENDENT ROUTINE COMPUTES THE
* 8-BIT QUOTIENT OF TWO 8-BIT POSITIVE INTEGERS
* USING A NONRESTORING DIVISION ALGORITHM.
* ROUTINE USES A, B, AND CCR.
* N ADDITIONS AND SUBTRACTIONS ARE REQUIRED WHERE
* N IS NUMBER OF BITS.

* STACK PICTURE ON ENTRY
*         U + 0          OLD STACK MARK
*         U − 1          COUNT ( = −8 INITIALLY)
*         U − 2          DIVISOR
*         U − 3          DIVIDEND
*
* STACK PICTURE ON EXIT
*         U + 0          OLD STACK MARK
*         U − 1          REMAINDER
*         U − 2          QUOTIENT
*
* CALLING ROUTINE SAVES STACK SPACE, STACK MARK
* AND PASSES PARAMETERS
*         PSHS           U
*         TFR            S,U
*         LEAS           −3,S
*          .
*          .                                   STACK PARAMETERS
*          .
*         LBSR           NRDV
*         TFR            U,S
*         PULS           U,PC
*
* SUBROUTINE BODY FOR 8-BIT NONRESTORING DIVISION
*
NRDV      PSHS           B,A,CCR              STACK OLD MPU
          CLRA
          LDB            DIVD,U
          ASLB
          ROLA
          SUBA           DVSR,U
* SUBTRACT DIVISOR FROM DIVIDEND
LOOP      TSTA
          BMI            NEGA
* PARTIAL REMAINDER NOW POSITIVE, SUBTRACT DIVISOR
          ASLB
          ROLA
          INCB
          SUBA           DVSR,U
```

```
* SKIP OVER
            BRA         ENDCHK
* ADD DIVISOR SINCE PARTIAL REMAINDER BECAME NEGATIVE
NEGA        ASLB
            ROLA
            ADDA        DVSR,U
* N LOOP CHECK
ENDCHK  INC             CNT,U
            BLT         LOOP
            TSTA
            BMI         DONE
*
* END CORRECTION OF PARTIAL REMAINDER, ONE TIME ONLY
*
CORR        ADDA        DVSR,U
* STACK REMAINDER AND QUOTIENT
            STA         RMDR,U
DONE        STB         QUOT,U
            PULS        CCR,A,B,PC
* END OF SUBROUTINE BODY

* STACK OFFSET VALUES FOR COUNTER, DIVISOR, DIVIDEND
* QUOTIENT, AND REMAINDER
*
CNT         EQU         -1              COUNT
DVSR        EQU         -2              DIVISOR
DIVD        EQU         -3              DIVIDEND
RMDR        EQU         -1              REMAINDER
QUOT        EQU         -2              QUOTIENT
```

EXAMPLE 5.11   Reentrant 16-Bit Divide

```
* THIS SUBROUTINE DIVIDES TWO 16-BIT POSITIVE INTEGERS
* GIVING A 16-BIT RESULT. SUCCESSIVE TRIAL SUBTRACTIONS
* ARE USED, WITH DIVIDEND RESTORATION AT EACH TRIAL IF
* C FLAG IS CLEARED. DIVISION NEED NOT BE NORMALIZED
* (.I.E., MSB = 1) AT ENTRY.
* SUBROUTINE USES A, B, AND CCR
* STACK PICTURE AT ENTRY:
*           U + 0       OLD STACK MARK
*           U - 1       COUNTER ( = 1 INITIALLY)
*           U - 2       MSB DIVISOR
*           U - 3       LSB DIVISOR
*           U - 4       MSB DIVIDEND
*           U - 5       LSB DIVIDEND

* STACK PICTURE ON EXIT:
*           U - 4       QUOTIENT (MSB)
*           U - 5       QUOTIENT (LSB)

* CALLING ROUTINE GENERATES STACK STORAGE, SAVES STACK MARK
*           PSHS        U               SAVE STACK MARK
*           TFR         S,U
```

```
*         LEAS      -5,S
*          .
*          .                          SET UP DIVISOR,
*          .                          DIVIDEND, AND COUNTER
*         LBSR      DIVG              CALL DIVIDER
*          .
*          .
*          .
*         TFR       U,S               CLEAN UP STACK
*         PULS      U,PC

* SUBROUTINE BODY FOR 16-BIT DIVISION
DIVG      PSHS      B,A,CCR           WE NEED THEM
          TST       MDVSR,U           DIVISOR NORMALIZED?
          BMI       NORMAL            YES, GO AHEAD
* NORMALIZE DIVISION TILL LEAD BIT IS 1, COUNTING LEFT SHIFTS
NNORM     INC       CNT,U
          ASL       LDVSR,U           SHIFT LSB DIVISOR
          ROL       MDVSR,U           NOW MSB
          BMI       NORMAL
          LDA       CNT,U
          CMPA      #17
          BNE       NORMAL            NORMAL?
* GET DIVIDEND IN D, CLEAR QUOTIENT
NORMAL    LDD       MDIVD,U
          CLR       MDIVD,U
          CLR       LDIVD,U
* BEGIN DIVISION BY SUCCESSIVE SUBTRACTION METHOD
* TESTING CARRY FLAG EACH TIME
DVD       SUBD      MDVSR,U           TRIAL SUBTRACTION
          BCC       SETC              OK?
          ADDD      MDVSR,U           NO, RESTORE DIVIDEND
          ANDCC     #$FE              CLEAR CARRY
          BRA       LINUP             SKIP NEXT INSTRUCTION
* SET CARRY BIT
SETC      ORCC      #$01              TRIAL SUBTRACTION OK
*LINE UP QUOTIENT, DIVIDEND, AND DIVISOR FOR NEXT TRIAL
LINUP     ROL       LDIVD,U           ADJUST QUOTIENT
          ROL       MDIVD,U           AND DIVIDEND
          LSR       MDVSR,U           ADJUST DIVISOR
          ROR       LDVSR,U
          DEC       CNT,U             DONE?
          BNE       DVD               NO
* RESTORE MPU REGISTERS AND EXIT
DONE      PULS      CCR,A,B,PC        YES, RETURN

* STACK OFFSET VALUES FOR COUNTER, DIVISOR, DIVIDEND
CNT       EQU       -1                COUNT
MDVSR     EQU       -2                MSB DIVISOR
LDVSR     EQU       -3                LSB DIVISOR
MDIVD     EQU       -4                MSB DIVIDEND
LDIVD     EQU       -5                LSB DIVIDEND
```

EXAMPLE 5.12: Floating-Point Addition and Subtraction

```
* THIS SUBROUTINE USES 16-BIT MANTISSAS (POSITIVE
* ONLY) AND 8-BIT BIASED EXPONENTS. THE EXPONENT RANGE
* IS 2⁻¹²⁸ (SMALLEST) TO 2⁺¹²⁷ (LARGEST). BIAS IS 200₈.
*
* BIT 7 OF THE EXPONENT IS USED FOR BIAS, NOT FOR
* ALGEBRAIC SIGN. INSTR IS POSITIVE FOR ADDITION, ZERO FOR
* SUBTRACTION. LEXP IS LOCAL STORAGE FOR LARGEST EXPONENT.
* EXPONENT OVERFLOW FLAG = $FF IN STACK. MAXEXP IS A
* CONSTANT = FF.
*
* STACK PICTURE ON ENTRY AND EXIT
*          U + 0       OLD STACK MARK
*          U − 1       ERROR FLAG (=$FF IF OVERFLOW)
*          U − 2       INSTR FLAG (1 IF ADD, 0 IF SUBTRACT)
*          U − 3       LSB MANTISSA 1
*          U − 4       MSB MANTISSA 1
*          U − 5       LSB MANTISSA 2
*          U − 6       MSB MANTISSA 2
*          U − 7       EXPONENT 1
*          U − 8       EXPONENT 2
*          U − 9       LSB MANTISSA RESULT
*          U − 10      MSB MANTISSA RESULT
*          U − 11      EXPONENT RESULT
*          U − 12      TRIAL LARGEST EXPONENT
*
* CALLING ROUTINE
*          PSHS        U
*          TFR         S,U
*          LEAS        −12,S
*            .
*            .                              STACK PARAMETERS
*            .
*          LBSR        FPASSR
*          TFR         U,S
*          PULS        U,PC
*
*
* SUBROUTINE BODY
*
FPASSR    PSHS        X,A,B,CCR
          LDA         EXP2,U
          LDB         EXP1,U
          STA         LEXP,U
          SUBB        EXP2,U
          BLS         EQEXM
          LDA         EXP1,U
          STA         LEXP,U
* ADJUST SMALLER EXPONENT BEFORE MANTISSA OPERATION
EQEXM     TSTB
EQEXP     BGE         EGEZ
```

```
* EXP1 SMALLER, INCREASE IT; DECREASE MANTISSA
          LSR       MMAN1,U
          ROR       LMAN1,U
          INCB
          BRA       EQEXP
EGEZ      BEQ       ASMAN
* EXP2 SMALLER, INCREASE IT; DECREASE MANTISSA
          LSR       MMAN2,U
          ROR       LMAN2,U
          DECB
          BRA       EQEXP
* EXPONENTS NOW EQUAL! ADD OR SUBTRACT ? CHECK INSTR.
ASMAN     LDD       MMAN1,U
          TST       INSTR,U
          BLT       SUBINS
          ADDD      MMAN2,U              ADD MANTISSA
          BRA       CONT
SUBINS    SUBD      MMAN2,U              SUBTRACT MANTISSA
*         STORE RESULT MANTISSA IN STACK
CONT      STD       LMANR,U
          LDB       LEXP,U
* MANTISSA ERROR CHECK
MOUA      BVC       ZREAD
          LSR       MMANR,U
          ROR       LMANR,U
          INCB
* EXPONENT TOO LARGE ?
          CMPB      MAXEXP
          BGT       ERROR
          BRA       RETURN
* EXPONENT TOO SMALL ?
ZREAD     LDX       MMANR,U
          CMPX      #00
          BNE       RENORM
* SET EXP OF RESULT TO ZERO, YES, LEAVE SUBROUTINE, ALL DONE
          CLRB
          BRA       RETURN
* EXPONENT OF RESULT NOT ZERO
* ADJUST MANTISSA OF RESULT BETWEEN 1/2 AND 1
RENORM    CMPX      #01
          BLT       RETURN
* INCREASE MANTISSA OF RESULT SO MSB = 1
          ASL       LMANR,U
          ROL       MMANR,U
* DECREASE EXPONENT OF RESULT
          DECB
          BLT       ERROR
          BRA       RENORM
* EXPONENT OF RESULT OVERFLOWED, SET OVERFLOW FLAG
ERROR     LDA       MAXEXP
          STA       ERRF,U
          STB       EXPR,U
RETURN    PULS      CCR,A,B,X,PC
* END OF SUBROUTINE
*
```

Modern Programming Methods

```
*
* STACK OFFSET VALUES FOR PARAMETERS
ERRF    EQU     -1                      ERROR FLAG
INSTR   EQU     -2                      ADD/SUBTRACT FLAG
LMAN1   EQU     -3                      LSB MANTISSA 1
MMAN1   EQU     -4                      MSB MANTISSA 1
LMAN2   EQU     -5                      LSB MANTISSA 2
MMAN2   EQU     -6                      MSB MANTISSA 2
EXP1    EQU     -7                      EXPONENT 1
EXP2    EQU     -8                      EXPONENT 2
LMANR   EQU     -9                      LSB RESULT MANTISSA
MMANR   EQU     -10                     MSB RESULT MANTISSA
EXPR    EQU     -11                     EXPONENT RESULT
LEXP    EQU     -12                     TEMPORARY LARGEST EXP.
MAXEXP  EQU     $FF                     MAX EXP VALUE
```

EXAMPLE 5.13: Negative Handler for 16 × 16 MULTIPLY

Prepares values for the 16 × 16 Multiply in Example 5.14. Converts any negative value to its 2's complement. NEGFLG will be zero if both values are positive or both negative. So, upon return if NEGFLG is not zero, the product must be converted to its 32-bit 2's complement. (Note that the only complement operation available to the 6809 is the 8-bit 1's complement.)

```
                CLR     NEGFLG      / clear flag
                TST     AA          / test MSB of first value
                BGE     CHECK2      / branch if positive (or zero)
                INC     NEGFLG      / increment NEGFLG
                LDD     ZERO        / begin 2's complement
                SUBD    AA          /     subtract AA from 0
                STD     AA          /     store result in #AA
CHECK2          TST     BB          / test MSB of second value
                BGE     ENDCHK      / branch if positive
                DEC     NEGFLG      / decrement NEGFLG
                LDD     ZERO        / begin 2's complement
                SUBD    BB
                STD     BB

ENDCHK          JSR     ABC         / jump to 16X16 Multiply

                TST     NEGFLG      / if 0, Z=1
                BEQ     ENDSGN      / branch if 0, result positive
                LDX     #C          / load address of result
                COM     ,X+         / take 1's complement of 32-bit
                COM     ,X+         /     result, 1 byte at a time
                COM     ,X+         / starting with LSB
                COM     ,X+
LOOP            INC     ,-X         / add 1 to LSB for 2's complement
                BCC     ENDSGN      / branch if carry clear
                CMPX    #C          / compare X with original address
                BNE     LOOP        / branch to adjust other bytes
ENDSGN          BRA     *           / end of routine
```

```
                ZERO    EQU     $0          / constant, used for 2's complement
                NEGFLG  NOP
                *
```

EXAMPLE 5.14:   16 × 16 MULTIPLY[5]

```
00230
00231          *   ************************************************
00232          *   MULTIPLY TWO 16-BIT POSITIVE VALUES
00233          *   TO GENERATE A 32-BIT PRODUCT.
00234          *   AT TERMINATION, BOTH INPUT VALUES
00235          *   AND THE RESULT WILL BE IN USER
00236          *   STACK.
00237          *
00238          *   (A:B) X (C:D) =             BDH:BDL
00239          *                      +     BCH:BCL
00240          *                      +     ADH:ADL
00241          *                   + ACH:ACL
00242          *                   -------------------
00243          *   SETUP:         3 LN, 10 BY,   10 CY
00244          *   OPERATION:  25 LN, 46 BY, 154 CY
00245          *   TOTAL:        28 LN, 56 BY, 164 CY
00246          *   ************************************************
00247

00249  1185  8E    11BF  3 ABC  LDX   #AA  POINTER TO A (MS BYTE)
00250  1188  108E  11C1  4      LDY   #BB
00251  118C  CE    11C3  3      LDU   #C   ADDRESS OF PRODUCT

00253  118F  6F    C4    6      CLR   0,U
00254  1191  6F    41    7      CLR   1,U
00255  1193  A6    01    5      LDA   1,X  : #A LS BYTE
00256  1195  E6    21    5      LDB   1,Y  : #B LS BYTE
00257  1197  3D          11     MUL
00258  1198  ED    42    6      STD   2,U
00259  119A  A6    84    4      LDA   0,X  : #A MS BYTE
00260  119C  E6    21    5      LDB   1,Y  : #B LS BYTE
00261  119E  3D          11     MUL
00262  119F  E3    41    7      ADDD  1,U
00263  11A1  ED    41    6      STD   1,U
00264  11A3  24    02    3      BCC   AB1
00265  11A5  6C    C4    6      INC   0,U
00266  11A7  A6    01    5 AB1  LDA   1,X  : #A LS BYTE
00267  11A9  E6    A4    4      LDB   0,Y  : #B MS BYTE
00268  11AB  3D          11     MUL
00269  11AC  E3    41    7      ADDD  1,U
00270  11AE  ED    41    6      STD   1,U
00271  11B0  24    02    3      BCC   AB2
00272  11B2  6C    C4    6      INC   0,U
00273  11B4  A6    84    4 AB2  LDA   0,X  : #A MS BYTE
00274  11B6  E6    A4    4      LDB   0,Y  : #B MS BYTE
00275  11B8  3D          11     MUL
```

[5] This program is provided courtesy of Motorola Semiconductor Products, Inc., Austin, Tex.

```
00276   11B9   E3   C4      6      ADDD   0,U
00277   11BB   ED   C4      5      STD    0,U

00279   11BD   20   FE      3      BRA    *

00281   11BF        03E8   AA      FDB    1000
00282   11C1        01F4   BB      FDB    500
00283   11C3        0000   C       FDB    0,0
```

EXAMPLE 5.15:   Factorial Program with Recursive Methods[6]

```
           *
           * FAC IS THE RECURSIVE ROUTINE TO CALCULATE FACTORIAL
           *      TO 32-BIT ACCURACY (N! = N * N−1!).
           *
           *      ENTRY: ACCB = DESIRED FACTORIAL
           *             2,S − 5,S = RETURN PARAMETER AREA
           *
400C   FAC       PSHS    B,A      SAVE REGISTERS TO BE USED
400E             CMPB    #1       1!?
4010             BHI     FAC1
           * WANT 1!,AND WE'VE GOT IT!
4012             LDD     #0
4015             STD     4,S
4017             LDD     #1
401A             STD     6,S
401C             PULS    A,B,PC

           * WANT N!, N ALREADY SAVED
401E   FAC1      DECB             N−1
401F             LEAS    −4,S     RETURN AREA
4021             BSR     FAC      GET ACCB FACTORIAL
           * NOW HAVE N−1! IN 0,S − 3,S
           * WANT TO RETURN N! IN 8,S-11,S
           * FIRST, INIT THE MS BYTES
4023             LDD     #0
4026             STD     8,S
           * NOW DO 8 X 32 MULTIPLY (32-BIT RESULT)
           * LS BYTE FIRST

4028             LDA     5,S      SAVED N
402A             LDB     3,S      RETURNED LS BYTE
402C             MUL
402D             STD     10,S     NO CARRY POSSIBLE
           * NEXT MOST SIGNIFICANT BYTE
402F             LDA     5,S      SAVED N
4031             LDB     2,S      RETURNED BYTE
4033             MUL
4034             ADDD    9,S
4036             STD     9,S
4038             BCC     FAC2
403A             INC     8,S      NO OVERFLOW POSSIBLE
```

[6] This program is provided courtesy of Terry Ritter, Motorola Semiconductor Products, Inc.

```
          *  ALMOST MS-BYTE
403C  FAC2    LDA    5,S
403E          LDB    1,S
4040          MUL
4041          ADDD   8,S
          *  NOTE:    OVERFLOW POSSIBLE MODULO 2**32
4043          STD    8,S
          *  NOW THE MS-BYTE
4045          LDA    5,S
4047          LDB    0,S
4049          MUL
404A          ADDB   8,S
          *  OVERFLOW POSSIBLE AGAIN
404C          STB    8,S
404E          LEAS   4,S
4050          PULS   A,B,PC
```

Our calling routine, FACSET, reserves four stack locations for the final result (with the MSB in S-4 and the LSB of N! in S). The FAC routine computes N, N-1, N-2, , , , , 0, saving working stack space above each computed value of N, N-1, , , , When N-I=1 has been reached, the routine begins to calculate 1!, then 2!, and so on, until N! has been calculated. We start the stacking process at a numerically high end of the memory space. Later, we consecutively retrieve 0, 1, 2, ... from the stack moving in the opposite direction, stopping when N! has been computed. We start the stacking process at a numerically high end of the memory space. Later, we consecutively retrieve 0, 1, 2, ... from the stack moving in the opposite direction, stopping when N! has been computed.

We continuously build onto the stack with PSHS B,A and LEAS -4,S, executed at locations 400C and 401C. A neat feature of this program is that no matter how large N is, the final result, N!, will always be found at the same location, exactly where you initially reserved space with your calling module. We use LEAS -4,S at program location 402F for this purpose.

SUMMARY

If you have read this chapter only once, read it again. Modern programming is an all-important topic that cannot be taken too lightly. Microprocessor hardware is a relatively low cost item in the total microcomputer. So, software costs still dominate by several orders of magnitude. The primary culprit is the continued generation of crudely documented ill-structured, nonportable programs. Only in very private libraries should such code exist, but this is not always true.

In most applications someone else will utilize your routine and eventually modify it or at least maintain it. Documentation is vital to the development of quality programs. Even the documentation itself can enhance structured attributes of programs.

Structure means that your code is modular. The programs obey a consistent set of programming rules. Modern programs partition the segments into reasonable lengths, always less than one page. Each segment should be identified hierarchically. There should be calling routines, one of which could be the highest-level module and called routines on the subroutines lower-level modules. Interrupt handlers and I/O routines are typical of the low-order modules in structured programming. This modular approach requires us to manipulate parameters consistently. We must identify global as well as local variables and the source and range of destinations for such variables.

All modules must be fully understood by looking at the module alone, not referring to distant unrelated program segments. The best procedure for handling parameters is through the various stack addressing modes found in the 6809. Lower-level module or subroutine linkage must also take on particular attributes. We should make only occasional use of the JSR instruction. Instead, the stack mark pointer should be used and used consistently (PSHS D, CCR, ,,, and PULS CCR, D, etc.) to mark the place where the parameter passage zone begins. Only when lower-level modules must access such parameters should the stack mark pointer be passed.

In most of the programming examples of this chapter you will find header comments relating to the calling routine for the module. This is shown to encourage you to develop structure in your coding. Obviously, most of your header statements will not include these comments about the calling routine in every instance. Of course, this mechanism must appear at least once in the microcomputer software. Structured code is only one important feature of modern programming. At the same time you should develop a facility for writing position-independent and reentrant code. Such programs reduce the unexpected influence of one lower-level module upon another. Reentrant code is always interruptable and restartable—code in the purest sense of the word.

Some modern programming pundits argue that structured programming (i.e., use a limited but complete set of program structures and only in a structured setting) is paramount to efficient programming. While debugging is simple and structured code tends to be self-documented, such practices are difficult in typical dedicated microprocessor applications. Furthermore, programs are not rapidly executable. Keep in mind that an additional system design step is required. Because a limited although complete set of structures is slow and inherently constrains the microprocessor system designer, structured programming may find little application in real-time microprocessor applications. However, where large software projects are imminent, we have no alternative.

As a final comment, compare Examples 5.9 and 5.15. Notice how difficult Example 5.9 is to understand. The paucity of line comments doesn't help. Also, the program structure is less clear in Example 5.9. In summary, Example 5.15 is far superior to Example 5.9.

EXERCISES

Now it is your turn to demonstrate your understanding. Try the following exercises.

1. Write reentrant code to call the ASCII-decimal program in this chapter. Assume position independency.

2. Example 5.9 could be improved if we closely follow the proposed 6809 documentation standards. Change the program to do so.

3. Does the 6809 have only two stack pointers?

4. How do you stack double words?

5. The high-level language subroutine linkage does not have a proper header. Generate a high-quality header for this code.

6. What is a stack mark pointer?

7. When would you use the S hardware pointer, and when would you use the U pointer?

8. Write a program to add a sequence of decimal digits. Use X to point to the input, U to point to the result, and ACCB to count the digits.

9. Write a program to copy a text line to a new location. Use X to point to the byte, Y to store it. Check carriage return for end of line.

10. Write a program to subtract a sequence of decimal digits in the Y and S stacks. Store the result in the U stack. ACCB contains the number of digits.

11. Write a program to pack four right-justified 6-bit characters in the X stack into three packed 8-bit bytes in the Y stack.

12. Revise Example 5.13 to make it PIC.

BIBLIOGRAPHY

ANDREWS, MICHAEL, AND THOMAS MRAZ. "Unified Elementary Function Generator," *Microprocessors and Microsystems*, vol. 2, Oct. 1978, pp. 270–276. Explains software to generate elementary functions. A routine for the sine and cosine using the 6800 is described.

"BASIC Can Implement Any Design, but First Learn Its Fundamentals," *Electronic Design News*, June 5, 1977, pp. 141–150. Describes the operators, functions, and statements in the BASIC language.

BASILI, VICTOR R., AND ROBERT W. REITER, JR. "An Investigation of Human Factors in Software Development," *Computer*, vol. 12, Dec. 1979, pp. 21–38. Collective behavior of "low-level" effects to determine significant human factors are offered to predict error rates above some critical level. Analyzes structured programming via control structures.

BERHARD, ROBERT. "Computers: Emphasis on Software," *IEEE Spectrum*, vol. 17, Jan. 1980, pp. 32-37. The introduction of high-level languages (PASCAL, etc.) to the microprocessor suggests that a functional programming (FP) language is better.

"Correct Program Notation Greatly Aids the Design Process," *Electronic Design News*, June 5, 1977, pp. 123-130. Documentation, strategically placed within code, flow charts, and finite-state machine graphs increase productivity rate.

"Data/Procedure Trade-offs Affect the Entire Design Cycle," *Electronic Design News*, June 5, 1977, pp. 77-82. Topical program designs require a clear understanding of data and procedure structures.

FISH, LARRY. "Block-Structured Language for Microcomputers," *Kilobaud Microcomputing*, Feb. 1979, pp. 24-28. A viable alternative to BASIC using XPLO is described. This block-structured high-level language is designed for 8-bit microprocessors requiring 16K to 24K of memory without a disc.

GALLACHER, JOE, AND PETER WAKEFIELD. "Software Organization of a Microcomputer-Based Data Acquisition System," *Microprocessors and Microsystems*, vol. 2, Apr. 1978, pp. 59-64. Describes useful programming techniques to apply standard modular hardware in data-acquisition applications involving thermocouples and strain gauges.

"Getting a BASIC Program to Run Proves Easy If You're Organized," *Electronic Design News*, June 5, 1977, pp. 153-158. Describes developing a formal design description, writing an equate table, and translating each segment of program design into a BASIC program.

GLADSTONE, BRUCE. "Software Development: It Pays to Have the Right Tool at the Right Time," *Electronic Design News*, June 20, 1976, pp. 91-99. Describes the editor software development tool including use of CRT access.

GLADSTONE, BRUCE. "Software Development: Some Tools Do Big Jobs Automatically," *Electronic Design News*, Aug. 20, 1976, pp. 45-54. The assembler software development tool is pictorially explained again, through the CRT.

HOKANSON, ROGER. "Choosing a High Level Language for Microprocessor Development Systems," *Digital Design*, Feb. 1979, pp. 28-34. Previews a spectrum of high-level languages for microprocessors, including PASCAL, FORTRAN, COBAL, and FORTH for possible microprocessor software.

JENSEN, RANDALL W., AND CHARLES C. TONIES. *Software Engineering*. Englewood Cliffs, N.J.: Prentice-Hall, 1979. This intermediate-level text describes the many design principles involved in standard structures for developing programs. Included are numerous examples illustrating continuous verification and validation, the human solving process, and software testing methodologies.

KORN, GRANINO A. "Microdare: Fast, Direct-Executing High-Level Language System for Small Computers," *Computer*, vol. 12, Oct. 1979, pp. 61-71. High-level software, such as Microdare, can ease development of application software in differential/ integral solvers.

"Let Systems Software Perform All Routine Work," *Electronic Design News*, June 5, 1977, pp. 195-200. Emphasizes the application of monitors, I/O control systems software, and supervisory systems code to routine tasks such as multiprocessing.

LEVENTHAL, LANCE A. "Microcomputer Software," *Digital Design*, Dec. 1979, pp. 86-87. Discusses the trends in the management control of software for microprocessors using high-level languages.

LEVENTHAL, LANCE A. "Structured Programming Formulates Microprocessor Program Logic," *Digital Design*, Oct. 1978, pp. 30–36. Explains the use of loops and linear structures to produce modern code for microprocessors. Gives an example using the keyboard data-entry program for the 8080 and 6800.

LEVENTHAL, LANCE A., AND WILLIAM C. WALSH. "Purchasing Microcomputer Software Isn't Easy," *Digital Design*, May 1979, pp. 107-111. Highlights the issues involved with judging software warranties, agreements, and vendor records in determining purchase of microcomputer software.

"Maintain Essential Documentation at Each Point in the Design Cycle," *Electronic Design News*, June 5, 1977, pp. 133-138. Describes how to use the working design manual (WDM), which includes a distribution list, design team, subject index, and program copy.

MCCRACKEN, DANIEL D. *A Guide to PL/M Programming for Microcomputer Applications*. Reading, Mass.: Addison-Wesley, 1978. Several examples demonstrate the use of high-level language in a typical microcomputer system with PL/M. These include array processing, interpolation routines, and sorting routines, with occasional references and some control programs for practical devices, such as a furnace.

OGDIN, CAROL A. "Microcomputer Programming Languages: When to Use Which, and Why?" *Electronic Design News*, Nov. 20, 1977, pp. 125-128. Examines the different levels of programming languages for microprocessor application. The essential trade-off involves the cost of program development versus life-cycle cost in production.

POPPER, C. "SMAL—A Structured Macro Assembly Language for a Microprocessor," *Proceedings of the Computer Convention*, 1974, p. 147. Describes a helpful software development tool for microprocessors employing a new language, SMAL.

"Procedures Combine Operations to Implement Desired Functions," *Electronic Design News*, June 6, 1977, pp. 103-108. Procedures define statements that process data. Separate data and control registers are necessary for clear code.

"Put Data and Procedures to Work in Well-Defined Algorithms," *Electronic Design News*, June 5, 1977, pp. 111-119, Objectives, well defined, point to the proper mix of data and procedural statements for a top-down design.

RITTER, TERRY, AND JOEL BONEY. "A Microprocessor for the Revolution: The 6809, Part I: Design Philosophy," *Byte Magazine*, Jan. 1979, pp. 14-40. Describes the design philosophy for the 6809 microprocessor, including the justification for the hardware features that support position-independent coding. The 6809 autoincrementing procedure and array subscript calculations are explained. A short routine describes a hardware process synchronization using the SYNC instruction.

RITTER, TERRY, AND JOEL BONEY. "A Microprocessor for the Revolution: The 6809, Part II: Instruction Set Deadends, Old Trials and Apologies," *Byte Magazine*, Feb. 1979, pp. 32-42. Describes the rationale for many instructions found in the 6809.

RITTER, TERRY, AND JOEL BONEY. "A Microprocessor for the Revolution: The 6809, Part III: Final Thoughts," *Byte Magazine*, Mar. 1979, pp. 46-52. Explains the proper use of conditional and unconditional branches in the 6809.

ROSENFELD, PAUL. "Is There a High-Level Language in your Microcomputer's Future?" *Electronic Design News*, May 20, 1976, pp. 62-67. PL/M is described and justified by developing a formula for the increased cost for incremental changes in programs developed with and without PL/M.

SHAW, CAROL B. "Making Microcomputer Programming Easier," *Digital Design*, Nov. 1977, pp. 66-72. Describes the advantages to employing a disc operating system

(DOS) in developing software through the various tools available in such a system. Multitask-event-driven operating systems are described in a two-terminal configuration.

"Software Consists of Much More than Just Coding Programs," *Electronic Design News*, June 5, 1977, pp. 69–73. Proper documentation is necessary to assure complete software without costly redesign.

"Software Design Tools Greatly Simplify the Programming Task," *Electronic Design News*, Nov. 20, 1976, pp. 299–307. Describes how to use monitors, assemblers, and operating systems in the microprocessor environment.

Solomon, Larry A., and Dennis Block. "Microcomputer Software Lowers Parts Count," *Digital Design*, May 1979, pp. 98–105. Compares an all-hardware with an all-software technique for a keyboard decode problem.

"System Software—Programs Everywhere, but Which to Choose?" *Electronic Design News*, Nov. 20, 1977, pp. 209–216. Describes the strengths and weaknesses of software development tools. Compares high-level languages (APL, BASIC, COBOL, FORTRAN IV, PASCAL).

"Testing Tricks and Techniques Are Really Only Common Sense," *Electronic Design News*, June 5, 1977, pp. 161–168. Describes error classifications (catastrophic and major) to be found and inductive testing to enhance program verification.

"Well-Defined Data Structures Make Later Manipulations Easier," *Electronic Design News*, June 5, 1977, pp. 87–95. Data types, properly invoked, increase the reliability of programs. This article describes how to build data types, arrays, lists, and items.

"What Can Other Languages Offer Your Application?" *Electronic Design News*, June 5, 1977, pp. 171–178. Compares actual code in several high-level languages.

"You Need Sophisticated Software to Handle Real-Time Interfaces," *Electronic Design News*, June 5, 1977, pp. 185–191. Vital requests require immediate response, but casual requests should be placed in queues. Bad interrupt handlers are described. Explains the use of initial task-table states.

Zeidler, Michael E. "Self Propagating Computer Programs, Key to Low-Cost Software?" *Digital Design*, Aug. 1978, pp. 22–26. Describes an operating system built around the F8 microprocessor to accommodate device control, user interaction file management, and program execution through the mechanisms of stacks and virtual memory.

Zelkowitz, Marvin, Allan C. Shaw, and John D. Gannon. *Principles of Software Engineering and Design*. Englewood Cliffs, N.J.: Prentice-Hall, 1979. Chapter 2 develops design strategies for structured programming and top-down design. Many examples of modern programming in high-level are described in later chapters. The text focuses on structure to aid in the generation of high-quality code.

6

Microprocessor Interfaces

6.1 BASIC INPUT/OUTPUT

In most third-generation microprocessors (such as the 6809), microprocessors are interfaced to peripheral devices directly from the data bus of the MPU chip or through special devices or chips designed for that purpose. In future microprocessors, peripheral device functions will migrate into the microprocessor chip. In either case, this interface constitutes the input/output structure of a microprocessor. Microprocessor input/output may be single-line, multiline, parallel, or serial. In this first section we look at some very simple input/output interfaces, the single and multiline. These interfaces are useful for devices that are not clocked or synchronized to the 6809 clock.

A Basic Output

The single-line input/output is the most basic form of interface to a microprocessor. Figure 6.1 depicts a very simple single-line output. This circuit uses a 7474 D flip-flop. This 1-bit latch will save the signal on D0 of the 6809 data bus when the clock input is asserted in the 7474. The clock input is derived from the inverted ANDed version of A0, A1, A15, E, and R/$\overline{W}$. We output ACCA information by the simple instruction STA $8001. Note that STA $8005, STA $8009, . . . also output ACCA information here!

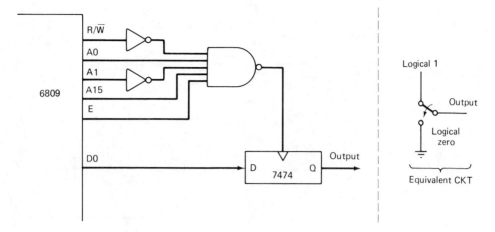

Figure 6.1. Single-Line Output STA $8001.

The equivalent circuit shown in the figure switches from logical 1 to logical 0, and vice versa.

This output could also conveniently serve as a control signal to some device. When the device reads a logical 0 on the Q output it takes one particular course of action. If it reads a logical 1, it takes the opposite course of action. Obviously, this single-wire output can only drive a device into one of two states at any given time. The signal is available after the address bus and the E signal (from the MPU) clock the device. Recall that the following edge of E can strobe a data word after the address bits have stabilized.

We could use the single-wire output to generate either a positive or negative pulse. Example 6.1 generates a positive pulse using the circuit.

EXAMPLE 6.1: Positive-Pulse Generator

With the following code we generate a positive pulse out of the device shown in Figure 6.1.

```
        LDB    #1        Generates pulse
        STB    $8001     Sends a '1'
        LDA    #$10      Delay value
UP      DECA
        BNE    UP
        COMB
        STB    $8001     Sends a '0'
```

A Basic Latching Input

Suppose that we need to capture (latch) data on a single wire from a device that may not keep its data on the line forever, as in Figure 6.2. In this case, we could connect the output of a latching device to a three-state buffer.

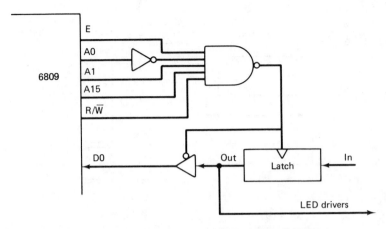

Figure 6.2. Single-Line Input STA $8002.

Our latch uses the rising edge of E to capture the input at that instant. Next, the three-state device is enabled. In this case to read a signal into D0 of the 6809, we are using the instruction LDA $8002 (or $8006, $800A, . . .). Our approach meets the minimal requirements for input (e.g., decode/timing via three-state buffers) and also performs as a latch.

We can extend Figure 6.2 from a single-wire to a multiwire input structure if parallel signals were received. Figure 6.3 depicts one such 8-bit input port which uses one chip. Again, eight latches are tied in parallel to the data input pins of the 6809. These latches are clocked all simultaneously by address pins, R/$\overline{\text{W}}$, and E. To read a signal from these latches we use the instruction LDA $8002 (or $8006, $800A, . . .).

If devices require only a circuit as simple as this, the application must be rather straightforward. However, many devices require some sort of

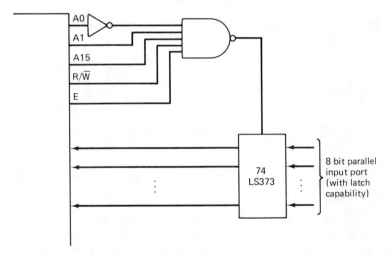

Figure 6.3. 8-Bit Parallel Input Port LDA $8002.

Microprocessor Interfaces

acknowledgment or *handshaking* between the device and the microprocessor. This coupling phenomenon tells the microprocessor that the device either has data ready for the microprocessor or, vice versa, the microprocessor has data ready for the device. Handshake occurs when the "other" unit responds with an acknowledging signal. The specific interpretation of the control signals is called the *protocol*. An orderly exchange is desired. Protocols can become elaborate when the byte and message formats as well as the message sequence are to be specified. For more sophisticated interfaces, microprocessors use interface circuits, two of which are shown in the next sections. Handshaking is, then, easily handled by resources in the peripheral devices.

6.2 PARALLEL INTERFACES

When parallel interfaces are desired with handshaking, the 68xx systems frequently employ a 6821 *Peripheral Interface Adapter* chip, or PIA. We show in Figure 6.4 a dual input/output port structure. PIA 1 will serve as a dual output port with ports A and B each as 8-bit outputs. PIA 2 will serve as a dual-input port with ports A and B as inputs. You might tie these input/output ports to a set of LEDs and a keyboard shown in Figure 6.4b and c. Such a configuration works well in development systems in which ports A

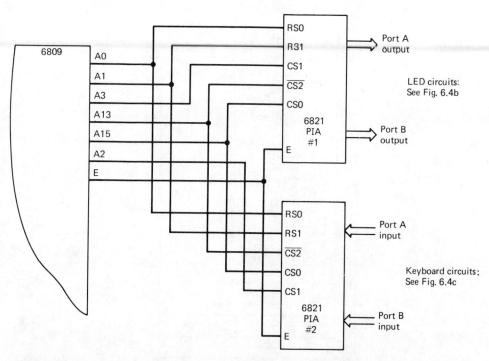

Figure 6.4. Parallel Input/Output Ports and LED and Keyboard Circuits. (Courtesy of Motorola Semiconductor Products, Inc.)

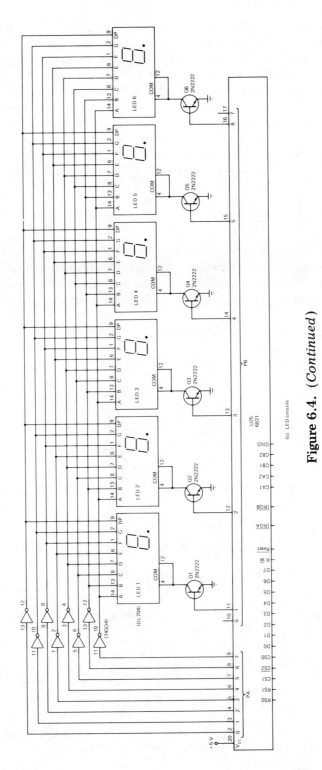

Figure 6.4. (*Continued*)

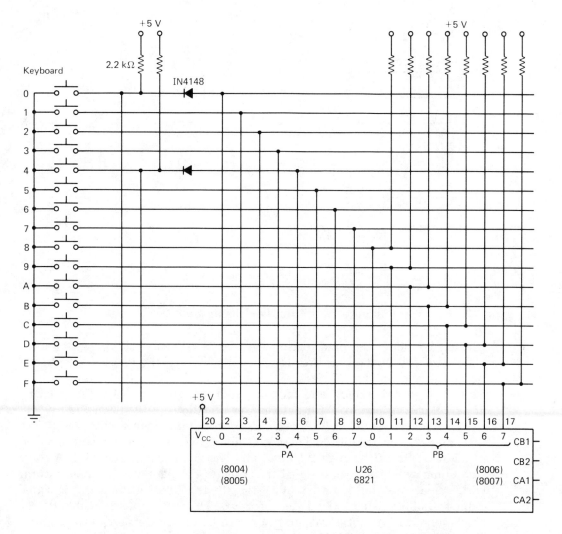

(c) Keyboard circuits

Figure 6.4. (*Continued*)

and B are tied to the rows and columns of the keyboard decoder in PIA 2. Ports A and B outputs of PIA 1 then drive some display circuitry.

A 6821 Interface

The 6821 is a programmable parallel interface I/O device. Each 6821 has two parallel 8-bit interface data ports with two associated control lines for each port. We can change the port designation from input to output as well as redefine the function of control signals that enter or exit from each PIA chip. In Figure 6.5 we see that the port A data register (DRA) would be selected by 8004, the control register for port A (CRA) input would be

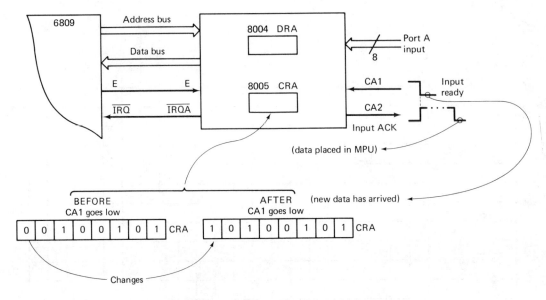

Figure 6.5. Port Handshake Input.

selected by 8005, the data register for port B (DRB) would be selected by 8006, and the control register for port B (CRB) of the PIA 2 or keyboard would be selected by 8007. PIA 1 would have location 800A for the data register of port B (DRB) and location 800B for the control register (CRB) of port B (see Appendix C for detailed specifications of the 6821 PIA).

Note that we select PIA registers by using input pins RS0, RS1, CS0, CS1, and $\overline{CS2}$ on the 6821. These pins are connected to some combination of address bits A0 through A15 and are decoded accordingly. All PIA chips have some synchronization signal that latches the data at the proper instant with respect to the MPU. A 6821 tied to the 6809 utilizes the E signal from the 6809 tied to the E pin of the 6821. Every programmable device needs some sort of initialization. Upon RESET all registers are automatically cleared in the 6821. This makes ports A and B input ports. If we want to change this mode, we need to program the data direction register (DDRA and DDRB) and possibly the control register bit patterns in CRA and CRB.

Since our entire microprocessor system is RESET simultaneously on POWER-UP, there could be ambiguous timing signals arriving at various interface circuits from the 6809 as RESET is asserted. The 6809 is designed to prevent this problem. When we reset the 6809 and 6821 and nearly all other 68xx peripheral devices, the 6809 will be the last device to come out of reset, hence peripheral devices will be ready to operate when the 6809 sets them up. Random data or control words will not be inadvertently latched into registers of programmable peripheral devices such as the 6821.

Input Handshake: Suppose that we desire to use a 6809 with one of several PIAs as an input port. Furthermore, let us assume that the device wishes to inform the MPU that data have arrived. Our signals for this protocol can be conveniently provided by the CA1 and CA2 control pins on the PIA. Let us choose the signal format of Figure 6.5 and set up the control register program accordingly. Suppose that port A addressed at location 8004 is an 8-bit input port from some device, and A's control register, CRA, is location 8005. Let us assume that the IRQA pin is connected to the IRQ of the MPU. When the device has valid input data, it also sends a signal to CA1 which makes a positive-to-negative transition on the PIA. This is the "input ready" signal originating from a device. This indicates that new data have arrived. When CA1 goes low, bit 7 of CRA is set to 1. The microprocessor is then interrupted. The microprocessor will take an interrupt vector into an interrupt routine. The microprocessor software in the interrupt routine would examine CRA registers of all PIA chips to determine which has set bit 7. We can use the simple branch BMI or branch on minus instruction to test bit 7, since that is in the sign bit of the word.

Our simple routine to read the data into accumulator A of the 6809 would be the single instruction LDA $8004. Now the word in port A has been loaded into accumulator A. When the MPU reads the data in location 8004, the PIA will send a positive-going signal out CA2, indicating to the device that the data have been taken from the MPU. It also clears bit 7 of control register A after reading in this data register which releases the IRQ line. This is a typical handshake protocol using a 6821 as an input port. Many others are possible. We could use the circuit of Figure 6.5 in the following example.

EXAMPLE 6.2: Input Handshake (see Figure 6.5)

Upon reception of an interrupt via IRQA, the MPU executes the following interrupt handler to read data from a device connected to port A of a PIA whose data register address is 8004. The prior contents of ACCA are saved (and restored after this routine). The word is loaded into ACCA. Then it is stored in RDATA. Before leaving the interrupt, the I flag is cleared.

```
INTA  LDA    $8004   Input word
      STA    RDATA   Store data
      ANDCC  #$EF    /Enable interrupts
      RTI
```

Output Handshake: A similar procedure applies if we want to establish an 8-bit output port with handshake protocol. Let us suppose, as in Figure 6.6, that port B of a PIA chip serves as an 8-bit output port and control lines CB1 and CB2 are to be used as "output requests" (device needs another word) and "output ready" (MPU loaded data word into data register), respectively. When CB1 goes low, bit 7 of this control register will be set to a 1. When the 6809 has been interrupted via IRQB, the interrupt software should search bit 7 in all PIA control registers. The 6809 software interrupt service routine should then respond to the interrupt by placing a data word in location 800A with a simple instruction such as STA $800A. This places the data

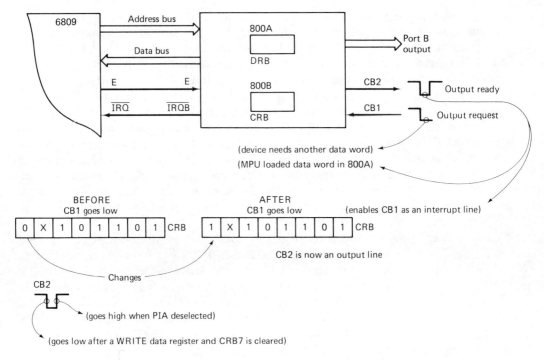

Figure 6.6. 6821 Output Port Handshake.

word from ACCA into the data register of port B of our PIA. Similarly, as with the input port handshake protocol, if we program the control register properly with this protocol, the CB2 line will be set to its high state upon loading of the data word in location 800A.

The handshake protocols for Figures 6.5 and 6.6 are established by programming the control registers CRA and CRB in locations 8005 and 800B, respectively. The programmed control word is shown in each figure. The 6821 is a versatile programmable device because we could change the interpretation of the input control lines (CA1, CB1) and output control lines (CA2, CB2). The details are found in the data sheets for the 6821 in the Appendix. Example 6.3 is an illustration of a simple procedure to send the number 25 out the PIA.

Establishing a protocol among a microcomputer and devices is simply coming to terms on a mutually consistent handshaking. Protocols possess the following capabilities:

1. A device initiates a request for some task or service.
2. The requested system acknowledges this request.
3. The device is subsequently serviced.
4. Finally, the device acknowledges the completion of the service received.

In practice, these capabilities exist as actual steps taken (although the roles of each hardware may reverse), commonly in the order listed. A distinct control or acknowledge signal is used at each step. Such signals are typically called "INPUT READY" and "INPUT ACK," "OUTPUT READY," and "OUTPUT REQUEST."

EXAMPLE 6.3: Output Handshake (see Figure 6.6)

Upon reception of an interrupt via IRQB, the MPU executes the following interrupt handler to output data to a device connected to port B of a PIA whose data register is 800A. The number 25 will be placed in the PIA.

```
INTB  LDA    #$25
      STA    $800A      Output 25
      ANDCC  #$EF       Clear I mask
      RTI               Return
```

Analog Conversion

Important interfaces to devices that accept or generate analog signals are the analog-to-digital conversion (ADC) and digital-to-analog conversion (DAC) interfaces, respectively. In Figure 6.7 we see a typical 12-bit analog-to-digital conversion interface. This uses a Teledyne 8705 12-bit ADC. The 6821 PIA captures the converted data from the ADC via 8 bits of port A and 4 bits of port B. An analog-to-digital converter requires a "start conversion" signal. A positive pulse on CA2 from the 6821 serves as the start conversion command to the ADC. ADCs generate a control signal which indicates the "end of conversion" or "data valid." We have tied this line to CA1 of the 6821. When this line goes high, data have been fully converted in the ADC and are available to the 6821.

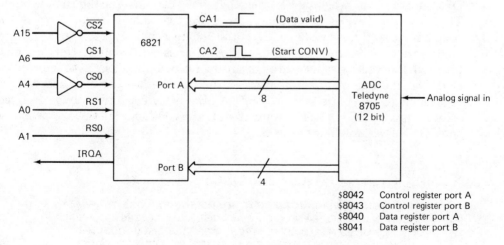

Figure 6.7. 12-Bit ADC Interface.

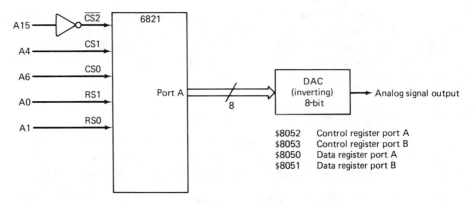

Figure 6.8. 8-Bit DAC Interface.

For our particular address selection via the chip select (CS) and register select (RS) pins of the 6821 we use locations 8040 through 8043 for control registers and data registers of ports A and B. In Example 6.4 we use this PIA and ADC interface to convert analog signals within the range −5 to +10 V. Our main program tests the ADC circuit shown in Figure 6.7 and the DAC circuit shown in Figure 6.8.

Notice that in Figure 6.8 another 6821 chip is tied directly to the DAC. This DAC uses no control signals. It automatically converts 8-bit data to the analog equivalent. We need to keep the data stable while the DAC is converting. Port A of this 6821 uses registers 8050 and 8052. The selection is made with chip select and register select pins via the address bus.

In Example 6.4 we see that the main program tests both the ADC and the DAC. It essentially reads a signal from the ADC and outputs it directly to the DAC. The routine converts only the high-order 8 bits of the 12-bit converted value. We could use this program to actually diagnose an ADC/DAC board. Our program assumes that the DAC inverts the digital input. That is, a positive number generates a negative analog signal. To use the program correctly, we need to invert the analog signal prior to transfer to the ADC input. A simple operational amplifier is sufficient. After we have inverted the analog signal through an operational amplifier, the subroutine COMP at the end of Example 6.4 determines whether the digitized value is equivalent to the value sent to the DAC. Every time the two values disagree, a local variable COUNT is incremented. If the ADC and DAC work properly, the COUNT variable must equal 0.

EXAMPLE 6.4: Program to Test an ADC/DAC Board

```
* THIS MODULE TESTS AN ADC/DAC BOARD FOR FAILURE THAT MAY
* OCCUR IN EITHER THE ADC OR DAC.  THE MODULE, TEST, CONSISTS
* OF A SET OF JUMPS TO SOME FIVE LOWER-LEVEL SUBROUTINES
* WHICH FIRST INITIALIZE THE PIA INTERFACES, THEN GENERATE
* A SAWTOOTH SIGNAL, STORING INTO THE DAC, CHECKING THE
```

```
* ADC SIGNAL TO VERIFY THAT THE OUTPUT SIGNAL CONVERTED
* BACK TO ITS DIGITAL ANALOG IS EQUIVALENT.  ANY ERRORS
* CAUSE LOCATION, /COUNT/, TO CONTAIN A NONZERO VALUE.  THE
* ROUTINE, TEST, CALLS SUBROUTINES PINIT, GINIT, DAC, ADC,
* AND CHCK.
*
*
* PINIT INITIALIZES DAC OUTPUT PORT A
* GINIT INITIALIZES ADC INPUT PORTS A, & B
* DAC   OUTPUTS    A WORD TO DAC VIA PORT A
* ADC   INPUTS     A WORD FROM 12 BIT ADC VIA PORT
*                  A ( MSB ) AND PORT B ( LSB )
* CHCK COMPARES  THE ADC DIGITAL VALUE WITH THE ORIGINAL
*        DAC VALUE, INCREMENTING /COUNT/ IF NO MATCH. ELSE
*        /COUNT/ IS ZERO.

* SINCE DAC IS INVERTING, AN ANALOG CIRCUIT MUST BE USED TO
* INVERT THE SIGNAL BACK TO ITS ORIGINAL POLARITY BEFORE
* ADC


* STACK PICTURE ON ENTRY AND EXIT

*         U + 0      OLD STACK MARK
*         U – 1      DAC OUTPUT VALUE
*         U – 2      ADC INPUT VALUE
*         U – 3      ERROR COUNT
*
* CALLING ROUTINE
TEST    PSHS       U,B,A,CCR
        TFR        S,U
        LEAS       –3,U
        CLR        VALOUT,U
        CLR        COUNT,U
        LBSR       PINIT
        LBSR       GINIT
LOOP    LBSR       DAC           OUTPUT TRIAL VALUE
        LBSR       ADC           RETRIEVE ANALOG VALUE
        LBSR       CHCK          COMPARE
        INC        VALOUT,U      CHANGE SIGNAL
        BNE        LOOP          REPEAT TEST
        TFR        U,S
        PULS       CCR,A,B,U,PC  RETURN
* END CALLING ROUTINE
*
*
* SUBROUTINE, PINIT, TO INITIALIZE PIA FOR DAC INTERFACE
*
PINIT   PSHS       A
        CLRA
        STA        PIA2AC        SET UP DDRA
        COMA
        STA        PIA2AD
        LDA        #$04          SET UP DATA
        STA        PIA2AC        REGISTER ADDRESS
        PULS       A,PC
```

```
* END OF SUBROUTINE, PINIT.
*
PIA2AC   EQU       $8052              CONTROL REGISTER
PIA2AD   EQU       $8050              DATA REGISTER
*
*
*
* SUBROUTINE, GINIT, INITIALIZES PIA FOR ADC INTERFACE
*
GINIT    PSHS      A
         CLRA
         STA       PIA1AC             SET UP CONTROL REG A
         STA       PIA1AD             SET UP DATA REG A
         STA       PIA1BC             SET UP CONTROL REG B
         STA       PIA1BD             SET UP DATA REG B
         LDA       #$04
         STA       PIA1AC             SET UP A DATA REG ADDR
         STA       PIA1BC             SET UP B DATA REG ADDR
         PULS      A,PC
* END SUBROUTINE, GINIT.
*
PIA1AC   EQU       $8042              A CONTROL REG ADDR
PIA1BC   RQU       $8043              B CONTROL REG ADDR
PIA1AD   EQU       $8040              A DATA REG ADDR
PIA1BD   EQU       $8041              B DATA REG ADDR
*
*
*
* SUBROUTINE, DAC, OUTPUTS CURRENT ACCA VALUE VIA PORT A
*
DAC      PSHS      A
         LDA       VALOUT,U
         STA       PIA2AD
         PULS      A,PC
* END OF SUBROUTINE DAC
*
* SUBROUTINE, ADC, CONVERTS ANALOG SIGNAL TO
* DIGITAL EQUIVALENT.  CHECKS ONLY HIGH ORDER
* 8 BITS OF POSSIBLE 12 BIT DIGITIZED VALUE
*
ADC      PSHS      B,A,CCR
         LDA       #$36               LOWER START -
                                      CONVERSION LINE
         STA       PIA1AC
         LDB       #$3E               PULL IT HIGH
         STB       PIA1AC             NOW LOW
         STA       PIA1AC
* CLEAR CRA7 TO SET UP END OF CONVERSION
* TEST BY DUMMY READ
         LDA       PIA1AD
* NOW WAIT TILL CONVERSION IS COMPLETE
WAIT     LDA       PIA1AC             CA1 HI ?
         BPL       WAIT               NO
* SET ADC VALUE INTO ACCB AND RETURN
         LDB       PIA1AD             YES
```

```
            STB         VALIN,U
            PULS        CCR,B,A,PC
* END OF SUBROUTINE ADC.
*
* SUBROUTINE, CHCK, CHECKS DIGITIZED VALUE FROM ADC
* WITH ORIGINAL VALUE FROM ACCA CONVERTED TO ANALOG.
* /COUNT/ IS SET TO NONZERO IF NO MATCH
*
*
CHCK    PSHS        B,A,CCR
        LDA         VALOUT,U        GET ANALOG VALUE
        CMPA        VALIN,U         COMPARE TO DIGIT-
        BEQ         OUT             IZED VERSION
        INC         COUNT,U
OUT     PULS        CCR,A,B,PC
* END OF SUBROUTINE CHCK.
*
*
*
VALOUT EQU          -1              DAC OUTPUT VALUE
VALIN   EQU         -2              ADC INPUT VALUE
COUNT   EQU         -3              ERROR FLAG
```

Buffer Storage

Sometimes it is desirable to store a block of data in some temporary memory of short length (8, 16, 32, or 64 words deep) because the microprocessor or I/O device cannot keep up with the data transmission rate. In this situation we could use a first-in-first-out (FIFO) stack to buffer the data. These stacks are available from peripheral device manufacturers. In the next example we look at the Am2813 FIFO memory (see Figure 6.9a). This 32-word × 8- or 9-bit FIFO has completely independent read and write controls and three-state outputs controllable by an output enable pin.

Data on the data input pins to the FIFO are written into FIFO memory by a pulse on a load pin called parallel load or PL. The data word automatically ripples through the memory until it reaches the output or another data word. Data are read from memory by applying a shift-out pulse to a parallel dump or PD pin. This dumps the word on the output and moves the next word in the buffer to the output. An output ready signal, OR, indicates that data are available at the output and also provides a memory empty signal. An input ready signal, IR, informs the microprocessor that the device is ready to accept data. IR also provides a memory full signal.

A master reset input, $\overline{MR}$, clears all the data from the device and a flag signal goes high when the memory contains more than 15 words.

Input FIFO: In Figure 6.9b we have assumed that a PIA is connected to the Am2813 used as an input FIFO via port B of this same PIA. Our algorithm employs the interrupt signal IRQA tied to the 6809 FIRQ. When

CA1 goes high, an interrupt has occurred and our interrupt handler should do the following:

1. Read data.
2. Pulse CA2 to PD (shift the next word into position).
3. Return from interrupt.

In Example 6.5 our input FIFO code is a READ subroutine called INFIFO. This subroutine is called from the general interrupt service routine. Note the particular PIA control register code. Can you verify that the control word is consistent with the protocol?

EXAMPLE 6.5: An Input FIFO

```
* THE SUBROUTINE INFIFO, RECEIVES A DATA WORD FROM
* A FIFO VIA PORT A OF A PIA WHEN IRQA GOES LOW
* VIA CA1 GOING HIGH.  MPU ACKNOWLEDGES WITH CA2 GOING LOW
* CONNECTED TO PARALLEL DUMP OF FIFO.
* THE INTERRUPT SERVICE ROUTINE IS ENTERED IF
* FIRQ GOES LOW.  THE SERVICE ROUTINE CALLS INFIFO.


INFIFO   PSHS    B,A,CCR
         LDA     PIADRA          GET NEW WORD
         STA     MEM
         LDB     PIAC1           GENERATE NARROW PULSE
         STB     PIACRA          ON PD OF FIFO
         LDB     PIAC2
         STB     PIACRA
```

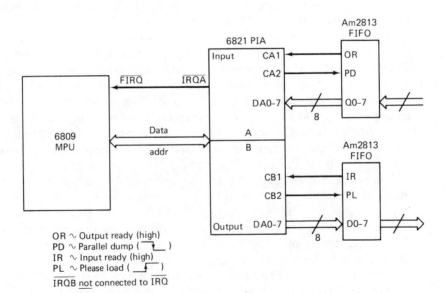

Figure 6.9. Am2813 FIFO Memory.

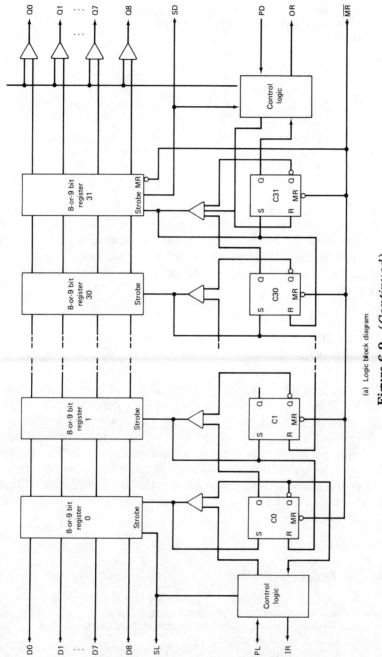

(a) Logic block diagram

Figure 6.9. (*Continued*)

```
          LDB       PIAC1
          STB       PIACRA
          PULS      CCR,A,B,PC              RETURN
* THE SUBROUTINE, PIAINIT, INITIALIZES THE PIA INPUT PORT
* PIA INITIALIZATION ( PORT A AS INPUT )
PIAINIT   PSHS      A,CCR
          CLRA
          STA       PIACRA
          STA       PIADRA                 PORT NOW INPUT
          LDA       PIAC1                  SET UP CRA
*                                          FOR HANDSHAKE
          PULS      CCR,A,PC               RETURN

PIACRA    EQU       ?                      CONTROL REGISTER A
PIADRA    EQU       ?                      PORT A DATA REGISTER
PIAC1     EQU       #$37                   DOWN PULSE
PIAC2     EQU       #$3F                   UP PULSE
```

Output FIFO: We can use a FIFO as an output stack as in Example 6.6. We could use a subroutine as well as an interrupt driven routine to be called whenever the data are ready to be output to the FIFO. To be sure that data can be stored in the FIFO, we observe CRB7 (bit 7) of the port B control register; CRB7 will be set when CB1 goes high. Our subroutine should do the following:

1. Write data into the ACCA.
2. Pulse CB2.
3. Return from interrupt.

As long as CRB7 is high, we continue to write data into ACCA. When CRB7 goes low, we must terminate this sequence. The FIFO is full. The code shown in Example 6.6 for this output buffer uses a subroutine, OUTFIF instead of an interrupt driven routine as in Example 6.5. This subroutine could be called whenever the data are ready to be transmitted by the MPU. Notice again how we have coded the control register for this port. Can you verify that the control word is valid for our protocol? How would you change the code if an interrupt driven routine were used instead of our subroutine?

EXAMPLE 6.6:   An Output FIFO

```
* THE SUBROUTINE, OUTFIF, SENDS A NEW DATA WORD OUT
* A FIFO VIA PIA PORT B WHEN CRB7 IS SET.
* A NARROW PULSE IS GENERATED VIA CB2 TO COMMAND THE
* FIFO TO ACCEPT THE WORD.
* CALLING ROUTINE MUST CHECK CRB7.  IF SET,
* CONTINUE TO OUTPUT ANOTHER WORD VIA SUBROUTINE,
* OUTFIF, STOP WHEN CRB7 IS CLEARED, INDICATING
* FIFO IS FULL.
```

```
OUTFIF   PSHS   B,A,CCR
         LDB    PIACRB        DATA WORD READY?
         BPL    OUTFIF        NO, GO BACK
         LDA    MEM
         STA    PIADRB        YES, STORE IN LATCH
         LDB    PIACW1        GENERATE NARROW PULSE
         STB    PIACRB        FOR FIFO
         LDA    PIACW2
         STA    PIACRB
         STB    PIACRB
         PULS   CCR,A,B,PC    RETURN
*
THE SUBROUTINE, PIASET, INITIALIZES THE PIA FOR THE
* TRANSFER
*
* PIA INITIALIZE ROUTINE
*
PIASET   PSHS   A,CCR
         CLRA                 CONNECT WITH DDR
         STA    PIACRB        CLEAR BIT 2
         COMA
         STA    PIADRB        NOW DDR HERE
         LDA    PIACW1
         STA    PIACRB
         PULS   CCR,A,PC      RETURN

PIACRB   EQU    ?             CONTROL REGISTER B
PIADRB   EQU    ?             PORT B DATA REGISTER
PIACW1   EQU    #$36          UP PULSE
PIACW2   EQU    #$3E          DOWN PULSE
```

6.3 SERIAL INTERFACES

Many serial interfaces for a microprocessor expect to see a typical data stream as in Figure 6.10. This character format requires a start bit followed by 8 information bits, and 1 or 2 stop bits (2 are shown here) which follow the 8 information bits. A "mark" or a constant binary value of 1 indicates to the device and to the MPU that the transmission is in the *idle* mode (no characters transmitted). Notice that the "start" bit is always a "space" or a 0. Eleven bits are required in order to transmit every character in this format. There are other versions of serial data formats, although this is very common.

If we desire to send this character format out across a 10-character/ second line, we could use the program in Example 6.7. This example can employ the single-wire output configuration that we saw earlier in Figure 6.1. Note that this transmission is accomplished via software and that no special hardware is required for the interface.

Suppose that we wish to output the serial data stream of Figure 6.10 using the single-wire output configuration of Figure 6.1. The software necessary for this appears in the program for Example 6.7. The subroutine uses a delay routine to space apart the pulses out at 9.1 ms (necessary for 10-

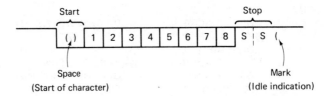

Figure 6.10. Asynchronous Terminal Character Format.

character/second interface). The 6809 is running at 1 megahertz (MHz) (1 μs per clock cycle).

EXAMPLE 6.7: Serial Data Output

```
* THIS ROUTINE SENDS A SERIAL CHARACTER OUT THROUGH
* THE LEAST SIGNIFICANT BIT D(0) OF LOCATION $8001.
* USES DATA WHERE ADDRESS IS ON THE STACK AT /CHAR/
* STACK PICTURE ON ENTRY AND EXIT
*        U + 0       OLD STACK MARKER
*        U − 2       ADDRESS OF CHARACTER
*        U − 4       OUTPUT KEY ( 8001 )
*
* SUBROUTINE BODY
OUTTY   PSHS      B,A,CCR
        LDB       #11               SET COUNTER TO 11
        LDA       [CHAR,U]          GET CHAR INTO ACCA
        ANDCC     #$FE              CLEAR CARRY FLAG
        ROLA                        CARRY INTO A(0)
SENDIT  STA       [OUT,U]           TRANSMIT BIT
        LBSR      DELAY             WAIT 9 MILLISECONDS
NEXT    RORA                        POSITION NEXT BIT
        ORCC      #$01              PLACE STOP BITS
        DECB                        COUNTDOWN
        BNE       SENDIT
        PULS      CCR,A,B,PC        RETURN
* END OF SUBROUTINE
* STACK PARAMETER OFFSET VALUES

CHAR    EQU       −2                ADDRESS OF CHARACTER
OUT     EQU       −4                OUTPUT KEY
* DELAY ROUTINE OF 9.1 MILLISECONDS
* ASSUMES NO INTERRUPTS OR WAITS ON MPU
* COMPUTE DELAY WITH CLOCK CYCLE TIMES
*                 #$0A TIMES #$64
DELAY   PSHS      Y,X
        LDX       #$0A              INITIALIZE X1 COUNTER
X1      LDY       #$64              INITIALIZE X2 COUNTER
X2      LEAY      ,−Y               COUNTDOWN X2
        BNE       X2                ZERO?
        LEAX      ,−X               COUNTDOWN X1
        BNE       X1                ZERO?
        PULS      X,Y,PC            YES, RETURN
```

For higher-performance serial data transmissions, the *asynchronous communications interface adapter* or 6850 ACIA device (Figure 6.11) is commonly used. This special interface chip takes the 8 bits in parallel from the data bus of the MPU and converts them to serial mode for a device connected to the TXD pin in Figure 6.12. A device that is sending data to the MPU is connected to RXD. This serial data stream is converted to parallel mode inside the 6850 automatically and is transferred to the data bus as an 8-bit word.

The important control signals include CTS, clear to send; RTS, ready to send; and DCD, data carrier detect. These signals are used by modems and other serial data devices to inform the MPU to set particular flags in the status register of the 6850 (see Appendix D). Serial data devices may transmit and receive at different clock rates; hence the 6850 accepts two clocks, a transmit and receive clock, which it uses to spool or stream out and capture serial data respectively.

If we use the ACIA as in Figure 6.12, it is simple to program output data serially using the sequence of steps in Figure 6.13. Example 6.8 demon-

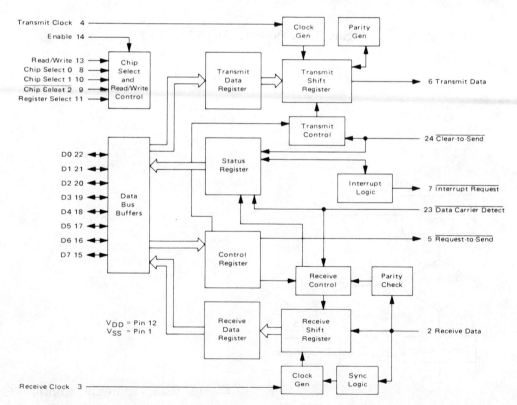

Figure 6.11. 6850 ACIA Device. (Courtesy of Motorola Semiconductor Products, Inc.)

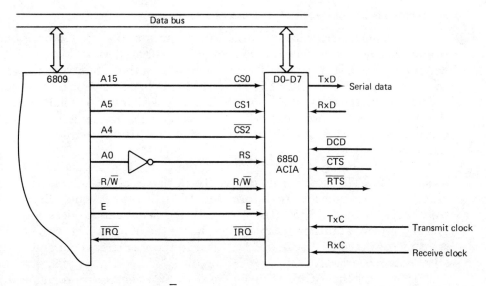

8021   read status if R/$\overline{W}$ = 1
8020   store into transmit data register if R/W = 0

Figure 6.12. 6809-to-ACIA Interface.

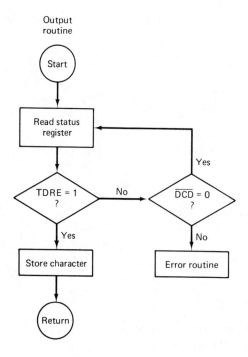

Figure 6.13. Transmit Routine for ACIA.

Microprocessor Interfaces

strates the procedure. We are using the control signals and the check bit in the status word, TDRE, to check whether the transmit data register is empty or not and if the ACIA will accept 8 bits from the MPU. The carrier detect flag $\overline{DCD}$ indicates that the carrier frequency is being transmitted. Location 8021 contains the ACIA status, and location 8020 accepts the 8-bit parallel data word from the MPU register ACCB.

EXAMPLE 6.8:

```
* THIS ROUTINE OUTPUTS A DATA WORD THROUGH AN ACIA, CHECKING
* THE CARRIER DETECT FLAG, DCD, BRANCHING TO AN (ERR)
* ERROR ROUTINE IF CARRIER IS LOST.  THE SUBROUTINE USES
* MPU REGISTERS A, B, AND CCR.
*
*
*        ACIA      STATUS REGISTER          8021
*        ACIA      TRANSMIT DATA REGISTER   8020
*
*
* SUBROUTINE BODY
ACIATR   PSHS      B,A,CCR           SAVE MPU REGISTERS
         LDA       ACIAST            CHECK TDRE BIT
         ASRA
         ASRA
         BCS       TXDRY             TRANSMIT DATA
         ASRA                        REGISTER EMPTY?
         ASRA                        NO
         BCC       ACIATR            CHECK DCD FLAG
         LBRA      ERR               CARRIER OK?
TXDRY    STB       ACIADA            NO
         PULS      CCR,A,B,PC        YES, READY TO SEND
                                     RETURN
ACIAST   EQU       $8021
ACIADA   EQU       $8020
```

6.4 STANDARD INTERFACES

Universally standard interfaces have yet to be devised for the microprocessor world. The majority of standards are either de facto or proposed. De facto standards include the popular S-100 bus, MULTI-BUS (Intel), and the LSI-11. Proposed standards now include the CAMAC IEEE 583 bus, the IEEE 488, and the RS 232 standard. Except for the RS 232, all these buses are parallel I/O standards.

The specifications for standard interfaces should include a wire list or pinout, a state diagram, pin designations, and signal parameter tolerances. Most of the current standards include such documentation, although not all are explicitly defined. For instance, the S-100 bus includes some undefined pins (contacts). Unfortunately, its present configuration has few ground and supply contacts, and it is suited primarily for the 8080 environment. Despite these shortcomings, the S-100 is extremely popular. Many peripheral devices can be obtained with S-100 bus compatibility in the microprocessor world. The IEEE society is also studying a standard specification for the S-100.

Types of Standards

The major types of standard interfaces come in two varieties. Generally, we can identify either a *master-slave* relation among the MPU and I/O or a *talker-listener* relation among them. In the former, a bus master module drives command and address lines. This is very common for single-board computers, which then become the bus master controlling other slave or I/O boards. Since the slave cannot control the bus, memory and I/O are typical slaves. Many masters may exist in a typical interface, hence standard specifications incorporate a protocol among the several masters requesting buses simultaneously. When so specified, a bus clock becomes a timing reference to help resolve bus contention among multiple master requests.

An elaborate interface standard incorporates a talker-listener relationship among the various modules, as found in the 488 standard. Since the bus basically operates in one of these two major modes, a system controller must establish which device "talks" and which one (or more) "listens." The system controller also terminates the networking process. The 488 bus standard assumes that one or more listeners can acquire the bus.

Some Considerations

A consideration when choosing one bus interface over another is the structure of power distribution, especially for microcomputer systems that are available on a single board. When "crated" in a chassis, we need to know whether power is to be centralized or distributed. Centralized power supplies are well regulated. Distributed power supplies require on-board regulation on each board in the chassis. We choose centralized or distributed power distribution, depending on the noise environment and the length of the actual power distribution circuits. Power distribution is one facet of the electrical specifications in a bus standard. Bus standards also specify an allowable variation (tolerance) in power supply voltages and currents. Tolerances for each electrical signal are also specified. The most rigorously specified crating configuration can be found in the CAMAC standard. This standard specifies:

1. Standard-dimension functional modules
2. A chassis or card cage with a fixed number of pin connectors (25 stations)
3. A module-connector linkage between the mother board and the back plane
4. The actual controller board

Microprocessors are found in many instrument controllers today. They simplify instrument front-panel human-factor problems between the instrument and the user. Microprocessors also enhance distributed instrumentation through efficient handshake and I/O from instrument to instrument. As a result, microprocessors can be found in numerous instruments. The IEEE 488-1978 standard has been proposed to eliminate I/O incompatibility among instrument manufacturers.

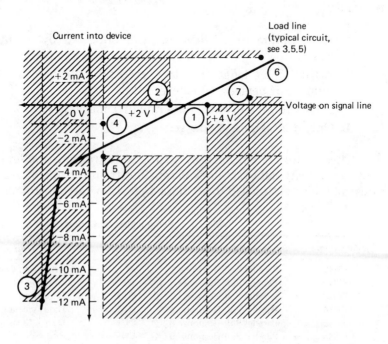

Note: The slope of the dc load line should, in general correspond to a resistance not in excess of 3 kΩ

Each signal line interface within a device shall have the following dc load characteristics and shall fall within the unshaded area of Fig. 6.14.
 (1) if I ⩽ 0 mA, V shall be < 3.7 V
 (2) if I ⩾ 0 mA, V shall be > 2.5 V
 (3) if I ⩾ −12.0 mA, V shall be > −15 V
(only if receiver exists)
 (4) if V ⩽ 0.4 V, I shall be < −1.3 mA
 (5) if V ⩾ 0.4 V, I shall be > −3.2 mA
 (6) if V ⩽ 5.5 V, I shall be < 2.5 mA
 (7) if V ⩾ 5.0 V, I shall be > 0.7 mA or the small-signal Z shall be ⩽ 2 kΩ at 1 MHz

Figure 6.14. DC Load Boundary Specification. (Courtesy of IEEE.)

In the past, the 488 standard was seldom implemented, owing primarily to the complexity of the logic protocol and the inavailability of low-cost ICs. This is no longer true. Manufacturers now provide us with 488-type controllers on a single chip to implement the 488 standard. The 488 standard finds its greatest usage in programmable measurement instrument systems. The general specification includes rules for defining circuits, cables, connectors, and control. But the greatest contribution to standardization can be found in the message repertoire, which assures unambiguous data transfer between devices. A system that employs the 488 standard specifications has:

1. A maximum of 15 devices, interconnected by a single contiguous bus.
2. A total cable length not to exceed 20 meters (m) or 2 m times the number of devices, whichever is less.
3. A maximum allowable data rate of 1 megabit/s.
4. Only digital data exchange.

These rules are enforced by a structured transmission line system which consists of eight data bus lines permitting transmission of ASCII (asynchronous and bidirectional), three data byte transfer control lines (I/O hand-

Table 6.1   Remote Message Coding

Mnemonic	Message Name	Mnemonic	Message Name
PPR1	Parallel Poll Response 1	ACG	Addressed Command Group
PPR2	Parallel Poll Response 2	ATN	Attention
PPR3	Parallel Poll Response 3	DAB	Data Byte
PPR4	Parallel Poll Response 4	DAC	Data Accepted
PPR5	Parallel Poll Response 5	DCL	Device Clear
PPR6	Parallel Poll Response 6	END	End
PPR7	Parallel Poll Response 7	EOS	End of String
PPR8	Parallel Poll Response 8	GET	Group Execute Trigger
PPU	Parallel Poll Unconfigure	GEL	Go To Local
REN	Remote Enable	IDY	Identify
RFD	Ready For Data	IFC	Interface Clear
RQS	Request Service	LAG	Listen Address Group
SCG	Secondary Command Group	LLO	Local Lock Out
SDC	Selected Device Clear	MLA	My Listen Address
SPD	Serial Poll Disable	MTA	My Talk Address
SPE	Serial Poll Enable	MSA	My Secondary Address
SRQ	Service Request	NUL	Null Byte
STB	Status Byte	OSA	Other Secondary Address
TCT	Take Control	OTA	Other Talk Address
TAG	Talk Address Group	PCG	Primary Command Group
UGG	Universal Command Group	PPC	Parallel Poll Configure
UNL	Unlisten	PPE	Parallel Poll Enable
UNT	Untalk	PPD	Parallel Poll Disable

Source: Motorola Semiconductor Products, Inc.

Table 6.2   Basic Interface Functions

Function	Description
TALKER	
Basic Talker	To let an instrument send data to another instrument.
Talk Only	To let an instrument operate in a system without a controller.
Unaddress if my listen address (MLA)	To prevent an instrument capable of functioning as both a talker and a listener from talking to itself.
Extended Talker (TE)	Same as talker function with added addressing capability.
Serial Poll	To send a "status byte" to the controller and identify itself as the source of a service request.
LISTENER	
Basic Listener	To let an instrument receive data from another instrument.
Listen Only	To let an instrument operate in a system without a controller.
Unaddress if my talk address (MTA)	To prevent an instrument capable of functioning as both talker and listener from listening to itself.
Extended Listener (LE)	Same as listener function with added addressing capability.
SOURCE HANDSHAKE	To synchronize the transmission of information on the data bus by the talker when sending instrument-generated data and by the controller when sending interface messages.
ACCEPTOR HANDSHAKE	To synchronize the receipt of information on the data bus for all interface functions when receiving interface messages and for the listener function when receiving instrument-generated data.
CONTROLLER	
System Controller	To let an instrument send the interface clear (IFC) or remote enable (REN) messages.
Send Interface Clear (IFC)	To let a system controller take charge from another controller and/or initialize the bus.
Send Remote Enable (REN)	To let a system controller enable instruments to switch to remote control.
Respond to Service Requests (SRQ)	To let a controller respond to service requests.
Send Interface Messages	To let the controller send multiline interface messages.
Receive Control	To let the controller accept control on the bus from another controller.
Pass Control	To let the controller pass control of the bus to another controller.
Parallel Poll	To let the control execute a parallel poll.
Take Control Synchronously	To let the controller take control of the bus without destroying a data transmission in progress.

Source: Motorola Semiconductor Products, Inc.

shake), and five general interface management signal lines. All lines can be either open-collector or three-state driven. The IEEE standard unambiguously and completely defines the bus line designations or callouts. Definitions of the terminology for a standard bus include a controller (a device that can address other devices to listen or to talk), a listener (a device addressed by an interface message to receive device-dependent messages), and a talker (a device addressed by an interface message to send device-dependent mes-

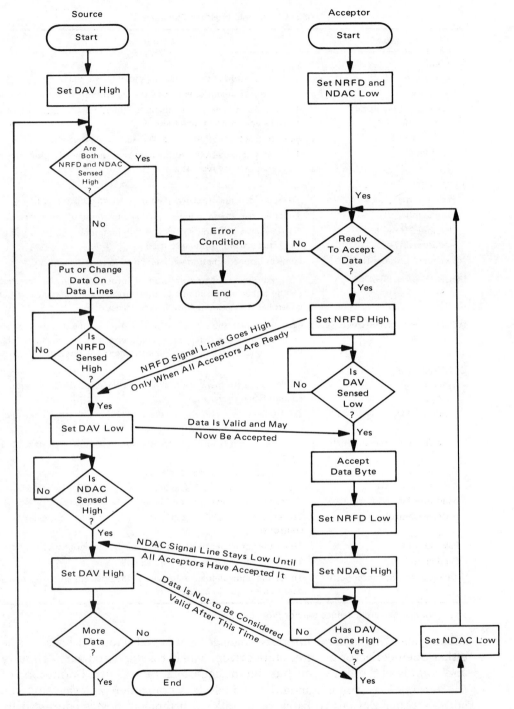

Flow diagram outlines sequence of events during transfer of data byte. More than one listener at a time can accept data because of logical-AND connection of NRFD and NDAC lines.

Figure 6.15. 488 Data Transfer. (Courtesy of Motorola Semiconductor Products, Inc.)

sages). Among the many definitions include local message, remote message, state notation, linkage, and timing specifications. The electrical specifications are shown in Figure 6.14 for a typical bus load line.

The 488 system is divided into three major functional parts: the device function, interface function, and message coding logic. A device function is simply an application such as a voltmeter, signal generator, logic-state analyzer, or counter. The interface function allows us to perform the basic linking between devices. Message coding is the process of converting remote messages among the interface signal lines. Two types of messages exist, the UNILINE (message sent over a single line) and MULTILINE (messages over groups of lines). Remote message coding and basic interface functions are tabulated in Tables 6.1 and 6.2. From these tables we have an enormous variety of coding protocol and basic interface functions. The mnemonic for each message and function is also included. Typical data transfer is indicated by the data transfer flow chart in Figure 6.15.

6.6 THE 68488 GENERAL-PURPOSE INTERFACE ADAPTER

The 488 standard instrument bus has been embodied in an LSI NMOS device available as the 68488 general-purpose interface adapter (GPIA) chip. Coupled with other peripheral devices, the 68488 and 6809 can perform stand-alone control operations. Among the possible interface protocols available in the 68488 are single- or dual-address capability, secondary address capability, complete source acceptor handshake, and complete talker-listener control. The 68488 includes additional capabilities. Among these are the programmable interrupts, trigger output DMA lines, and two transmit/receive buffer control outputs for transceivers. The system configuration is shown in Figure 6.16. Basic software-talker and software-listener programs are shown in Examples 6.9 and 6.10, courtesy of Motorola Semiconductor Products, Inc.

EXAMPLE 6.9: Basic Software Talker Configuration

```
*                        The MC68488 is at address location $5000.
LDA      $5004           READ the device's address on the ADDRESS SWITCHES.
STA      $5004           WRITE the address into the ADDRESS REGISTER.
*                        The device's address was $0A.
*                           (AD5–AD1 corresponds to 01010, respectively.)
LDA      #$00            LOAD ACC A with zeros.
STA      $5003           This clears the reset bit.
STA      $5000           Mask all interrupts (if desired) in the INTERRUPT MASK
*                           REGISTER.
STA      $5002           Select no special features in the ADDRESS MODE REGISTER.
*                        At this time the controller will address the device to TALK in
*                           the following manner.
*                        ENABLE ATN and send mta (my talk address) on the DIOI–8
*                           lines which would be X1001010 ($4A). Now DISABLE ATN.
```

The 68488 General-Purpose Interface Adapter   191

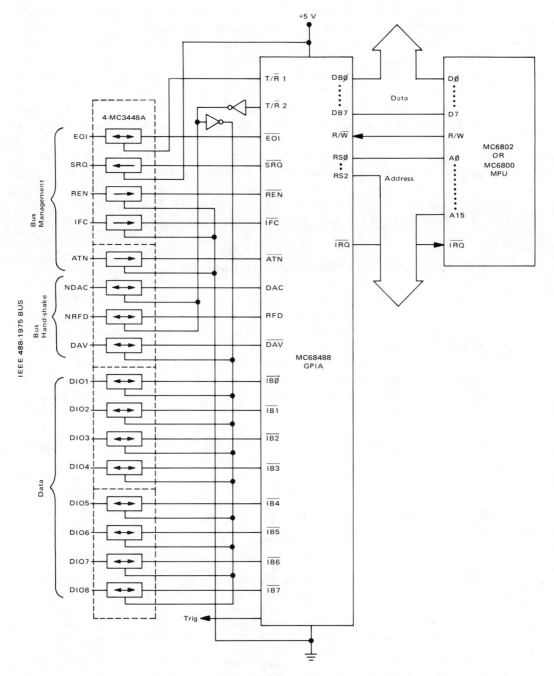

Figure 6.16. 68488 Interface. (Courtesy of Motorola Semiconductor Products, Inc.)

```
       *                            A READ of $5002 ADDRESS STATUS REGISTER will
       *                            show:
       *                            $89 ma (Bit 7), TACS (Bit 3), and TPAS (Bit 0) will be set
       *                            HIGH. At this time the device is ready to TALK.
       *                            BO (Bit 6) of the INTERRUPT STATUS REGISTER will be
       *                            HIGH. Writing a byte to $5007 DATA OUT REGISTER will
       *                            reset BO to ZERO. BO is set HIGH when the device(s)
       *                            listening accepts the data. A possible software approach to
       *                            output five bytes of data from memory pointed to by the
       *                            INDEX REGISTER to the 488 bus is as follows:
         LDB    #$04               Counter.
LOOP     LDA    $5000              LOAD ACCUMULATOR A with contents of INTERRUPT
       *                            STATUS REGISTER.
         CMPA   #$50               Check for Bit (BO) to be set.
         BEQ    LOOP               If BO is Zero, keep checking.
         LDA    0,X                Get a byte of data (BO went set).
         STA    $5007              Output to DATA OUT REGISTER and on to bus.
         INX                       Increment pointer.
         DECB                      Decrement counter.
         BNE    LOOP               If not finished, loop back.
         LDA    #$20               Load ACCUMULATOR with 20.
         STA    $5003              SET EOI (this precedes last byte of data).
         LDA    0,X                Remove last byte from buffer.
         STA    $5007              Writes to DATA OUT REGISTER and bus.
         RTS                       End of Subroutine.
```

EXAMPLE 6.10:   Basic Software Listener Configuration

```
       *                            The MC68488 is at address location $5000.
         LDA    $5004              READ the device's address on the ADDRESS SWITCHES.
         STA    $5004              WRITE the address into the ADDRESS REGISTER.
       *                            The device's address was $06.
       *                               (AD5–AD1 corresponds to 00110, respectively.)
         LDA    #$00               LOAD ACC A with zeros.
         STA    $5003              This clears the reset bit.
         STA    $5000              Mask all interrupts (if desired) in the INTERRUPT MASK
       *                            REGISTER.
         STA    $5002              Select no special features in the ADDRESS MODE
       *                            REGISTER.
       *                            At this time the controller will address the device to LISTEN
       *                            in the following manner:
       *                            ENABLE ATN and send mla (my listen address) on the
       *                            DIOI–8 lines which would be X0100110 ($26). Now
       *                            DISABLE ATN. A READ of $5002 ADDRESS STATUS
       *                            REGISTER will show $86 ma (Bit 7), LACS (Bit 2), and
       *                            LPAS (Bit 1) will be set HIGH. At this time the device is
       *                            ready to LISTEN.
       *                            BI (Bit 0) of the INTERRUPT STATUS REGISTER will be
       *                            LOW. BI will go HIGH to indicate that a data byte is
       *                            available in the DATA-IN REGISTER at $5007. Reading
       *                            the DATA-IN REGISTER will reset BI (Bit 0). A possible
       *                            software approach could be as follows: Accept data from
       *                            the 488 bus to a memory buffer pointed to by INDEX
       *                            REGISTER.
```

```
LOOP 1    LDA      $5000      Load ACC A with contents of INTERRUPT STATUS
          *                      REGISTER.
          TFR      A,CCR      Transfers ACC A contents to CONDITION CODE
          *                      REGISTER.
          BCC      LOOP 1     LOOP until carry bit is set. This indicates BI is set in ROR.
          BVS      LOOP 2     BRANCH to LOOP 2 if overflow is set, indicating END,
          *                      bit 1, of ROR has set (i.e., Controller has sent EOI).
          LDA      $5007      LOAD DATA-IN REGISTER into ACC A. This resets bit BI.
          STA      0,X        STORE the data byte in the buffer.
          INX                 Increment pointer.
          BRA      LOOP 1     BRANCH back to LOOP 1 and check to see if BI is set.
LOOP 2    INX                 Increment pointer.
          LDA      $5007      Get the last byte of data from the DATA-IN REGISTER.
          STA      0,X        Put last byte in the buffer.
          RTS                 End of Subroutine.
```

Example Address Map

Hexadecimal Address	MC68488 Registers ($R/\overline{W}$)
$5000	Interrupt Status/Interrupt Mask
$5001	Command Status/—
$5002	Address Status/Address Mode
$5003	Auxiliary Command/Auxiliary Command
$5004	Address Switch/Address
$5005	Serial Poll/Serial Poll
$5006	Command Pass-thru/Parallel Poll
$5007	Data In/Data Out

6.7 THE RS-232 STANDARD INTERFACE

Many mechanical input/output devices, which are rather slow compared with the microprocessor clock rate and generally physically distant from the microcomputer system, employ a serial data communications interface. Also, many applications require a minimum number of wires from microprocessor to device. The RS232C is a popular standard interface specification found in such applications. Voltages in the RS-232 can vary from a 3-V minimum to a 25-V maximum but must terminate with an impedance ranging from 3 to 7 kilohms (kΩ). Negative logic is assumed; the OFF control state is a logical 1 while the ON state is a logical 0. Transmitting data characters requires use of the TRANSMIT, RECEIVE, and SIGNAL ground pins in the pin out shown in Table 6.3. The RS-232 interface standard is seeing increasing replacement by the RS-422 simply because of the short-cable-length specifications in the RS-232 (usually 50 ft or less).

6.8 A KEYBOARD INTERFACE

A keyboard is a collection or matrix of switches that generate a "1" or "0" value if they are mechanically functioning properly. Designing an interface for a keyboard depends on many human factors such as multiple key depres-

Table 6.3 RS232C Interface

Circuit	Conn. Pin Number	Voltage (V)	Signal Name and Symbol	Function
AA	1	–	PROTECTIVE GROUND	Connects modem or coupler frame to control unit frame for use with a common ground if desired.
AB	7	–	SIGNAL GROUND (COMMON RETURN) 0V	Establishes common reference point for all circuits connected to control unit.
BA	2	±12	TRANSMITTED DATA TD	Transfers telegraph modulation from control unit to modem or coupler (from TTY).
BB	3	±5 TO ±25	RECEIVED DATA RD	Transfers telegraph modulation from modem or coupler to control unit (to TTY).
CA	4	±12	REQUEST TO SEND RG	When signal (+) is received from circuit CD, it sends the signal (+) to modem or coupler, which causes carrier wave to be emitted and reply received on circuit CB (from TTY).
CB	5	±5 TO ±25	CLEAR TO SEND OR READY TO SEND RS	Transfers to control unit the signal (+) "clear to send" (connected on line; carrier wave emitted). The RS lamp lights. This is the response (suitably delayed) to signal "request to send" sent to modem or coupler on circuit CA (to TTY).
CC	6	±5 TO ±25	DATA SET READY OR MODEM READY IT	Transfers to control unit the signal (+) "DATA SET READY." The MR signal Lamp lights (to TTY).
CD	20	±20	DATA TERMINAL READY OR CONNECT TO LINE CL	Transfers to modem or coupler the signal (+) which controls line switching (from TTY).
CE	22	–	RING INDICATOR	
CF	8	±5 TO ±25	RECEIVE LINE SIGNAL DETECTOR CD	Transfers to control unit the signal (+) when the carrier is received. The signal (–), i.e., carrier absent, causes the signal lamp CD to light and resets control unit (to TTY).
–	10	–	Unassigned	–
–	11	–	Unassigned	–

Source: *EDN* magazine.

sions, key bounce, and key rollover. The keys may represent data, instructions, control signals, scale factor, and so on. Basic functions of the related software require us to:

1. *Test for depression of any key.* This can be done by comparing with all 1's in the following code (assume that a depressed key generates a zero value) in Example 6.11.

EXAMPLE 6.11: **Key Depression Test**

```
WAIT      LDA     PIADRA      READ PORT A
          CMPA    #$FF        KEY PRESSED?
          BEQ     WAIT        NO, WAIT
FOUND      .                  YES
           .
           .
```

2. *Identify the depressed key.* This means searching for the zero bit. Simple shift and count can find the key with the following code in Example 6.12.

EXAMPLE 6.12: **Key Identification**

```
FOUND     LDB     #7          INITIALIZE COUNTER
TEST      LSLA                TEST BIT[B]
          BCC     DONE        IS IT ZERO?
          DECB                NO,
          BRA     TEST        TEST NEXT BIT
DONE       .                  YES, KEY IN ACCB
           .
           .
```

3. Jump to program code that implements specific key request.

Basically, keyboards can be organized in two configurations. They are:

1. Independently connected switches
2. Matrix-organized

Each of these may be encoded. Scanning methods, however, will be different depending on the configuration and the encoding technique. Let us look at the first configuration.

Independently Connected Switches

Each switch is connected to a different input line as shown in Figure 6.17. When a switch is closed the corresponding line is pulled down (set

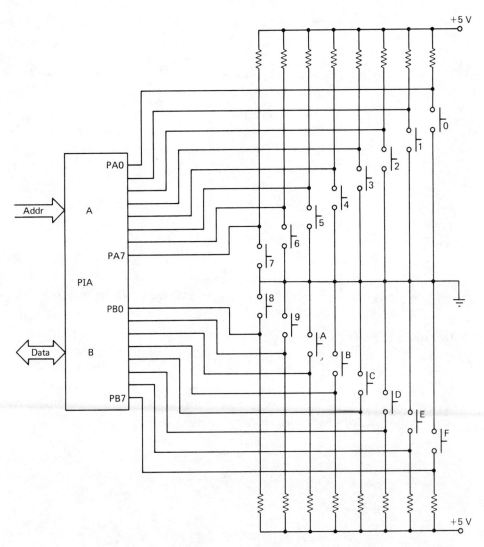

Figure 6.17. Independently Connected Switches.

to zero). To determine which key is depressed, you will have to scan port A continuously, checking for any zero bits. If a bit is zero, a key has been pressed. Identify the key by finding the zero bit, that is, by shifting the byte until you get a zero bit into the carry, while counting the number of shifts. The count represents the digit corresponding to the key pressed.

Debouncing: Because the actual mechanical behavior of a switch does not generate a clear, crisp level change instantly (the signal to the microprocessor "oscillates" for a few milliseconds), we must wait until the switch settles. The solution is to implement a program delay as follows in Example 6.13.

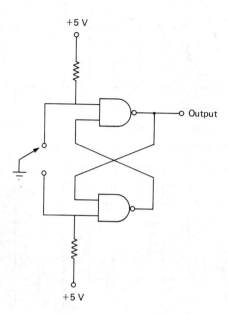

Figure 6.18. Debouncing SPDT Switch.

EXAMPLE 6.13: Key Debounce Delay

```
              LDX      #N        CHOOSE N FOR 2 ms
    DELAY     LEAX     -1,X
              BNE      DELAY
```

The MPU cycles taken by each instruction are

```
              LDX      5
              LEAX     5
              BNE      3
```

for a total delay of

$$T_c(N(5 + 3) + 5) = (8N + 5)T_c$$

where T_c is the processor clock period. For 2-ms delay with your 1-MHz processor

$$(8N + 5) * 10^{-6} \cong 2 * 10^{-3} \quad \text{for} \quad N = 256 \text{ (approx.).}$$

If you have SPDT switches, debouncing can also be done in hardware. Two cross-coupled NAND gates are used to latch the output as shown in Figure 6.18. When the switch is normally closed (NC), the output is 0. When the switch is normally open (NO), the output is 1. However, when the switch is neither closed nor open (bouncing state), the output remains the same. A program corresponding to Figure 6.17 is given in Example 6.14.

EXAMPLE 6.14: Full Keyboard Scanner with 2-ms Debounce

```
* THIS ROUTINE SCANS THE 16 INDEPENDENTLY CONNECTED
* KEYBOARD SWITCHES TIED TO LINES PA0 - PA7
* AND PB0 - PB7
* SEE FIGURE 6.17.
KBDIC     PSHS      CCR,X
          LBSR      PIAINIT     CONFIGURE PIA
SCAN      LDA       PIADRA      READ PORT A
          LDB       PIADRB      READ PORT B
          CMPD      #$FFFF      ANY KEY PRESSED?
          BEQ       SCAN        NO, SCAN
          LBSR      DELAY       YES, DEBOUNCE
* NOW DECODE BY SHIFT AND COUNT METHOD
          LDX       #0          COUNT=0
DECODE    LSRA
          RORB
          BCC       DONE        ZERO BIT FOUND?
          LEAX      1,X         COUNT = COUNT +1
          BRA       DECODE
DONE      TFR       X,D         DIGIT IN ACCB
          PULS      X,CCR,PC    RETURN
* THE FOLLOWING ROUTINE INITIALIZES THE PIA
* PORT A = INPUT ; PORT B = INPUT
PIAINIT   CLR       PIACRA      ACCESS DDRA
          CLR       PIADDRA     ALL INPUTS
          LDA       #$04        ACCESS DRA
* DO SAME FOR PORT B
          CLR       PIACRB
          CLR       PIADDRB
          LDA       #$04
          STA       PIACRB
          PULS      PC
* SUBROUTINE DELAY PROVIDES 2ms DELAY
DELAY     LDX       #256
DLY       LEAX      -1,X
          BNE       DLY
          PULS      PC
```

The disadvantages of unencoded independently connected switches are that they require a large number of input lines and multiword operations as the number of switches increases. Encoding will greatly reduce these requirements, since 8 encoded bits (single word of your computer) can represent 256 keys. However, we need to know when the key is pressed and when it is not. You may solve this problem by using a priority encoder or producing a strobe signal. When we use a priority encoder, in order to have a "ground" code signifying no closure, a dummy switch on the least priority line may be kept closed constantly. Figure 6.19 depicts this. A program to accomplish this is listed in Example 6.15.

Another alternative is to produce a strobe by NANDing all the inputs, as shown in Figure 6.20.

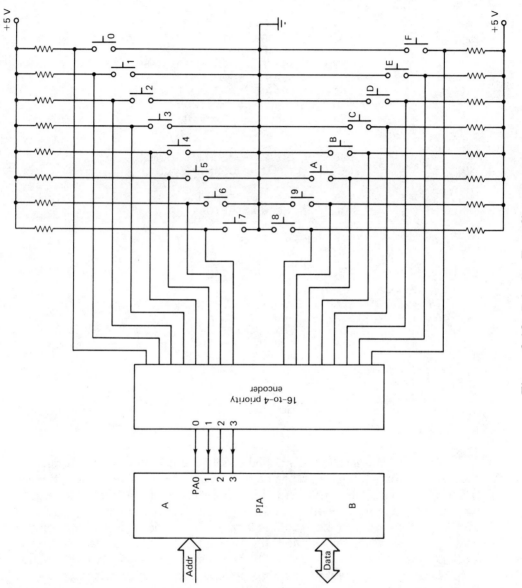

Figure 6.19. Priority Encoding.

Microprocessor Interfaces

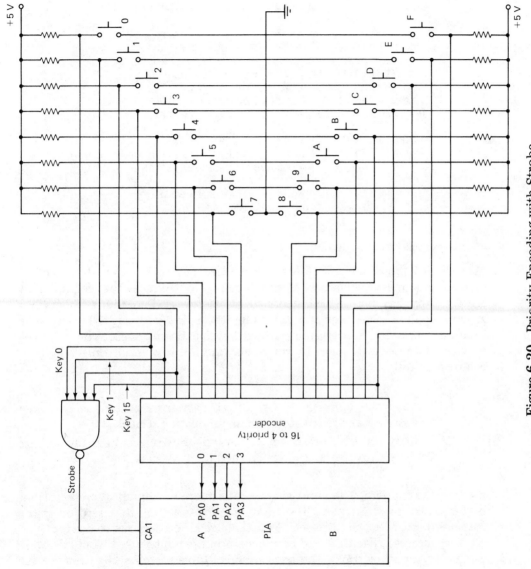

Figure 6.20. Priority Encoding with Strobe.

EXAMPLE 6.15: Strobed Keyboard Scan

```
* THIS ROUTINE SCANS AN ENCODED KEYBOARD WITH
* STROBE.  DECODING IS STRAIGHTFORWARD

KBDES    PSHS      CCR
         LBSR      PIAINIT
SCAN     TST       PIACRA      IS ANY KEY PRESSED?
         BPL       SCAN        NO, SCAN
         LDA       PIADRA      YES, READ PORT A
         ANDA      #$0F        MASK UPPER 4 BITS
         PULS      CCR,PC      RETURN, DIGIT IN ACCA
* PIAINIT SET UP PORT A INPUT, CONFIGURES CA1 AS
* AN INTERRUPT INPUT LINE.  A LOW TO HIGH
* TRANSITION ON CA1 WILL SET THE BIT CRA7, WHICH
* IS CLEARED AUTOMATICALLY WHEN PORT A IS READ.
*
PIAINIT  CLR       PIACRA      ACCESS DDRA
         CLR       PIADDRA     ALL INPUTS
         LDA       #%00000110  ACCESS DRA, SET
                               STROBE
         STA       PIACRA      ON RISING EDGE
         PULS      PC          RETURN
```

Matrix-Organized Keyboards

One of the disadvantages of independent switches is that they need as many input lines as switches. Matrix organization reduces that requirement greatly. Any key here is characterized by its row and column numbers. By grounding all the columns and examining the rows, you can tell if any keys have been pressed. To determine which key has been pressed, you will have to ground the columns one by one, checking the rows each time. The procedure is as follows.

1. Test for key depression. Ground all columns simultaneously. A key depressed makes a row-to-column connection. Check it.
2. Identify the depressed key. Ground only one column at a time. Test each row for a "0," which then identifies the key.

Be careful here. The numbers you read in are not binary representations of particular row numbers. The number corresponding to a zero bit is the row number of the key pressed. You then need a technique to convert it to a binary number. The shift and count method previously used would do well. Let us try another trick! The trick here is "table searching." Assemble the

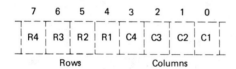

Figure 6.21. Byte Assignment.

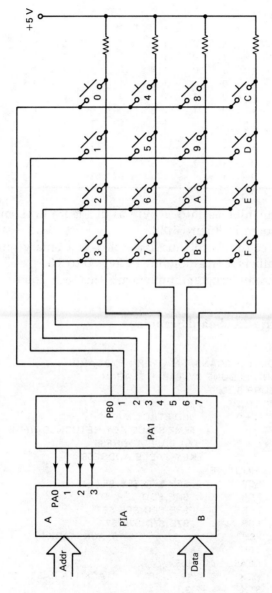

Figure 6.22. Matrix-Organized Keyboard.

Table 6.4   Key Search Table

Key	R4	R3	R2	R1	C4	C3	C2	C1	Hex Number
0	1	1	1	0	1	1	1	0	EE
1	1	1	1	0	1	1	0	1	ED
1	1	1	1	0	1	0	1	1	EB
1	1	1	1	0	0	1	1	1	E7
4	1	1	0	1	1	1	1	0	DE
5	1	1	0	1	1	1	0	1	DD
6	1	1	0	1	1	0	1	1	DB
7	1	1	0	1	0	1	1	1	D7
8	1	0	1	1	1	1	1	0	BE
9	1	0	1	1	1	1	0	1	BD
10	1	0	1	1	1	0	1	1	BB
11	1	0	1	1	0	1	1	1	B7
12	0	1	1	1	1	1	1	0	7E
13	0	1	1	1	1	1	0	1	7D
14	0	1	1	1	1	0	1	1	7B
15	0	1	1	1	0	1	1	1	77

row and column nibbles into a byte as in Figure 6.21 and use the matrix-organized keyboard in Figure 6.22.

To interpret the word thus assembled as a binary number, form Table 6.4 of such numbers, corresponding to keys 0 to 15.

The following program implements this technique.

EXAMPLE 6.16:   Matrix Keyboard Scanning

```
* THIS ROUTINE SCANS A MATRIX KEYBOARD
* DECODING IS DONE BY TABLE SEARCH
* SEE FIGURE 6.22.
* STACK PICTURE:
*              U + 0      OLD STACK MARK
*              U - 1      TEMP SPACE/KEY RETURNED HERE
*              U - 3      PIA BASE ADDRESS
*              U - 5      KEY TABLE ADDRESS
* CALLING ROUTINE:
* KTBL    FCB          $EE, $ED, $EB, $E7
*         FCB          $DE, $DD, $DB, $D7
*         FCB          $BE, $BD, $BB, $B7
*         FCB          $7E, $7D, $7B, $77
*         PSHS         U              STACK MARK
*         TFR          S,U
*         LEAS         -5,S
*         LDX          PIAADDR        STACK PIA BASE ADDR
*         STX          -3,U
*         LEAX         KTBL,PCR       STACK TABLE ADDR
*         STX          -5,U
*         LBSR         KBDMAT         CALL KBDMAT
*          .
*          .
```

```
*          TFR      U,S            RESTORE S
*          PULS     U,PC

* SUBROUTINE BODY
KBDMAT     PSHS     CCR,D,X
           LDX      -3,U           LOAD PIA ADDR
           LBSR     PIAINIT        CONFIGURE PIA
SCAN       LDA      #%11110111     TEST 4TH COLUMN
NXTCOL     STA      2,X            GROUND NEXT COL
           STA      -1,U
           LDA      2,X            READ PORT B
           CMPA     -1,U           ANY ROW ZERO?
           BNE      FOUND          YES, KEY DOWN
           ASRA                    NO, TEST NEXT COLUMN
           BCS      NXTCOL
           BRA      SCAN
* KEY FOUND IN THIS COLUMN, AND ROW.  SEARCH TABLE
FOUND      LDX      -5,U           GET TABLE ADDR
           CLRB                    COUNT=0
SEARCH     CMPA     B,X
           BEQ      DONE
           INCB
           BRA      SEARCH
DONE       STB      -1,U
           PULS     X,D,CCR,PC

* PIAINIT CONFIGURES PORT B AS
* COLUMNS PB0-PB3 : OUTPUTS
* ROWS PB4-PB7 : INPUTS
PIAINIT    CLR      3,X            ACCESS DDRB
           LDA      #0F            COL OUT, ROWS IN
           STA      2,X
           LDA      #$04           ACCESS DATA REG B
           STA      3,X
           PULS     PC
```

There are problems with this type of keyboard also. Among these are:

1. Scans increase linearly with the number of columns.
2. Testing bogs down when the processor word size is short.
3. Special care is needed for the cases where the closure ends before scanning is over.

At least the first and third problems can be solved adequately by switching the directions of I/O lines. First, ground all the columns and read the rows. Next, ground all the rows and read the columns. Assemble the code using the two words and search the table as before. The procedure is as follows.

1. Determine if any keys have been pressed. Ground all the columns. If any row line is zero, a column-to-row connection exists and a key has been pressed. Store the row word.

2. Identify the key. Reinitialize PIA to make rows outputs and columns inputs. Ground all the rows. Read the columns and store.
3. Assemble the code with the row and column words above.
4. Search the table for a match. The index of the match is the digit corresponding to the key pressed.

The program in Example 6.17 implements this method.

EXAMPLE 6.17: Matrix Keyboard Scan with Dynamic Configuration of PIA

```
* THIS ROUTINE SCANS AND DECODES A
* MATRIX ORGANIZED KEYBOARD
* USES TABLE SEARCH METHOD TO DECODE.
* PIA IS CONFIGURED DYNAMICALLY
*
* STACK PICTURE
*           U + 0    OLD STACK MARK
*           U - 1    KEY ON RETURN
*           U - 3    PIA BASE ADDR
*           U - 5    TABLE ADDRESS
* SUBROUTINE BODY
KBDDYN  PSHS    CCR,D,X
* MAKE COLUMNS OUTPUTS AND ROWS INPUTS
        LDX     PIADRA,U   GET PIA ADDR
        LBSR    PIACORI
        LDA     #$F0       GROUND ALL COLS
SCAN    STA     2,X
        LDA     2,X
        ANDA    #$F0       MASK COLS
        CMPA    #$F0       ANY ROW ZERO?
        BEQ     SCAN
        STA     TEMP,U     YES, STORE ROWS
* NOW MAKE COLUMNS INPUTS AND ROWS OUTPUTS
        LBSR    PIACIRO
* GROUND ROWS AND READ COLUMNS
        LDA     #$0F
        STA     2,X
        LDA     2,X
        ANDA    #$0F       MASK ROWS
        ORA     KEY,U      ASSEMBLE THE WORD
* SEARCH TABLE FOR MATCH
        LDX     KTBL,U     GET TABLE ADDR
        CLRB               KEY = 0
MATCH   CMPA    B,X        MATCHES ?
        BEQ     DONE
        INCB
        BRA     MATCH      NO, TRY NEXT KEY
DONE    STB     KEY,U      STORE RESULT
        PULS    X,D,CCR,PC
*
* PIACORI MAKES COLS OUT AND ROWS IN
```

```
PIACORI    CLR    3,X         ACCESS DDRB
           LDA    #$0F        COL OUT ROW IN
           STA    2,X
           LDA    #$04
           STA    3,X
           PULS   PC
*
* PIACORI MAKES COLS IN ROWS OUT
PIACIRO    CLR    3,X
           LDA    #$F0
           STA    2,X
           LDA    #$04
           STA    3,X
           PULS   PC
* STACK OFFSET VALUES
PIADRA     EQU    -3          PIA BASE ADDRESS
KTBL       EQU    -5          TABLE ADDRESS
KEY        EQU    -1          KEY VALUE ON RETURN
```

You have now seen how to scan a keyboard with various techniques. As with many microprocessor-based designs, the ultimate approach can be either heavily hardware or software oriented. The debounce also can be accomplished either by a delay routine or hardware. Similarly, the scanning method can be facilitated primarily in hardware or software.

SUMMARY

Simplicity is the key to successful microprocessor interfaces. The first few examples in this chapter illustrate this approach. Many applications do not require the programming power of a PIA or an ACIA, hence why not choose a simpler circuit?

But, even so, the trade-off in software for hardware (or vice versa) should never be taken lightly. The utility of elegant peripheral devices such as the PIA, ACIA, and DMA controller chip can make your programming life very pleasant. All of these peripheral devices provide convenient I/O handshake, which is easily implemented through simple, short instructions. Such instructions can generally be placed in an initialization routine prior to any lower-level module call for these interfaces. Handshaking is an important aspect of microprocessor interfaces; therefore, the flexibility of peripheral devices that provide such convenient handshaking should not be overlooked.

As we shall see in Chapter 7, many devices operate at incompatible rates with the MPU clock. One solution you have already seen is to employ a FIFO. This data buffering technique is demonstrated in the 2813 interface of this chapter.

This chapter demonstrates a variety of interfacing techniques, which can be very much hardware or software. It is this dual nature of the microprocessor environment that allows us to seek many design options.

EXERCISES

1. What is the duration of the positive pulse in Example 6.1?

2. Change the code in Example 6.1 to generate a negative pulse.

3. Write a program using Figure 6.1 in the text to generate a square wave with a 100-MPU clock cycle period.

4. Write a program to generate a low-going pulse out of CA2 for Figure 6.5.

5. For Example 6.2, generate code to initialize the PIA.

6. For Example 6.3, generate code to initialize the PIA.

7. Assume that FIRQ is connected to IRQA of the PIA in Example 6.2. Recode Example 6.2 to handle this implementation.

8. Repeat Exercise 7 with SYNC instruction.

9. In Examples 6.1 to 6.3, multiply addresses can access the devices. Why?

10. In Examples 6.1 to 6.3, design device selection circuits to uniquely select each device.

11. In Figure 6.2, two tasks are performed. What are they?

12. In Example 6.1, the following code will not work. Why?

```
        LDB    #1
        STB    $8001
        LDA    #$10
UP      DECA
        BNE    UP
        COM    $8001
```

13. Recode Example 6.2 to perform handshake in the following manner:
    a. Low to high transition on CA1 (Input Ready) and high to low transition on CA2 (Input Acknowledge).
    b. Low to high transition on CA1 (Input Ready) and low to high transition on CA2 (Input Acknowledge).
    c. Use CRA6 instead of CRA7.

14. In Examples 6.1 and 6.2, can a 74S100 be used? Why or why not?

15. Suppose that the circuit of Figure 6.23 is used instead of Figure 6.2. Do the timing waveforms agree with the intended usage?

16. Recode Example 6.3 to perform handshake in the following manner:
    a. High to low transition on CB1 (Output Request) and low to high transition on CB2 (Output Ready).
    b. Low to high transition on CB1 (Output Request) and low to high transition on CB2 (Output Ready).
    c. Use CRB6 instead of CRB7.

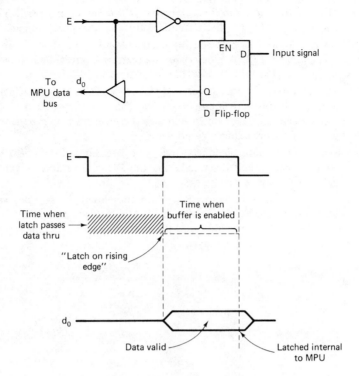

Figure 6.23. Timing Waveforms.

17. If the control word in ports A and B of Examples 6.2 and 6.3 is

    %10100111

    what handshake transitions are assumed?

18. Using the interface circuits of Figure 6.4, generate a program to read out the letter A on LED1 when KO is depressed.

19. Using the interface circuits of Figure 6.4, generate a program to blink the letter A at periodic intervals. Assume that the 6809 is clocked at rated speed, and determine the blink rate of your program.

BIBLIOGRAPHY

CUSHMAN, ROBERT H. "Microcomputer Support Chip Directory: Solutions Keep Pouring Forth," *Electronic Design News*, Nov. 20, 1977, pp. 91–100. A table of the peripheral devices available to the microprocessor world is generated.

GOOZE, MITCHELL, AND HENRY DAVIS. "Peripheral Addressing in Microprocessor Systems," *Digital Design*, Feb. 1980, pp. 22–27. Describes four addressing techniques: parallel I/O, isolated I/O, memory mapped, and command-driven programmed I/O (serial I/O) using the T19900 microprocessor.

IEEE, *Digital Interface for Programmable Instrumentation*, IEEE STD 488-1975. New York: IEEE, 1975. The IEEE standard for 488 bus specifications.

"Interfacing—A Contest between Input and Output," *Electronic Design News*, Nov. 20, 1977, pp. 173-182. A glossary of standard interfaces, including RS232, IEEE 488, and CAMAC (IEEE 583), and IBM Selectric code is described.

JENKINS, DAVID C., AND JOSEPH McCAULEY. "Cassette Interfacing: A Multilingual Approach," *Kilobaud Microcomputing*, Jan. 1979, pp. 78-81. Describes a CPU to cassette deck language which increases the efficiency of programming this important interface. Data encoding is described.

Motorola Semiconductor Products, Inc., "Getting Aboard the 488-1975 Bus," Motorola, Phoenix, Ariz. Circuit diagrams using the MC68488 interface adapter are developed, together with several examples.

MUNT, ROGER. "Microprocessor Keyboard and Coding," *Microprocessors and Microsystems*, Vol. 2, Apr. 1978, pp. 67-70. A block diagram of a keyboard and coder with the MC6810 RAM and 2651 USART connected to a 2650 microprocessor is described and a conversion program given.

7

Input/Output
Programming

7.1 INTRODUCTION

From the preceding chapters we have explored the intimate hardware details of the microprocessor chip itself and the powerful instruction sets that are available in modern microprocessors. But a microprocessor, like any computer, is beneficially employed when it actually transforms data, even though microprocessors can remember, decide, and alter data. But where do data come from? The main source (if not the only source) is the real world. To acquire these data we connect or interface the microprocessor with the world. We have already seen the hardware approach to interfacing a microprocessor to peripheral devices in Chapter 6. Now we study how programs could be developed for particular interfacing tasks.

Independent I/O

In the past, computers were thought of solely as a central processing unit, a memory unit, and an I/O unit. With this distinct partition, manufacturers and users assumed that the instructions as well as the control signals should be distinct for each unit. This led to the independent I/O configuration. As we see in Figure 7.1, a user would expect memory devices to have a particular set of control signals that are activated only for memory units. Data transfer to peripheral devices (which are not memory devices) would

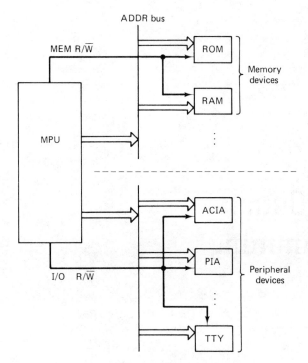

Figure 7.1. Independent I/O.

have another independent set of control signals. This notion of independence carried over to the two distinct control signals now found in microcomputer systems. In Figure 7.1 we see the memory read/write (MEM R/W) signal controlling the data direction for memory devices. However, the data direction control for peripheral devices would have the I/O read/write (I/O R/W) control signal.

Memory-Mapped I/O

In later-generation microprocessors, a memory-mapped I/O configuration is commonly found. Here the MPU draws no distinction between memory devices and peripheral devices. In fact, a single data direction control signal, the read/write ($R/\overline{W}$) signal, is typically employed, as we see in Figure 7.2. In contrast to the independent I/O configuration, the memory-mapped I/O configuration does not use special memory map instructions. Only a small set of input/output instructions accesses information in memory as well as peripheral devices. We then look at memory and I/O devices as "peripheral" devices that contain one or more registers which temporarily or permanently store data. Obviously, a memory unit such as a RAM or ROM contains many memory registers and a PIA- or ACIA-type device contains only a few registers. The essential point is that the MPU draws no distinction between a memory device and an I/O device.

Input/Output Programming

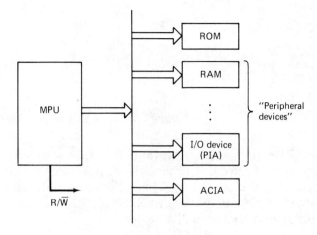

Figure 7.2. Memory-Mapped I/O.

There are, of course, advantages and disadvantages of each I/O configuration. Designers who employ an independent I/O configuration claim that the wiring plan is clear, hardware is easier to debug because separate control wire connect to functionally different devices, and distinctly different microprocessor instructions (memory reference versus input/output instructions) help the programmer to identify the functions of particular program segments. Memory-mapped I/O designers argue that the additional instructions and additional wires complicate matters both for the programmer and the system designer. Moreover, they assert that many tasks are simply executed by nondistinct memory reference I/O instructions. In either case, the choice is not clear. One configuration does not appear to have an edge over another nor do their respective instruction sets. In the 6800 family of microprocessor architectures, the memory map I/O is employed.

I/O Programming Classes

We have already seen how microprocessors are interfaced to the real world from the timing viewpoint. All of our previous remarks have focused upon typical control signals that communicate between the MPU and the peripheral devices. But input/output can be examined also by looking at its requirements within a programming context as well as those found within the timing context already seen. If we look at input/output from this programming viewpoint, we find three classes of input/output data transfer. These are unconditional input/output, conditional input/output, and program interrupt input/output.

Unconditional Transfer: The unconditional transfer is the simplest and most straightforward technique. In this approach we make some very critical assumptions. The first assumption is that the device is ready to transmit or receive data. The second assumption is that the control or status information is not necessary. Third, the data themselves have settled and are valid in

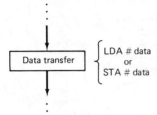

Figure 7.3. Unconditional Transfer.

some register or memory location. The typical sequence for data transfer appears as in Figure 7.3. The only instructions we employ are the simple load (LDA) and store (STA). This simple data transfer requires one and only one input/output instruction. In Example 7.1, the unconditional transfer for the 6809 does a read on a PIA device.

EXAMPLE 7.1: 6809 Unconditional Data Transfer

```
                         .
                         .
                         .
        LDA $PIADRA      fetch data
                         .
                         .
```

Conditional Transfer: In many peripheral devices we must check the device status before executing a data transfer. In that case, our input/output programming task requires a conditional transfer. This two-step process first checks the device status and next performs the data transfer as in Figure 7.4. Now, two or more instructions are required. If we are using a 6821 PIA we first read the control status register in the particular port. After a successful interrogation we proceed with the data transfer. The same procedure holds for the 6850 ACIA, and, in fact, most peripheral devices would assume that we are performing a conditional transfer. Even so, for many tasks the condi-

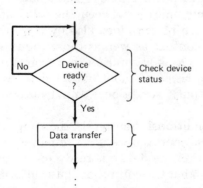

Figure 7.4. Conditional Transfer.

Input/Output Programming

tional transfer may not be required yet we would still employ the PIA or the ACIA (for later system expansion). In Example 7.2 we see how the 6809 performs a conditional data transfer, reading a word from a PIA once bit 7 in the respective control register of the PIA has been cleared.

EXAMPLE 7.2:

```
                                    .
                                    .
            NRDY   LDA   $PIACRA     Fetch PIA control word
                   BPL   NRDY        Bit 7 set?
                   LDA   $PIADRA     Yes, fetch data word
                                    .
                                    .
                                    .
```

Program Interrupt Transfer: Both the unconditional and conditional I/O programming techniques suffer from one or more drawbacks. The unconditional transfer makes the critical assumption that the device is ready at the time of data transfer. The conditional transfer requires the microprocessor to wait for the device, thus inhibiting further microprocessor tasking. If our devices are asynchronous, this delay may become unacceptable. In that case, you can employ the program interrupt input/output technique. Now our microprocessor can perform many tasks, including data transfer with peripheral devices without hanging up in a wait loop. The sequence would appear as in Figure 7.5. Interrupt programs if properly written will allow the main program to be executed without any trace of interruption, except for a slight delay in timing. To accomplish this transparent or invisible activity, the interrupt program must save any MPU registers it is about to use before such usage. At the end of the interrupt program the old contents of the MPU registers must be restored. This preservation and restoration is automatically accomplished in most microprocessors by the hardware. In the 6809 it is accomplished quite rapidly by simple instructions or the hardware itself.

To enforce this transparent behavior of the interrupted program, your

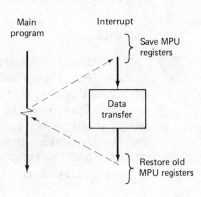

Figure 7.5. Interrupt Transfer.

main program, typically a high-level calling routine as well as lower-level modules (subroutines), must be properly programmed. Code should always be reentrant. That is, any module, either calling routine or subroutine, should permit interruption (branching to an interrupt service routine and return) which destroys neither active MPU registers nor current data in stacks or memory locations. Reentrant code permits us to do just that. From Chapter 5 we have seen that stacks and the use of a stack mark pointer for parameter passage are vital to reentrant programming. Consistent use of such techniques is encouraged. The following programming practices also apply to program interrupt transfer code.

1. Use reentrant code throughout.
2. Save only those MPU registers affected by the interrupt.
3. Employ stacks for limited data storage in a consistent manner and only when necessary.

7.2 INTERRUPT-DRIVEN SYSTEMS

In many situations it is not possible to reconcile a difference in speed between the microprocessor and the peripheral device. This incompatibility costs time when we are locked into a wasteful wait loop necessary for the conditional transfer. Because of this speed difference and the asynchronous nature of activity, the natural solution is to allow the device to initiate the data transfer activity. Interrupt-driven systems do just that. In interrupt-driven systems, microprocessors can execute the main programs without hanging up on slow devices. System activity periodically examines interrupt lines to determine device needs. This automatic monitor of the interrupt lines is (and should be) transparent to the user.

In Figure 7.6 we see the typical flow activity for a generic microprocessor and the detailed flow activity for the 6809. Here we see that an MPU alternates between checking for interrupts and executing program instructions. All microprocessors complete the execution of the current instruction before entering the interrupt state, and this diversion from the main program is accomplished automatically by the hardware.

The Dilemma

Although this activity appears simple, the program structure does not. In fact, from Figure 7.7 we see that a main program which can execute tasks or instructions A, B, C, and so on, can be interrupted at any point in this activity. Therefore, the interrupting program potentially links to the main program after every instruction! Upon return from the interrupt, this unlinking also generates an equally large number of paths between the interrupt program and the main program. Such potentially numerous links cannot be simply portrayed as a clear program structure. Modern programming techniques do not provide useful conceptual tools to handle interruption. This dilemma unfortunately demands the best of any of us. No debugging tools are available, and program verification is an exhaustive exercise because program flow grows enormously as program complexity increases. For these reasons, programmers shy away from interrupt-driven systems. Yet in many applications, we have no recourse but to employ program interrupt transfer.

How Do Interrupt-Driven Systems Operate?

Interrupt-driven systems are implemented in either the hardware or the software control structure of a microprocessor. This control structure con-

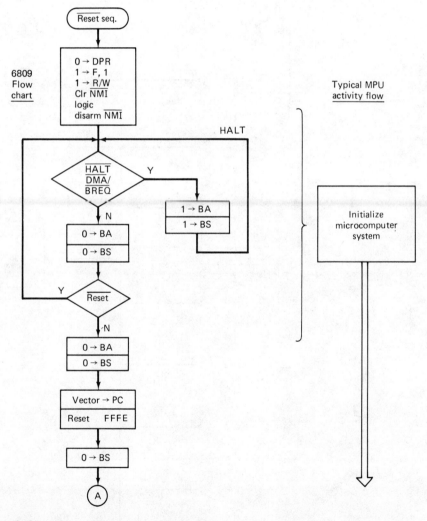

Figure 7.6. Microprocessor Flow Activity. (Courtesy of Motorola Semiconductor Products, Inc.)

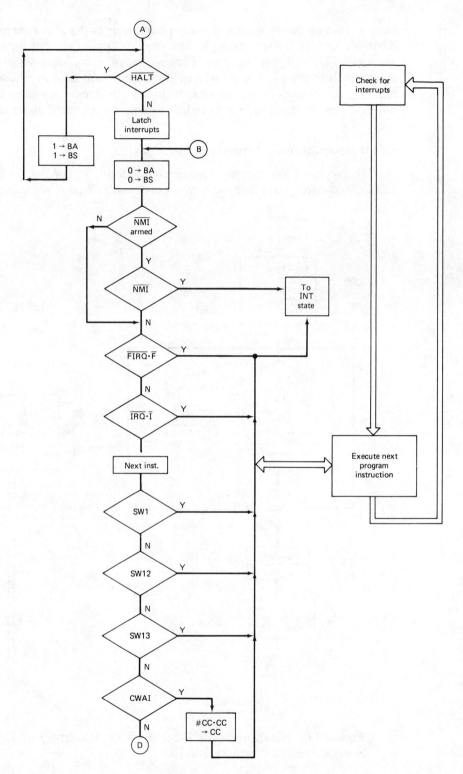

Figure 7.6. (*Continued*)

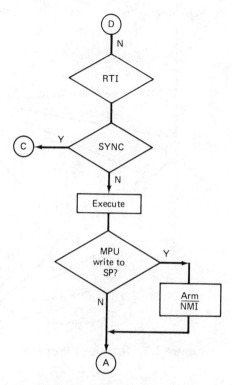

Figure 7.6. (*Continued*)

sists of linkage, priority, and masking mechanisms. Such mechanisms enable us to design both the hardware and software which allow a program to be interrupted temporarily (suspending normal data processing), jump to a predefined location in memory to handle the interrupt device, and return to the interrupted point in the normal data processing task.

Interrupt Linkage

We maintain the integrity of the microprocessor machine state before interruption (and after) by invoking the preservation-restoration cycle just mentioned. This interrupt linkage is quite similar to the necessary linkage for subroutine handling, but not identical. The main difference is that we know exactly the state of the machine, its control register contents, the MPU register states, and stack activity when we enter a subroutine simply because we programmed it accordingly. Interruption is a different matter. No preknowledge of the machine state (status register, MPU registers, memory) is known at the time of interruption. Therefore, to keep the program state intact, a minimal amount of interrupt linkage is required. At the least, we must save the current program counter contents and possibly the condition code register. Nearly all microprocessors do this automatically with hardware. Upon return from the interrupt program we restore these registers. In many

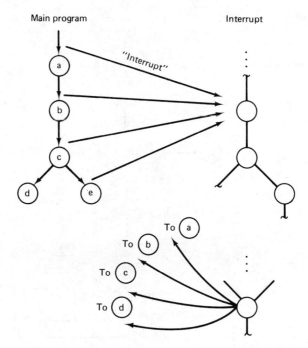

Figure 7.7. Interrupt Program Structure.

microprocessors, we can save and restore more than just the PC and CCR. Additional instructions can save some or all of the active MPU registers. In the 6809 we have the option of saving more than one register by employing either the IRQ (normal interrupt) or FIRQ (fast interrupt). These separate interrupt lines to the MPU will automatically save all the MPU registers or simply the PC and CCR, respectively.

Stacking Order: In the 6809 the hardware stack pointer after interruption is first decremented and then the respective MPU registers are stored on the stack. In Figure 7.8 we observe the registers saved by the FIRQ request. The stacking order for an IRQ interrupt is shown in Figure 7.9. Here we see that the stacking order is identical to that found in the push (PSHS) instruction execution of all MPU registers. A consistent policy for stack ordering among interrupts and subroutines (where we employ the push instruction) is very important. This consistency aids implementation of structured programming.

The automatic hardware linkage generates less overhead time with the FIRQ interrupt than with the IRQ. Should you find it necessary to reduce the program execution time for responding to a particular device, the FIRQ interrupt can be beneficially used. However, caution is advised since you are only partially preserving the microcomputer machine state. Where program resilience (the ability to execute a program in any unexpected event) is crucial, the IRQ interrupt should be employed.

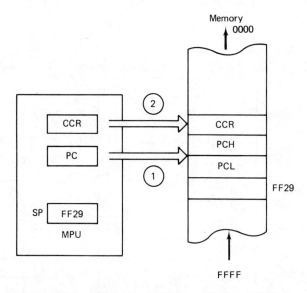

Figure 7.8. Registers "Preserved" by FIRQ in 6809.

Interrupt Priority

Seldom do all peripheral devices in your microcomputer system require immediate attention simultaneously. Some devices may even allow themselves to be interrupted. Some situations may not allow any further interruption. For instance, loss of microprocessor power or cooling demand an immediate and uninterruptable response from the microprocessor. Upon impending loss of power, the microprocessor must immediately save all MPU registers and place the microprocessor in a predictably returnable state. Some interrupt-driven systems permit the microprocessor to switch to a battery-driven power supply. These different interruption requests are implemented with a priority schedule.

Internal Priority: In microprocessor hardware we find the single-priority hardware level or multiple-priority hardware level, as shown in Figure 7.10. In the single-priority hardware level, only one input pin is available to the MPU. In the multiple-priority hardware, additional interrupt pins are provided. In the 6809 we have a nonmaskable interrupt (NMI), a normal interrupt (IRQ), and a fast interrupt (FIRQ). Hardware internal to the MPU automatically determines the priority of interruption. In the 6809 the nonmaskable interrupt has the highest priority. The FIRQ interrupt has the next highest priority, and the IRQ has the lowest priority.

External Priority (Polling): The previous scheme is typical of the internal control structure of an MPU in interrupt-driven systems. Interrupt priority can also be established externally through extra hardware as well as software. When minimal hardware is desired at the expense of more software, you can establish priority through software polling. This is accomplished by monitor-

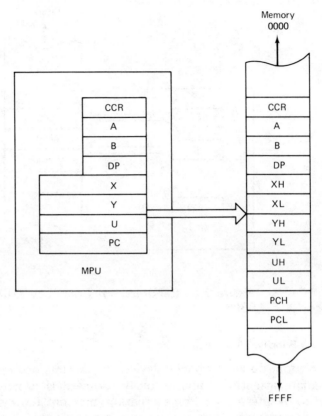

Memory
0000

FFFF

Figure 7.9. Registers "Preserved" by IRQ in 6809.

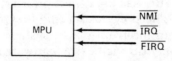

(a) Single-priority hardware level

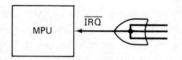

(b) Multiple-priority hardware level

Figure 7.10. Interrupt Priorities.

Input/Output Programming

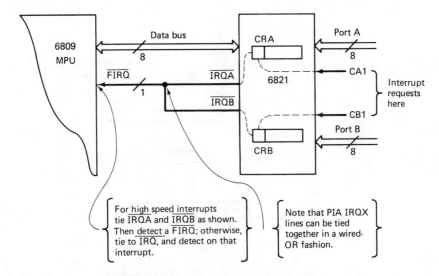

Figure 7.11. PIA Interrupt Interface.

ing interrupt flags outside the MPU device. In the 6809 system, we can employ control register bit 7 (or bit 6) in the control word of the PIA as shown in Figure 7.11. Here bit 7 of ports A and B of the same PIA are wire ORed through the IRQA and IRQB output pins from the PIA to the FIRQ pin of the 6809. Devices could interrupt the microprocessor via input control wires CA1 and CB1 of the PIA. The software polling scheme would appear as shown in Figure 7.12. By simply placing each bit 7 test in some relative order we establish the priority of ports A and B. In our case, we have given port A a higher priority than port B.

Program Interrupt Controller

We can also establish priority through external hardware provided by special peripheral chips such as the priority interrupt controller (PIC) device shown in Figure 7.13. In a 6809 configuration the low-order address bits, A1 through A4, are connected to the 6828. A0 and A5 through A15 are tied directly to memory devices or the address bus. Output from the 6828 generates a "new" A1 through A4. Upon interruption from device A, B, or C (up to eight devices), the 6828 (so programmed) automatically determines the priority level of the device, thus disabling further interrupts from lower-level devices. The 6828 then interrupts the 6809 via IRQ of the 6809. Such devices determine priority by programming the PROM inside the actual PIC. Many such priority controller devices support additional operations. For instance, in the 6828 we can stretch the system clock to match the device response time to that of the microprocessor system.

Another convenient feature of the 6828 is its automatic generation of the vector address for each interrupt. Vector interrupts assume that the de-

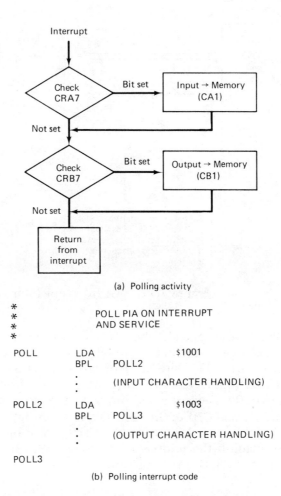

(a) Polling activity

```
*                        POLL PIA ON INTERRUPT
*                        AND SERVICE
*
*
POLL       LDA                    $1001
           BPL       POLL2
           :         (INPUT CHARACTER HANDLING)
           :

POLL2      LDA                    $1003
           BPL       POLL3
           :         (OUTPUT CHARACTER HANDLING)
           :

POLL3
```

(b) Polling interrupt code

Figure 7.12. Software Polling Scheme.
(Courtesy of Motorola Semiconductor
Products, Inc.)

vice identifies (or directly causes) the starting location of the interrupt program handler immediately after interrupt acknowledge. Nonvectored interrupt mechanisms use a fixed location in the memory map for the interrupt process. Vectored interrupt mechanisms enhance implementation of multiple entry locations for interrupts. The 6828 can vector to eight locations. This automatic address generation circuitry is typical of the hardware approach to vectored interrupts.

Masking

A necessary property of interrupt-driven systems is the ability to mask interrupts. In microprocessors we commonly find all further interrupts automatically masked by the MPU during the current interrupt. In addition,

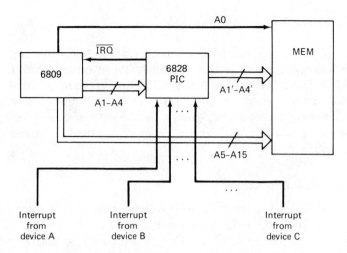

Figure 7.13. Hardware Priority Interruption.

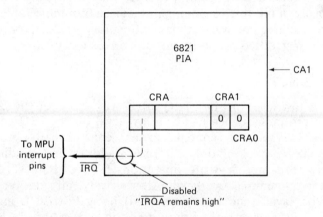

Figure 7.14. External Interrupt Masking.

software instructions are provided which can set or clear masks. These are internal mechanisms, which alter the interrupt behavior inside the MPU.

We can also mask interrupts externally (outside the MPU). Recall that in the PIA, CRA7 is the interrupt flag (the latch external to the MPU which remembers an interrupt) for a peripheral device. This interrupt flag is connected to the IRQ pin of the microprocessor. If we program a particular PIA to inhibit interruption at that PIA we are effectively masking further interrupts from that PIA. To do so we need simply set bit 0 of the control register to a 0, as in Figure 7.14. This prevents CA1 from writing into CRA7. Hence, the output IRQ from the PIA is thus disabled and will remain high regardless of the input interrupt signals coming from the devices. In effect, this masking feature dynamically alters the priority of interrupting devices.

7.3 6809 INTERRUPTS

The 6809 has six vectored interrupts, three hardware and three software. Of the hardware, there is the nonmaskable interrupt ($\overline{NMI}$), the fast maskable ($\overline{FIRQ}$), and the maskable ($\overline{IRQ}$). The software interrupts consist of SWI, SWI2, SWI3. When an interrupt is accepted, the MPU registers are pushed onto the hardware stack, except in the case of $\overline{FIRQ}$, where only the return address and CCR are saved. Program control is transferred through the interrupt's vector.

Nonmaskable Interrupts

$\overline{NMI}$ is edge-sensitive in the sense that if it is sampled LOW one cycle after it has been HIGH, an $\overline{NMI}$ interrupt will occur. Because $\overline{NMI}$ is not masked by execution of an $\overline{NMI}$, it is possible to take another $\overline{NMI}$ interrupt before executing the first instruction of the $\overline{NMI}$ routine. A potentially fatal error exists if an $\overline{NMI}$ is allowed to occur regularly before completing the RTI of the previous $\overline{NMI}$, since the stack may eventually overflow. The $\overline{NMI}$ is especially applicable to gaining immediate (noninhibitable) MPU response for power failure, software dynamic memory refresh, or other nondelayable events. When used properly, no fatal errors will occur.

Fast Interrupts

A low level on the $\overline{FIRQ}$ input with bit F of the CCR cleared triggers the interrupt sequence just as a low level on the $\overline{IRQ}$ with the I bit cleared causes its respective sequence to take control. $\overline{FIRQ}$ provides fast interrupt response by stacking only the return address and condition codes. This enhances read–modify–write operations (i.e., CLR, TST, INC, DEC, rotates, etc.) with minimal overhead. Alternatively, any desired subset of registers may be saved (and later recovered) using PSH/PUL instructions. But any active MPU not disturbed should not be tampered with, so that the return to normal program execution can be continued rapidly.

After accepting a $\overline{FIRQ}$ interrupt, the processor will clear the E flag, save the return address and CCR, then automatically set both the I and F bits to mask out the present $\overline{FIRQ}$ and further $\overline{IRQ}$ and $\overline{FIRQ}$ interrupts. After clearing the original interrupt, the user may reset the I and F bits to allow multiple-level (nested) interrupts.

Normal Interrupts

$\overline{IRQ}$ provides a slower response to interrupting devices than $\overline{FIRQ}$, but stacks the entire machine state. This means that interrupting routines can use all MPU resources without damaging processing of the interrupted routine even while in an interrupt subroutine. An $\overline{IRQ}$ interrupt, having lower priority than the $\overline{FIRQ}$, is prevented from interrupting the $\overline{FIRQ}$ handling routine by automatic setting of the I flag.

Input/Output Programming

Table 7.1   Memory Map for Interrupt Vectors

Memory Map for Vector Location		Interrupt Vector Description
MS	LS	
FFFE	FFFF	RESET
FFFC	FFFD	$\overline{\text{NMI}}$
FFFA	FFFB	SWI
FFF8	FFF9	$\overline{\text{IRQ}}$
FFF6	FFF7	$\overline{\text{FIRQ}}$
FFF4	FFF5	SWI2
FFF2	FFF3	SWI3
FFF0	FFF1	Reserved

NOTE: $\overline{\text{NMI}}$, $\overline{\text{FIRQ}}$, and $\overline{\text{IRQ}}$ requests are latched by the falling edge of every Q except during cycle stealing operations (e.g., DMA), where only $\overline{\text{NMI}}$ is latched. From this point, a delay of at least one bus cycle will occur before the interrupt is serviced by the MPU.

Source: Motorola Semiconductor Products, Inc.

After accepting an $\overline{\text{IRQ}}$ interrupt, the processor sets the E flag, saves the entire machine state, and then sets the I mask bit to mask out the present and further $\overline{\text{IRQ}}$ interrupts. After clearing the original interrupt, the user may reset the I mask bit to allow multiple-level $\overline{\text{IRQ}}$ interrupts.

All interrupt-handling routines should return to the formerly executing task using an RTI instruction. RTI recovers the saved machine state from the hardware stack and control is returned to the interrupting program. If the recovered E bit is CLEAR, it indicates that $\overline{\text{FIRQ}}$ has occurred, so that only the return address and CCR are to be recovered by RTI. The memory map for 6809 interrupts and the vector addresses are tabulated in Table 7.1.

Polling Interrupts

Sometimes, you will need to combine normal ($\overline{\text{IRQ}}$) and fast ($\overline{\text{FIRQ}}$) interrupts in a system. In the next example, we assume that some devices can interrupt via $\overline{\text{IRQ}}$, whereas others can interrupt via $\overline{\text{FIRQ}}$. The program is designed to poll devices that can interrupt via $\overline{\text{IRQ}}$. But even during this polling, an $\overline{\text{FIRQ}}$ is permitted and can be handled accordingly. Example 7.3 demonstrates a typical polling routine (for $\overline{\text{IRQ}}$ interrupts) with additional code to handle $\overline{\text{FIRQ}}$ interrupts as well.

EXAMPLE 7.3:   Polled Interrupt Scan

Suppose that several devices at memory locations CAT, DOG, . . . , BIRD are interfaced to the 6809. Each device has a CRA associated with it and sets bit 7 when the device interrupts. Assume that CAT sent an $\overline{\text{IRQ}}$ to the 6809 and that the I mask bit is clear. The entire machine state is saved, then control goes to vector FFF8, after which it jumps to $100, where the devices are tested according to a priority schedule set by the testing routine. The program branched to the CAT handler at $500.

While the CAT handler is being executed, suppose that BIRD sends a $\overline{\text{FIRQ}}$. Since $\overline{\text{FIRQ}}$ has higher priority, the CAT routine will be interrupted, the return address and CCR will be pushed onto the hardware stack, and control will go through the $\overline{\text{FIRQ}}$ vector FFF6 to the device handler at $200. Notice that we do *not* need a TST BIRD in the polling routine section as we do for CAT and DOG, because in our example system the $\overline{\text{FIRQ}}$ is enabled only by one device, whereas $\overline{\text{IRQ}}$ can be enabled by several devices.

```
                ORG    $FFF8         vector for IRQ
                FDB    $100          for device testing
                 .
                 .
                 .

* Polled Interrupt Scan, check PIA control registers, bit 7.
                ORG    $100          start of polling routine
                TST    CAT           bit 7 of CAT CRA7 set?
                BMI    CHDLR         yes, go to handler
                TST    DOG           bit 7 of DOG CRA7 set?
                BMI    DHDLR         yes, go to handler
                 .
                 .
                 .
                RTI
                 .
                 .
                 .

* Interrupt handler gets ASCII character, stores in X indexed buffer.
                ORG    $500
CHDLR           LDA    MODEM         clears ACIA IRQ, gets char from device
                STA    ,X+           store char
                CMPA   $EOL          end of line?
                BNE    CHDLR         more characters to get?
                RTI                  no, return
EOL             EQU    $0D           ASCII CR (Carriage Return)
                 .
                 .

                ORG    $FFF6         vector for FIRQ
                FDB    $200          for device testing

                ORG    $200          start of BIRD handler
BHDLR           STD    SAVED         save accumulators, FIRQ doesn't save them
                LDD    O,BBFR        load numbers
                MUL
                STD    BUFOUT        store result in out buffer
                LDD    SAVED         restore accumulators
```

```
GOBAK    RTI
          .
          .
          .
         ORG    $010      This is RAM space now
FLAG     NOP              >0 for multiplication
SAVED    FDB    0         for saving accumulators
BBFR     FDB    0         will contain numbers from BIRD
BUFOUT   FDB    0         will contain product
MODEM    FCB    0
```

Upon executing RTI, the return address, and CCR are restored, control goes back to CHDLR via the saved return address (the old PC), and continues executing there. After it executes RTI in that routine, all the MPU registers are restored to the MPU from the hardware stack(s) and control returns to the main program. These short segments illustrate the ease of programming the 6809 to handle polled interrupts. Although the code starts at $100 for the polling routine, this segment, as well as the handlers, can be placed anywhere in the memory space by changing the instruction FDB $200 to FDB $NEW. NEW would be the new starting location for the polling routine.

The relative placement of each TST $LOC in the polling routine implicitly specifies the interrupt priority, with the first TST having the highest priority. This polling priority is overridden by the hardware priority between $\overline{\text{IRQ}}$ and $\overline{\text{FIRQ}}$. $\overline{\text{FIRQ}}$ has a higher priority and will interrupt the MPU if the F flag is clear, even during an $\overline{\text{IRQ}}$.

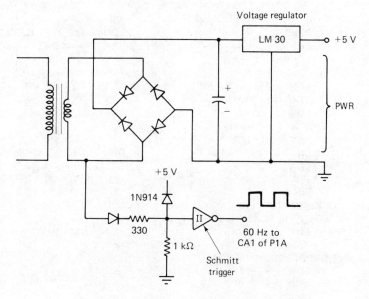

Figure 7.15. Real-Time Clock Circuit.

Real Time Clock

Example 7.4 demonstrates a useful interrupt subroutine, the real-time clock. Here CA1 must be programmed as an interrupt input line whose signal is derived from the wave-shaping circuit shown in Figure 7.15. When $\overline{IRQ}$ occurs, you must vector to the clock routine. The PIA is set up by writing $07 into the A side control register. This will generate an $\overline{IRQ}$ on every rising edge of the CA1 clock signal. The following code initializes the PIA and creates space for seconds, minutes, hours, and 60th's of a second. You can read time at location TIME after starting the clock, which is pointed to by the U pointer.

EXAMPLE 7.4:   Real-Time Clock

```
* CLOCK ROUTINE
* USES 60 HZ PULSE INPUT TO CA1 TO GENERATE
* INTERRUPT (IRQ) OF PROCESSOR
* TIME IS KEPT IN LOCATIONS ON THE STACK
* POINTED BY U-POINTER
* STACK PICTURE:
*         U + 0       60'S
*         U – 1       SECONDS
*         U – 2       MINUTES
*         U – 3       HOURS
*         U – 4       WORKSPACE
*
* CALL INIT ROUTINE TO SET UP PIA FOR THE INTERRUPT AND
* START THE REAL TIME CLOCK.
* INIT CREATES SPACE FOR TIME ON S-STACK
* U POINTS TO 60'S LOCATION.  OTHERS CAN BE ACCESSED BY
* CONSTANT OFFSETS FROM U.
INIT      PULS      X                 RECONFIGURE RETURN ADDR
          LEAU      1,S               CREATE SPACE FOR TIME
          LEAS      –5,S
          PSHS      X                 RETURN ADDR HERE
          LDX       CLOCK,PCR         SET UP IRQ VECTOR
          STX       IRQ
          LDX       #0                RESET CLOCK
          STX       –3,U
          STX       –1,U
          LDX       #PIAADDR          LOAD PIA BASE ADDR
          LDA       #07               INITIALIZE PIA
          STA       X                 AND THE CLOCK STARTS!
          PULS      PC
* CLOCK ROUTINE
* ENTERED VIA 60HZ INTERRUPT, USING IRQ
CLOCK     LDA       PIADRA            CLEAR INTERRUPT BY
*                                     DUMMY READ
* INCREMENT 60'S
          LDA       0,U
          ADDA      #01
          DAA
          STA       0,U
```

```
* NOW UPDATE THE CLOCK
            LDA     #$60              SET UP MAX 60',
            STA     -4,U              SECONDS & MIN VALUE
            CLRB                      POINT TO 60'S
            LBSR    UPDATE            UPDATE 60'S
            DECB
            LBSR    UPDATE            UPDATE SECONDS
            DECB
            LBSR    UPDATE            UPDATE MINUTES
            LDA     #$24              SET UP MAX HOUR VALUE
            DECB
            LBSR    UPDATE            UPDATE HOURS
            RTI
* UPDATE ROUTINE UPDATES 60'S, SECONDS, MINUTES, AND HOURS
* IF APPROPRIATE.  WHEN NO FURTHER UPDATE IS NEEDED IT
* RETURNS FROM INTERRUPT DIRECTLY.
UPDATE      LEAY    B,U
            LDA     Y
            CMPA    -4,U              IS UPDATE NEEDED?
            BNE     RETURN            NO, EXIT INTERRUPT
            CLR     Y                 YES, ZERO THE TIME UNIT
            LDA     -1,Y              INCREMENT NEXT UNIT
            ADDA    #01
            DAA                       DECIMAL ADJUST
            STA     -1,Y
            PULS    PC                CHECK NEXT UNIT
RETURN      LEAS    2,S
            RTI
```

7.4 REAL-TIME PROGRAMMING

Real-time programming is an activity that requires special care. A real-time environment is rather peculiar. At times a peripheral demands an immediate response from the MPU; other times it can wait forever. Most real-time applications are demanding in terms of MPU response when the response is requested. Software time-outs, program control interrupts, and hardware interrupts are typical tools in real-time programming.

A common solution is to use the interrupt of a microprocessor to solve your real-time problems. This solution as we have already seen requires a careful software design. Interrupts request a break in the current sequence of events to respond to an unexpected situation. You, as the software designer, must generate programs for any contingency, any unexpected event beforehand.

Software Time-out

The objective of the software time-outs is to delay program execution in the MPU for some peripheral requirements. For example, we might command a DAC to begin a conversion, then desire to delay the program until conversion is complete. If at all possible, we should write the code without any unnecessary bytes (NOPS, etc.) which would waste memory space. When we cannot use the natural timing of an existing program, we may introduce software delays. We can put a software timer in a program. By carefully counting the number of clock cycles to execute a loop, we can then synchronize to a hardware device. Should a device begin execution but take significant amounts of time indicating that it is in a busy state, our time-out program will then respond only after the busy state is terminated and the device is ready for another operation from the microprocessor. The software timer essentially makes the microcomputer wait until the I/O device is ready. You always time your program for the worst possible (longest interval) event. This makes software timeouts the least-efficient of all techniques for synchronizing to an I/O system, even though it takes the least amount of hardware.

In Example 7.5, we synchronize the microprocessor to the slow device, and the MPU reads two bytes from the device. The MPU latches the word in index register X temporarily and then places that data into a location determined by the user stack pointer. Next, the delay count is decremented until the device is ready. After that, the routine checks to see if the last word has been received. If not, it returns to the starting location (MORE). Notice how we employ the user stack pointer in the post-increment mode.

EXAMPLE 7.5:   Software Time-out

```
* This routine delays program execution at MORE until the device is ready.
* Counting clock cycles in this position is crucial to performance.
* X      temporarily holds word from input
* U      points to buffer which is finally saving words for device
* B      contains length of time-out
* A      contains number of words to save

        MORE    LDX     DEVICE      read data from device
                STX     ,U++        store in buffer indexed by X,
                                    and increment address
        WAIT    DECB                time-out?
                BNE     WAIT        no
                DECA                end of data?
                BNE     MORE
```

Software Synchronization

Suppose, however, that we cannot really accurately time a device response. Also, assume that the microprocessor must be clocked at a specific clock rate which is not an integral value compatible with the device. Worse yet, even integral values of MPU clock cycles will not help. What other alternatives exist?

One neat feature of the 6809 is the SYNC instruction. This instruction essentially provides software synchronization with an external hardware process. Upon encountering this instruction, the CPU remains in a stopped state until an interrupt is received. When enabled, the CPU handles the interrupt in a normal fashion, even though the CPU was in the stopped state. Upon return from the interrupt service routine, the stopped state is cleared and your program continues. But if the interrupt were disabled or masked off (by a CCR mask), the stopped state is simply cleared and the program simply continues without branching to the interrupt service routine. Example 7.6 shows how simple it is.

EXAMPLE 7.6: Software Synchronization

```
* This routine delays program execution at MORE until device interrupts.
* Then a 16-bit word from DEVICE is loaded into X to be stored
* in a buffer.
* Mask off proper interrupt flag before executing this code.
* X       index register temporarily latches data
* U       points to buffer
* A       contains length of buffer
                    .
                    .
                    .
       MORE   SYNC                    wait for interrupt
              LDX    DEVICE           get data from device
              STX    ,U++             store and increment address
              DECA                    last data?
              BNE    MORE             no
                    .
```

7.5 DIRECT MEMORY ACCESS

There will always be some devices that need immediate and continuous attention. The floppy disc and memory drum are two examples. Here we want to pass data between the disc and microprocessor memory at a very high speed in some synchronized fashion. Also, we do not want the microprocessor program to interfere with this activity unexpectedly. Our main concern is that a continuous record on the disc becomes a contiguous block of data transfer. It is seldom possible to speed up the overall system operation by loading and unloading memory using an MPU control program. Devices such as discs require much faster and continuous access. The direct memory access (DMA) is one convenient way to provide both an immediate and continuous response to such peripheral devices. Direct memory access means that we can couple the RAM memory in the microcomputer system directly to the peripheral device without having to go through an MPU register (such as an accumulator). With extra hardware, we can employ a DMA controller chip in a DMA channel to generate the needed response.

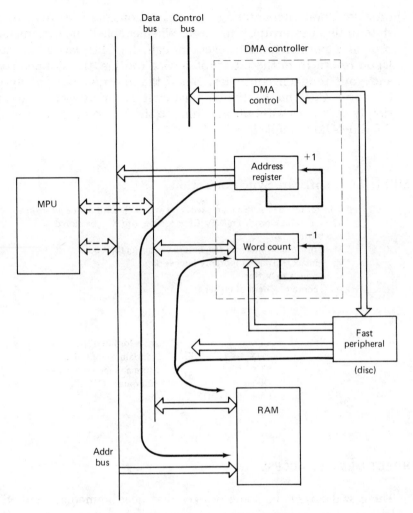

Figure 7.16. DMA Channel.

DMA Controllers

From Figure 7.16 we see that a DMA controller has an automatic address generator and update circuitry, a word count register (normally decremented toward 0 upon completion of block transfer), and a data register or means for coupling the fast peripheral device data lines to the RAM in the microcomputer system. The DMA flow activity is depicted in Figure 7.17. Upon DMA request and acknowledge, the data and address buses are granted to the DMA channel. The address register is initialized to point to the starting location of the data space. A data word is transferred and the word count register is checked. DMA continues until the count equals 0, at which time the DMA channel is disabled and all buses are returned to the microprocessor system.

Input/Output Programming

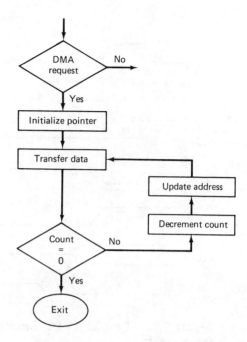

Figure 7.17. DMA Flow Activity.

DMA Implementations

There are many variations of DMA. In microcomputer systems we can generally employ three techniques. First, we can perform DMA during an MPU HALT state. This permits an indefinite number of data transfer cycles but requires a considerable delay start time for the MPU to release the bus. The second method, called reverse cycle-stealing or burst mode, assumes that the microprocessor will release the data and address bus for a predetermined number of cycles. We implement this second technique in the 6809 using the DMA/BREG input line of the MPU. In this mode we can obtain 14 DMA cycles, as shown in Figure 7.18. In this technique the address and data pins of the MPU are placed in the off state (which puts the

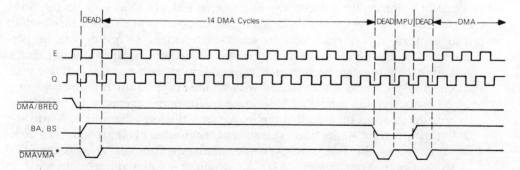

Figure 7.18. Auto-Refresh DMA Timing. (Courtesy of Motorola Semiconductor Products, Inc.)

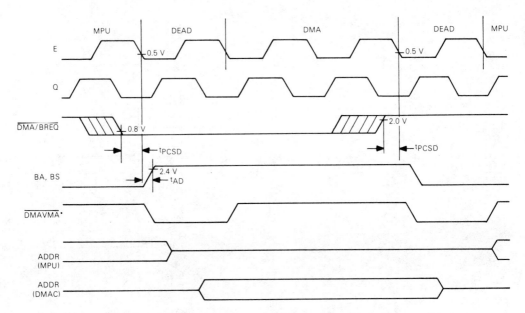

Figure 7.19. Typical DMA Timing. (Courtesy of Motorola Semiconductor Products, Inc.)

MPU buffers effectively in high impedance). In the third technique, we transfer data synchronously while the MPU is running (cycle stealing). In Figure 7.19 we see a typical DMA timing cycle for the 6809 running in the cycle stealing DMA mode. This last mode is almost transparent to other MPU activity but is slower than the two preceding techniques. The first technique, transferring data during the HALT state, seriously degrades program execution in the microprocessor but provides for continuous DMA indefinitely. The burst-mode procedure is a compromise between these two extremes.

6844 Controller

DMA controller devices are available as a single chip such as the 6844 device shown in Figure 7.20. This device can operate in all three modes with four separate DMA channels. In addition, channel priorities can be programmed in the 6844. Address increment or decrement update is automatic and each channel can be separately programmed with control bits for each channel. DMA access is terminated with an interrupt to the microprocessor.

Obviously, the first DMA technique allows the memory to operate at its maximum rate. In fact, this technique uses the least amount of hardware, but stops program execution. The second technique, cycle stealing, is a compromise among the DMA transfer rate, hardware complexity, and the MPU execution rate. Your choice of DMA technique is solely device-dependent in most cases. However, to circumvent the cost of program stoppage, the HALT mode technique is not likely to be used.

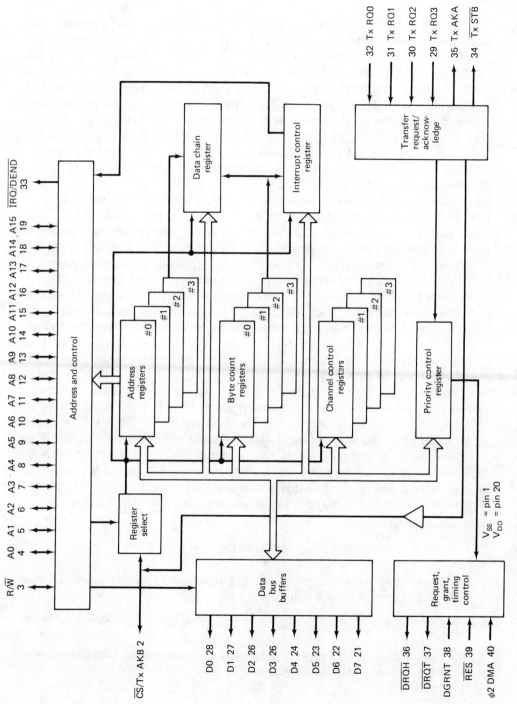

Figure 7.20. 6844 Block Diagram. (Courtesy of Motorola Semiconductor Products, Inc.)

SUMMARY

In this chapter we describe three types of input/output program data transfers: the unconditional data transfer, the conditional data transfer, and program interrupt transfer. The simplest in hardware and software is the unconditional transfer. However, its greatest drawback is that the device must be ready at the time of input/output program execution. Unless this is possible, we must, at least, employ the conditional data transfer. Here we essentially suspend program execution and wait for the device. We have seen a variety of techniques, including the powerful SYNC instruction in the 6809. In many applications assuming that a device is always ready, or suspending program execution, is unreasonable. We must then resort to the program interrupt transfer method.

Such interrupt-driven systems can be very hardware or very software intensive, depending on the relative costs of each approach. Software solutions rely heavily on polling. Hardware solutions rely on special peripheral devices to control priority and access.

Interrupt-driven systems are commonly employed in real-time programming problems. Other procedures are also available. These include software synchronization by counting the precise number of instructions executed between data transfers and attempting to synchronize transfer with the natural timing of the program. Some devices, however, are very demanding, requiring not only immediate response but continuous attention. In that case, we employ a DMA channel into our microcomputer system.

The topics in this chapter are difficult to weave into the fabric of modern programming. We cannot easily stitch program structure into interrupt-driven systems or real-time programs. Inherently, the haphazard nature of this data transfer activity inhibits invocation of structure into a flow chart. If we attempt to do so, we find that a potential number of structural links between the calling routine and the interrupt software are impossible to enumerate. Even our attempts to debug the code fail unless we resort to totally exhaustive testing, but this is unreasonable for a program of moderate size. Hence, caution is advised when generating code for such applications.

EXERCISES

1. Define the three types of input/output data transfers and identify the weak points and the strong points of each technique.

2. Interrupt-driven systems have a number of advantages and disadvantages. Describe them.

3. For each of the following devices, identify the best input/output programming technique in each case. Justify you selection.
    a. Disc
    b. Drum
    c. X/y plotter

    d. Slow dynamic RAM (needs periodic refresh)

    e. Line printer

    f. Teletype

    g. CRT

4. In the 6809 we can employ the SYNC instruction to temporarily suspend program execution for a device data transfer. Simulate this SYNC instruction with other 6809 instructions.

    a. Use a minimal number of bytes.

    b. Use a minimal number of instruction cycles.

5. What are three types of DMA? How do they work?

6. In Exercise #5, identify the advantages and disadvantages of each type of DMA.

7. Why is it difficult to employ modern programming techniques to real-time programming?

8. In the 6800 the resulting delay for the DMA technique using the HALT state may require as many as 13 clock cycles. This maximum delay occurs if the HALT line goes low after a 100-ns window (the leading edge of phase one in the last cycle of an instruction). If this happens, the MPU will not halt at the end of the current instruction, but will halt at the end of the next instruction. If we employ this DMA technique in the 6809, what will be the longest delay?

9. It is possible to use phase 1 of the two-phase clock system in the 6800 for DMA access since only phase 2 is used for data transfer. Can such a time-multiplex operation be used for DMA in the 6809?

BIBLIOGRAPHY

FERGUSON, ROBERT. "This 6800 System Handles Clock Stealing," *Digital Design*, Oct. 1978, pp. 60–68. Describes the use of the 6875 clock chip with the 6800 microprocessor in the cycle stealing DMA mode. Schematic of an HDLC-DMA loop board is given using the 6844 and 6854 peripheral devices.

KNOBLOCK, D. E., AND CHRIS A. VISSERS. "Insight into Interfacing," *IEEE Spectrum*, May 1975, pp. 50–57. Describes an interfacing system definition approach to programmable bench instruments which require vital communications capabilities among independently manufactured products. The discussion is centered around the IEEE 488 bus notation.

KRAFT, GEORGE S., AND WING N. TOY. *Mini/Microcomputer Hardware Design*. Englewood Cliffs, N.J.: Prentice-Hall, 1979. A good description of the interrupt mechanism for small computers is given in Chapter 8. The idea of multilevel priority interrupt is developed at the chip level. A two-dimensional multilevel priority level facility is described in great detail. This text is suggested for the hardware designer at the small computer level.

LEVENTHAL, LANCE A. *Introduction to Microprocessors: Software, Hardware, Programming*. Englewood Cliffs, N.J.: Prentice-Hall, 1978. A fundamental discussion of microprocessor interrupt systems is provided in Chapter 9, including a discussion of the inability to structure interrupt-driven systems. In later chapters other microprocessor interrupt systems are described, including the 8080 and 6800.

LOUGHRY, DON. "Don Loughry on ANSI/IEEE Standard 488 and the HP Interface Bus," *Hewlett-Packard Journal*, Dec. 1979, pp. 27–28. The 488 standard is contrasted with the HPIB standard, claimed to be more than just a 488 bus. Generalized formats expand the HPIB beyond that of the 488.

MOTOROLA SEMICONDUCTOR PRODUCTS, INC., MICROCOMPUTER APPLICATIONS ENGINEERING. *M6800 Microprocessor Applications Manual*. Phoenix, Ariz.: Motorola, 1975. Detailed specifications for DMA interface and timing can be found in this manual. Many useful 6800 interfaces are described which have applicability in the 6809.

SOUCEK, BRANKO. *Microprocessors and Microcomputers*. New York: Wiley, 1976. The three IOTs are further described in this test in Chapter 5, including block diagrams of the essential hardware features of the device side of the interface. Introductory material on the DEC PDP-11 and other minicomputer interfaces are also provided.

8

Data Acquisition

8.1 THE SYSTEM

The real world seldom permits us to interface a microprocessor directly to the signals we observe naturally. In fact, most of these signals are incompatible with any machine measurement. Some are even downright hostile (approaching thousands of volts)! Therefore, we usually think of a "system" that either measures signals or controls activity which is part of some process. The system we use is depicted in Figure 8.1 with three major elements: a controller, a process that we want to observe and/or control, and the measurement device. If we operate in open loop the input feeds the control, which could come from either the process block or the measurement block. When we desire closed-loop control, the measurement output is usually linearly combined with the input, thus serving as a primary signal for the control. *The microprocessor plays a primary role in both the control block and the measurement block.*

In this chapter we focus on classes of signals we could expect in the real world. In addition, we look at the signal conditioning that is required to transform raw, primary, or measured signals into a form compatible with microprocessor interface. For the most part we stress the measurement aspects of the system. Chapter 9 covers the control aspects.

You should keep in mind that, in most systems, the control block can be merged with the measurement block. Our figure simply partitions the

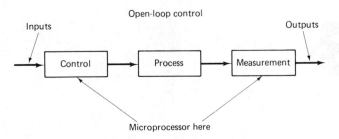

Figure 8.1. The System.

tasks into recognizable elements which perform some measurement/control operations on real signals.

8.2 SIGNAL TYPES

What, then, are commonly encountered signals we expect to see in measurement and control? Typical physical signals are temperature, pressure, humidity, force, proximity, or displacement. These are the "measured" signals. Seldom are these signals directly compatible with the microprocessor interface because microprocessors observe electrical signals. Other "measured" signals are physiochemical signals which provide desired properties for chemical analysis such as:

Electrical conductivity

Thermal conductivity

Mass spectrum

Diffusion coefficient (chromatography)

The earlier physical signals and these later physiochemical signals are not the only signals we may encounter, although they are the most common. It is quite probable that we may need to monitor physical properties, such as viscosity, density, vibrational frequency, and mass. However, these properties are generally observed indirectly by the physical signals that we have listed.

Transducers

We translate these incompatible physical signals to a compatible form by employing a transforming device called the transducer. Commonly, the transducer generates an electrical signal that can be eventually digitized and monitored by a microprocessor. Most electrical instrumentation systems employ some type of transducer. These transducers are typically thermocouples, strain gauges, thermistors, position indicators, servo force balance devices, and accelerometers. Transducers obviously monitor physical proper-

Data Acquisition

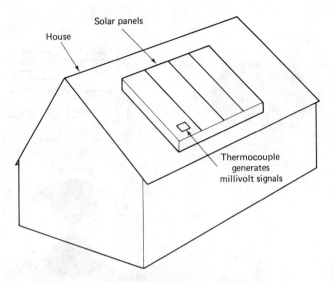

Figure 8.2. Measurement of Temperature.

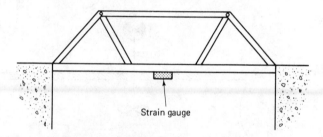

Figure 8.3. Indirect Measurement of Deformation.

ties, such as heat, force, or pressure, converting them to either a voltage or a current source. A transducer, then, is an integral part of the input circuit to the system we have just observed. It might be found in the control block or in the measurement block. We find transducers employed also in applications depicted in Figures 8.2 to 8.4.

8.3 SIGNAL CONDITIONING

Even if we use transducers as shown in Figures 8.2 to 8.4, the signal from the transducer itself is not necessarily useful until we have modified its output further. Typically, we must amplify, attenuate, filter, or translate the electrical quantity. Microprocessors interface with TTL logic. This means that a microprocessor likes to see 0 or +5 V; the 0 representing a Boolean value of 0 and 5 V representing a Boolean value of 1 (for positive logic). The negative logic convention assumes that Boolean 0 is equivalent to +5 V and that

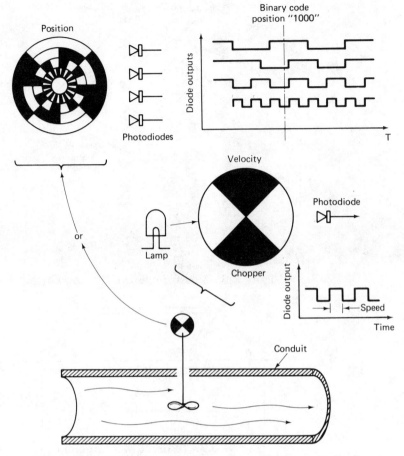

Figure 8.4. Measuring Position, Flow Rate, or Velocity.

Boolean 1 is equivalent to 0 V. Few transducer devices generate such large voltage transitions. We need to modify the signal, and this modification is called *signal conditioning*. Some of the signal conditioning may be performed by analog devices prior to interfacing with a microprocessor. Some of the conditioning may be performed by the microprocessor itself.

In general, signal conditioning consists of the following:

1. Amplification
2. Filtering
3. Input Protection
4. Isolation
5. Common Mode Rejection
6. Cold Junction Compensation
7. Transient Excitation

Isolation is necessary when we must avoid ground loops and transient voltage spikes. For balanced input systems, unwanted voltages across both inputs must be suppressed via common mode rejection techniques. Thermocouple interfaces sometimes employ cold junction compensation to accurately reference input readings. Most of the above conditioning is readily accomplished by peripheral devices external to the microprocessor chip. Let us look at the signal conditioning that a microprocessor typically performs.

Static Computations

Our conditioning operations depend on whether signals are static or dynamic, that is, whether they are rather slowly varying or fast-varying, respectively. On the very slow varying signals or dc signals, we execute static signal conditioning operations. This simply means that we may perform a conversion, linearization, or amplification. Remember that a common voltage range is 0 to 5 V (this may differ for CMOS). If our input signal does not swing between 0 and 5 V but has some offset, our conditioning must remove this offset in order to generate the proper signal range. This conditioning is simply a translation process.

Linearization

Linearization is necessary when the signal does not behave in a linear fashion. Thermocouples behave this way. In fact, a standard conversion formula of millivolts output versus temperature input is now commonly accepted industry-wide. The thermocouple output typically operates as shown in Figure 8.5. We desire to have the measured signal behave linearly.

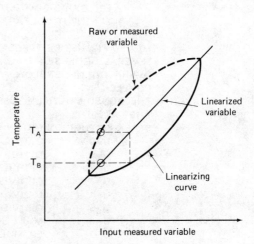

Figure 8.5. Linearization of Thermocouples.

So we must compensate for the nonlinear behavior by introducing a linearizing curve. This is a rather simple task for a microprocessor. When we want to use a voltage output that is linear with temperature as in digital display, it is necessary to use a linearizing curve, as shown in Figure 8.5.

Linearizing a Thermocouple Reading: Suppose that we observe the temperature T_A. From Figure 8.5 we see that this is much too high. In fact, we are supposed to see T_B, but we don't. Well, in order to do that we must subtract ΔT_A from T_A to obtain T_B. The linearizing curve can be a stored set of values or a computed set of values of ΔT_I for the various input temperatures T_I which when subtracted from the measured value give us the desired linear quantity itself.

The microprocessor could either store the linearized curve in memory as a set of values or approximate the linearizing curve by a set of straight lines which can compute the correction factor ΔT_A, depending on the amount of curvature. Or else, we can compute the actual value by a small set of straight-line segments that approximate the linearizing curve. Then the microprocessor could use a subroutine that determines which linear segment to use and eventually computes the correction factor ΔT_I. The routine in Example 8.1 performs a linearization. Notice that we are using special subroutines (SDVD and SMULT to handle signed division and signed multiplication of 16-bit operands found in the U stack.) The example assumes that the thermocouple is operated with a conventional resistive bridge.

EXAMPLE 8.1: A Thermocouple Linearization Program

```
* THIS MODULE CONVERTS THE NONLINEARITY OF THERMOCOUPLE
* FUNCTIONS WITH A STANDARD EQUATION
*
*          TCORR = A + E0 (B + C * E0/EI)/EI
*
* WHERE A,B,C ARE BRIDGE PARAMETERS
*        E0 = BRIDGE OUTPUT VOLTAGE
*        EI = INPUT VOLTAGE
*
* E0 AND EI MUST BE APPROXIMATELY SCALED (NORMALLY
* SEVERAL ORDERS OF MAGNITUDE DIFFERENCE) TO PREVENT
* OVERFLOW, UNDERFLOW.  ALL VARIABLES ARE 16 BITS,TWOS
* COMPLEMENT
* THE SIGNED MULTIPLY SUBR, SMULT, AND SIGNED DIVIDE SUBR, SDVD
* ARE CALLED
* STACK PICTURE ON ENTRY AND EXIT
*        U+0          OLD STACK MARK
*        U−1          DIVIDE ROUTINE COUNT          NDCNT
*        U−2          EI DIVISOR MSB                MEI
*        U−3          EI DIVISOR LSB                LEI
*        U−4          C DIVIDEND MSB                MDIVD
*        U−5          C DIVIDEND LSB                LDIVD
*        U−6          MULT COUNT                    NMCNT
*        U−7          E0, MULTIPLIER MSB            MEO
*        U−8          E0, MULTIPLIER LSB            LEO
```

```
*        U–9         MULTIPLICAND MSB              MCAND
*        U–10        MULTIPLICAND LSB              LCAND
*        U–11        B CORRECTION TERM MSB         MBCORR
*        U–12        B CORRECTION TERM LSB         LBCORR
*        U–13        A CORRECTION TERM MSB         MACORR
*        U–14        A CORRECTION TERM LSB         LACORR
*        U–15        TCORR MSB                     MTCORR
*        U–16        TCORR LSB                     LTCORR
*
* CALLING MODULE CONVERTS EQUATION FROM RIGHT TO LEFT
* DIVISOR IS EI, DIVIDEND IS C, MULTIPLIER IS E0
LINRO    PSHS        X,B,A,CCR
         LBSR        SDVD
* QUOTIENT IS NOW C/EI FOUND IN MDIVD,U
         LDX         MDIVD,U
         STX         MCAND,U
         LBSR        SMULT
* PRODUCT IS NOW C * E0/EI FOUND IN MCAND,U
         LDD         MCAND,U
         ADDD        MBCORR,U                      ADD B
         STD         MDIVD,U
         LBSR        SDVD
* QUOTIENT IS NOW (B + C * E0/EI)/EI FOUND IN MDIVD,U
         LDX         MDIVD,U
         STX         MCAND,U                       MULT BY E0
         LBSR        SMULT
* PRODUCT IS NOW E0 ( B + C * E0/EI)/EI FOUND IN MCAND,U
         LDD         MCAND,U
         ADDD        MACORR,U                      ADD A
         STD         MTCORR,U                      STORE RESULT
         PULS        CCR,A,B,X,PC                  RETURN
* END OF MODULE
* STACK OFFSET PARAMETERS
NDCNT    EQU         –1
MEI      EQU         –2
LEI      EQU         –3
MDIVD    EQU         –4
LDIVD    EQU         –5
NMCNT    EQU         –6
MEO      EQU         –7
LEO      EQU         –8
MCAND    EQU         –9
LCAND    EQU         –10
MBCORR   EQU         –11
LBCORR   EQU         –12
MACORR   EQU         –13
LACORR   EQU         –14
MTCORR   EQU         –15
LTCORR   EQU         –16
```

Flowmeter Linearization: Another important application which requires linearization is the calculating of flow rate of moving fluids. We must calculate the square root of a variable here. In Figure 8.6 we see a typical orifice submerged in a fluid being transmitted through some pipe. The Q function

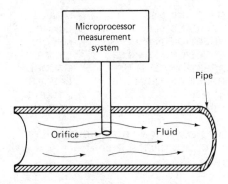

Q = Flow (volume per second)

A = Orifice area

C = Orifice coefficient

G = Gravitational coefficient

ΔH = Pressure difference across orifice

$Q = CA\sqrt{2G\ \Delta H}$

Figure 8.6. Flow Measurement.

or the volume per second function depends on the square root of the pressure difference across the orifice. In this situation we could use the microprocessor as the linearizing device to obtain the square root. The routine in Example 8.2 employs two subroutines (SMULT and SQRT to perform signal multiply and square rooting) to calculate flow rate. SMULT is a signed 16×16 multiplication, exiting with the product in ACCD. One operand must reside in ACCA before the call. The other operand is a parameter in the macro call. SQRT obtains the square root of the operand in ACCA, exiting with the result in ACCA.

EXAMPLE 8.2:   A Flowmeter Calculation Routine

```
* THIS MODULE COMPUTES THE FLOW RATE THROUGH A
* PIPE USING AN ORIFICE IN THE FORMULA
*        Q= C * A * SQRT (2 * G * PDIFF)
* WHERE Q = FLOW (VOLUME PER SECOND)
*        A = ORIFICE AREA
*        C = ORIFICE COEFFICIENT
*        G = GRAVITY (9.81 M/S/S)
*        PDIFF = PRESSURE DIFFERENTIAL
* MODULE CALLS TWO SUBROUTINES, SMULT AND SQRT
* SMULT IS SIGNED 16 * 16 BIT MULTIPLICATION AND SQRT
* IS SQUARE ROOT.  C, A, G ARE 8 BIT VALUES.  SMULT USES
* STACK PARAMETERS.  SQRT USES 16 BIT ARGUMENTS IN REGISTER D LEAVING
* AN 8 BIT RESULT IN ACCA
* STACK UPON ENTRY                              ON EXIT
*        U – 0          STACK MARKER
*        U – 1          MCOUNTER
*        U – 2          MULTIPLIER MSB           COEFFICIENT
*        U – 3          MULTIPLIER LSB
```

Data Acquisition

```
*          U-4          MULTIPLICAND MSB       FINAL RESULT FLOW
*          U-5          MULTIPLICAND LSB       IN CUBIC M/S
*          U-6          AREA
*          U-7          COEFFICIENT (ORIFICE)
*          U-8          CONSTANT (GRAVITY)
* CALLING MODULE COMPUTES EQUATION FROM RIGHT TO LEFT
* MULTIPLIER IS G, MULTIPLICAND IS 2 * PDIFF
FLOW       PSHS         U,B,A,CCR
           TFR          S,U
           LEAS         -8,U
           CLRB
           LDA          GRAV,U
           STD          MPLIER,U
           ASL          PDIFF,U
           LDA          PDIFF,U
           STD          MCAND,U
           LBSR         SMULT
* SUBROUTINE CALCULATES 2 * G * PDIFF. PRODUCT FOUND IN MCAND,U
           LDD          MCAND,U
           LBSR         SQRT
* SUBROUTINE CALCULATES SQRT OF 2 * G * PDIFF, RESULT FOUND IN A,B
           CLRB
           STD          MCAND,U
           LDA          AREA,U
           STD          MPLIER,U
           LBSR         SMULT
* SUBROUTINE CALCULATES A * SQRT (2 * G * PDIFF) PRODUCT IN MCAND,U
           CLRB
           LDA          COEFF,U
           STD          MPLIER,U
           LBSR         SMULT
* SUBROUTINE CALCULATES C * A * SQRT (2 * G * PDIFF) PRODUCT FOUND
* IN MCAND,U
           LEAS         8,U
           PULS         CCR,A,B,U,PC                RETURN
* END OF MODULE
*
* STACK OFFSET VALUES FOR PARAMETER PASSAGE
MCNT       EQU          -1
MPLIER     EQU          -2
LPLIER     EQU          -3
MCAND      EQU          -4
LCAND      EQU          -5
AREA       EQU          -6
COEFF      EQU          -7
GRAV       EQU          -8
```

8.4 DERIVED QUANTITIES

Linearization is not the only important signal-conditioning operation you
will perform on signals. On occasion you will find it necessary to modify
your signal for reasons other than to compensate for the nonlinear behavior
of the transducer itself. The microprocessor may perform computations

Table 8.1   Functional Diagrams for Instrument and Control Systems

Function and symbol	Math equation	Graphic representation	Definition
Summing Σ	$m = X_1 + X_2 + \ldots + X_n$		The output equals the algebraic sum of the inputs.
Averaging Σ/h	$m = \dfrac{X_1 + X_2 + \ldots + X_n}{n}$		The output equals the algebraic sum of the inputs divided by the number of inputs.
Difference Δ	$m = X_1 - X_2$		The output equals the algebraic difference between the two inputs.
Proportional X or P	$m = KX$		The output is directly proportional to the input.
Integral $\int$ or I	$m = \dfrac{1}{T_t} \int X \, dt$		The output varies in accordance with both magnitude and duration of the input. The output is proportional to the time integral of the input.
Derivative d/dt or o	$m = \tau_o \dfrac{dX}{dt}$		The output is proportional to the rate of change (derivative) of the input.
Multiplying X	$m = X_1 X_2$		The output equals the product of the two inputs.
Dividing $\div$	$m = \dfrac{X_1}{X_2}$		The output equals the quotient of the two inputs.
Root extraction $\sqrt{}$	$m = \sqrt{X}$		The output equals the root (i.e., square root, fourth root, 3/2 root, etc.) of the input.
Exponential X^n	$m = X^n$		The output equals the input raised to a power (i.e., second, third, fourth, etc.).
Nonlinear or unspecified function f(X)	$m = f(X)$		The output equals some nonlinear function of the input.

Table 8.1   (Continued)

Function symbol	Math equation	Graphic representation	Definition
Time function $t(t)$	$m = X\,f(t)$ $m = f(t)$		The output equals the input times some function of time or equals some function of time alone.
High selecting $>$	$m = \begin{cases} X_1 \text{ for } X_1 \geq X_2 \\ X_2 \text{ for } X_1 \leq X_2 \end{cases}$		The output is equal to that input which is the greatest of the inputs.
Low selecting $<$	$m = \begin{cases} X_1 \text{ for } X_1 \leq X_2 \\ X_2 \text{ for } X_1 \geq X_2 \end{cases}$		The output is equal to that input which is the least of the inputs.
High limiting $\not>$	$m = \begin{cases} X \text{ for } X \leq H \\ H \text{ for } X \geq H \end{cases}$		The output equals the input or the high limit value whichever is lower.
Low limiting $\not<$	$m = \begin{cases} X \text{ for } X \geq L \\ L \text{ for } X \leq L \end{cases}$		The output equals the input or the low limit value whichever is higher.
Reverse proportional $-K$ or $-P$	$m = -KX$		The output is reversely proportional to the input.
Velocity limiter $V \not>$	$\dfrac{dm}{dt} = \dfrac{dX}{dt} \begin{cases} \dfrac{dX}{dt} \leq H \text{ and} \\ m = X \end{cases}$ $\dfrac{dm}{dt} = H \begin{cases} \dfrac{dX}{dt} \geq H \text{ or} \\ m \neq X \end{cases}$	$\dfrac{dX}{dt} > H$ $\quad$ $\dfrac{dm}{dt} = H$	The output equals the input as long as the rate of change of the input does not exceed a limit value. The output will change at the rate established by this limit until the output again equals the input.
Bias, $+, -,$ or $\pm$	$m = X \pm b$		The output equals the input plus (or minus) some arbitrary value (bias).
Analog signal generator A	$m = A$	Does not apply	The output is an analog signal developed within the generator.
Transfer T	$m = \begin{cases} X_1 \text{ for state 1} \\ X_2 \text{ for state 2} \end{cases}$	State 1 State 2	The output equals the input which has been selected by transfer. The state of the transfer is established by external means.
Signal monitor $H/$	State 1 $\quad X < H$ State 2 (energized or alarm state) $\quad X > H$	State 1 State 2	

Table 8.1 (Continued)

Function symbol	Math equation	Graphic representation	Definition
/L	State 1 (energized or alarm state) $X < L$ State 2		
H/L	State 1 (first output m_1 energized or alarm state) $X < H/L$ State 2 (second output m_2 energized or alarm state) $X > H/L$		The output has discrete states which are dependent on the value of the input. When the input exceeds (or becomes less than) an arbitrary limit value the output changes state.
H//L	State 1 (first output m_1 energized or alarm state) $X < L$ State 2 (both outputs inactive or de-energized) $L < X < H$ State 3 (second output m_2 energized or alarm state) $X > H$		

Note: The variables used in the table are:

A,	an arbitrary analog signal	m,	analog output variable
b,	analog bias value	n,	number of analog inputs or value of exponenet
d/dt,	derivative with respect to time	t,	time
H,	an arbitrary analog high limit value	T_D,	derivative time
$1/T_1$,	integrating rate	X	analog input variable
L,	an arbitrary analog low limit value	$X_1, X_2, X_3, \ldots, X_n$,	Analog input variable (1 to n in number)

Source: Extracted from SAMA Standard PMC22–11–1966.
Functional Diagramming of Instrument and Control Systems, with permission of the publisher, PMC Section, SAMA

similar to those listed in Table 8.1. These brief definitions of signal processing are standards recognized by industry. These have been extracted from the Scientific Apparatus Makers Association standard on functional diagramming of instrumentation and control systems. Let us examine two such functions.

Low-Selecting

Your microprocessor will monitor signals after some signal preconditioning, but such signals will sometimes undergo further signal conditioning to generate what we commonly call *derived quantities*. The outputs from the mathematical equations in Table 8.1 represent derived quantities that can be used in the measurement and control process itself. For example, let us look at the function called LOW-SELECTING. The purpose of this function is to choose the lesser value of two inputs. The microprocessor makes a decision on these two inputs either sequentially or in parallel. Then by a simple comparison, the microprocessor selects and generates an output that is the least of both inputs.

Bias

Another simple function is the BIAS function. Here we assume that some input is offset from zero and we wish to add or subtract a fixed bias or constant to the input signal in order to return its zero crossover point back to zero. This is commonly encountered in isothermal correction of thermocouples. Only if the thermocouple junction is referenced to a nominal value (commonly 32°F) will we have no problem. In any event, there will exist an inherent bias which we must remove computationally. It is simple for a microprocessor to either add or subtract a known constant to the input signal each time the input is read. Note that this differs from the graphic representation in Table 8.1. The table entry assumes that the input signal does cross zero origin, whereas we wish to offset it to the positive or negative side. Derived quantities are also called *auxiliary variables*. This is simply because they can often be computed from static mathematical models of the process. Notice that many mathematical models also require multiplication, division, and square root. Hence, it is important to have an accurate algorithm which performs these elementary algebraic operations, sometimes very fast.

8.5 DYNAMIC SIGNAL CONDITIONING

If signal conditioning was simply static, our solutions with microprocessors would be straightforward. That is not the case. The world is full of nonstatic signals. Although it may be true that the linearization curve for thermocouples won't change with time, that is certainly not true for most physical devices. In fact, when our transducer itself changes with time or drifts, we need to be concerned with other signal-conditioning computations.

Physical devices also have time lags associated with them because of inertial effects surrounding the process. For instance, if a thermocouple which is essentially measuring temperature is immersed in a fluid bath, it takes a finite amount of time before a thermocouple reads the actual temperature. This time lag or delay is associated with the physical properties of the process itself. This thermal delay must be compensated for by the microprocessor or else our readings may be erroneously low if the actual temperature of the device is decreasing, and high otherwise. We also call such a delay transportation delay or transport lag. This is a dynamic problem that we resolve by performing dynamic signal conditioning.

Phase Lag

A thermocouple output signal is nearly static. But if some device generates a signal that is changing rapidly and has a high frequency associated with it, it is possible to erroneously measure properties such as the maximum amplitude because of the phase shift or the variation of signal lag with frequency. For signals that contain only one frequency which is precisely known we could easily calculate the phase shift beforehand. A delay time equal to a complete period of the wave is just the phase shift of 360 degrees. Proportionally longer or shorter lags can be easily calculated, and the true amplitude can then be determined. If the signal contains many frequencies, the phase-shift calculation and the resultant amplitude determination is no longer simple. Methods, however, do exist.

Digital versus Analog

Before microprocessors became available we dealt with dynamic conditioning by solely employing analog circuits to condition signals. Analog circuits have some drawbacks. For instance, they cannot remember values too long. They themselves introduce considerable measurement error and the dynamic range of the analog circuits is very narrow. Digital signals are employed to overcome drawbacks found with analog circuits. Microprocessors that monitor signals can remember forever as long as the power is applied or nonvolatile memory is used. The dynamic range can be modified by software to suit the application. Finally, most microprocessors can now keep up with fast signals encountered in most process measurement and control.

Dynamic signal conditioning for microprocessors for the most part means that we are dealing with transport lags, sampling rates, slew rates, and filtering problems. In this section we look at typical signal-conditioning operations required for transport lags and sampling.

Transport Lag

We begin with transport lag. The delays associated with transport lag occur in instances where the signal velocity usually causes delays independent of the nature of the signal itself. (One exception is a lag that is dependent upon the signal or process variable frequency. This occurs when an energy-storage device—thermal, electrical, or mechanical—exists. The phase-shift phenomenon we saw earlier is a form of delay that is dependent upon the frequency content.) When a process has a single storage element, we can expect a first-order lag. In electrical terms, this is a simple RC filter shown in

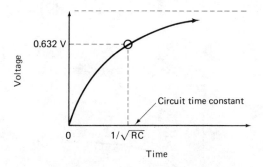

Figure 8.7. First-Order Lag Circuit.

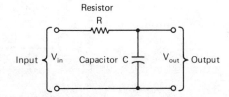

Figure 8.8. Response of First-Order Lag Circuit to Step Function.

Figure 8.7. The response of this filter is equivalent to a first-order lag, shown in Figure 8.8. The curves represent an exponential function.

First Order Response

Many physical phenomena obey first-order behavior, so it is of considerable interest. For instance, a thermometer bulb in a bath tends to appear as a first-order lag circuit, as shown in Figure 8.9. When a thermometer bulb is immersed in a bath, it will rise up to the bath temperature in a predictable but finite time. If bath A is at temperature T_A, the response curve, A in Figure 8.9, models the process behavior of the thermometer bulb. Similarly, if the bath temperature is at T_B, response curve B models the behavior. But in both curves, observe that the thermometer bulb has reached 63.2% of its final value in the same length of time. We call this time the lag coefficient t_c. This is an important time constant which is independent of the bath temperature and is analogous to the time constant, the square root of RC, found in the electrical circuit containing a resistor and capacitor.

Temperature First-Order Equation

We can immediately derive the equation for the thermometer bulb response once we know t_c, as in

$$T_0 = T_A \left[1 - \exp \left(-\frac{t}{t_c} \right) \right]$$ (8.1)

where

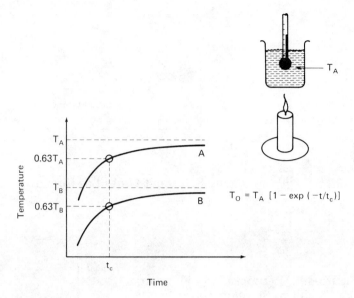

Figure 8.9. Thermometer Bulb First-Order Response.

$$T_0 = T_A\,[1 - \exp(-t/t_c)]$$

T_0 = output temperature
t_c = thermal time constant
T_A = final bath temperature

This is intuitively obvious because our physical system is a single energy storage, which implies a first-order lag system. The thermometer then exhibits a first-order time lag. Of course, equation (8.1) represents the behavior of the thermometer bulb only if subjected to a sudden rise in its ambient temperature (a step function).

The microprocessor designer, given t_c, can predict the lag response in a given system when the thermometer bulb is subjected to a step increase in temperature. However, in many cases the total system design requires us to first determine t_c itself. This will depend on many factors. Here we must be concerned with the area, overall heat-transfer coefficient, and the actual rate of heat transfer as well as properties of the thermometer bulb.

Duality in Nature

First-order lag processes can be found in many systems. The process variables for the electrical, thermal, and fluid flow problems are listed in Table 8.2. If you are familiar with the electrical model using current and potential or voltage but are required to develop a heat-flow model, use the dual of each variable in the domains you are familiar with to generate the correct equation in the unfamiliar domain.

Table 8.2a Physical Analogs

	Electrical	Heat Flow	Fluid Flow
Quantity	Q, charge	Q (Btu)	Volume (ft^3)
Flow	I	q (Btu/min)	Q (ft^3/s)
Potential	V	ΔT ($^\circ$F)	h, head (ft)
Resistance	R	$1/UA$ ($^\circ$F/Btu)	h/Q
Capacitance	C	C_p (Btu/$^\circ$F) (= $q/\Delta T$)	Volume/h = A for constant cross section
Time constant	RC	C_p/UA	$\doteq A/C_u$ for small Δh

Table 8.2b Translational and Rotational Mechanical System Analogs

Translational	Rotational
Force, f	Torque, τ
Acceleration, a	Angular acceleration, α
Velocity, u	Angular velocity, Ω
Displacement, x	Angular displacement, θ
Mass, M	Moment of inertia, I_θ
Damping coefficient, D	Rotational damping coefficient, D_θ
Compliance, K	Torsional compliance, K_θ

Table 8.2c Force-Voltage Analogs

Mechanical system	Electrical system (f-v analogy)
Force, f	Voltage, v
Velocity, u	Current, i
Displacement, x	Charge, q
Mass, M	Inductance, L
Damping coefficient, D	Resistance, R
Compliance, K	Capacitance, C

Sampling Rate

The first-order lag phenomenon really means that the raw signal moves so fast or changes so rapidly that our measurement system cannot respond quickly enough. In the previous discussion we assumed that a step input was applied and that the first-order lag phenomenon exhibited some delay which was ultimately interpreted as an error. Well, suppose now that the signal is constantly changing instead of abruptly changing only once (as if a step input was applied). What, then, must we do? For constantly changing signals we need to determine an acceptable sampling rate. We know from theory (using the Nyquist sampling theorem) that we need to sample more than twice as fast as the highest frequency component we can expect in the signal.

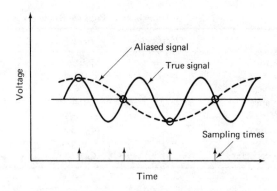

Figure 8.10. Effect of Slow Sampling Rate.

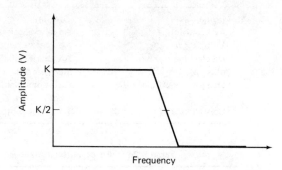

Figure 8.11. Low-Pass Filter.

If we are monitoring a single frequency, we must periodically sample faster than twice that frequency.

Aliasing

If we attempt to sample at or slower than twice the highest frequency, we will encounter a harmful phenomenon called *aliasing*, which would appear as shown in Figure 8.10. Notice that our aliased interpretation of the true signal is actually half of the frequency of the signal itself. Choosing the sampling rate is therefore a simple matter once we know the highest frequency to expect. In most cases we don't. In practice, to ensure that we do not erroneously identify an aliased frequency, a low-pass filter (see Figure 8.11) is employed ahead of the microprocessor. This low-pass filter is basically the first-order lag circuit we saw in Figure 8.8. If we select a low-pass filter, we need to compensate for the additional delay caused by the filter if this is a significant transport lag.

Remember that the function of our measurement block in Figure 8.1 is to acquire data and in some sense convert those data to a compatible format. These measurement blocks are sometimes called *data-acquisition and conversion modules*. Microprocessors make excellent data-acquisition and conversion devices. Some vendors provide a complete single board system with microprocessor, ADC and DAC, power supply and interface circuitry. The RTI 1230 micromodule available from Analog Devices, Norwood, Massachusetts is typical of such a system. The RTI 1230, however, has no signal conditioning circuitry on-board. The Analog Devices μ MAC 4000 does provide signal conditioning.

Quantization

Microprocessors depend upon the proper *descretization* or *quantizing* of the signal itself as well as a satisfactory sampling rate. Quantizing analog signals distorts the actual signal information. We need to be aware of this. A quantizing error is shown in Figure 8.12 for the typical quantization rule we have assumed (Figure 8.13).

Let us say that we are going to use a 3-bit binary code which has eight levels in an analog signal from -5 to $+5$ V. We call $Q/2$ the quantization error and it represents a "distance." The distance between the decision levels is Q, the quantization size or bit size of our quantizer. Hence a quantizer with a binary output code of $2n$ discrete output levels makes $2n - 1$ decisions. Since this decision has a finite uncertainty associated with it, a quantization error arises. We say that the peak value of the quantization noise (distortion caused by the quantizer) is $Q/2$. The root-mean-square (rms) value is $Q/2\sqrt{3}$. Even though the quantization noise can be reduced by increasing the resolution of the quantizer, there will always be a quantization uncertainty of $\pm Q/2$ for any quantizer.

Aperture Time

Quantization also affects the data acquisition in the following manner. Any signal to be sampled will require a minimum and finite amount of time to convert that analog signal to its digital equivalent. This conversion time has a lower bound. We call it the *aperture time*, T_a. If we try to ascertain a reading in less time we will encounter an uncertainty in a reading of the signal value we are observing, as shown in Figure 8.14. We can easily derive the required aperture time for sampling sinusoids in the following manner. The worst time to sample a sinusoid is at the zero crossing of the waveform. This is where the rate of change is a maximum over the entire period. From equation (8.2) we can derive the percentage resolution, $\Delta V/V$, as a function of aperture time. We see that percent resolution is simply a function of the

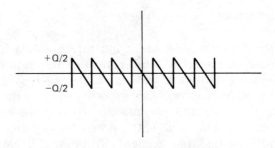

Figure 8.12. Quantizing Error.

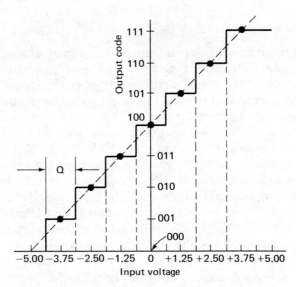

Figure 8.13. Transfer Function for Bipolar 3-Bit ADC Converter.

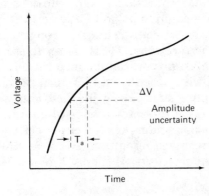

Figure 8.14. Aperture Time, T_A, and Amplitude Uncertainty.

Table 8.3		Decimal Equivalents of 2^n and 2^{-n}	
n	2^n	2^{-n}	dB
0	1	1	0
1	2	0.5	−6
2	4	0.25	−12
3	8	0.125	−18.1
4	16	0.0625	−24.1
5	32	0.03125	−30.1
6	64	0.015625	−36.1
7	128	0.0078125	−42.1
8	256	0.00390625	−48.2
9	512	0.001953125	−54.2
10	1,024	0.0009765625	−60.2
11	2,048	0.00048828125	−66.2
12	4,096	0.000244140625	−72.2
13	8,192	0.0001220703125	−78.3
14	16,384	0.00006103515625	−84.3
15	32,768	0.000030517578125	−90.3
16	65,536	0.0000152587890625	−96.3

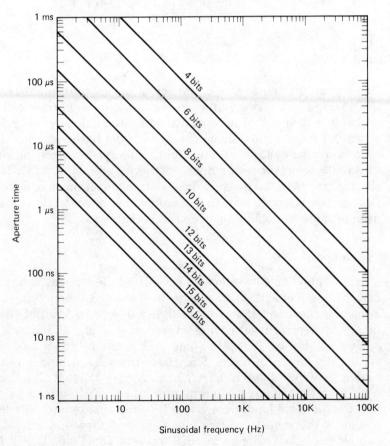

Figure 8.15. Aperture Time Required for a Given Frequency and Resolution.

frequency w and the aperture time T_a. (Compute the derivative of the waveform and set $t = 0$.)

$$\Delta V = \frac{d}{dt} [V \sin wt] \times T_a \qquad \text{at } t = 0 \tag{8.2}$$

EXAMPLE 8.3:   Determine the Aperture Time for Sampling Sinusoids

Suppose that we want to digitize a 1-kHz signal to 10 bits of resolution. Ten bits of resolution also specify our quantization which is a percent resolution. We see from Table 8.3 that this is equivalent to 0.1%. Since 2 raised to the power -10 is 0.000976, the least significant bit can still be in doubt. Hence, $\Delta V/V$ is 0.001 and from equation (8.3) we find that T_a is $0.001/2(3.14)(1000) = 160$ ns. For your convenience the aperture time required for any given frequency in resolution has been plotted in Figure 8.15.

$$\frac{\Delta V}{V} = 2(3.1416)(f)(T_a) \tag{8.3}$$

8.7 DIGITAL CODE

One important transducer is the actual device that quantizes or descretizes the analog signal. This is the *analog-to-digital converter* (ADC). The ADC is simply a device that accepts a single-wire analog signal and converts it to a parallel N-bit binary signal. Everything we have examined about aperture time and quantization so far applies also to the specification of the ADC. The 6809 microprocessor does not have an on-chip ADC. Hence, we must specify our ADC separately in a data acquisition and conversion system. Besides the aperture-time and sampling-rate specifications for the ADC, we need to know which digital code is acceptable to us.

Popular Codes

For popular converters we have listed the straight binary, offset binary, and 2's-complement binary code in Tables 8.4 and 8.5. In Table 8.4 an 8-bit unipolar converter assumes that a 0- to +10-V input signal is used. All binary 0's represent an analog voltage of 0 V and all binary 1's represent an analog voltage of 9.95 V. Some ADCs can be purchased as *bipolar* converters, as shown in Table 8.5. Here, the zero voltage input level is represented by a 10000000 in binary base. A +5-V input is all 1's and a -5 V is all 0's. This offset binary code is no more than a shifted binary code where one-half the full-scale binary corresponds to the analog zero. The 2's-complement coding is the same as offset binary except that the most significant bit is complemented. We depict the BCD code in Table 8.6. The BCD code is quite

Table 8.4   Binary Coding for 8-Bit Unipolar Converters

Scale	+10 V Full Scale	Straight Binary		Complementary Binary	
		MSB	LSB	MSB	LSB
+FS − 1LSB	+9.96	1111	1111	0000	0000
+3/4FS	+7.50	1100	0000	0011	1111
+1/2FS	+5.00	1000	0000	0111	1111
+1/4FS	+2.50	0100	0000	1011	1111
+1/8FS	+1.25	0010	0000	1101	1111
+1LSB	+0.04	0000	0001	1111	1110
0	0.00	0000	0000	1111	1111

Table 8.5   Binary Coding for 8-Bit Bipolar Converters

Scale	±5 V Full Scale	Offset Binary		2's Complement	
		MSB	LSB	$\overline{MSB}$	LSB
+FS − 1LSB	+4.96	1111	1111	0111	1111
+3/4FS	+3.75	1110	0000	0110	0000
+1/2FS	+2.50	1100	0000	0100	0000
0	0.00	1000	0000	0000	0000
−1/2FS	−2.25	0100	0000	1100	0000
−3/4FS	−3.75	0010	0000	1010	0000
FS + 1LSB	−4.96	0000	0001	1000	0001
−FS	−5.00	0000	0000	1000	0000

Table 8.6   BCD Coding for Two-Digit Unipolar Converter

Scale	+10 V Full Scale	BCD	
		MSD	LSD
+FS − 1LSD	+9.9	1001	1001
+3/4FS	+7.5	0111	0101
+1/2FS	+5.0	0101	0000
+1/4FS	+2.5	0010	0101
+1LSD	+0.1	0000	0001
0	0.0	0000	0000

useful for direct digital display from the ADC. It is not always useful for direct interface to the microprocessor itself. The 8-bit bipolar converter which generates a 2's-complement form is most common.

Another important transducer is the digital-to-analog converter, or DAC. This device works in the opposite way from the ADC. It takes an N-bit parallel signal from the microprocessor and converts it to a single-wire analog voltage. Specifying a DAC is similar to specifying an ADC but much simpler. The DAC is useful when we want our microprocessor to command or control a process. The ADC is used when we want to measure or monitor a signal.

8.8 BASIC DESIGN STEPS FOR SIGNAL CONDITIONING

We now have enough information to summarize a list of typical design steps we are going to encounter when we must determine the signal conditioning requirements for the microprocessor. The crucial steps are:

1. Specify the signal range and quantization levels.
2. Select the appropriate numerical representation.

These two steps are necessary for determining the static computations of the signal conditioning. The design steps for considering the dynamic behavior also include:

1. Specify the minimum sampling rate.
2. Determine the aperture time for our system sampling rate.

There is, of course, much to designing a measurement system, and we have ignored problems encountered with noise, cross-coupling, and ill-posed models themselves. At times these can be major problems. However, for most situations we are already well on our way. Transducer manufacturers provide excellent literature which addresses these issues.

8.9 A LOW-COST ADC TECHNIQUE

Sometimes, hardware costs override all other considerations, including speed. This is quite common when we must perform analog-to-digital conversion. When speed is not important, less costly ADC techniques are sought. The successive-approximation-register (SAR) method is one solution. Here, a DAC and analog comparator circuit in conjunction with an MPU output PORT perform the ADC by making successively larger or smaller guesses at the actual analog signal value. In Figure 8.16, a SAR circuit using the Burr-Brown MP11 implements the flow activity in Figure 8.17 using the microprocessor program of Example 8.4. We are using only one DAC output of the MP11, whose PORT is selected by address FFF0. The MP11 also houses the register which latches the current "guess." Trial guesses continue checking each successively smaller value, retaining the current value if PB0 (data bit 0 of PORT B of PIA) is reset. A counter in location $400 keeps track of all bits tested. The final digitized value resides in location $401 when V_{in} is equal to V_{ref}.

EXAMPLE 8.4: SAR Analog/Digital Conversion

```
SAR     LDX     #$0000      INITIALIZE MP11
        STX     $FFF2       LOCATED AT FFF0
        STX     $FFF4       INITIALIZE PIA
```

```
            STX      $FFF6              LOCATED AT FFF4
            LDX      #$FFFF
            STX      $FFF0
            STX      $FFF2
            CLR      $0400              CLEAR MEM 0400
            CLRA
            ORCC     #01                SET CARRY
START       ROR      $0400
            BCS      EXIT
            ADDA     $0400              ADD BIT POINTER TO ACCA
            STA      $FFF0              OUTPUT ACCA TO D/A
            LDB      #6
LOOP        DECB
            BNE      LOOP               DELAY LOOP
            LDB      $FFF4              READ COMPARATOR – PAO
BIT
            BITB     #01
            BNE      START
            SUBA     $0400
            JMP      START
EXIT        STA      $0401
            RTS
```

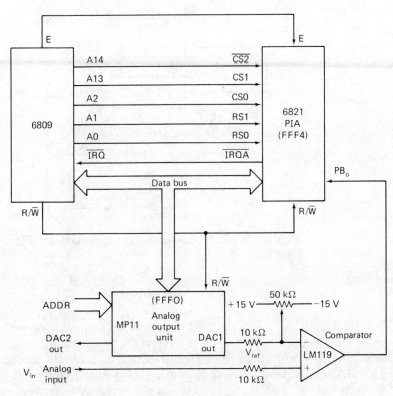

Figure 8.16. Successive Approximation Interface for ADC.

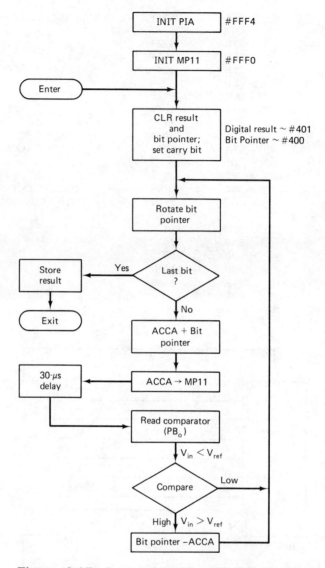

Figure 8.17. Successive Approximation Flow Chart.

SUMMARY

Invariably, microprocessors find their way into signal processing and control. In so doing, they must essentially interface to an analog world. Microprocessors must also monitor analog signals as well as generate analog signals. ADCs and DACs are merely translators for such signals. However, signals contain information as well as noise. In some designs it is convenient to filter the noise before the ADC. In others, we let the microprocessor perform digital filtering on the signal spectrum.

Knowing how to filter out which part of the signal spectrum is important in data acquisition. In this chapter we look at the signal-conditioning tasks found in microprocessor data acquisition systems. These tasks can be considered as either static computations or dynamic computations. The difference depends on the signal characteristics. Conversion, linearization, and amplification are static computations. Drift compensation, filtering, and phase shifting are dynamic computations. In process control, manufacturers use derived quantities or quantities which are modified raw signals. Derived quantities can be generated by the microprocessor or by the front-end analog circuits.

The transducer is the simplest front-end circuit in the analog world. Transducers inherently possess certain physical attributes. They may obey a first-order law which means that a single time-constant lag response is expected. More complex transducers such as accelerometers possess second-order effects.

ADCs and DACs as transducers are conversion devices which also have peculiar properties. They introduce quantization noise, observe signals within some window (aperture time), and generate digital code of several types. The typical ADC can generate unipolar, bipolar, and offset bipolar codes, although seldom simultaneously.

The basic design steps for signal processing consider signal range and quantization levels to determine an appropriate numerical representation. These static signal-conditioning requirements are modified when dynamic signals are encountered. For dynamic signals, we must consider the minimum sampling rate and the aperture time of our overall system.

EXERCISES

1. Why are we concerned about the physical properties of the measured signals?

2. What are typical physical tasks?

3. What are some of the tasks involved in designing with the microprocessor for measurement or data acquisition?

4. What signals are directly compatible with a microprocessor?

5. How do we interface the physical signals?

6. What are typical transducers, and what do they do?

7. What is the equation for behavior of a thermometer that exhibits a first-order time lag?

8. Suppose that you wish to fill a cylindrical reservoir at the same time that it is being drained. You want to keep a desired level in the tank at all times within certain

limits by manipulating a valve. You want to control this valve with a microprocessor. Design the necessary sequence of steps to be executed by the microprocessor.

9. Suppose that you are sampling a 100-kHz signal and desire 12 bits of resolution. What aperture time is required?

10. List some reasons for buying an ADC that generates BCD code.

11. If you use an offset binary coded ADC with a 2's complement microcomputer, how would you convert the binary code in the microcomputer to ensure that negative analog signals become negative binary numbers, positive analog signals become positive binary numbers, and zero analog signals become 00 . . . 0 binary in the microcomputer?

12. In Example 8.1, assume we are operating a 6809 at 1 MHz. Calculate the maximum time to make one linearized computation of a thermocouple. Can you reduce this time? How? What are you sacrificing?

13. Repeat excerise 12 for Example 8.2.

BIBLIOGRAPHY

ALDRIDGE, DON. "A/D Conversion Systems . . . Let Your Microprocessor Do the Working," *Electronic Design News*, May 5, 1976, pp. 75–80. Describes useful 6800 to 6820 PIA interfaces for an 8-bit and 4-bit successive approximation A/D and D/A conversion. 6800 programs and a high-accuracy dual ramp A/D procedure are also given.

ANALOG DEVICES. *Data Acquisition Products Catalog*, Norwood, Mass.: Analog, 1978. This large catalog contains numerous device specifications for analog-to-digital and digital-to-analog converters, operational amplifiers, low-pass filters, and other analog devices useful for data acquisition. There is a short discussion of the theoretical aspects of A/D and D/A conversion in tutorial form.

BASS, H. G. *Introduction to Engineering Measurements*. New York: McGraw-Hill, 1971. This elementary text explains by numerous illustrations typical signals to be measured in the real world, including pressure, time, motion, vibration, temperature, flow, and viscosity. Ends with a discussion of the useful topics in the dynamic performance of transducers responding to standard test inputs, such as stamps, ramps, and sinusoids.

CLIFF, R. A. "Digital Multiplexing of Analog Data in a Microprocessor Controlled Data Acquisition System," *IEEE Transactions on Computers*, vol. C-29, Feb. 1980, pp. 200–201. An alternative design uses multiple comparators (one per input) followed by a digital multiplexor to make the sequential conversion of inputs perform faster than interrupt-driven conversions.

COLLETT, C. V., AND A. D. HOPE. *Engineering Measurements*. New York: Pitman, 1974. Strain gauges and strain gauge measurements are described. Interferometry parameters and measurements are explained in the applications of dimensional and angular measurements. An important data-acquisition system utilizes the assessment of surface finish of machined areas to determine the roughness and waviness caused by the tool marks. Describes such applications through many real-world examples.

ELLIS, M. J., G. R. HOVEY, AND T. E. STAPINSKI, "MTEC: A Microprocessor System for Astronomical Telescope and Instrument Control," *IEEE Transactions on Com-*

puters, vol. C-29, Feb, 1980, pp. 208–211. A flexible, modular control system using an 8-bit microprocessor operates via UART serial links in a telescope control system.

ENOCHSON, LOREN D., AND ROBERT K. OTNES. *Programming and Analysis for Digital Time Series Data.* The Shock and Vibration Information Center, U.S. Department of Defense, Code 8404, Naval Research Laboratory, Washington, D.C., 20390, 1968. Many useful algorithms to perform Fourier computations, digital filtering and the analysis thereof, including stationary and nonstationary processes, are described in this handbook. A theoretical discussion is provided for spectral-density-function computations, which help us to determine the input signal spectrum, including the noise. This is an advanced compendium of important filtering topics.

GLASGOW, BARRY. "Choose a Microcomputer Analog-Interface Board with This Handy Selection Guide," *EDN*, May 20, 1979, pp. 169–175. Describes packaged one-board solutions to data-acquisition interfaces for microprocessors.

KIRK, FRANKLIN W., AND NICHOLAS R. RIMBOI. *Instrumentation.* Chicago: American Technical Society, 1975. This introductory text describes through numerous illustrations the transducers found in measuring several physical signals, including pressure, level transmission, temperature, and flow. A table of industry standard instrumentation symbols is provided in the appendix. These Instrument Society of America (ISA) symbols are commonly used in the industry. Primary element, function, general instrument, control valve body, and actuator symbols are listed.

MARZALEK, MICHAEL S. "Some Microprocessor Contributions to Spectrum Analyzer Performance," *Hewlett-Packard Journal*, Aug. 1979, pp. 15–16. The author briefly describes microprocessor control front-panel and frequency calculations in a spectrum analyzer instrument.

MIDDELHOEK, SIMON, JAMES B. ANGELL, AND DAVE J. W. NOORLAG. "Microprocessors Get Integrated Sensors," *IEEE Spectrum*, vol. 17, Feb. 1980, pp. 42–46. One-chip microprocessors are eliminating some transducer tasks. This article describes photoconductive, photovoltaic, piezoresistive, and other transducers on a microprocessor chip.

MOLINARI, FRED, PAUL SEVERINO, AND EDWIN KROEKER. "Shopping for the Right Analog I/O Board: Software Considerations Come First," *Electronic Design*, vol. 21, Oct. 11, 1978, pp. 238–243. Describes a memory-mapped technique to do software control for real-time programs using analog input/output boards in a microcomputer system with multitasking software. The use of the control and status register in this application is described for an interrupt-driven system.

MORRISON, ROBERT L. "Data Acquisitions, A Software Approach," *Digital Design*, Mar. 1979, pp. 66–71. Data acquisition through use of a practical voltage-to-frequency converter system is described. Also included is a flow chart for thermocouple interface software, and a successive approximation logic flow chart for A/D conversion all in the 6800.

MROZOWSKI, ANDRIJ. "Analog Output Chips Shrink A-D Conversion Software," *Electronics*, June 23, 1977, pp. 130–133. The program and flow chart for a successive approximation solution to A/D conversion for the 6800 microprocessor using the Burr-Brown MP11 analog output unit is described.

ZUCH, EUGENE L. "Compensate for Temperature Drift in Data-Converter Circuits," *Electronic Design News*, Apr. 20, 1979, pp. 195–198. Explains the effects of temperature drift in A/D and D/A converters. A nomagraph is provided for effects of ambient temperature on the differential linearity error.

ZUCH, EUGENE L. *Data Acquisition and Conversion Handbook*. Mansfield, Mass.: Datel Intersil, 1979. This practical applications manual describes numerous data acquisition solutions to a variety of disciplines from electrical engineering to process control. The many buzz words of the industry are also identified. Detailed discussion of the intimate hardware inside A/D and D/A converters are also provided. A large glossary of data conversion terms is provided.

9

Process Control
Digital Algorithms

9.1 INTRODUCTION

The primary topics of this chapter focus on developing microcomputer code for process control applications. The material is directed at specific applications where much of the theoretical analysis has been previously completed. That is, we have assumed that important phases of the problem, such as

1. Plant or process modeling
2. Identification of control and observable parameters
3. Performance of the controlled system

have been completed beforehand. Therefore, in this chapter, we begin our study with available models provided in mathematical terminology using the Laplace transform. Details of important phases described above can be found in several existing texts, some of which are listed at the end of the chapter.

This chapter introduces simple procedures for generating algorithms in microprocessor-based controllers where straightforward techniques can be identified and applied. Invocation of modern programming methods ensure programs understandable to the casual user. Here, in the setting of process control, where noncomputer specialists abound, you must vigilantly practice modern programming. For, in the current situation, the microprocessor code will undergo several iterations (probably by only occasional users

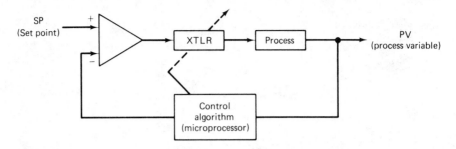

Figure 9.1. Process under Control.

of microprocessors). All of the programs now developed possess some degree of modularity and position independence, the hallmarks of high-quality programs. Let us begin with the simplest control application, that of set-point control.

We can depict a process to be controlled by Figure 9.1. Here we see the process or plant in a loop with a controller ahead of the process. The control algorithm, and in our case the digital control algorithm, is embedded in a feedback loop. The purpose of the control algorithm is to actuate the controller mechanism ahead of the process, thus changing the process variable, PV. The input variable, SP, or *set point*, and the *process variable*, PV, are used in equation (9.1) to generate an error signal, E. We want PV to follow SP. So our controller tries to make E as small as possible.

$$E = SP - PV \qquad (9.1)$$

We execute a control algorithm with a microprocessor. This microprocessor actually generates a digital control algorithm, in contrast to circuits which generate an analog control algorithm. There are many advantages to implementing digital control in microprocessors:

1. Infinite memory time
2. Flexibility through simple program changes
3. Accurate response to long reaction times
4. Accurate controls not possible in some analog problems (for instance, deadtime control)

We select the control algorithm being guided by several criteria. They include the permissible value of the set points, the range of supply and demand in the feedback or process variables, and the system or environment considerations. Most of these are interdependent criteria and subject to considerable analysis. For this chapter we are going to assume that such tasks have been accomplished.

9.2 FIRST-ORDER LAG

A very important fundamental tool is the first-order lag or low pass filter. We saw an implementation of this circuit in Chapter 8 in a different setting (data acquisition). In data acquisition, as well as in control, filtering or smoothing signals before they enter the control process is frequently necessary. A simple filter, called a first-order lag filter, suppresses high noises. We simply wish to prevent high-frequency noises from entering our system, and we can do this with the expression shown in equation (9.2). This is the transfer function of a first-order lag. A transfer function relates the output of some system or process to its input. The function is actually a Laplace transfer function.

$$\frac{\text{Output}}{\text{Input}} = \frac{1}{T_1 S + 1} \tag{9.2}$$

The time constant in this circuit is T_1. This Laplace transform is not directly implementable in a microprocessor. In fact, the expression we can use is the following difference equation:

$$D_N = D_{N-1} + K(X - D_{N-1})$$

$$K = \frac{T_S}{T_S + T_1} \tag{9.3}$$

This recursive equation uses the input X to calculate an output D_N. After each evaluation D_N replaces D_{N-1}. The microcomputer now simply has to subtract, scale, and add D_{N-1} to obtain a new output D_N. The scale factor K is a function of sampling time, T_S, and the first-order lag-time constant, T_1.

The flexibility of the microprocessor to implement this first-order filter is now evident. If T_1 or T_S changes, a simple program entry is required. This is much easier than changing the analog equivalent if we were to use electrical circuits. In the electrical analog equivalent, a capacitor or an inductor must be changed physically, possibly requiring an expensive modification of the electronic circuitry itself.

9.3 DIGITAL CONTROL ALGORITHMS

Section 9.2 has covered a first-order lag process. We implemented this filter with a difference equation derived from the Laplace transfer function. In the simplest processes we would analyze the problem in a similar fashion starting with a transfer function and, later, generating a difference equation for the digital control algorithm.

There are many digital control algorithms. The most popular are the on–off, proportional, derivative, and integral control. In Section 9.5 we will

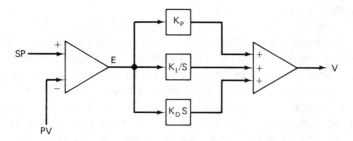

Figure 9.2. Ideal Proportional, Integral, Differential Control.

examine a PID digital control algorithm (proportional, integral, derivative). The PID digital control algorithm is often used where complete knowledge of the process or plant is lacking. Here, we would be delighted to control the process *within* a certain range (if enough information about the process is available). This is easy for the PID algorithm. We essentially tune the parameters in the algorithm to the process. However, this is not an exact solution, only an approximation. Still, it is often used.

For processes or plants that do not require full PID control, we can use one or more of the individual controls in the PID algorithm. For instance, if we desire simple proportional control, we could eliminate the derivative and integral control terms shown in equation (9.4). The equivalent block diagram for (9.4) is depicted in Figure 9.2.

$$\frac{\text{Output}}{\text{Input}} = K \left(1 + \underbrace{\frac{1}{T_I S}}_{} + \underbrace{T_D S}_{} \right) = \frac{V}{E} \tag{9.4}$$

Derivative term

Integral term

where

$$K_p = K$$
$$K_I = K/T_I$$
$$K_D = KT_D$$

Equation (9.4) represents an ideal noninteractive or Jordan canonical form of the PID algorithm in its Laplace form. We will use this Laplace transform later to derive the difference-equation expressions directly implementable in a microprocessor.

9.4 DERIVING DIGITAL CONTROL ALGORITHMS

The following procedure to derive digital control algorithms, although not exactly precise, suffices for many process control applications. As mentioned earlier, it is common to work with incomplete knowledge of the process or plant. Sometimes, an intuitive feeling for the plant behavior is all that is available. Often, only a model of the complex plant is assumed. In such circumstances, our first attempt is to use the PID algorithm or a crude version of it. We use the following steps to derive a digital control algorithm:

1. Obtain the analog transfer function of the control (Laplace expression).
2. Convert the analog transfer function to a differential-equation expression.
3. Convert the differential equation to a difference form.
4. Solve the expression for the present variables in terms of the past variables.

In step 1 the analog transfer function is a Laplace transform. The Laplace transforms of many transfer functions have been tabulated.[1] In step 2 we convert the Laplace equation to a differential equation.

In step 3 we change the expression from a differential equation to a difference form using equation (9.5).

$$\frac{dD}{dT} \cong \frac{D_N - D_{N-1}}{T_S} \tag{9.5}$$

The output D is a function of the previous value D_{N-1} and the sampling period T_S. The differential form on the left-hand side can be approximated by the difference form on the right-hand side. In the differential equation, substitute the right-hand side wherever the differential expression is found in step 3. Step 4 is merely a rearranging of the variables in the expression so so that the microprocessor can conveniently compute the present values in terms of past values alone.

The best way to understand this derivation technique is by example. Let us do just that. Note that every physically realizable process can eventually be described by a single differential equation or a set of differential equations. If we want to employ a digital computer to control a process, we must use a model. This mathematical model is the differential equation. To find the proper differential equation, we portray process behavior by a block diagram with input X and output Y, as shown in Figure 9.3.

The process behavior is described by a transfer function in Laplace notation. For example, the first-order lag in Section 9.2 has the transfer function

| STEP 1 |

$$\frac{Y}{X} = \frac{1}{T_1 S + 1} \tag{9.6}$$

---

[1] M. Abramowitz and I. A. Stegun, *Handbook of Mathematical Functions*, National Bureau of Standards AMS-55, U.S. Government Printing Office, Washington, D.C. June 1954.

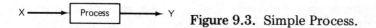

Figure 9.3. Simple Process.

S is an "operator" which can be replaced by d/dt after rearranging terms. For equation (9.6),

$$(T_1 S + 1) Y = X$$

or

STEP 2 $\qquad\qquad T_1 \dfrac{dY}{dt} + Y = X$ $\qquad\qquad$ (9.7)

Now the difference form is obtained by substituting for dY/dt as follows:

$$\frac{dY}{dt} \approx \frac{\Delta Y}{\Delta T} = \frac{Y_N - Y_{N-1}}{T_S}$$ $\qquad$ (9.8)

where T_S is the sampling period:

$$\Delta T = T_N - T_{N-1} = T_S$$ $\qquad$ (9.9)

For equation (9.7) we have

STEP 3 $\qquad\qquad T_1 \dfrac{Y_N - Y_{N-1}}{T_S} + Y_N = X$ $\qquad\qquad$ (9.10)

Now we rearrange equation (9.10) so that only Y_N appears on the left-hand side:

STEP 4 $\qquad\qquad Y_N = Y_{N-1} + \left(\dfrac{T_S}{T_S + T_1} \right) (X - Y_{N-1})$ $\qquad$ (9.11)

This is our difference equation suitable for implementation in the digital computer. To find the difference equation for any process, you follow steps 1 through 4.

A 6809 program that implements the first-order difference equation is shown in Example 9.1. We are using a macro called MULT which multiplies signed arguments in ACCA and a parameter passed by MULT. The product is found in ACCD. We could also have used the SMULT subroutine of Chapter 7, but we would then have to place operands on the U stack.

EXAMPLE 9.1:

```
* IMPLEMENTATION OF THE DIGITAL FILTER
* DESCRIBED BY
*    DN = DNM1 + K (XN − DNM1)
* WHERE,
```

```
*        DN = CURRENT OUTPUT
*        DNM1 = PREVIOUS OUTPUT
*        K = FILTER CONSTANT
*        XN = CURRENT INPUT
* ALL VARIABLES ARE LOCAL
* DNM1 IS INITIALIZED APPROPRIATELY
* AT THE START OF THE PROCESS BY THE CALLING
* PROGRAM
*
* STACK PICTURE ON ENTRY AND EXIT
*        U-0      STACK MARK
*        U-1      DNM1, PREVIOUS OUTPUT
*        U-2      DN, CURRENT OUTPUT
*        U-3      XN, CURRENT INPUT
*        U-4      K, MULTIPLIER
*        U-5      CAND, MULTICAND (PRODUCT AT EXIT)
* CALLING ROUTINE USES 8 * 8 SIGNED MULTIPLY
* SUBROUTINE, MULT, WHICH GENERATES AN 8 BIT UP-ROUNDED PRODUCT
* CALLING ROUTINE BODY (K ALREADY IN MULTIPLIER)
DIGFIL  PSHS       A,CCR
        LDA        DN,U
        STA        DNM1, U
        LDA        XN,U
        SUBA       DNM1,U
* OVERFLOW POSSIBLE!  BRANCH IF V=1 TO ERROR PRINTOUT
        LBVS       OVFL
        LDA        CAND,U
        LBSR       MULT
* SUBROUTINE, MULT, COMPUTES K(XN-DNM1) WITH
* PRODUCT IN ACCA AND CAND,U
        ADDA       DNM1,U
* NOW COMPUTE DNM1 + K(XN - DNM1), CHECK FOR OVERFLOW!
        LBVS       OVFL
        STA        DN,U
DONE    PULS       CCR,A,PC
* END OF CALLING ROUTINE
*
* STACK OFFSET VALUES FOR PARAMETERS
DNM1    EQU        -1
DN       "         -2
XN       "         -3
PLIER    "         -4
CAND     "         -5
```

9.5 A PID ALGORITHM FOR MICROPROCESSORS

In practice we find that most controls require a low-pass filter ahead of the process. Hence, the Laplace transform in equation (9.12) is more likely implemented than equation (9.4).

$$\frac{V}{E} = \left(\frac{K}{1 + T_F S}\right)\left(1 + \frac{1}{T_I S} + T_D S\right) \tag{9.12}$$

where T_F is the time constant of the low-pass filter.

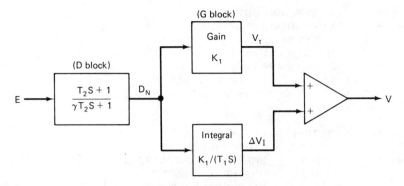

Figure 9.4. Interactive PID Algorithm for Microprocessors.

The low-pass filter is represented by the first factor in parentheses on the right-hand side of equation (9.12). The second set of terms on the right-hand side is the PID. The block diagram implementing the real or interactive form for this equation can be seen in Figure 9.4. The first block is now a "differential" block. By rearranging the terms according to Figure 9.4, we can easily implement this modified PID algorithm in a microprocessor. The difference expression for the D block is

$$D_N \cong D_{N-1} + \frac{1}{\gamma}(E_N - E_{N-1}) + \left(\frac{T_S}{\gamma T_2 + T_S}\right)(E_N - D_{N-1}) \qquad (9.13)$$

where we are assuming that T_S is much smaller than T_2. T_2 is the real derivative time constant and γ is a rate amplitude constant. If we must employ a low-pass filter as in equation (9.12), then $T_F = \gamma T_2$. The difference expression for the integral or I block is

$$V_I = K_1 \left(\frac{T_S}{T_1}\right) D_N \qquad (9.14)$$

The gain block expression is simple. From Figure 9.4 we see that $V_t = (K_1)(D_N)$. See Exercise 9 at the end of the chapter for details.

In Example 9.2 we have coded the 6809 to compute the transfer function of the differential block in Figure 9.4. Two macros, MULT and DIVIDE, are used in this routine. The MULT macro performs a signed 16-bit $\times$ 16-bit multiply on ACCA and the parameter transferred in the macro call. The product is found in ACCD. DIVIDE is a macro that divides two signed arguments, ACCA (dividend) and the parameter (divisor). The quotient is found in ACCA, and the remainder can be found in ACCB.

EXAMPLE 9.2: A Derivative Block

```
* IMPLEMENTATION OF DERIVATIVE BLOCK (DERBLK)
* DESCRIBED BY THE EQUATION
*
```

```
*                    1                    TS
* DN = DN-1 + — (EN - EN-1) + ——————— (EN - DN-1)
*                    R                 R*T2 + TS
* WHERE,
*           DN    = CURRENT OUTPUT
*           DN-1 = PREVIOUS OUTPUT
*           R     = RATE AMPLITUDE CONSTANT
*           T2    = REAL DERIVATIVE TIME CONSTANT
*           EN    = CURRENT INPUT
*                    TS
* LET K1 = ——————
*                 R*T2 + TS
*
*
* STACK PICTURE
*           U + 0           OLD STACK MARK
*           U - 1           DN
*           U - 2           DNM1
*           U - 3           EN
*           U - 4           ENM1
*           U - 5           R
*           U - 6           T2
*           U - 7           K1
*
* SUBROUTINE BODY
DERBLK  PSHS        B,A,CCR
        LDA         DN,U                    DEFINE OLD OUTPUT
        STA         DNM1,U
        LDA         EN,U
        SUBA        DNM1,U
        MULT        K1,U                    SCALE WITH TIME CONST.
        PSHS        A                       STACK SECOND TERM
        LDA         EN,U
        SUBA        ENM1,U
        DIVIDE      R,U                     ACCA ← ACCA/R, MACRO
        ADDA        DNM1,U
        ADDA        ,S+
        STA         DN,U                    OUTPUT READY
        LDB         EN,U
        STA         ENM1,U                  REDEFINE OLD INPUT
        PULS        CCR,A,B,PC
*
*
STACK OFFSET VALUES
DN      EQU         -1
DNM1    EQU         -2
EN      EQU         -3
ENM1    EQU         -4
R       EQU         -5
T2      EQU         -6
K1      EQU         -7
```

The integral block found in Figure 9.4 is implemented by the program in Example 9.3. Here again, we use the macros introduced in the previous examples. The algorithm implemented in code uses a simple rectangular integration rule. Two end points of each interval are used to calculate the area under the curve. Hence, N in the summation is just equal to 1. Better integration rules are available, one of which is found in Example 9.5.

EXAMPLE 9.3: An Integral Block

```
*
*               Y(t) = ∫₀^TN  D(t) dt
*
* IN DISCRETE FORM :
*
*               Y(t) = TS Σ_{i=0}^{n} Di
*
* STACK PICTURE
*         U + 0     OLD STACK MARK
*         U - 1     YN    : CURRENT INTEGRAL VALUE
*         U - 2     YNM1  : PREVIOUS INTEGRAL VALUE
*         U - 3     DN    : CURRENT INPUT
*         U - 4     TS    : SAMPLING PERIOD
*
INTBLK   PSHS    CCR, A
         LDA     YN, U              REDEFINE OLD INTEGRAL
         STA     YNM1, U
         DIVIDE  TS, U              MACRO CALL
         ADDA    DN, U              UPDATE SUM
         MULT    TS, U              GET INTEGRAL, MACRO CALL
         STA     YN, U              DONE
         PULS    A, CCR, PC
*
* STACK OFFSET VALUES
YN       EQU     -1
YNM1     EQU     -2
DN       EQU     -3
TS       EQU     -4
```

9.6 BETTER ALGORITHMS

In the previous examples we have used very simple derivative and integral forms. In practice, the derivative form previously seen is a first difference which can be quite noisy, since differentiation tends to accentuate high-frequency noise. A better difference form is the four-point central difference expression shown in equation (9.15) and reexpressed for microprocessor implementation in equation (9.16).

$$\tilde{E} = \frac{E_N + E_{N-1} + E_{N-2} + E_{N-3}}{4} \qquad (9.15)$$

$$\frac{\Delta E}{T_S} = \frac{1}{6T_S}(E_N - E_{N-3} + 3E_{N-1} - 3E_{N-2}) \qquad (9.16)$$

With this simple improvement we achieve some degree of smoothing by using three previous values of the signal instead of one. Example 9.4 lists the actual code.

EXAMPLE 9.4: 4-Point Central Difference

```
* IMPROVED DERIVATIVE COMPUTATION
* 4-POINT CENTRAL DIFFERENCE
* DELTAE = ( En – En–3 – 3*En–2 + 3*En–1 )/(6Ts)
* STACK PICTURE
*          U + 0      OLD STACK MARK
*          U – 1      EN
*          U – 2      ENM1
*          U – 3      ENM2
           U – 4      ENM3
*          U – 5      TS
*          U – 6      DELTAE
*
IMPDER PSHS        B,A,CCR
       LDA         ENM1,U
       SUBA        ENM2,U
       MULT        3              MACRO: ACCA ← 3*ACCA
       SUBA        ENM3,U
       ADDA        EN,U
       DIVIDE      6              MACRO: ACCA ← ACCA/6
       STA         DELTAE,U       OUTPUT READY
       LDB         ENM2,U         REDEFINE OLD VALUES
       STB         ENM3,U
       LDB         ENM1,U
       STB         ENM2,U
       STA         ENM1,U
       PULS        CCR,A,B,PC
*
STACK OFFSET VALUES
EN         EQU      –1
ENM1       EQU      –2
ENM2       EQU      –3
ENM3       EQU      –4
TS         EQU      –5
DELTAE EQU          –6
```

The integration algorithm seen in Example 9.3 can also be improved since this rectangular integral algorithm is the crudest form of integration for a digital computer. A better integration routine uses the trapezoidal rule:

$$\int_0^N e(t) \approx \sum_{i=0}^N \frac{e_{i+1} + e_i}{2} \tag{9.17}$$

The program in Example 9.5 lists an integration routine using a trapezoidal rule. The scaling factor, T_S, as found in Example 9.3 is not shown here and must be included.

EXAMPLE 9.5: Trapezoidal Integration

```
* IMPROVED INTEGRAL COMPUTATION
* THE RECTANGULAR INTEGRAL
*
*           N
*          ___
*          \   (e )
*          /__   i
*          i=0
*
* CAN BE REPLACED BY TRAPEZOIDAL RULE
*
*           N
*          ___
*          \   (e  + e   )/2
*          /__   i    i-1
*          i=0
*
* PRICE OF IMPROVEMENT IS MORE MEMORY
* AND COMPUTATIONAL TIME
*
* STACK PICTURE
*          U + 0         OLD STACK MARK
*          U - 1         EN
*          U - 2         ENM1
*          U - 3         INTEG
*
BINT      PSHS          A,B,CCR
          LDA           ENM1,U
          ADDA          EN,U
          ASRA
          ADDA          INTEG,U        INTEG HAS OLD VALUE
          STA           INTEG,U        INTEG GETS NEW VALUE
          LDB           EN,U
          STB           ENM1,U         REDEFINE OLD INPUT
          PULS          CCR,B,A,PC
*
* STACK OFFSET VALUES
EN        EQU           -1
ENM1      EQU           -2
INTEG     EQU           -3
```

9.7 DEADTIME COMPENSATION ALGORITHMS

In certain applications it is important to compensate for processes that simply do not respond to inputs or controls for a predictably finite period of time. This delay or deadtime is the time where no apparent action takes place in the system even though a control has been asserted. This is common in the steel industry, where a control attempts to form steel bars from rough feedstock when the event occurs after a delay, inherent in the process of forming steel bars. The process with deadtime control is shown in Figure 9.5. This procedure has been investigated by Smith[2] and Bibbero[3] who have shown that equations 9.18 through 9.21 can compensate for many deadtime effects.

[2] O. J. M. Smith, "Closer Control of Loops with Dead Time," *Chemical Engineering Progress*, vol. 53, 1957, pp. 217–219.
[3] R. J. Bibbero, *Microprocessors in Instruments and Control* (New York: Wiley-Interscience, 1977, pp. 165–168.)

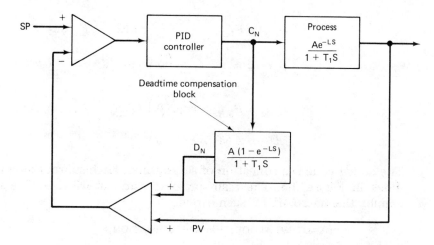

Figure 9.5. Process with Deadtime under Microprocessor Control.

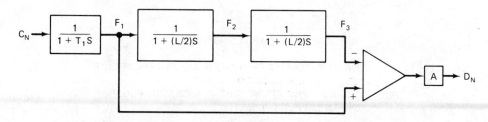

Figure 9.6. Deadtime Algorithm Partitioned for Microprocessor Implementation.

A program implementing the procedure (shown in Figure 9.6) suitable for microprocessors is given in Example 9.6. In this example we have coded the 6809 to approximate the deadtime algorithm required for Figure 9.5. We are implementing the deadtime compensation block of Figure 9.5 by partitioning this block into smaller blocks, as depicted in Figure 9.6. Equations, (9.18) to (9.21), which apply to the code, are represented by the four blocks in Figure 9.6. The actual code is a set of low-level modules, each of which is position-independent. Each low-level module implements a respective block in Figure 9.6. The higher-level module, DTALG, is the calling routine to each lower-level module.

EXAMPLE 9.6:   A Deadtime Computer Algorithm

In this example we have coded in the 6809 an approximation of the deadtime algorithm required for Figure 9.5. We are implementing the deadtime compensation block of Figure 9.5 by partitioning this block into smaller blocks shown in Figure 9.6. We use the following equations:

$$F_{1,N} = F_{1,N-1} + \frac{T_S}{T_1 + T_S} (C_N - F_{1,N-1}) \tag{9.18}$$

$$F_{2,N} = F_{2,N-1} + 2\left(\frac{T_S}{L}\right)(F_{1,N} - F_{2,N-1}) \tag{9.19}$$

$$F_{3,N} = F_{3,N-1} + 2\left(\frac{T_S}{L}\right)(F_{2,N} - F_{3,N-1}) \tag{9.20}$$

$$D_N = A(F_{1,N} - F_{3,N}) \tag{9.21}$$

The actual code is a collection of subroutines. Each subroutine implements a block in Figure 9.6. The main program starts at DTALG. The subroutines employ the macro MULT seen earlier.

```
* DEADTIME ALGORITHM APPROXIMATION
*
* EMPLOYS FOUR SUBROUTINES TO EVALUATE THE
* OUTPUT DN AT TIME t=NTS, GIVEN THE INPUT
* CN. THE LAPLACE TRANSFER FUNCTION IS
*
* D      A        ⎡        1          ⎤
* ─ = ────────── ⎢1 - ──────────────⎥
* C   T₁S + 1    ⎣    (1 + (L/2)S)**2 ⎦
*
* ONCE INITIATED THIS PROGRAM TAKES CARE OF
* THE PROCESS INDEFINITELY
* READS INPUT FROM PORT A AND SENDS OUTPUT
* THROUGH PORT B
*
* STACK PICTURE
*          U + 0        OLD STACK MARK
*          U – 1        F1N   : BLOCK 1 OUTPUT t=NTS
*          U – 2        F2N   : BLOCK 2 OUTPUT t=NTS
*          U – 3        F3N   : BLOCK 3 OUTPUT t=NTS
*          U – 4        DN    : OUTPUT          t=NTS
*          U – 5        F1NM1 : BLOCK 1 OUTPUT t=(N–1)TS
*          U – 6        F2NM1 : BLOCK 2 OUTPUT t=(N–1)TS
*          U – 7        F3NM1 : BLOCK 3 OUTPUT t=(N–1)TS
*          U – 8        CN    : INPUT          t=NTS
*          U – 9        K2    : BLOCK 1 CONSTANT
*          U – 10       K3    : BLOCK 2 CONSTANT
*          U – 11       A1    : BLOCK 4 CONSTANT
*
* CALLING ROUTINE SAVES SPACE, STACK MARK,
* AND PASSES PARAMETERS
* CALLING SEQUENCE :
*          PSHS         U              SAVE U
*          TFR          S,U            STACK MARK
*          LEAS         –11,S          RESERVE SPACE
*          .                           STACK PARAMETERS
*          .
*          .
*          LBSR         DTALG
```

```
*         TFR         U,S
*         PULS        U,PC
* DTAA ROUTINE BEGINS
*
DTALG  CLR         F1N,U                    INITIALIZE THE SYSTEM
       CLR         F2N,U
       CLR         F3N,U
WAIT   LDA         PIACRA                   CHECK INPUT STATUS
       BPL         WAIT
       LDA         PIADRA                   READ IN PORT A
       STA         CN,U
       LBSR        DTBLK1                   FIND F1N
       LBSR        DTBLK2                   FIND F2N
       LBSR        DTBLK3                   FIND F3N
       LBSR        DTBLK4                   FIND DN
       LDA         DN,U                     OUTPUT DN THROUGH
       STA         PIADRB                   PORT B
       BRA         WAIT
*
*
* IMPLEMENTATION OF LAG BLOCK 1 :
*
* F1         1
* ── = ───────
* C    T₁S + 1
* WHOSE DISCRETE SOLUTION IS
*
*                    Tₛ
* F1,N = F1,N−1 + ─────── (CN − F1,N−1)
*                  Tₛ + T₁
*
* LET Tₛ/(T₁ + Tₛ) BE DENOTED BY K2
*SINCE Tₛ ≪ T₁, K2 ≅ Tₛ/T₁ (APPROX.)
*      Tₛ = SAMPLING PERIOD
*      T₁ = FILTER LAG
DTBLK1 LDA         F1N,U                    CURRENT OUTPUT BECOMES
       STA         F1NM1                    OLD OUTPUT
       LDA         CN,U                     FIND NEW OUTPUT
       SUBA        F1NM1,U
       MULT        K2,U                     A ← A * K2
       ADDA        F1NM1,U
       STA         F1N,U                    OUTPUT READY
       PULS        PC                       EXIT
* IMPLEMENTATION OF BLOCK 2
*
* F2            1
* ── = ───────────
* F1    1 + (L/2)S
*
* WHOSE DISCRETE SOLUTION IS
*
* F2,N = F2,N−1 + 2 * (Tₛ/L) * (F1,N − F2,N−1)
*
* LET (Tₛ/L) = K3
*
```

```
DTBLK2  LDA     F2N,U           REPLACE OLD VALUE
        STA     F2NM1,U         WITH CURRENT VALUE
        LDA     F1N,U
        SUBA    F2NM1,U
        MULT    K3,U
        ASLA
        ADDA    F2NM1,U
        STA     F2N,U           OUTPUT READY
        PULS    PC              RETURN
*
*
*
* IMPLEMENTATION OF BLOCK 3
*
* F3          1
* ── = ───────────
* F2     1 + (L/2)S
*
* WHOSE DISCRETE SOLUTION IS
*
```

$*\ F3,N = F3,N-1 + 2 * (T_s/L) * (F2,N - F3,N-1)$

```
*
DTBLK3  LDA     F3N,U
        STA     F3NM1,U         DEFINE OLD OUTPUT
        LDA     F2N,U
        SUBA    F3NM1,U
        MULT    K3,U
        ASLA
        ADDA    F3NM1,U
        STA     F3N,U           OUTPUT READY
        PULS    PC              RETURN
*
*
*
* IMPLEMENTATION OF BLOCK 4
*
* DN = A1 * (F1,N - F3,N)
*
DTBLK4  LDA     F1N,U
        SUBA    F3NM1,U
        MULT    A1,U
        STA     DN,U            OUTPUT READY
        PULS    PC              RETURN
*
*
STACK OFFSET VALUES
*
F1N     EQU     -01
F2N     EQU     -02
F3N     EQU     -03
DN      EQU     -04
F1NM1   EQU     -05
F2NM1   EQU     -06
F3NM1   EQU     -07
CN      EQU     -08
```

```
K2      EQU     -09
K3      EQU     -10
A1      EQU     -11
PIADRA  EQU     ?               PIA PORT A ADDRESS
PIADRB  EQU     ?               PIA PORT B ADDRESS
PIACRA  EQU     ?               PIA PORT A CONTROL REG
```

9.8 INPUT/OUTPUT MODULES FOR MICROPROCESSOR-BASED CONTROLLERS

In this section by example we demonstrate a procedure to interface I/O modules to the microprocessor. Our problem is to convert a stage in a batch-processing plant to a microprocessor-controlled system using the I/O modules. As we do so, many incompatible voltages will be encountered. To help us, the industry supplies various types of I/O modules: (1) output modules that convert the output voltage of an MPU or discrete logic system into a driving source for an external device, and (2) input modules that convert a relatively high voltage from an external source into a 5- or 15-V dc signal for an MPU or a logic system. Characteristics of the I/O modules available from Motorola are given in Tables 9.1 and 9.2 and their internal structures are shown in Figure 9.7.

Output modules directly drive machines that manipulate large voltages and/or currents and devices with small power requirements. They can drive fractional horsepower motors, small heaters, solenoid valves, or lamps directly. If you wish to drive large loads, an intermediate driver is necessary. Optocoupling, often used with the I/O modules, provides very high insulation between input and output signals and is a very satisfactory alternative.

Interfacing the I/O modules is straightforward. Usually, the module is in series with the load and a fuse is provided for protection. A TTL output will be able to drive the module directly. The circuit in Figure 9.7a can be used for standard TTL Schottky (S), low-power Schottky (LS), and high-speed (H) series devices. A buffer is needed for low-power TTL (L) devices. Figure 9.7a shows a LED in series with the input, which acts as status indicator. The LED is turned on when the module is driving the load (logic input = 1).

Table 9.1	Output Modules	
Type Number	Logic Input (V dc)	Output
OAC5	5	140 V ac
OAC5A	5	280 V ac
OAC15	15	140 V ac
OAC15A	15	280 V ac
ODC5	8	60 V dc
ODC15	15	60 V dc

Table 9.2	Input Modules	
Type Number	Input	Logic Output (V dc)
IAC5	140 V ac	5
IAC5A	280 V ac	5
IAC15	140 V ac	15
IAC15A	280 V ac	15
IDC5	32 V dc	5
IDC15	60 V dc	15

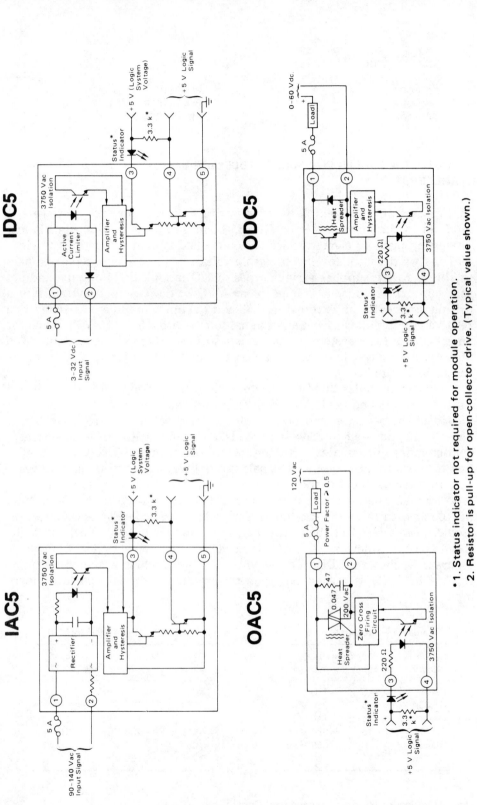

Figure 9.7. Typical I/O Module Circuits and Examples of External Interface Components. (Courtesy of Motorola Semiconductor Products, Inc.)

Interfacing the modules to MOS logic requires more circuitry because we must buffer the MOS. A TTL device may be used as buffer and this is sufficient for most NMOS devices. For CMOS operating on 5 V, a low-power Schottky device may be used as buffer. Another way to interface the modules with MOS devices is to use a single saturating transistor. This is shown in Figure 9.7b. By changing the value of R1 to 39 kΩ, the circuit in Figure 9.7b can be used to interface a CMOS operating at 15 V with 15-V logic modules OAC15, OAC15A, and ODC15. Since input modules are open-collector, it is very simple to interface them. All you need is a pull-up register (Figure 9.7c and d). An optional status indicator LED is also shown.

Let us suppose that you want to automate a typical industrial application, a mixing tank in a batch-processing plant (Figure 9.8). Liquids pass through several stages before they are said to be processed. The mixing tank is one of several stages. Three liquids from three inlet valves pour into the tank. After the tank is filled, the stirring motor is started and the immersion heater is turned on. This continues until the mixture is raised uniformly to a preset temperature. Then the outlet valve is opened to pass the mixture to next stage. The liquid level in the tank is sensed by level sensors while a thermostat senses the temperature. The characteristics of the equipment are as follows:

1. Stirring Motor: $\frac{3}{4}$ hp, 120 V ac, one-phase; starter 120 V ac, 250 mA.
2. Three inlet valves: dc-solenoid-operated, 24 V dc, 1.2 A.
3. Outlet valve: dc-solenoid-operated, 24 V dc, 2.0 A.
4. Immersion heater: 200-W resistive coil, 120 V ac, 1.7 A.

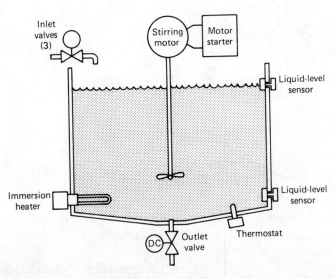

Figure 9.8. Mixing Tank with Makeup Heater. (Courtesy of Motorola Semiconductor Products, Inc.)

5. Two liquid-level sensors: SPST N.C. contacts.

6. Thermostat: SPST N.C. contacts.

EXAMPLE 9.7: A Mixer Tank Process Controller

```
* INTERFACING OF I/O MODULES AS IN FIGURES 9.7 AND 9.9
* THIS ROUTINE CONTROLS THE MIXER TANK THROUGH
* ONE PORT OF A PIA
* BANG-BANG CONTROL (SIMPLE ON/OFF) IS ASSUMED.
* THIS CODE IS POSITION-INDEPENDENT.
* PORT A USAGE:
*          PAO-3      OUTPUT        INLET VALVES
*          PA3        OUTPUT        OUTLET VALVE
*          PA4        OUTPUT        HEATER
*          PA5        OUTPUT        STIRRER
*          PA6-7      UNUSED
* PORT B USAGE:
*          PBO        INPUT         UPPER LEVEL SENSOR
*          PB1        INPUT         LOWER LEVEL SENSOR
*          PB2        INPUT         THERMOSTAT
*          PB3-7      UNUSED
* INITIALIZE PIA
```

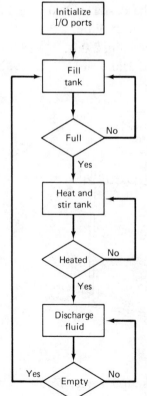

Figure 9.9. Interface Connections to Power Sources and PIA. (Courtesy of Motorola Semiconductor Products, Inc.)

```
TANK     LDX      #PIADRA        LOAD PIA BASE ADDRESS
         LBSR     PIAINIT
* FILL THE TANK
REPEAT   LDA      #%00000111     CLOSE OUTLET VALVE,
                                 SHUT OFF HEATER &
                                 STIRRER
         STA      X              OPEN INLET VALVES
FILL     LDA      2,X            READ PORT B
         ANDA     #01            IS TANK FULL?
         BEQ      FILL           NO, GO FILL
* START MIXING AND HEATING
         LDA      #%00110000     YES, CLOSE INLET VALVES
         STA      X              START HEATER & STIRRER
HEAT     LDA      2,X            CHECK FOR TEMPERATURE
         ANDA     #04            HEATED?
         BEQ      HEAT           NO, HEAT
* EMPTY THE TANK
         LDA      #%00001000     YES, STOP MIXING
         STA      X              & OPEN OUTLET VALVE
EMPTY    LDA      2,X
         ANDA     #02            IS TANK EMPTY?
         BNE      EMPTY          NO, EMPTY IT
         BRA      REPEAT         YES, REPEAT ACTIONS
* ROUTINE PIAINIT INITIALIZES PIA FOR THE
* CONFIGURATION DESCRIBED ABOVE
PIAINIT  LDA      #$FF           MAKE PORT A OUTPUT
         CLR      1,X            ACCESS DDRA
         STA      X
         LDA      #$04
         STA      1,X
         CLR      3,X            MAKE PORT B INPUT
         CLR      2,X
         STA      3,X
         PULS     PC
```

SUMMARY

In this chapter we have illustrated simple procedures (by example) for the digital computer control algorithms using PID control. We have ignored several theoretical issues, including the Laplace transform, and the more elaborate procedures for control, such as the Z transform, optimal control, and stability. These important theoretical topics are necessary for your understanding in developing new algorithms. Also, our procedure for deriving digital control algorithms is only one of several powerful methods. However, all of these issues have been addressed in the literature.

Many of the theoretical considerations for developing digital control algorithms can be found in several texts. The equations used in this chapter can be found in the book by Bibbero.[3] The theoretical concepts of sampled

[3] R. J. Bibbero, *Microprocessors in Instruments and Control* (New York: Wiley–Interscience, 1977.

data techniques can be found in the books by Tou[4] and Koppel.[5] The intent of this chapter is to show you that the microprocessor can effectively implement digital algorithms for a process control system.

EXERCISES

1. An important tool in process control is the lead–lag compensation shown in Figure 9.10.

$$D_N = D_{N-1} + \frac{T_S}{T_1 + T_S}(X_N - D_{N-1}) \qquad \text{lag equation}$$

$$C_N' = \frac{T_2(D_N - D_{N-1})}{T_S} + D_N \qquad \text{lead equation}$$

$$C_N = KC_N' \qquad \text{gain equation}$$

Given the expression for the lag, lead, and gain block, generate microcomputer code for the

a. Lag block
b. Lead block
c. Gain block

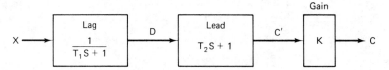

Figure 9.10. Lead–Lag Compensation.

2. Suppose that sample time, T_S, is equivalent to T_2, the real derivative time constant. Rederive equation (9.13).

3. The PID algorithm will "bump" (exhibit a harmful, abrupt change in output) when step inputs occur. Generate a "bumpless" or velocity algorithm for the PID controller. Assume that the Laplace transform is

$$\left(\frac{T_2 S + 1}{\gamma T_2 S + 1}\right)\left(K_1 S + \frac{K_1}{T_1}\right)\left(\frac{1}{S}\right)$$

How would you depict this bumpless real PID algorithm in a block diagram?

4. Generate the difference expression for the noninteractive or separated-mode PID algorithm of equation (9.13).

[4] J. T. Tou, *Digital and Sampled-Data Control Systems* (New York: McGraw-Hill, 1959).
[5] L. B. Koppel, *Introduction to Control Theory* (Englewood Cliffs, N.J.: Prentice-Hall, 1968.

5. A PID algorithm also suitable for microprocessors is

$$V_N = KE_N + K_i \sum_{i=0}^{N} E_i T_s + K_D \left(\frac{E_N - E_{N-1}}{T_S} \right) + V_m$$

where $K_I = K/T_I$, $K_D = KT_D$, and V_m is the average set-point value. Generate a program to implement this expression.

6. All programs in this chapter could be speeded up. What methods are possible? What are you sacrificing?

7. In Example 9.1 assume that a 6809 is running at 1 MHz. How fast does this program update DN. Assume SMULT is handled by the signed multiply routine found in Chapter 5.

8. Except for Example 9.1, we have not checked for overflow. If you do not scale your input scales properly, what must you do in

a) Example 9.2   c) Example 9.4
b) Example 9.3   d) Example 9.5

9. Figure 9.4 does not follow directly from equation (9.12). Historically, the analog form for the "real" or interactive PID is

$$\frac{V}{E} = \frac{T_2 S + 1}{\gamma T_2 + 1} K_1 \left(1 + \frac{1}{T_1 S} \right)$$

where T_1 = real integral time constant and T_2 = real derivative time constant. This form is interactive because the parameters are related and cannot be set or "tuned" separately. If $T_F = \gamma T_2$, show that the real form and equation (9.12) are identical if

$$K = K_1 \frac{T_1 + T_2}{T_1} \qquad T_D = \frac{T_1 T_2}{T_I}$$

$$T_I = T_1 + T_2$$

What happens if $T_2 \ll T_1$?

BIBLIOGRAPHY

ANDREWS, MICHAEL. *Principles of Firmware Engineering in Microprogram Control.* Maryland: Computer Science Press, 1980. Chapter Six demonstrates a useful design technique, the Algorithmic State Machine or ASM, applied to controlling numerical control machinery (vertical miller).

BAKER, PAUL W. "The Solution of Differential Equations on Short Word Length Computing Devices," *IEEE Transactions on Computers,* vol. C-78, Mar. 1979, pp. 205-215. The numerical solution of differential equations for dynamic simulation is described in microprocessor word lengths. A theoretical analysis of the truncation error and possible controls in the digital differential analyzer (DDA) to suppress truncation error is offered.

CADZOW, JAMES A. *Discrete-Time Systems*. Englewood Cliffs, N.J.: Prentice-Hall, 1973. This engineering text describes methods that employ the transform for modeling transfer-function system response. The material is nicely developed from the Laplace transform and should serve as a comprehensive introduction to the material required for developing mathematical models for real systems.

CADZOW, JAMES A., AND HINRICH R. MARTENS. *Discrete-Time and Computer Control Systems*. Englewood Cliffs, N.J.: Prentice-Hall, 1970. The powerful notions of state-variable techniques using the inverse Z transform and one-sided Z transform is described. Many open-loop and closed-loop sampled data systems are developed for low-order processes. The appendix contains useful Fortran computer programs for dead beat control.

KUO, BENJAMIN. *Analysis and Synthesis of Sampled-Data Control Systems*. Englewood Cliffs, N.J.: Prentice-Hall, 1963. This advanced-level textbook covers useful design and synthesis procedures for digital controllers, including nonlinear sampled data control systems. A procedure for statistical analysis and design is examined using the mean-square-error criterion. The important topic of multirate and skip sampling is also covered.

LANDAU, JACK V. "State Description Techniques Applied to Industrial Machine Control," *Computers*, Feb. 1979, pp. 32–40. Describes the state language for developing control software and using structured programming techniques for microprocessors with application to sewing machines.

LIPTAK, BELAG, ED. *Instrumentation in the Processing Industries*. Philadelphia: Chilton, 1973. This handbook is a collection of papers addressing the fundamental issues of control in the chemical, steel, electrical, and glassmaking industries. Several monographs related to the control process are provided in the many papers. The discussion is generally at the intermediate or advanced level, so that only a specialist in each discipline can fully understand the material. However, an occasional introductory paper is provided. Few mathematical relationships are established.

SEELY, SAMUEL, NORMAN H. TARNOFF, AND DAVID HOLSTEIN. *Digital Computers in Engineering*. New York: Holt, Rinehart and Winston, 1970. This textbook advances numerous programs to solve a number of filtering, correlation, and noise-reduction problems for data acquisition and control systems. Discusses Fourier transforms and integration techniques such as the Runge–Kutta. This is an intermediate- to advanced-level text readable by most practicing engineers. A short section on adaptive control, including error checking and roundoff, is provided.

Appendices

A

General Loading Considerations

A.1 RULE OF THUMB FOR TTL

Choose loads to outputs of 6809 to ensure unequivocal interpretation of both a logical "1" (that is, greater than 2.4 V for TTL) and a logical "0" (less than 0.4 V for TTL).

Ensure that worst-case path delay caused by capacitive loading does not cause race conditions in the hardware. The TTL family loading rules follow.

The Thévenin equivalent circuits for the loading specifications of Tables A.1 and A.2 are shown in Figures A.1 and A.2, respectively.

Table A.1   **Output Drive**

	Logic Family $\longrightarrow$	74LSxx	74xx	74Sxx
1	Minimum guaranteed source current with output pulled down to 2.4 V	400 μA	400 μA	1000 μA
0	Minimum guaranteed sink current with output pulled up to 0.4 V	9 mA	16 mA	20 mA

Logic Family →	74LSxx	74xx	74Sxx
1 Maximum current with input pulled up to 2.4 V	20 μA	40 μA	50 μA
0 Maximum current with input pulled down to 0.4 V	0.36 mA	1.6 mA	2.0 mA

Output drive
(worst-case circuits)

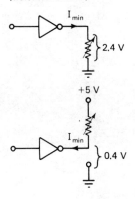

Figure A.1. TTL Output Loads.

Input loading
(worst-case circuits)

Figure A.2. TTL Input Loads.

A.2 RULE OF THUMB FOR CMOS

Since a CMOS input looks like an open circuit (a CMOS input draws 10 pA!), ensure that the expected voltage from an unloaded output (say, from the 6809) meets the design specification for the chosen operating range of the CMOS device.

EXAMPLE A.1:   A 6809 to CMOS load

CMOS devices operate over a wide voltage range (3 to 15 V). In fact, a CMOS inverter curve looks as shown in Figure A.3 for a 5-V power source. Suppose that we operate our CMOS at 5 V.

Rule of Thumb for CMOS

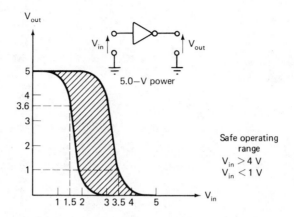

Figure A.3. CMOS Inverter Curve.

Can a 6809 output line drive this CMOS inverter and a 74xx load at the same time?

Answer: At a logical "1," a 6809 output line can deliver 205 μA at 2.4 V to externals. From Table A.2 the 74xx could need (worst case) 40 μA. The CMOS input is essentially an open circuit so we will not exceed this specification. But we are not done. We also want to know what the 6809 does at 4 V output, not 2.4V.

Suppose that it delivers only 50 μA at 4 V (you will need to verify this with the 6809 manufacturer). At 4 V, the 6809 with a CMOS and TTL load does not work under our assumption. For completeness, let us check what happens at logical "0." The 6809 can accept 2.0×10^{-3} A, I_{LOAD}, when $V_{OL} = V_{SS} + 0.5$. If $V_{SS} = 0$, then $V_{OL} \leqslant 0.5$. From Table A.2, at 0.4 V, a 74xx input could leak or "source" back to the 6809, 1.6 mA, and the 6809 will still "say" that a logical "0" appears at the line (recall that the 6809 will stay below 0.4 V at logical "0" only if the load does not try to push more than 2 mA into the 6809 *output* line when the power supply voltage is 5 - 0.25 or 4.75 V. Hence, we have no problem at logical "0" with mixed loads on a 6809 output line.

6809 outputs that are said to be TTL-compatible will support TTL and CMOS together at the logical 0 requirement. However, the 6809 output cannot support both TTL and CMOS at the logical 1 level. So mixing TTL and CMOS on the same output line is not advised.

Notice that a specification which tells us that the output can source 40 μA at 2.4 V (typical of TTL specifications) does not help us to answer a CMOS question.

6809
Product Specifications[1]

MAXIMUM RATINGS

Rating		Symbol	Value	Unit
Supply Voltage		V_{CC}	-0.3 to $+7.0$	Vdc
Input Voltage		V_{in}	-0.3 to $+7.0$	Vdc
Operating Temperature Range		T_A	0 to $+70$	°C
Storage Temperature Range		T_{stg}	-55 to $+150$	°C
Thermal Resistance	Ceramic	Θ_{JA}	50	°C/W
	Plastic		100	°C/W

ELECTRICAL CHARACTERISTICS (V_{CC} = 5.0 V ±5%, V_{SS} = 0, T_A = 0 to 70°C unless otherwise noted)

Characteristic		Symbol	Min	Typ	Max	Unit
Input High Voltage	Logic, EXtal, $\overline{RESET}$	V_{IH}	$V_{SS} + 2.0$ $V_{SS} + 4.0$	— —	V_{CC} V_{CC}	Vdc
Input Low Voltage	Logic, EXtal, $\overline{RESET}$	V_{IL}	$V_{SS} - 0.3$	—	$V_{SS} + 0.8$	Vdc
Input Leakage Current (V_{in} = 0 to 5.25 V, V_{CC} = max)	Logic	I_{in}	—	1.0	2.5	μAdc
Output High Voltage (I_{Load} = -205 μAdc, V_{CC} = min) (I_{Load} = -145 μAdc, V_{CC} = min) (I_{Load} = -100 μAdc, V_{CC} = min)	D0-D7 A0-A15, R/$\overline{W}$, Q, E BA, BS	V_{OH}	$V_{SS} + 2.4$ $V_{SS} + 2.4$ $V_{SS} + 2.4$	— — —	— — —	Vdc
Output Low Voltage (I_{Load} = 2.0 mAdc, V_{CC} = min)		V_{OL}	—	—	$V_{SS} + 0.5$	Vdc
Power Dissipation		P_D	—	—	1.0	W
Capacitance # (V_{in} = 0, T_A = 25°C, f = 1.0 MHz)	D0-D7 Logic Inputs, EXtal	C_{in}	— —	10 7	15 10	pF
	A0-A15, R/$\overline{W}$, BA, BS	C_{out}	—	—	12	pF
Frequency of Operation (Crystal or External Input)	MC6809 MC68A09 MC68B09	f_{XTAL}	— — —	— — —	4 6 8	MHz
Three-State (Off State) Input Current (V_{in} = 0.4 to 2.4 V, V_{CC} = max)	D0-D7 A0-A15, R/$\overline{W}$	I_{TSI}	— —	2.0 —	10 100	μAdc

[1] Reprinted courtesy of Motorola Semiconductor Products, Inc.

READ/WRITE TIMING

Characteristic	Symbol	MC6809			MC68A09			MC68B09			Unit
		Min	Typ	Max	Min	Typ	Max	Min	Typ	Max	
Cycle Time	t_{CYC}	1000	–	–	667	–	–	500	–	–	ns
Total Up Time	t_{UT}	975	–	–	640	–	–	480	–	–	ns
Peripheral Read Access Time $t_{UT} - t_{AD} - t_{DSR} = t_{ACC}$	t_{ACC}	695	–	–	440	–	–	320	–	–	ns
Data Setup Time (Read)	t_{DSR}	80	–	–	60	–	–	40	–	–	ns
Input Data Hold Time	t_{DHR}	10	–	–	10	–	–	40	–	–	ns
Output Data Hold Time	t_{DHW}	30	–	–	30	–	–	30	–	–	ns
Address Hold Time (Address, R/$\overline{W}$)	t_{AH}	20	–	–	20	–	–	20	–	–	ns
Address Delay	t_{AD}	–	–	200	–	–	140	–	–	110	ns
Data Delay Time (Write)	t_{DDW}	–	–	225	–	–	180	–	–	145	ns
E_{low} to Q_{high} Time	t_{AVS}	–	–	250	–	–	165	–	–	125	ns
Address Valid to Q_{high}	t_{AQ}	50	–	–	25	–	–	15	–	–	ns
Processor Clock Low	t_{PWEL}	450	–	–	295	–	–	210	–	–	ns
Processor Clock High	t_{PWEH}	450	–	–	280	–	–	220	–	–	ns
MRDY Set Up Time	t_{PCSM}	125	–	–	125	–	–	125	–	–	ns
Interrupts Set Up Time	t_{PCS}	200	–	–	140	–	–	110	–	–	ns
HALT Set Up Time	t_{PCSH}	200	–	–	140	–	–	110	–	–	ns
RESET Set Up Time	t_{PCSR}	200	–	–	140	–	–	110	–	–	ns
DMA/BREQ Set Up Time	t_{PCSD}	125	–	–	125	–	–	125	–	–	ns
Crystal Osc Start Time	t_{RC}	100	–	–	100	–	–	100	–	–	ms
E Rise and Fall Time	t_{Er}, t_{Ef}	5	–	25	5	–	25	5	–	20	ns
Processor Control Rise/Fall	t_{PCr}, t_{PCf}	–	–	100	–	–	100	–	–	100	ns
Q Rise and Fall Time	t_{Qr}, t_{Qf}	5	–	25	5	–	25	5	–	20	ns
Q Clock High	t_{PWQH}	450	–	–	280	–	–	220	–	–	ns

C

6821 Specifications: Internal Controls[1]

There are six locations within the PIA accessible to the MPU data bus: two peripheral registers, two data direction registers, and two control registers. Selection of these locations is controlled by the RS0 and RS1 inputs together with bit 2 in the control register, as shown in Table C.1.

Table C.1   Internal Addressing

RS1	RS0	Control Register Bit		Location Selected
		CRA-2	CRB-2	
0	0	1	X	Peripheral Register A
0	0	0	X	Data Direction Register A
0	1	X	X	Control Register A
1	0	X	1	Peripheral Register B
1	0	X	0	Data Direction Register B
1	1	X	X	Control Register B

X = Don't Care

[1] Reprinted courtesy of Motorola Semiconductor Products, Inc.

C.1 INITIALIZATION

A low reset line has the effect of zeroing all PIA registers. This will set PA0–PA7, PB0–PB7, CA2, and CB2 as inputs, and all interrupts disabled. The PIA must be configured during the restart program which follows the reset.

Details of possible configurations of the data direction and control register are as follows.

C.2 DATA DIRECTION REGISTERS (DDRA AND DDRB)

The two data direction registers allow the MPU to control the direction of data through each corresponding peripheral data line. A data direction register bit set at "0" configures the corresponding peripheral data line as an input; a "1" results in an output.

C.3 CONTROL REGISTERS (CRA AND CRB)

The two control registers (CRA and CRB) allow the MPU to control the operation of the four peripheral control lines: CA1, CA2, CB1, and CB2. In addition, they allow the MPU to enable the interrupt lines and monitor the status of the interrupt flags. Bits 0 through 5 of the two registers may be written or read by the MPU when the proper chip select and register select signals are applied. Bits 6 and 7 of the two registers are read only and are modified by external interrupts occurring on control lines CA1, CA2, CB1, or CB2. The format of the control words is shown in Table C.2.

Data Direction Access Control Bit (CRA-2 and CRB-2)

Bit 2 in each Control register (CRA and CRB) allows selection of either a peripheral interface register or the data direction register when the proper register select signals are applied to RS0 and RS1.

Table C.2   Control Word Format

	7	6	5	4	3	2	1	0
CRA	IRQA1	IRQA2	CA2 Control			DDRA Access	CA1 Control	

	7	6	5	4	3	2	1	0
CRB	IRQB1	IRQB2	CB2 Control			DDRB Access	CB1 Control	

Table C.3   Control of Interrupt Inputs CA1 and CB1

CRA-1 (CRB-1)	CRA-0 (CRB-0)	Interrupt Input CA1 (CB1)	Interrupt Flag CRA-7 (CRB-7)	MPU Interrupt Request IRQA (IRQB)
0	0	↓ Active	Set high on ↓ of CA1 (CB1)	Disabled — IRQ remains high
0	1	↓ Active	Set high on ↓ of CA1 (CB1)	Goes low when the interrupt flag bit CRA-7 (CRB-7) goes high
1	0	↑ Active	Set high on ↑ of CA1 (CB1)	Disabled — IRQ remains high
1	1	↑ Active	Set high on ↑ of CA1 (CB1)	Goes low when the interrupt flag bit CRA-7 (CRB-7) goes high

Notes: 1.   ↑ indicates positive transition (low to high)

2.   ↓ indicates negative transition (high to low)

3.   The Interrupt flag bit CRA-7 is cleared by an MPU Read of the A Data Register. and CRB-7 is cleared by an MPU Read of the B Data Register.

4.   If CRA-0 (CRB-0) is low when an interrupt occurs (Interrupt disabled) and is later brought high, IRQA (IRQB) occurs after CRA-0 (CRB-0) is written to a "one".

Interrupt Flags (CRA-6, CRA-7, CRB-6, and CRB-7)

The four interrupt flag bits are set by active transitions of signals on the four interrupt and peripheral control lines when those lines are programmed to be inputs. These bits cannot be set directly from the MPU data bus and are reset indirectly by a read peripheral data operation on the appropriate section.

Control of CA1 and CB1 Interrupt Input Lines (CRA-0, CRB-0, CRA-1, and CRB-1)

The two lowest-order bits of the control registers are used to control the interrupt input lines CA1 and CB1. Bits CRA-0 and CRB-0 are used to enable the MPU interrupt signals IRQA and IRQB, respectively. Bits CRA-1 and CRB-1 determine the active transition of the interrupt input signals CA1 and CB1 (Table C.3).

Control of CA2 and CB2 Peripheral Control Lines (CRA-3, CRA-4, CRA-5, CRB-3, CRB-4, and CRB-5)

Bits 3, 4, and 5 of the two control registers are used to control the CA2 and CB2 peripheral control lines. There bits determine if the control lines will be an interrupt input or an output control signal. If bit CRA-5 (CRB-5) is low, CA2 (CB2) is an interrupt input line similar to CA1 (CB1) (Table C.4). When CRA-5 (CRB-5) is high, CA2 (CB2) becomes an output signal that may be used to control peripheral data transfers. When in the output mode, CA2 and CB2 have slightly different characteristics (Tables C.5 and C.6).

Table C.4   Control of CA2 and CB2 as Interrupt Inputs
[CRA-5 (CRB-5) Is Low]

CRA-5 (CRB-5)	CRA-4 (CRB-4)	CRA-3 (CRB-3)	Interrupt Input CA2 (CB2)	Interrupt Flag CRA-6 (CRB-6)	MPU Interrupt Request $\overline{\text{IRQA}}$ ($\overline{\text{IRQB}}$)
0	0	0	↓ Active	Set high on ↓ of CA2 (CB2)	Disabled — $\overline{\text{IRQ}}$ remains high
0	0	1	↓ Active	Set high on ↓ of CA2 (CB2)	Goes low when the interrupt flag bit CRA-6 (CRB-6) goes high
0	1	0	↑ Active	Set high on ↑ of CA2 (CB2)	Disabled — $\overline{\text{IRQ}}$ remains high
0	1	1	↑ Active	Set high on ↑ of CA2 (CB2)	Goes low when the interrupt flag bit CRA-6 (CRB-6) goes high

Notes: 1. ↑ indicates positive transition (low to high)

       2. ↓ indicates negative transition (high to low)

       3. The Interrupt flag bit CRA-6 is cleared by an MPU Read of the A Data Register and CRB-6 is cleared by an MPU Read of the B Data Register.

       4. If CRA-3 (CRB-3) is low when an interrupt occurs (Interrupt disabled) and is later brought high, IRQA (IRQB) occurs after CRA-3 (CRB-3) is written to a "one".

Table C.5   Control of CB2 as an Output
(CRB-5 Is High)

CRB-5	CRB-4	CRB-3	CB2 Cleared	Set
1	0	0	Low on the positive transition of the first E pulse following an MPU Write "B" Data Register operation.	High when the interrupt flag bit CRB-7 is set by an active transition of the CB1 signal.
1	0	1	Low on the positive transition of the first E pulse after an MPU Write "B" Data Register operation.	High on the positive edge of the first "E" pulse following an "E" pulse which occurred while the part was deselected.
1	1	0	Low when CRB-3 goes low as a result of an MPU Write in Control Register "B".	Always low as long as CRB-3 is low. Will go high on an MPU Write in Control Register "B" that changes CRB-3 to "one".
1	1	1	Always high as long as CRB-3 is high. Will be cleared when an MPU Write Control Register "B" results in clearing CRB-3 to "zero".	High when CRB-3 goes high as a result of an MPU Write into Control Register "B".

Table C.6   Control of CA2 as an Output
(CRA-5 Is High)

CRA-5	CRA-4	CRA-3	CA2 Cleared	Set
1	0	0	Low on negative transition of E after an MPU Read "A" Data operation.	High when the interrupt flag bit CRA-7 is set by an active transition of the CA1 signal.
1	0	1	Low on negative transition of E after an MPU Read "A" Data operation.	High on the negative edge of the first "E" pulse which occurs during a deselect.
1	1	0	Low when CRA-3 goes low as a result of an MPU Write to Control Register "A".	Always low as long as CRA-3 is low. Will go high on an MPU Write to Control Register "A" that changes CRA-3 to "one".
1	1	1	Always high as long as CRA-3 is high. Will be cleared on an MPU Write to Control Register "A" that clears CRA-3 to a "zero".	High when CRA-3 goes high as a result of an MPU Write to Control Register "A".

D

The MC6850:
An Asynchronous
Communications
Interface Adapter

The 6850 is a general-purpose asynchronous communications interface adapter that does data framing for serial transmission (see Figures D.1 and D.2). The unit is also interfaced directly to the 6809 bus, for direct memory-mapped I/O. Data-stream conversion can occur in both directions, together with formatting and error detection. Variable word lengths, interrupt control, transceive control, modem control, and clock dividers provide a very versa-

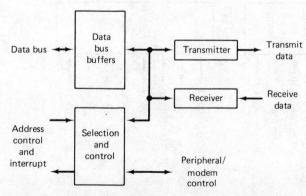

Figure D.1. MC6850 Asynchronous Communications Interface Adapter Block Diagram. (Courtesy of Motorola Semiconductor Products, Inc.)

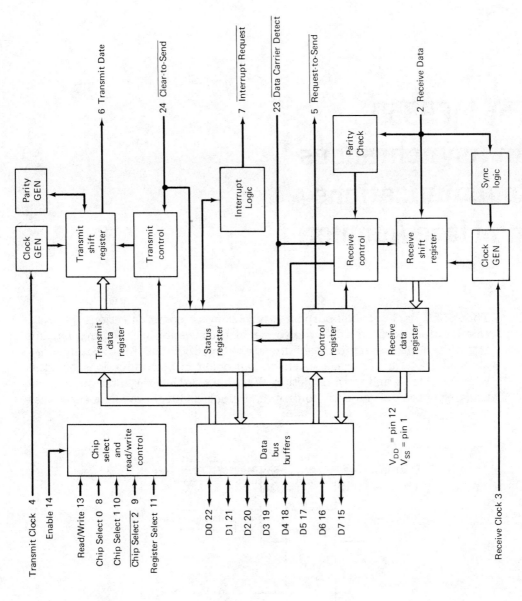

Figure D.2. Expanded Block Diagram of Figure D.1. (Courtesy of Motorola Semiconductor Products, Inc.)

The MC6850: An Asynchronous Communications Interface Adapter

tile type of converter. The unit does not have an on-board clock but may be used with the MC1411 clock generator.

D.1 POWER-UP

The 6850 chip has internal reset circuitry that hold the master reset bit in the control word low until set by the MPU. This assures that no activity occurs before the exact moment. CR0 and CR1 are the two bits that must be triggered before talking to the other control bits. The control register is selected by appropriate decoding of control lines from the MPU (see Table D.1 for details).

D.2 CONTROL REGISTER

The control register stipulates the operating mode of the ACIA, so programming must be specific. CR0 and CR1 control the clock divider and the master reset (Table D.2). The baud rate will most likely be set here. CR2, CR3, and CR4 control the type of transceiving. The types of parity, stop bits, and bit strings are defined by Table D.3. CR5 and CR6 control the transmit interrupt and the request-to-send line (Table D.4). The transmit

Table D.1   Definition of ACIA Register Contents

Data Bus Line Number	Buffer Address			
	RS • $\overline{\text{R/W}}$ Transmit Data Register	RS • R/W Receive Data Register	$\overline{\text{RS}}$ • $\overline{\text{R/W}}$ Control Register	$\overline{\text{RS}}$ • R/W Status Register
	(Write Only)	(Read Only)	(Write Only)	(Read Only)
0	Data Bit 0*	Data Bit 0	Counter Divide Select 1 (CR0)	Receive Data Register Full (RDRF)
1	Data Bit 1	Data Bit 1	Counter Divide Select 2 (CR1)	Transmit Data Register Empty (TDRE)
2	Data Bit 2	Data Bit 2	Word Select 1 (CR2)	Data Carrier Detect ($\overline{\text{DCD}}$)
3	Data Bit 3	Data Bit 3	Word Select 2 (CR3)	Clear-to-Send ($\overline{\text{CTS}}$)
4	Data Bit 4	Data Bit 4	Word Select 3 (CR4)	Framing Error (FE)
5	Data Bit 5	Data Bit 5	Transmit Control 1 (CR5)	Receiver Overrun (OVRN)
6	Data Bit 6	Data Bit 6	Transmit Control 2 (CR6)	Parity Error (PE)
7	Data Bit 7***	Data Bit 7**	Receive Interrupt Enable (CR7)	Interrupt Request (IRQ)

* Leading bit = LSB = Bit 0
** Data bit will be zero in 7-bit plus parity modes.
*** Data bit is "don't care" in 7-bit plus parity modes.
Source: Motorola Semiconductor Products, Inc.

**Table D.2   Word Select Bits (CR0 and CR1):
The Word**

CR1	CR0	Function
0	0	÷ 1
0	1	÷ 16
1	0	÷ 64
1	1	Master Reset

Source: Motorola Semiconductor Products, Inc.

**Table D.3   Word Select Bits (CR2 to CR4):
The Word**

CR4	CR3	CR2	Function
0	0	0	7 Bits + Even Parity + 2 Stop Bits
0	0	1	7 Bits + Odd Parity + 2 Stop Bits
0	1	0	7 Bits + Even Parity + 1 Stop Bit
0	1	1	7 Bits + Odd Parity + 1 Stop Bit
1	0	0	8 Bits + 2 Stop Bits
1	0	1	8 Bits + 1 Stop Bit
1	1	0	8 Bits + Even Parity + 1 Stop Bit
1	1	1	8 Bits + Odd Parity + 1 Stop Bit

Source: Motorola Semiconductor Products, Inc.

**Table D.4   Word Select Bits (CR5 and CR6):
The Word**

CR6	CR5	Function
0	0	$\overline{RTS}$ = low, Transmitting Interrupt Disabled.
0	1	$\overline{RTS}$ = low, Transmitting Interrupt Enabled.
1	0	$\overline{RTS}$ = high, Transmitting Interrupt Disabled.
1	1	$\overline{RTS}$ = low, Transmits a Break level on the Transmit Data Output. Transmitting Interrupt Disabled.

Source: Motorola Semiconductor Products, Inc.

data register empty interrupt is set high on an empty register if the interrupt is enabled. CR7 controls the enabling of an interrupt if either the receive data register is full, there is a data string overrun, or there exists a low-to-high transition on the data carrier detect signal line.

D.3 STATUS REGISTER

The status register of the ACIA provides information for use in program branching. These bits can trigger a specific interrupt if enabled or they can provide operation information to the executing program. Bit zero indicates that the receive data register is full with current data. The bit is cleared after a read or a master reset. DCD being high causes bit zero to be low. Bit 1 indicates that the data in the transmit data register has been transferred out and is now ready for more data. Bit 2 indicates the presence of a carrier as detected by the modem, and will cause an interrupt request if enabled. Bit 2 is cleared by a read status, read data sequence. If the bit is still high after the interrupt has been cleared, it will follow its input. Bit 3 is the clear-to-send bit, and if it is off, disables the TDRE bit, which effectively inhibits transmission. Bit 4 is a framing error bit and is available any time the associated character string is in the receive buffer. This bit indicates a synchronization error, faulty transmission, or a break condition. Bit 5 is the receiver overrun bit. An overrun condition is such that one or more characters in a data string were not read before the incoming characters started filling the receive data register. This error is cleared by reading the RDR. Bit 6 is a parity error bit and indicates that the number of 1's in the character is not the programmed sum, either odd or even. The bit is available as long as the data is in the RDR. Bit 7 is the composite interrupt bit, and any interrupt will be reflected in this bit. This bit can be cleared by a RDR read or a TRD write.

EXAMPLE D.1: Modem Interface

This application will be inclusive in the 6860 application and will go into modem control for communication over long-distance communication media.

Following is typical code for this application to initialize the 6860.

```
* IN THIS MODULE INITIALIZATION WILL OCCUR,
* ALL LABELS MUST BE
* DEFINED.
         LDA     #$AF
         STA     CR          DO A MASTER RESET ON CONTROL REGISTER
         ANDA    #$AC
         STA     CR          ACTIVATE DIVIDE BY ONE SEQUENCE
   TST   LDA     STATREG     LOAD STATUS REGISTER
         ANDA    #$8         MASK OUT CTS BIT
         BEQ     GO          PERFORM DATA TRANSFER
         .
         .
         .
```

E

Special Interfaces

The 68xx architectural series is supported by several peripheral devices, some of which are explained in this appendix. A brief description of each device with an example is given in each section. Many excellent diagrams have been furnished by Motorola, for which the author is grateful. The author is also indebted to Jonathan Dust, Colorado State University, for the examples demonstrating the potential of the 68xx peripheral devices.

E.1 MC6828: A PRIORITY-INTERRUPT CONTROLLER

The 6828 is a versatile chip that can be implemented in small systems as an eight-level interrupt prioritizing unit (see Figure E.1 and Table E.1). It has encoded capabilities to vector the host MPU to a specific address in the case of interrupt detection on its input ports. The unit finds most applicability in a system that is required to service several hardware devices on a priority basis that cannot use time-costly port-polling routines. The unit provides very quick interrupt servicing with a minimum of MPU time. It provides a good interface for the MPU to a variety of hardware peripheral interrupt lines.

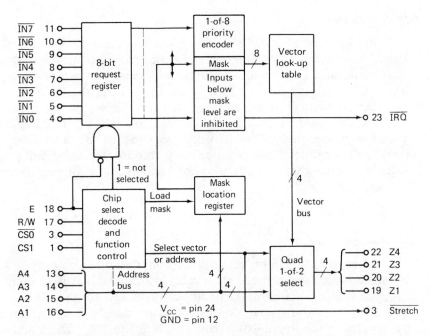

Figure E.1. 6828 Block Diagram. (Courtesy of Motorola Semiconductor Products, Inc.)

Table E.1   Truth Table for M6800 Microprocessor Systems

		Output When Selected				Equivalent to Bits 1-4 of B0, B1 . . . , B15	Address ROM Bytes
Active Input		Z4	Z3	Z2	Z1	Hex Address	Contain Address of:
Highest	IN7	1	0	1	1	F F F 6 or 7	Priority 7 Routine
	IN6	1	0	1	0	F F F 4 or 5	Priority 6 Routine
	IN5	1	0	0	1	F F F 2 or 3	Priority 5 Routine
	IN4	1	0	0	0	F F F 0 or 1	Priority 4 Routine
	IN3	0	1	1	1	F F E E or F	Priority 3 Routine
	IN2	0	1	1	0	F F E C or D	Priority 2 Routine
	IN1	0	1	0	1	F F E A or B	Priority 1 Routine
Lowest	IN0	0	1	0	0	F F E 8 or 9	Priority 0 Routine
	None	1	1	0	0	F F F 8 or 9	Default Routine*

*Default routine is the response to interrupt requests not generated by a prioritized input. The default routine may contain polling routines or may be an address in a loop for an interrupt driven system.

Source: Motorola Semiconductor Products, Inc.

General Description

The 6828 is a bipolar LSI design that operates with TTL-level buffers and operates with a power consumption of 625 mW on a 5-V bus. The unit is a 24-pin DIP configuration available in a plastic or ceramic package. The unit is used primarily with the 68xx level of micros but can be interfaced to other manufacturers' products. It is built to present an interrupt to the MPU on detection of the interrupt signal, and upon receipt of a chip select goes about modifying the appropriate address lines.

Mask Generation

In the case of a system with priority devices, it should first be determined how many interrupts are needed in the system. To do this an interrupt mask must be created. This mask will cause requests below a predefined level to be ignored by the PIC. When interfacing the 6828 to the system, note that when the chip is selected, the mask is set by writing to a specific address. The control lines in this address are A1–A4. The writing can consist of anything, just so the R/$\overline{W}$ line goes low at the correct address. If the mask indicates that there is no priority routine, the MPU will proceed to a default routine that services a nonprioritized interrupt (see Tables E.2 and E.3 and Figure E.2).

Interrupt Sequence

After the interrupt mask has been generated, the system becomes operable on a request basis. If a valid interrupt signal is recognized by the PIC, an interrupt request is made immediately to the MPU by the PIC. The MPU saves the system configuration on the stack and replies to the PIC by putting FFF8 on the bus and enabling the PIC. The PIC decodes the vector address and switches it onto the address output lines for the MSB of vector address. The LSB part of the vector address is read from the modified FFF9 address read. After this address is read, the execution of the interrupt routine begins.

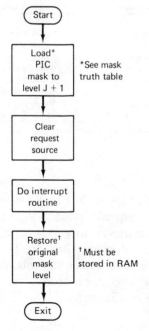

Figure E.2. Mask Flow Chart. (Courtesy of Motorola Semiconductor Products, Inc.)

Table E.2 Interrupt Masks

Write Anything to This Address:	and Address Bus Lines A1–A4 will Have This Value:	Which will Inhibit All Interrupts, Including and Below:
FFE0 or FFE1	0000	All interrupts enabled
FFE2 or FFE3	0001	IN1
FFE4 or FFE5	0010	IN2
FFE6 or FFE7	0011	IN3
FFE8 or FFE9	0100	IN4
FFEA or FFEB	0101	IN5
FFEC or FFED	0110	IN6
FFEE or FFFF	0111	IN7
FFF0 through FFFF	1000 through 1111	All interrupts disabled

Source: Motorola Semiconductor Products, Inc.

Table E.3 Mask Truth Table

Mask Register Contents				Response to Priority Inputs 1 = Response to Input, 0 = No Response							
M4	M3	M2	M1	IN7	IN6	IN5	IN4	IN3	IN2	IN1	IN0
1	1	1	1	0	0	0	0	0	0	0	0
1	1	1	0	0	0	0	0	0	0	0	0
1	1	0	1	0	0	0	0	0	0	0	0
1	1	0	0	0	0	0	0	0	0	0	0
1	0	1	1	0	0	0	0	0	0	0	0
1	0	1	0	0	0	0	0	0	0	0	0
1	0	0	1	0	0	0	0	0	0	0	0
1	0	0	0	0	0	0	0	0	0	0	0
0	1	1	1	1	0	0	0	0	0	0	0
0	1	1	0	1	1	0	0	0	0	0	0
0	1	0	1	1	1	1	0	0	0	0	0
0	1	0	0	1	1	1	1	0	0	0	0
0	0	1	1	1	1	1	1	1	0	0	0
0	0	1	0	1	1	1	1	1	1	0	0
0	0	0	1	1	1	1	1	1	1	1	0
0	0	0	0	1	1	1	1	1	1	1	1

Source: Motorola Semiconductor Products, Inc.

EXAMPLE E.1: Timer Interface

For this application the circuit will consist of a system that is monitoring a timer input on the highest priority for a CRT update, and a parallel port that is bringing in new picture data. The parallel input will be secondary and will be serviced when possible. Refer to the schematic and flow chart for a further understanding of the application (Figure E.3).

We can use the following code to generate an interrupt mask.

```
* FIRST THE INTERRUPT MASK FOR THE CHIP SHOULD BE GENERATED.
* ALL NAMES HAVE BEEN DEFINED.
      CLRA
      STA        $FFEA    /DISABLES INTERRUPTS 5 AND BELOW
* NOW INITIALIZE THE INTERRUPT VECTORS
      LDA        $01
      STA        $FFE8
      CLRA
```

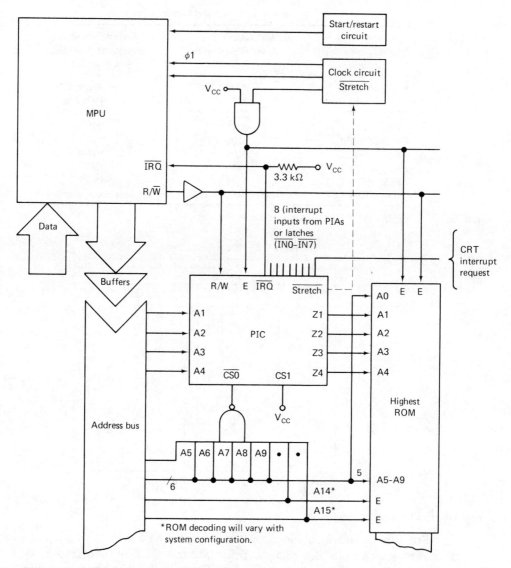

Figure E.3. Typical MPU Interface to 6828. (Courtesy of Motorola Semiconductor Products, Inc.)

```
STA       $FFE9
LDA       $05
STA       $FFEA
LDA       $FFEB    /VECTOR ADDRESSES INITIALIZED!
```

The following questions frequently arise when using the 6828.

1. What chip should be used when using an external clock circuit and phase 2 stretch circuits, and when is this circuit necessary?

Answer: The 6809E should be used when designing with external clocks, because it has no on-board oscillator. The stretch circuit is implemented when slow-access memory devices are used in the system design. It "stretches" or lengthens the response time needed by the ROM or RAM to present valid data to the bus. The MRDY input control signal to the 6809 is useful here.

2. What lines are significant in the description of the interrupt mask to the PIC?

Answer: A1–A4 and the R/$\overline{W}$ lines are the significant lines used in mask description.

3. What is a default routine when used with a PIC?

Answer: A default routine is vectored to on receipt of a nonprioritized interrupt by the MPU. This input would probably be in parallel with the $\overline{\text{IRQ}}$ line of the MPU.

4. In the code above, what are the priority 1 and 2 vectors?

Answer: The priority 1 vector is 0100H and the priority 2 vector is 0501H. Use Figure E.2 to determine the priority.

E.2 THE MC6840: A PROGRAMMABLE TIMER MODULE—PTM

The 6840 is a versatile system component that is oriented to small microsystems. The MC6840 has three 16-bit binary counters, three control registers, and a status register (see Figure E.4). The MC6840 generates output signals, timing signals, or interrupts to the system. Applications include event counters, frequency measurement, pulse-width modulators, pulse-train generators, and delay generators.

General Description

The chip is an *N*-channel MOS design that operates on a 5-V bus with a power dissipation of about 550 mW. It is available in a plastic or ceramic 28-pin DIP package, with fully compatible TTL buffers. Internal control of the chip's functions are related directly to the control registers. Three control registers exist with direct access first made to the control register 2. The LSB of this register selects which of the other two registers is accessed when one addresses the shared port at register select (RS)=0. See Table E.4 for a detailed description of the RS addressing. The RS lines are hardware decode lines for memory-mapped I/O. These lines work with the R/$\overline{W}$ line to determine which operation column to read from. Once the desired register

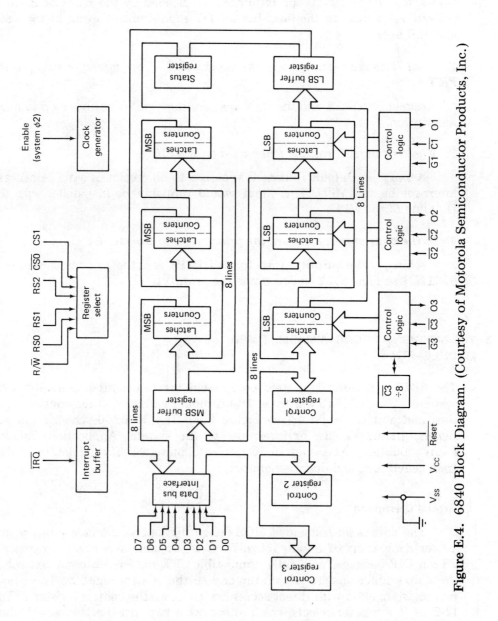

Figure E.4. 6840 Block Diagram. (Courtesy of Motorola Semiconductor Products, Inc.)

Table E.4   Register Selection

RS2	RS1	RS0	R/W̄ = 0	R/W̄ = 1
Register Select Inputs			Operations	
0	0	0	CR20 = 0 Write Control Register #3 CR20 = 1 Write Control Register #1	No Operation
0	0	1	Write Control Register #2	Read Status Register
0	1	0	Write MSB Buffer Register	Read Timer #1 Counter
0	1	1	Write Timer #1 Latches	Read LSB Buffer Register
1	0	0	Write MSB Buffer Register	Read Timer #2 Counter
1	0	1	Write Timer #2 Latches	Read LSB Buffer Register
1	1	0	Write MSB Buffer Register	Read Timer #3 Counter
1	1	1	Write Timer #3 Latches	Read LSB Buffer Register

Source: Motorola Semiconductor Products, Inc.

is determined, we must go to Table E.5 to find the exact bit function for that register. The top of Table E.5 indicates the LSB of all the control registers. Note that they have functions such as CR10, which determines the initialization or operation of the counters. CR30 determines if special pre-scaler hardware is patched into this counter. The next two rows of the table describe the bits that have the same function independent of the control register selected. For example, control bit 1 selects whether an internal clock (enable line) or an external clock (CX input) will decrement the counters. Control bit CRX2 selects whether the binary information is treated as an 8-bit or 16-bit word. A time-out will occur on the 16-bit word after $N + 1$ counts, where N is the 16-bit binary number in the counter latches. In the dual 8-bit mode a time-out occurs after the MSB+1 and the LSB+1 have decremented to zero. Control bits X3, X4, and X5 will be discussed in the section on Table E.6. CRX6 determines whether the composite

Table E.5   Control Register Bits

CR10 Internal Reset Bit	CR20 Control Register Address Bit	CR30 Timer #3 Clock Control
0 All timers allowed to operate	0 CR #3 may be written	0 T3 Clock is not prescaled
1 All timers held in preset state	1 CR #1 may be written	1 T3 Clock is prescaled by ÷ 8
CRX1*	Timer #X Clock Source	
0	TX uses external clock source on C̄X̄ input	
1	TX uses Enable clock	
CRX2	Timer #X Counting Mode Control	
0	TX configured for normal (16-bit) counting mode	
1	TX configured for dual 8-bit counting mode	
CRX3 CRX4 CRX5	Timer #X Counter Mode and Interrupt Control (See Table 3),	
CRX6	Timer #X Interrupt Enable	
0	Interrupt Flag masked on ĪR̄Q̄	
1	Interrupt Flag enabled to ĪR̄Q̄	
CRX7	Timer #X Counter Output Enable	
0	TX Output masked on output OX	
1	TX Output enabled on output OX	

*Control Register for Timer 1, 2, or 3, Bit 1.
Source: Motorola Semiconductor Products, Inc.

interrupt flag in the status register will be masked or not. CRX7 determines whether or not the timer interrupt flag will be masked or not.

Flags

The MC6840 has an internal status register which contains four interrupt flags. Bit 0 is timer flag 1, bit 1 is timer flag 2, and bit 2 is flag 3. Bit 7 is the composite flag that is an "OR" function of all the counter flags, if enabled by the appropriate CRX6. An interrupt flag is cleared by an internal reset CR10, an external reset (RESET), a sequential read status register, and a read timer counter. An individual interrupt I1, I2, or I3 is also cleared by a write timer latch command or counter initialization command to that counter.

Initialization

To initialize a 16-bit counter, two bytes must be passed to the PTM. The upper part of the counter must be put in the write MSB buffer register. The port must then be incremented and the LSB of the word must then be written. After writing to the write timer latch port, the entire 16-bit word is loaded into the appropriate counter latch.

Operation

Operation of the counter is triggered by an internal reset operation or through the use of a specific command in a specific mode.

Gate Controls

The gate inputs on the PTM can replace the loading or recognition of inputs using the enable line. The input is not considered valid until either the enable or gate line has gone through four pulses. This ensures necessary minimum setup times. The input gating pulse is selected by CRX1.

Operating Modes

Some operating modes of the chip are controlled by CRX3, CRX4, and CRX5. Refer to Table E.6. The different modes of operation—continuous, single-shot, frequency comparison, and pulse width comparison—are controlled by the following bit configurations.

Continuous Mode

The first mode in Table E.6 is the continuous mode. We select this mode by putting a zero in CRX3 and CRX5, and one can obtain a square wave or a variable-duty-cycle waveform. The actual type depends on the

Table E.6   Operating Modes

Control Register			Timer Operating Mode
CRX3	CRX4	CRX5	
0	*	0	Continuous
0	*	1	Single-Shot
1	0	*	Frequency Comparison
1	1	*	Pulse Width Comparison

*Defines Additional Timer Functions
Source: Motorola Semiconductor Products, Inc.

mode of counter operation (either 8 or 16 bits). In this mode, a write timer latches commands to be selected by clearing CRX4. Refer to Table E.7 for specific continuous operating modes and initialization schemes that are implemented by programming bits CRX2 and CRX4.

Monostable Mode

The single-shot mode described in Table E.8 is very similar to the continuous mode except for three major aspects. First, the output is enabled for only one pulse until it is reinitialized (see counter initialization). Second, the counter enable does not rely on a low *value* as in the continuous mode. Third, if LSB=MSB=0 or N=0 in the counter load, the counter is disabled.

Table E.7   Continuous Operating Modes

CONTINUOUS MODE (CRX3 = 0, CRX5 = 0)			
Control Register		Counter Initialization	Initialization/Output Waveforms
CRX2	CRX4		*Timer Output (OX) (CRX7 = 1)
0	0	$\overline{G}\downarrow + W + R$	
0	1	$\overline{G}\downarrow + R$	
1	0	$\overline{G}\downarrow + W + R$	
1	1	$\overline{G}\downarrow + R$	

$\overline{G}\downarrow$ = Negative transition of $\overline{Gate}$ input.

W = Write Timer Latches Command.

R = Timer Reset (CR10 = 1 or External $\overline{Reset}$ = 0).

N = 16-Bit Number in Counter Latch.

L = 8-Bit Number in LSB Counter Latch.

M = 8-Bit Number in MSB Counter Latch.

T = Clock Input Negative Transitions to Counter.

t_0 = Counter Initialization Cycle.

TO = Counter Time Out (All Zero Condition).

*All time intervals shown above assume the the Gate ($\overline{G}$) and Clock ($\overline{C}$) signals are synchronized to Enable (System $\varphi2$) with the specified setup and hold time requirements.

Source: Motorola Semiconductor Products, Inc.

SINGLE-SHOT MODE (CRX3 = 0, CRX7 = 1, CRX5 = 1)			
Control Register		Initialization/Output Waveforms	
CRX2	CRX4	Counter Initialization	Timer Output (OX)
0	0	$\overline{G}\!\downarrow + W + R$	$\vdash$ (N+1)(T) $\dashv$ (N+1)(T) $\dashv$ $\vdash$ (N)(T) $\dashv$
0	1	$\overline{G}\!\downarrow + R$	t_0 ___ TO ___ TO
1	0	$\overline{G}\!\downarrow + W + R$	$\vdash$ (L+1)(M+1)(T) $\dashv$ (L+1)(M+1)(T) $\dashv$ $\vdash$ (L)(T) $\dashv$
1	1	$\overline{G}\!\downarrow + R$	t_0 ___ TO ___ TO

Symbols are as defined in Table E.7.
Source: Motorola Semiconductor Products, Inc.

Time Interval Modes

By using CRX4 and CRX5, we can specify a functional time interval useful for interrupt generation. The interrupt flags are a function of the gate period and counter time-outs. Refer to Table E.9 for the bit patterns and PTM functions. Specific counter initializations, resets, and interrupt flags depend on the state of CRX5. See Table E.10 for the frequency comparison mode and Table E.11 for the pulse-width comparison mode. An important distinction between the two modes occurs when the interrupt flag is set with respect to the transition of the gate signal.

Table E.9   Time Interval Modes

CRX3 = 1			
CRX4	CRX5	Application	Condition for Setting Individual Interrupt Flag
0	0	Frequency Comparison	Interrupt Generated if $\overline{\text{Gate}}$ Input Period (1/F) is less than Counter Time Out (TO)
0	1	Frequency Comparison	Interrupt Generated if $\overline{\text{Gate}}$ Input Period (1/F) is greater than Counter Time Out (TO)
1	0	Pulse Width Comparison	Interrupt Generated if $\overline{\text{Gate}}$ Input "Down Time" is less than Counter Time Out (TO)
1	1	Pulse Width Comparison	Interrupt Generated if $\overline{\text{Gate}}$ Input "Down Time" is greater than Counter Time Out (TO)

Source: Motorola Semiconductor Products, Inc.

Table E.10   Frequency Comparison Mode

CRX3 = 1, CRX4 = 0				
Control Reg Bit 5 (CRX5)	Counter Initialization	Counter Enable Flip-Flop Set (CE)	Counter Enable Flip-Flop Reset (CE)	Interrupt Flag Set (I)
0	$\overline{G}\!\downarrow \cdot \overline{I} \cdot (\overline{CE} + TO \cdot CE) + R$	$\overline{G}\!\downarrow \cdot \overline{W} \cdot \overline{R} \cdot \overline{I}$	$W + R + I$	$\overline{G}\!\downarrow$ Before TO
1	$\overline{G}\!\downarrow \cdot \overline{I} + R$	$\overline{G}\!\downarrow \cdot \overline{W} \cdot \overline{R} \cdot \overline{I}$	$W + R + I$	TO Before $\overline{G}\!\downarrow$

I represents the interrupt for a given timer.
Source: Motorola Semiconductor Products, Inc.

Special Interfaces

CRX3 = 1, CRX4 = 1				
Control Reg Bit 5 (CRX5)	Counter Initialization	Counter Enable Flip-Flop Set (CE)	Counter Enable Flip-Flop Reset (CE)	Interrupt Flag Set (I)
0	$\overline{G}\downarrow\cdot\overline{I}+R$	$\overline{G}\downarrow\cdot\overline{W}\cdot R\cdot\overline{I}$	$W+R+I+G$	$\overline{G}\uparrow$ Before TO
1	$\overline{G}\downarrow\cdot\overline{I}+R$	$\overline{G}\downarrow\cdot\overline{W}\cdot R\cdot\overline{I}$	$W+R+I+G$	TO Before $\overline{G}\uparrow$

Source: Motorola Semiconductor Products, Inc.

Usability

This chip is very effective for real-time programming. Let us see how it interfaces to a 6809 system and use it to determine whether a signal is in a certain frequency range.

EXAMPLE E.2:   A Scan-Rate Tester

Currently, many companies are interested in automated test stations. In our test a comparison is being made between a standard vertical scan rate and test point A, which is on a TV vertical oscillator board (see Figures E.5 and E.6). The system that we design samples the incoming frequency, compares it to a known standard, and then pulses a stepper motor in the correct direction to adjust a slug in an inductor. This will change the frequency of the oscillator iteratively until the board's frequency is within range.

Refer to Figure E.6. Note that the 6809 has been connected to a 6840. It is assumed that the 6809 also connects to other devices (i.e., ROM, RAM, etc.).

The code for this application follows.

```
* ENABLE REGISTER 1, USE INTERNAL CLOCK, 16-BIT MODE.
* SINGLE SHOT MODE, INITIALIZES ONE SHOT ON A LATCH
* WRITE OR AN INTERNAL RESET.  DISABLE COUNTER TWO
* FLAG, ENABLE OUTPUT.
            LDA    #$00
            STA    MSB1
            STA    MSB2

            STA    LSB2
            STA    MSB3
            STA    LSB3
            LDA    #$85
            STA    CNTRL1    /STORE SAME CONTROL WORD IN CONTROL
* WORD ONE, DO A GENERAL RESET.
            ANDA   #$05      /A ACC IS NOW 05H.
            STA    CNTRL1    /RESET OCCURS, GET SET FOR OPERATION.
            STA    CNTRL2    /TALK TO CNTRL3 NEXT TIME.
            LDA    #$16      /NO PRESCALER, EXTERNAL CLOCK SOURCE ON,
* 16-BIT MODE, FOR FREQUENCY COMPARISON,
* INTERRUPT FLAG ON, OUTPUT DISABLED.
            STA    CNTRL1    /ACTUALLY STORING IN CNTRL3.
            LDA    #$FF
            STA    PRSTFLG   /STORE PREVIOUS STATE FLAG=.LT.
```

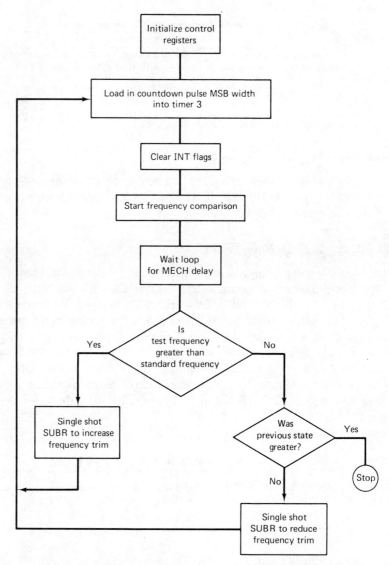

Figure E.5. Flow Chart for Micro-Controlled System.

```
* NOW PROGRAM ALL OF THE COUNTER PRESETS.
* START WITH REGISTER 3.
        LDA     #$AA
        STA     MSB3        /LOAD MSB OF #3 COUNTER.
* TIMER #3 LATCHES, THIS IS THE PULSE WIDTH
* OF THE STANDARD MEASUREMENT.
* ALL PARTS OF THE INITIALIZATION HAVE BEEN
* DONE.  NOW ENTRY IS MADE INTO THE MAIN MODULE
  FREQCMP   STA     LSB3        /START LOOKING FOR AN
* INTERRUPT IF TEST FREQ IS STANDARD FREQ.
        LDA·    #$FF
        STA     LOOP
```

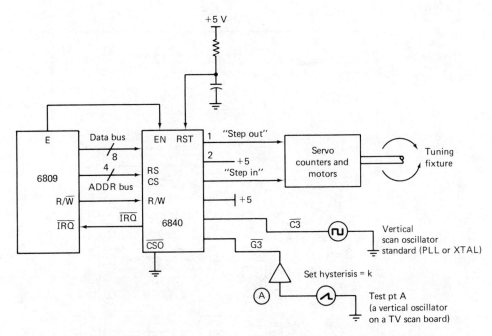

Figure E.6. Microprocessor-Controlled Scan-Rate Tester for TV Tuners.

```
WAIT          DEC      LOOP
              BNE      WAIT
              LDA      PRSTFLG
              CMPA     #$00
              BEQ      END
              LDA      #$80
              STA      LSB1          /STEP THE MOTOR IN TO INCREASE
* THE FREQUENCY.
              ORA      #$FF
              STA      PRSTFLG
              JMP      FREQCMP
END           RTS
INTRPT        LDA      CREG2
              LDA      MSB3          /THIS SEQUENCE WILL CLEAR THE COMPOSITE
* FLAG AND INDIVIDUAL FLAGS.
              LDA      LSB0
              STA      LSB2          /STEP THE MOTOR OUT TO DECREASE THE FREQ.
              CLRA
              STA      PRSTFLG
              JMP      FREQCMP
```

The following questions are often asked.

1. If the operating RAM is located in the low portion of memory and the ceiling is about 10K in a 16K system, where should the system, ROM, and memory-mapped I/O be located?

The MC6840: A Programmable Timer Module—PTM   **325**

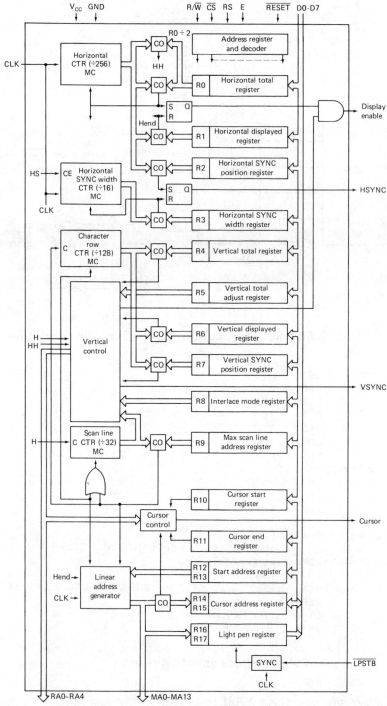

Figure E.7. CRTC Block Diagram. (Courtesy of Motorola Semiconductor Products, Inc.)

Answer: The system, ROM, and memory-mapped I/O should be placed at a location so as not to interfere with any operating room or stacks. Map out the system. Leave room for system expansion.

2. What lines in the schematic determine the port addresses that control the PTM?

Answer: The register select lines and the chip select lines are address decode lines that determine the port location in the system.

3. In this application, is the enable line to the PTM actually needed?

Answer: No, in this mode of operation we are comparing the frequencies between the clock input and the gate input.

E.3   THE MC6845: A CATHODE-RAY CONTROLLER

The CRTC chip is designed for controlling a variety of CRT display devices. It provides programmable formatting of three different types of raster-scan modes, which providing for options such as a light pen. The device can provide addressing of 16K of memory and will refresh dynamic memory. It has additional addressing for a 2515 character-generator ROM, and is designed to be operated most efficiently in a 6809 environment (see Figure E.7).

Pinout Description

Data Bus D0–D7.   The data bus lines are tri-state lines that pass parallel data to and from the CRTC control registers.

Enable Lines.   The enable line is a line that enables the data bus I/O drivers and clocks data to and from the CRTC.

Chip Select.   The chip select line enables communication to the CRTC internal register file when a valid device decode address is available from the processor.

Register Select.   The register select line selects either an address register or a data register within the internal register file of the CRTC.

R/W Line.   The read/write line determines whether the addressed register within the CRTC is written to or read by the MPU.

Vertical Sync.   This signal is necessary in the video processing unit for composite video generations. It indicates the start of a vertical scan page.

Horizontal Sync.   This signal is a pulse that is generated for the video display monitor or video processing unit to indicate the time when a scan line has begun.

Display Enable.   This signal indicates that the CRTC is providing addressing to information in the active display area.

Refresh Memory Addresses.   These 14 lines will refresh display within a 16K area of refresh memory. This area is the video display memory area.

Raster Addresses. These five lines address the character ROM for the row of the character that is to be displayed.

Cursor Line. This line indicates to external video processing logic that the cursor is to be displayed.

Clock Line. This line is the synchronizing signal that relates all CRTC signals.

Light Pen Strobe. This line will latch the current video display refresh memory address to indicate where the light pen was positioned on the screen.

Reset Line. The reset line clears all counters in the CRTC, puts all outputs to a low level, stops device operation, and leaves the control registers unchanged. See Table E.12 for a complete description of the reset line.

Register File Description

Address Register. The address register is an indirect register and indicates the address of some other register in the bank of 18 registers. RS must be low to select this register.

Horizontal Total Register. This register determines the horizontal scan frequency. It is expressed in character time units and is the period of one scan line.

Horizontal Displayed Register. This register indicates how many displayed characters are made per lines. It does not include horizontal retrace time.

Table E.12   Typical 80 × 24 Screen Format Initialization of CRTC

Reg. #	Register File	Program Unit	Calculation*	Programmed Value Decimal	Hex
R0	H Total	T_c	102 × .527 = 53.76 μs	102 − 1 = 101	N_{ht} = $65
R1	H Displayed	T_c	80 × .527 = 42.16 μs	80	N_{hd} = $50
R2	H Sync Position	T_c	86 × .527 = 45.32 μs	86	N_{hsp} = $56
R3	H Sync Width	T_c	9 × .527 = 4.74 μs	9	N_{hsw} = $09
R4	V Total	T_{cr}	25 × 645.12 = 16.13 ms	25 = 1 = 24	N_{vt} = $18
R5	V Total Adjust	T_{sl}	10 × 53.76 = .54 ms	10	N_{adj} = $0A
R6	V Displayed	T_{cr}	24 × 645.12 = 15.48 ms	24	N_{vd} = $18
R7	V Sync Position	T_{cr}	24 × 645.12 = 15.48 ms	24	N_{vsp} = $18
R8	Interlace Mode	—		—	$00
R9	Max Scan Line Address	T_{sl}		11	N_{sl} = $0B
R10	Cursor Start	T_{sl}		0	$00
R11	Cursor End	T_{sl}		11	$0B
R12	Start Address (H)	—			$00
R13	Start Address (L)	—		128	$80
R14	Cursor (H)	—			$00
R15	Cursor (L)	—		128	$80

Clock Period = T_c = .527 μs

Scan Line Period = T_{sl} = (N_{ht} + 1) × T_c = 102 × .527 μs = 53.76 μs

Character Row Period = T_{cr} = N_{sl} × T_{sl} = 12 × 53.76 μs = 645.12 μs

*These are typical values for the Motorola M3000 Monitor; values may vary for other monitors.

Source: Motorola Semiconductor Products, Inc.

Horizontal Sync Position. This register indicates where the horizontal sync pulse begins on the horizontal scan line.

Horizontal Sync Width. This register controls the pulse width of the horizontal sync pulse for customizing to a variety of CRT monitors.

Vertical Total. This register is a coarse control for the vertical scan frequency. It is normally set close to 50 or 60 Hz. Remember, it is also expressed as a time period. The time period is related to character line times.

Vertical Adjust. The vertical adjust is a fine control for the adjustment of the overall vertical period. This is expressed as a number of scan lines.

Vertical Displayed. This register indicates the number of actual displayed character rows on the screen.

Vertical Sync Position. This register indicates to the CRTC when the vertical sync pulse is generated in terms of the total vertical scan time. It is expressed in character row times.

Interlace Mode. This register selects one of three display modes, non-interlace or one of two types of interlace modes. Refer to Table E.13 for information on how to control the modes. When the same information is stored in both fields of a scan frame, the display is in the interlace mode. This mode is effective in improving the quality of the picture. If the even lines of a character are displayed in the even fields and the odd lines displayed in the odd fields, the mode is an interlace sync and video mode. This effectively doubles the character time density on the screen since no information is duplicated. These are some restrictions in interlace mode. See Motorola data sheets for specific details.

Maximum Scan Line Address. This register determines the number of scan lines per character row. This includes spacing between lines of the field.

Cursor Start Register. This register controls the cursor format (refer to Table E.13 for operation). Bit 6 is the blink enable control. Bit 5 is the blink rate and display control. The other five bits control which scan line starts the cursor display.

Cursor End. This register indicates the scan line that marks the end of the cursor display.

Start Address. These registers determine in video memory where the display starts after vertical blanking time.

Light Pen. These registers (high byte and low byte) indicate the con-

Table E.13   Cursor Start
Register

Bit 6	Bit 5	Cursor Display Mode
0	0	Non-Blink
0	1	Cursor Non-Display
1	0	Blink, 1/16 Field Rate
1	1	Blink, 1/32 Field Rate

Source: Motorola Semiconductor Products, Inc.

The MC6845: A Cathode-Ray Controller

tent of the video memory address register when the light pen option is implemented.

Cursor. These registers contain the location of the cursor in video memory, again high byte and low byte.

EXAMPLE E.3: An Interactive Terminal

The CRTC chip is used inside an interactive terminal. Primarily, connections will be made that reflect interfacing to a 6809 MPU.

The code[1] below, in conjunction with Table E.12, performs a typical register initialization for a common 80 X 24 line frame display.

```
        NAM   CRTINT
        ORG   $0
        CLRB                    /CLEAR COUNTER
        LDX   #$20              /POINT X TO CONSTANTS
CRTI1   STB   $9000             /CRTC ADDR REG
        LDA   0,X               /GET NEXT CONSTANT
        STA   $9001             /CRTC REG
        INX                     /MOVE POINTER
        INCB                    /ALL DONE?
        CMPB  #$10
        BNE   CRTI1
        SWI
        ORG   $20
CRTTAB  FCB   $65,$50,$56,$9    /CONSTANTS
        FCB   $18,$0A,$18,$18
        FCB   0,$0B, 0, $0B
        FDB   $80,$80
        END
```

The following types of questions are often asked.

1. Where is the video block information stored for the frame display?

Answer: The video block information is located in an access-protected area for storage of video information only.

2. How does the CRTC get its registers properly initialized?

Answer: During power-up of the MPU-CRTC circuit, the registers must be initialized by execution of a ROM-based routine that loads the registers correctly to the size of the display. See Table E.12 for correct register initialization for a common 80 X 24 line display.

---

[1] Reprinted Courtesy of Motorola Semiconductor Corp., ca. 1977. See MC6845 Data Specification Publication AD1-465.

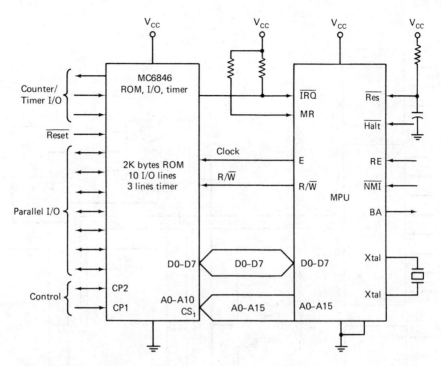

Figure E.8. Typical Microcomputer. (Courtesy of Motorola Semiconductor Products, Inc.)

E.4   THE MC6846: ROM–I/O–TIMER

The 6846 is a multipurpose chip that consists of on-board 2048 bytes of fully addressable ROM, an 8-bit bidirectional data port for parallel interfacing, two control lines, and a PTM similar to the 6840 chip. The chip is a custom chip in the sense that the ROM is masked at production, but it is very versatile as a building block in a small dedicated system. Applications include those of minimal chip count control systems, programmable frequency generators and counters, and pulse-train comparators. It is connected to a microprocessor as shown in Figure E.8.

General Description

The chip is an NMOS device that has a power dissipation of 0.1 W on a 5-V bus. The unit is fully TTL-compatible and operates up to 1 MHz. The on-board timer is one full channel that operates with continuous, single-shot, and time interval modes. The channel has a divide-by-8 prescaler, a count-down input, a control gate, and a timer output. Mask-programmable 2K ROM is available for factory programming. Also, the chip sports an entire I/O byte for external interfacing (see Figure E.9).

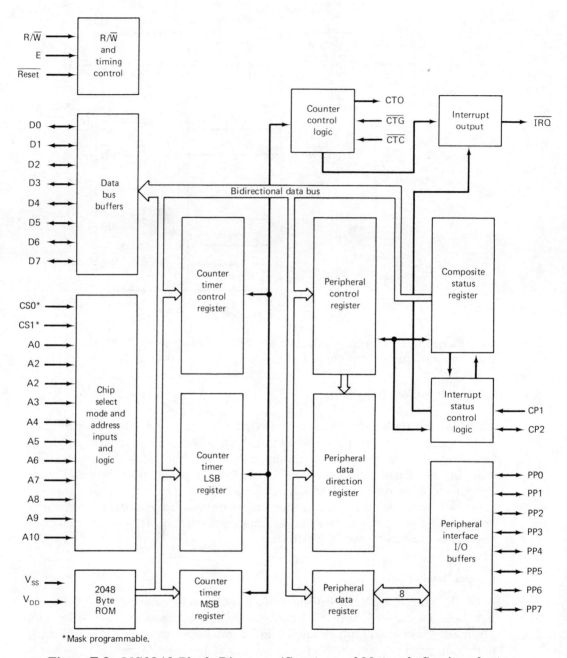

Figure E.9. MC6846 Block Diagram. (Courtesy of Motorola Semiconductor Products, Inc.)

*Mask programmable.

Masked Programmed Storage

The 6846 has a masked ROM organized in a 2048 × 8 matrix. Address inputs allow the matrix to be fully decoded in a unique program module. Selecting of the ROM is controlled by selecting either CS0 or CS1 depending on the mask specification.

Timer

The 6846 timer is very similar to the 6840 PTM timer 3. The 6840 has been previously studied and discussed in detail, so in this section a study of only the differences in operation will be shown. There are basically three differences between the timers. You will recall that in using the control registers in the 6840, control registers 1 and 3 are "buried" and that access must be made to control register 2 to control which one will be accessed. In the 6846 access is simplified, since the MPU can talk to all registers directly. The 6840 has a dual 8-bit continuous mode for generating nonsymmetrical waveforms. In the 6846 there is a similar mode called the cascaded one-shot mode. It is useful in generating nonsymmetrical waveforms longer than one time-out. See Tables E.14 to E.17 for the difference in control bits.

Cascaded Single-Shot Mode

This mode is the same as the single-shot mode except for two cases. In the first case the output waveform does not return to zero after a time-out; it remains at its initialized level until it is reprogrammed or changed by a time-out. The output waveform can be any multiple of time-outs. Again an interrupt is generated at the end of a time-out. The second exception is the method to change the output level. In this mode the timer output will be equal to the status of TCR7 at the end of a time-out—hence the ability to have long pulses greater than one time-out (see Table E.16). When a time-out interrupt is generated, a routine should be serviced to determine whether TCR7 should be reset or not. The interrupt flag should also be reset.

Table E.14   MC6846 Internal Register Addresses

A2	A1	A0	REGISTER SELECTED
0	0	0	Combination Status Register
0	0	1	Peripheral Control Register
0	1	0	Data Direction Register
0	1	1	Peripheral Data Register
1	0	0	Combination Status Register
1	0	1	Timer Control Register
1	1	0	Timer MSB Register
1	1	1	Timer LSB Register
X	X	X	ROM Address

Source: Motorola Semiconductor Products, Inc.

Table E.15 Composite Status Register

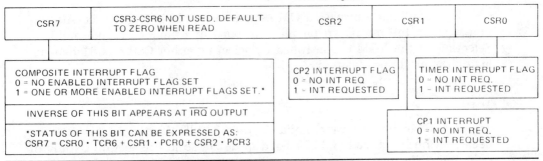

| CSR7 | CSR3-CSR6 NOT USED. DEFAULT TO ZERO WHEN READ | CSR2 | CSR1 | CSR0 |

COMPOSITE INTERRUPT FLAG
0 = NO ENABLED INTERRUPT FLAG SET
1 = ONE OR MORE ENABLED INTERRUPT FLAGS SET.*

INVERSE OF THIS BIT APPEARS AT $\overline{IRQ}$ OUTPUT

*STATUS OF THIS BIT CAN BE EXPRESSED AS:
CSR7 = CSR0 · TCR6 + CSR1 · PCR0 + CSR2 · PCR3

CP2 INTERRUPT FLAG
0 = NO INT REQ
1 = INT REQUESTED

TIMER INTERRUPT FLAG
0 = NO INT REQ.
1 = INT REQUESTED

CP1 INTERRUPT
0 = NO INT REQ.
1 = INT REQUESTED

Source: Motorola Semiconductor Products, Inc.

Table E.17 Peripheral Control Register

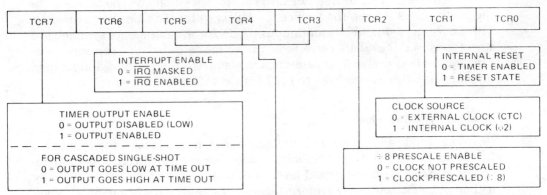

| TCR7 | TCR6 | TCR5 | TCR4 | TCR3 | TCR2 | TCR1 | TCR0 |

INTERRUPT ENABLE
0 = $\overline{IRQ}$ MASKED
1 = $\overline{IRQ}$ ENABLED

INTERNAL RESET
0 = TIMER ENABLED
1 = RESET STATE

TIMER OUTPUT ENABLE
0 = OUTPUT DISABLED (LOW)
1 = OUTPUT ENABLED

FOR CASCADED SINGLE-SHOT
0 = OUTPUT GOES LOW AT TIME OUT
1 = OUTPUT GOES HIGH AT TIME OUT

CLOCK SOURCE
0 = EXTERNAL CLOCK (CTC)
1 = INTERNAL CLOCK (φ2)

÷ 8 PRESCALE ENABLE
0 = CLOCK NOT PRESCALED
1 = CLOCK PRESCALED (÷ 8)

TCR3	TCR4	TCR5	TIMER OPERATING MODE	COUNTER INITIALIZATION	INTERRUPT FLAG SET
0	0	0	CONTINUOUS	$\overline{CTG}{\downarrow} + W + R$	T.O.
0	0	1	CASCADED SINGLE SHOT	$\overline{CTG}{\downarrow} + R$	T.O.
0	1	0	CONTINUOUS	$\overline{CTG}{\downarrow} + R$	T.O.
0	1	1	NORMAL SINGLE SHOT	$\overline{CTG}{\downarrow} + R$	T.O.
1	0	0	FREQUENCY COMPARISON	$\overline{CTG}{\downarrow} \cdot \overline{I} \cdot (W + T.O.) + R$	$\overline{CTG}{\downarrow}$ BEFORE T.O.
1	0	1		$\overline{CTG}{\downarrow} \cdot \overline{I} + R$	T.O. BEFORE $\overline{CTG}{\downarrow}$
1	1	0	PULSE WIDTH COMPARISON	$\overline{CTG}{\downarrow} \cdot \overline{I} + R$	$\overline{CTG}{\uparrow}$ BEFORE T.O.
1	1	1			T.O. BEFORE $\overline{CTG}{\uparrow}$

R = RESET CONDITION
W = WRITE TIMER LATCHES
T.O. = COUNTER TIME OUT
Source: Motorola Semiconductor Products, Inc.

$\overline{CTG}{\downarrow}$ = NEG TRANSITION OF PIN 17
$\overline{CTG}{\uparrow}$ = POS TRANSITION OF PIN 17
$\overline{I}$ = INTERRUPT FLAG (CSR0) = 0

Parallel Peripheral Port

The 6846 has an 8-bit port for parallel communication. It also has handshaking and interrupt capability to tie to an intelligent port. The unit consists of two peripheral control lines, a data direction register, and a peripheral control register. The port also directly affects 2 bits of the composite status register.

Special Interfaces

Table E.16   Timer Control Register

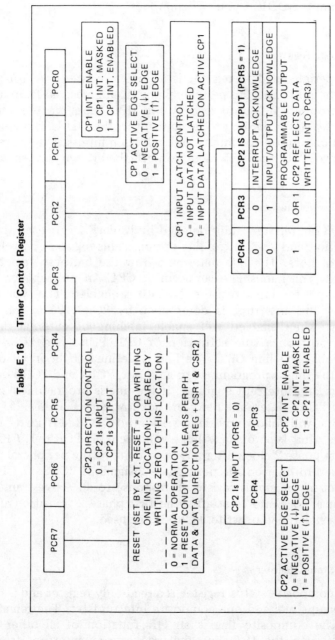

Source: Motorola Semiconductor Products, Inc.

Data Direction Register

The data direction register will configure the peripheral port bits for input (0) or an output (1). They are true bidirectional ports, but remember to reprogram the DDR if you switch modes.

Peripheral Data Register

The peripheral data register is a buffer register used for data transfer between the MPU and the peripheral port. Data received from inputs appear in the appropriate bits until read by the MPU. Data written here appear on the correct ports according to assignment in the DDR. The control register has a latching option for inputs and will latch inputs as they are input, until they are read. With the latching option off, the bits vary in real time.

Peripheral Control Register

This 8-bit register, fully detailed in Table E.17, is used to control the reset function and the control line options. This register controls the peripheral control lines. The bits determine how the hardware reacts to a handshake input. This handshake can occur on CP1. An interrupt can be generated in the composite status register if PCR0 is enabled. The type of edge that will trigger this interrupt is determined by PCR1. PCR2 has an optional mode that when enabled will enable latching of external data into the peripheral port on a true activation of CP1. PCR3 and PCR4 control the programmable I/O line CP2. The line is defined to be input or output by PCR5. If the line is programmed as an input, PCR4 and PCR5 determine the active edge and interrupt enabling. If the line is programmed as an output, PCR3 and PCR4 determine hardware acknowledge schemes. If PCR4 is high, the CP2 line will follow any data written into PCR3. If PCR4 is low, PCR3 determines what type of handshake will occur. If PCR3=1, CP2 will go low on the first phase 2 clock after a read or write to the peripheral data register. CP2 will return high on the next phase 2 signal. If PCR3=0, CP2 is set after CSR1 is set in the status register in response to an active transition of CP1. The response goes into reset after the first phase 2 transition after a peripheral data register read or write. PCR6 is not used.

Composite Status Register

The composite status register is a read-only register and is comprised of three interrupt bits and one composite interrupt bit. The remaining bits are unused. The composite flag is an OR function of all other flags, and it alone is tied to the IRQ line that requests an interrupt from the MPU. CSR0 is the timer interrupt flag; CSR1 and CSR2 relate to operation of the peripheral control lines.

EXAMPLE E.4:   Frequency Synthesis

This application implements a frequency synthesizer, one that could be used in several areas such as local oscillators, waveform generators, or transmitters (see Figure E.10). The oscillator output is fundamentally related to the time base of the system itself. The calibration of the VC0 is compared directly to a fixed-length wait period. The base frequency is constantly monitored with a feedback loop. The output frequency is counted in the internal counter. CP2 controls the clock output to the buffer selector, with CP1 a known state decode feedback. Notice that we are using the microprocessor in a closed-loop system, one that corrects and modifies itself in operation.

The code for this application is as follows:

```
* FIRST SET UP THE CP1 AND CP2 CONTROL LINES ON THE 6846.
        LDA    #$B1
        STA    PCR         /STORE THE PERIPHERAL CONTROL REGISTER.
* NOW LETS SET UP THE DATA DIRECTION REGISTER FOR ALL OUTPUTS.
        ORA    #$FF
        STA    DDR
* NOW ITS TIME TO SET UP THE VC0 FREQUENCY BY OUTPUTTING TO THE
* DAC.
        LDA    #$AA
        STA    PDR         /WRITE TO THE PERIPHERAL DATA REGISTER.
* ITS NOW TIME TO START INITIAL CALIBRATION PROCEDURE.  THIS IS
* DONE BY LOADING THE APPROX COUNTER PRESET AND THEN COUNTING
* THE INPUT FREQUENCY FOR A SPECIFIED AMOUNT OF MACHINE CYCLES.
        LDA    #$82         /RESET, USE EXTERNAL CLOCK, ENABLE PRESCALER,
* CONTINUOUS MODE, ENABLE TIMER INTERRUPT IN CASE
* THE FIRST VC0 LOAD IS TO FAR OFF.  DISABLE
* COUNTER OUTPUT-NO OUTPUT UNTIL AFTER CALIB.
        STA    TCR         /STORE IN THE TIMER CONTROL REGISTER.
        LDA    #$44
        STA    MSB         /STORE THE MSB INTO THE COUNTER.
        LDA    #$02
        STA    TCR         /PRESET THE TIMER.
        LDA    #$DD
        STA    LSB
* NOW THE TIME BASE COMPARISON
   WAIT DECA
        BNE    WAIT
   GO   LDA    MSB         /GET THE MSB REG FIND OUT IF IT IS CORRECT.
        CMPA   STND        /COMPARE THE MSB WITH THE STANDARD NUMBER.
        BEQ    OK
        BGT    REDUCE      /BRANCH TO REDUCE BASE FREQUENCY.
        BLT    INCREASE    /BRANCH TO INCREASE BASE FREQUENCY.
* THE SAME PROCEDURE IS DONE FOR COMPARING THE LSB TO SEE IF IT
* IS IN THE CORRECT RANGE.  AFTER THIS AREA THE PROGRAM ENTERS
* THE SPECIFIC APPLICATION PROPOSED BY THE USER.  A
* PERIODIC CHECK OF THE BASE FREQUENCY SHOULD BE REQUIRED.
* OTHER ACTIVITIES IN REAL TIME SHOULD RELATE SOMEHOW TO
* THE I/O DEVICES.
```

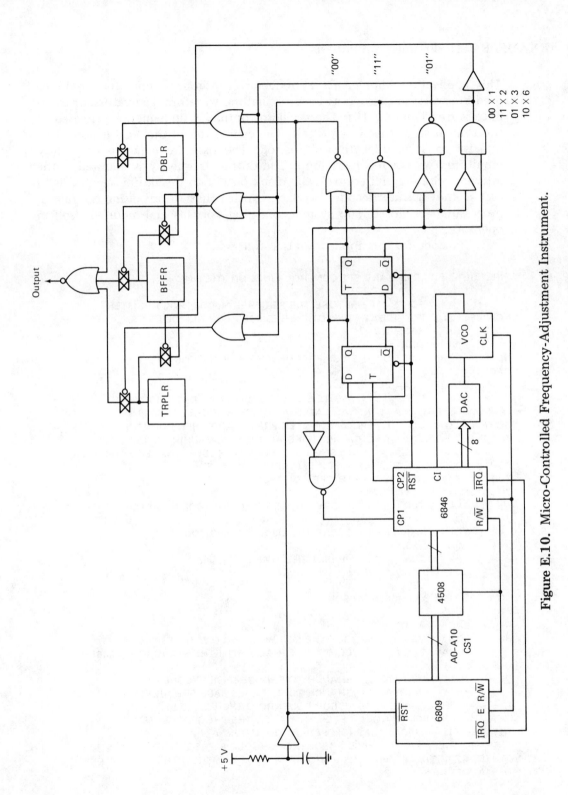

Figure E.10. Micro-Controlled Frequency-Adjustment Instrument.

E.5 THE MC6860: A 0-600 BPS DIGITAL MODEM

The 6860 is a 24-pin DIP that is based on a MOS design that dissipates about 150 mW. The unit is a subsystem designed to be used with the 6850 ACIA, an external threshold detector, and a CBT line interface (see Figure E.11). All data are transferred in a serial mode and modulated in a frequency-shift method. The unit provides for remote handshaking plus interface signals to the data coupler and the communication terminal. Several different modes of operation are available for modem use (see Figure E.12).

Answer Mode

The 6860 provides for an automatic answering mode. The mode is first initiated by receipt of a ring indicator. This input would come from either a CBS or a CPT data coupler, depending on the type of system to which it is interfaced. If the data terminal ready (DTR) line is low at this time, the answer phone output to the coupler goes high. Upon triggering the ap-

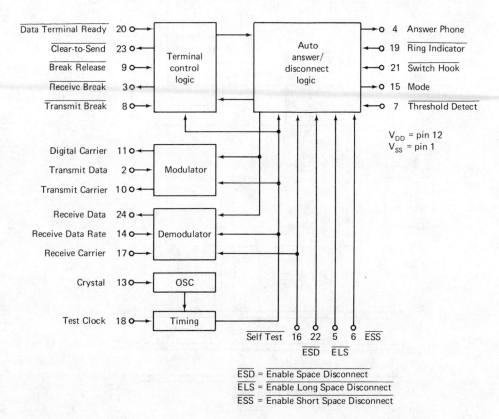

Figure E.11. 6860 Modem Block Diagram. (Courtesy of Motorola Semiconductor Products, Inc.)

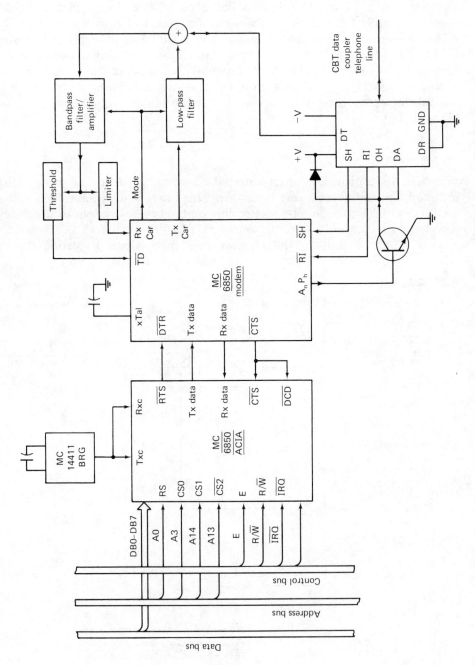

Figure E.12. Modem Interface. (Courtesy of Motorola Semiconductor Products, Inc.)

Special Interfaces

propriate switches in the coupler the 2225-Hz transmit carrier goes on. After the modem on the other end of the line detects the transmit carrier it starts a 1270-Hz answer modem carrier. After the 1270-Hz carrier has been detected for 150 ms, the receive input is unclamped from a high condition and frequency-shift data can be received. The absence of a threshold detect of the 1270-Hz carrier for more than 51 ms starts hang-up procedures, which will finally terminate 17 s after the RI line is released. The clear to send goes true 450 ms after the receipt of the answer carrier and data are transmitted.

Originate Mode

After the receipt of a switch hook command, the modem function is switched to the originate mode. If the DTR line is true, the 6860 will provide a true output to the answer phone connection of the coupler. The modem will now look for a 2225-Hz carrier from the answering modem for 17 s after the coupler releases the SH line. Disconnect procedures occur after this waiting period. If the 2225-Hz carrier threshold detect has been made at least 150 ms, the receive data output is enabled. 450 ms after receiving a 2225-Hz signal, a 1270-Hz originate carrier is transmitted to the remote site. 750 ms after the 2225-Hz carrier is received, a CTS output is made true to the data terminal interface.

Initiate Disconnect

An initiate disconnect command is used when the originate modem is used to tell the remote modem to hang up. The disconnect is implemented by bringing the DTR line high for greater than 34 ms. The local modem then transmits a 3-s duration space pulse and then hangs up. If the remote hangs up before the termination of the 3-s period, the threshold detect will detect its absence from the line, and send the CTS line high, which will in turn mark the line in the answer mode, and turn the carrier off in the originate mode.

Automatic Disconnect

The automatic disconnect feature is used when a modem should be hung up. If the modem receives a space of 150 ms or greater, it is assumed that data transmission is over and that disconnect procedures should start. A receive break is issued after 150 ms. If a break release is not given by the modem controller before 300 ms with the enable short space disconnect true, the modem hangs up. The space time before disconnect can be changed to 1.5 s if the enable long space disconnect line is true. ESS and ELS must not be both low.

The following questions are frequently asked.

For what reason is frequency shift keying used in the mod/demod circuitry?

Answer: The FSK method of data transceiving is more reliable, since this method is more resistant to major amplitude variations.

What is a data coupler, and why is it needed?

Answer: A data coupler is a device that directly controls the telephone line activity. It must meet FCC and local standards for telephone interface.

How is duplex activity accomplished via the two communicating modems?

Answer: The activity is accomplished by use of separate independent transmit and receive carriers for the FSK circuits.

How does one modem indicate to another modem to disconnect?

Answer: The modem signals the other modem to disconnect by transmitting a space of a certain duration.

Hexadecimal–Octal Conversion Chart

		LOWER HEX DIGIT															
		0	**1**	**2**	**3**	**4**	**5**	**6**	**7**	**8**	**9**	**A**	**B**	**C**	**D**	**E**	**F**
	0	0	1	2	3	4	5	6	7	8	9	10	11	12	13	14	15
		000	*001*	*002*	*003*	*004*	*005*	*006*	*007*	*010*	*011*	*012*	*013*	*014*	*015*	*016*	*017*
	1	16	17	18	19	20	21	22	23	24	25	26	27	28	29	30	31
		020	*021*	*022*	*023*	*024*	*025*	*026*	*027*	*030*	*031*	*032*	*033*	*034*	*035*	*036*	*037*
	2	32	33	34	35	36	37	38	39	40	41	42	43	44	45	46	47
		040	*041*	*042*	*043*	*044*	*045*	*046*	*047*	*050*	*051*	*052*	*053*	*054*	*055*	*056*	*057*
	3	48	49	50	51	52	53	54	55	56	57	58	59	60	61	62	63
		060	*061*	*062*	*063*	*064*	*065*	*066*	*067*	*070*	*071*	*072*	*073*	*074*	*075*	*076*	*077*
UPPER HEX DIGIT	**4**	64	65	66	67	68	69	70	71	72	73	74	75	76	77	78	79
		100	*101*	*102*	*103*	*104*	*105*	*106*	*107*	*110*	*111*	*112*	*113*	*114*	*115*	*116*	*117*
	5	80	81	82	83	84	85	86	87	88	89	90	91	92	93	94	95
		120	*121*	*122*	*123*	*124*	*125*	*126*	*127*	*130*	*131*	*132*	*133*	*134*	*135*	*136*	*137*
	6	96	97	98	99	100	101	102	103	104	105	106	107	108	109	110	111
		140	*141*	*142*	*143*	*144*	*145*	*146*	*147*	*150*	*151*	*152*	*153*	*154*	*155*	*156*	*157*
	7	112	113	114	115	116	117	118	119	120	121	122	123	124	125	126	127
		160	*161*	*162*	*163*	*164*	*165*	*166*	*167*	*170*	*171*	*172*	*173*	*174*	*175*	*176*	*177*
	8	128	129	130	131	132	133	134	135	136	137	138	139	140	141	142	143
		200	*201*	*202*	*203*	*204*	*205*	*206*	*207*	*210*	*211*	*212*	*213*	*214*	*215*	*216*	*217*
	9	144	145	146	147	148	149	150	151	152	153	154	156	157	158	160	161
		220	*221*	*222*	*223*	*224*	*225*	*226*	*227*	*230*	*231*	*232*	*233*	*234*	*235*	*236*	*237*

UPPER HEX DIGIT	LOWER HEX DIGIT															
	0	1	2	3	4	5	6	7	8	9	A	B	C	D	E	F
A	160 *240*	161 *241*	162 *242*	163 *243*	164 *244*	165 *245*	166 *246*	167 *247*	168 *250*	169 *251*	170 *252*	171 *253*	172 *254*	173 *255*	174 *256*	175 *257*
B	176 *260*	177 *261*	178 *262*	179 *263*	180 *264*	181 *265*	182 *266*	183 *267*	184 *270*	185 *271*	186 *272*	187 *273*	188 *274*	189 *275*	190 *276*	191 *277*
C	192 *300*	193 *301*	194 *302*	195 *303*	196 *304*	197 *305*	198 *306*	199 *307*	200 *310*	201 *311*	202 *312*	203 *313*	204 *314*	205 *315*	206 *316*	207 *317*
D	208 *320*	209 *321*	210 *322*	211 *323*	212 *324*	213 *325*	214 *326*	215 *327*	126 *330*	127 *331*	128 *332*	129 *333*	220 *334*	221 *335*	222 *336*	223 *337*
E	224 *340*	225 *341*	226 *342*	227 *343*	228 *344*	229 *345*	230 *346*	231 *347*	232 *350*	233 *351*	234 *352*	235 *353*	236 *354*	237 *355*	238 *356*	239 *357*
F	240 *360*	241 *361*	242 *362*	243 *363*	244 *364*	245 *365*	246 *366*	247 *367*	248 *370*	249 *371*	250 *372*	251 *373*	252 *374*	253 *375*	254 *376*	255 *377*

Let us demonstrate how to use this chart by converting the hex number FF to its octal equivalent. In the lower right-hand corner we see 377, the octal equivalent.

Now let us find the octal equivalent for FE. It is 376, or 1 less than 377. Now let us try a harder one, 3C in hex. From the thirteenth column and the fourth row, we find its octal equivalent, 74. Notice that the respective decimal equivalent is shown above each octal entry. 3C in hex is 60 in decimal.

Hexadecimal-Octal Conversion Chart

The Standard ASCII Code

BITS 4 thru 6 —		0	1	2	3	4	5	6	7
	0	NUL	DLE	SP	0	@	P		p
	1	SOH	DC1	!	1	A	Q	a	q
	2	STX	DC2	"	2	B	R	b	r
	3	ETX	DC3	#	3	C	S	c	s
	4	EOT	DC4	$	4	D	T	d	t
	5	ENQ	NAK	%	5	E	U	e	u
BITS 0 thru 3	6	ACK	SYN	&	6	F	V	f	v
	7	BEL	ETB	'	7	G	W	g	w
	8	BS	CAN	(	8	H	X	h	x
	9	HT	EM	)	9	I	Y	i	y
	A	LF	SUB	*	:	J	Z	j	z
	B	VT	ESC	+	;	K	[	k	{
	C	FF	FS	,	<	L	/	l	/
	D	CR	GS	-	=	M	]	m	}
	E	SO	RS	.	>	N	^	n	≈
	F	SI	US	/	?	O	—	o	DEL

Single-Board Microcomputer

Applications of microprocessors that demand immediate design solutions can often be handled by employing a built-up board of the particular micro-processor with attendant peripheral devices. The MEK 6809 D4 is one alternative to the popular method using "evaluation boards." This nearly self-contained single PC board houses the 6809, D4BUG firmware, system RAM of 512 bytes, user RAM of 512 bytes expandable to 4K, and several other support chips. Features of this single-board microcomputer are listed below. The MEK 6809D4 with MEK68KPD (keyboard) are depicted in Figure H.1.

1. System buffers are used between sections of the MEK6809D4 board and between the board and its edge connectors.
2. Hardware RAM and ROM page select register.
3. 4K static user RAM (eight sockets) may be mapped with jumpers to appear at any 4K block in the 64K basic memory space, and in addition may be jumpered to appear on a selected "RAM Page/or Pages" as controlled by a 3-bit hardware RAM Page register.
4. Eight 24-pin ROM sockets may be configured to accept combinations of ROM/EPROM types, including $1K \times 8$ single or triple supply EPROMs or ROMs, $2K \times 8$ single or triple supply EPROMs or ROMS, $4K \times 8$ ROMs or EPROMs, or $8K \times 8$ ROMs or EPROMs.
5. A ROM-based mapping technique is used to allow completely gen-

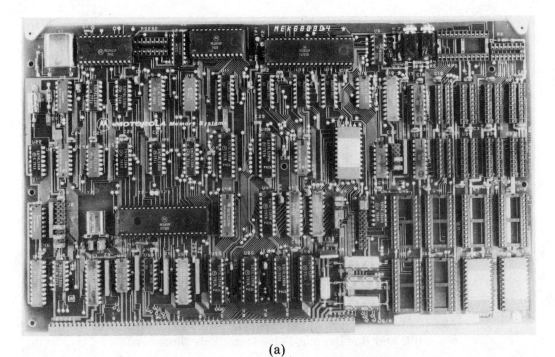

(a)

(b)

Figure H.1. MEK6809D4 with MEK68KPD Keyboard. (Courtesy of Motorola Semiconductor Products, Inc.)

eral address mapping of the eight ROM sockets anywhere in the 64K basic memory space with 1K resolution. In addition, the sockets may be mapped on any "ROM Page/or Pages" as controlled by a 3-bit hardware ROM page register.

6. All memory and I/O on the board is fully decoded, so that address space not specifically required on the D4 is available for off-board mapping.

7. A −12-V to −5-V regulator is provided to allow use of three supply EPROMs on the D4. Supply voltages of +12, −12, and +5 must be provided by the user.

8. Hardware is provided which allows Monitor software to store and recover Kansas City Standard 300-baud or 1200-baud format cassette tape data.

9. Interrupt driven stop-on-address comparator.

10. System clock derived from 3.579-MHz on-board XTAL or from a 4 × TTL compatible external source.

11. "Test" signal and logic provided to allow control of on-board memory and I/O from an external processor through the 70-pin edge connector.

12. Control and status lines provided for flexible hardware control of MPU and Bus Decode/Drive logic. This allows for:

Testing and Debug

Interrupts (RESET, NMI, IRQ, FIRQ)

Interrupt Vectoring by Device (IVE, STKOP)

Interrupt Disable (IRQE, FIRQE)

HALT and Bus Request (BREQ)

Slow Memory (MEMRDY)

DMA

The following features are standard on the MEK6809D4B and may be included as options on the MEK6809D4A:

1. RS-232 compatible serial port, including buffered handshake signals.

2. Baud-rate generator providing baud-rate clocks for 110-, 300-, 600-, 1200-, 4800-, and 9600-baud rates.

3. Address, data, and control lines fully buffered at bus interface.

I

The Proposed S-100 Bus Specifications

The S-100 standard proposed in 1980 applies to interfaces interconnected via a 100-line parallel backplane bus which follows the general guidelines below.

1. Data exchanged among the interconnected devices is digital (as distinct from analog).
2. The total number of interconnected devices is small (22 or fewer).
3. The total transmission path length among interconnected devices is electrically short (25 inches or less). That is, transmission-line propagation delays are not important.
4. The maximum data rate of any signal on the bus is low (less than or equal to 6 MHz).

A state-diagram notation is employed such as that shown in Fig. I.1. States are depicted as circles and transitions as arcs between states. The interface enters a state only if the expression on the entering arc is true. Each expression must contain a driven as well as a driving expression (separated by a slash /). The S-100 bus pin list is tabulated in Table I.1. The permanent master state diagram, slave interface diagram, and bus cycle fundamental timing relationships are depicted in Figures I.2, I.3, and I.4, respectively.

Table I.1   Proposed S-100 Bus Layout—Quick Reference

pin 1	+8 Volts (B)			pin 51	+8 Volts (B)	
pin 2	+16 Volts (B)			pin 52	−16 Volts (B)	
pin 3	XRDY (S)	H		pin 53	GND	
pin 4	V10* (S)	L		pin 54	SLAVE CLR* (B)	L
pin 5	V11* (S)	L		pin 55	DMA0* (M)	L
pin 6	V12* (S)	L		pin 56	DMA1* (M)	L
pin 7	V13* (S)	L		pin 57	DMA2* (M)	L
pin 8	V14* (S)	L		pin 58	sXTRQ* (M)	L
pin 9	V15* (S)	L		pin 59	A19	H
pin 10	V16* (S)	L		pin 60	SIXTN* (S)	L
pin 11	V17* (S)	L		pin 61	A20 (M)	H
pin 12	NMI* (S)	L		pin 62	A21 (M)	H
pin 13	PWRFAIL* (B)	L		pin 63	A22 (M)	H
pin 14	DMA3* (M)	L		pin 64	A23 (M)	H
pin 15	A18 (M)	H		pin 65	NDEF	
pin 16	A16 (M)	H		pin 66	NDEF	
pin 17	A17 (M)	H		pin 67	PHANTOM* (M/S)	L
pin 18	SDSB* (M)	L		pin 68	MWRT (B)	H
pin 19	CDSB* (M)	L		pin 69	RFU	
pin 20	GND			pin 70	GND	
pin 21	RFU			pin 71	NDEF	
pin 22	ADSB* (M)	L		pin 72	RDY (S)	H
pin 23	DODSB* (M)	L		pin 73	INT* (S)	L
pin 24	φ (B)	H		pin 74	HOLD* (M)	L
pin 25	pSTVAL* (M)	L		pin 75	RESET* (B)	L
pin 26	pHLDA (M)	H		pin 76	pSYNC (M)	H
pin 27	RFU			pin 77	pWR* (M)	L
pin 28	RFU			pin 78	pDBIN (M)	H
pin 29	A5 (M)	H		pin 79	A0 (M)	H
pin 30	A4 (M)	H		pin 80	A1 (M)	H
pin 31	A3 (M)	H		pin 81	A2 (M)	H
pin 32	A15 (M)	H		pin 82	A6 (M)	H
pin 33	A12 (M)	H		pin 83	A7 (M)	H
pin 34	A9 (M)	H		pin 84	A8 (M)	H
pin 35	DO1 (M)/DATA1 (M/S)	H		pin 85	A13 (M)	H
pin 36	DO0 (M)/DATA0 (M/S)	H		pin 86	A14 (M)	H
pin 37	A10 (M)	H		pin 87	A11 (M)	H
pin 38	DO4 (M)/DATA4 (M/S)	H		pin 88	DO2 (M)/DATA2 (M/S)	H
pin 39	DO5 (M)/DATA5 (M/S)	H		pin 89	DO3 (M)/DATA3 (M/S)	H
pin 40	DO6 (M)/DATA6 (M/S)	H		pin 90	DO7 (M)/DATA7 (M/S)	H
pin 41	D12 (S)/DATA10 (M/S)	H		pin 91	D14 (S)/DATA12 (M/S)	H
pin 42	D13 (S)/DATA11 (M/S)	H		pin 92	D15 (S)/DATA13 (M/S)	H
pin 43	D17 (S)/DATA15 (M/S)	H		pin 93	D16 (S)/DATA14 (M/S)	H
pin 44	sM1 (M)	H		pin 94	D11 (S)/DATA9 (M/S)	H
pin 45	sOUT (M)	H		pin 95	D10 (S)/DATA8 (M/S)	H
pin 46	sINP (M)	H		pin 96	sINTA (M)	H
pin 47	sMEMR (M)	H		pin 97	sWO* (M)	L
pin 48	sHLTA (M)	H		pin 98	ERROR* (S)	L
pin 49	CLOCK (B)			pin 99	POC* (B)	L
pin 50	GND			pin 100	GND	

Adapted from Table by IEEE Computer Society Microprocessor Standards Committee, Newport Beach, California.

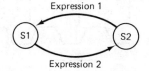

Figure I.1. State Diagram.

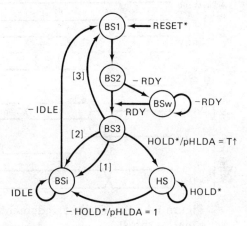

† There is a minimum specified time delay between hold and hold acknowledge:
[1] instruction execution complete = INT enable · INT request/interrupt accept
[2] instruction execution not complete + INT disabled + no interrupt request
[3] (instruction execution complete · −HOLD* · −interrupt accept) +
(instruction execution not complete · −IDLE)

Figure I.2. Permanent Master State Diagram.

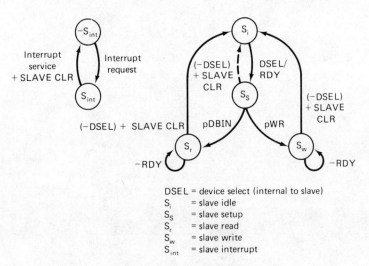

DSEL = device select (internal to slave)
S_i = slave idle
S_S = slave setup
S_r = slave read
S_w = slave write
S_{int} = slave interrupt

Figure I.3. Slave Interface State Diagram.

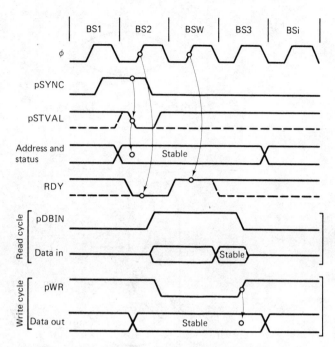

Figure I.4. Bus-Cycle Fundamental Timing Relationships.

J

The Pro Log STD
Bus Specifications

In April 1979, Pro Log introduced an industrial control bus specification[1] that has received widespread interest in the industrial process control community. Notable among its features are:

1. Standard motherboard, which allows any of four different cards in any slot.
2. Efficient handling of all internal bus management control signals.
3. Power supply pins for +24-V industrial control users.
4. Compatible functions grouped together.

The pinout is shown in Table J.1 on page 354.

---

[1] *Microprocessor User's Guide*, Pro Log Corp., Monterey, California © 1979, pp. 74-77.

Table J.1   STD BUS Pinout

		COMPONENT SIDE			CIRCUIT SIDE			
	PIN	MNEMONIC	SIGNAL FLOW	DESCRIPTION	PIN	MNEMONIC	SIGNAL FLOW	DESCRIPTION
LOGIC POWER BUS	1	+5V	In	+5 Volts DC (Bussed)	2	+5V	In	+5 Volts DC (Bussed)
	3	GND	In	Digital Ground (Bussed)	4	GND	In	Digital Ground (Bussed)
	5	-5V	In	-5 Volts DC	6	-5V	In	-5 Volts DC
DATA BUS	7	D3	In/Out	Low Order Data Bus	8	D7	In/Out	High Order Data Bus
	9	D2	In/Out	Low Order Data Bus	10	D6	In/Out	High Order Data Bus
	11	D1	In/Out	Low Order Data Bus	12	D5	In/Out	High Order Data Bus
	13	D0	In/Out	Low Order Data Bus	14	D4	In/Out	High Order Data Bus
ADDRESS BUS	15	A7	Out	Low Order Address Bus	16	A15	Out	High Order Address Bus
	17	A6	Out	Low Order Address Bus	18	A14	Out	High Order Address Bus
	19	A5	Out	Low Order Address Bus	20	A13	Out	High Order Address Bus
	21	A4	Out	Low Order Address Bus	22	A12	Out	High Order Address Bus
	23	A3	Out	Low Order Address Bus	24	A11	Out	High Order Address Bus
	25	A2	Out	Low Order Address Bus	26	A10	Out	High Order Address Bus
	27	A1	Out	Low Order Address Bus	28	A9	Out	High Order Address Bus
	29	A0	Out	Low Order Address Bus	30	A8	Out	High Order Address Bus
CONTROL BUS	31	WR*	Out	Write to Memory or I/O	32	RD*	Out	Read to Memory or I/O
	33	IORQ*	Out	I/O Address Select	34	MEMRQ*	Out	Memory Address Select
	35	IOEXP*	In/Out	I/O Expansion	36	MEMEX*	In/Out	Memory Expansion
	37	REFRESH*	Out	Refresh Timing	38	MCSYNC*	Out	CPU Machine Cycle Sync.
	39	STATUS 1*	Out	CPU Status	40	STATUS 0*	Out	CPU Status
	41	BUSAK*	Out	Bus Acknowledge	42	BUSRQ*	In	Bus Request
	43	INTAK*	Out	Interrupt Acknowledge	44	INTRQ*	In	Interrupt Request
	45	WAITRQ*	In	Wait Request	46	NMIRQ*	In	Non-Maskable Interrupt
	47	SYSRESET*	Out	System Reset	48	PBRESET*	In	Push Button Reset
	49	CLOCK*	Out	Clock from Processor	50	CNTRL*	In	AUX Timing
	51	PCO	Out	Priority Chain Out	52	PCI	In	Priority Chain In
POWER BUS	53	AUX GND	In	AUX Ground (Bussed)	54	AUX GND	In	AUX Ground (Bussed)
	55	AUX +V	In	AUX Positive (+12 Volts DC)	56	AUX -V	In	AUX Negative (-12 Volts DC)

*Low Level Active Indicator

Index